BLIND
SPOT

BLIND
SPOT

The Secret History

of American

Counterterrorism

TIMOTHY NAFTALI

BAS
BOOKS

A Member of the Perseus Books Group

New York

Books published by Basic Books are available at special discounts for bulk purchases
in the United States by corporations, institutions, and other organizations. For more
information, please contact the Special Markets Department at the Perseus Books
Group, 11 Cambridge Center, Cambridge MA 02142, or call (617) 252-5298,
(800) 255-1514 or e-mail special.markets@perseusbooks.com.

Design by Jane Raese
Text set in Baskerville Book

Library of Congress Cataloging-in-Publication Data
Naftali, Timothy J.
Blind spot : the secret history of American counterterrorism / Timothy J. Naftali.
p. cm.
Includes index.
ISBN 0-465-09281-0 (hardcover)
1. Terrorism—United States—Prevention—History.
2. Terrorism—Government policy—United States—History. I. Title.
HV6432.N34   2005
363.32'0973—dc22
2005003248

05 06 07 • 10 9 8 7 6 5 4 3 2 1

IN MEMORY OF MY FATHER,

JAMES D. NAFTALI

CONTENTS

PREFACE

AT 10:20 A.M. on September 11, 2001, I was entering the lobby at the University of Virginia's Miller Center of Public Affairs with a candidate I had just interviewed for a job. The interview had taken place at a café in downtown Charlottesville that did not have a radio or television set. Immediately, a colleague ran over to me nearly in tears: "Tim, one of the World Trade Center towers has fallen and the Pentagon is burning." Shocked, I hustled with the candidate over to a big plasma screen in a nearby room showing CNN. Before leaving my apartment that morning I had caught news of a plane apparently crashing into the center's north tower. No one at CNBC had then called it an act of terrorism, and I wondered whether the pilot had perhaps suffered a heart attack. Ninety minutes later, like millions around the world I watched that tower collapse and knew that this was terrorism, though on a scale never seen before.

There was more than the traumatic images and CNN's choice of thriller author Tom Clancy as a commentator that made this all seem unreal. Students of the Cold War knew that in theory, the United States government was prepared to respond to a Soviet nuclear missile attack. Warning would be a matter of minutes, and again, according to the theory, the president and the leadership of Congress were all to be whisked away to a safe location. On September 11, the president was out of communication with the American public for long stretches of time. The effect was an eerie official silence, as though the entire government were as paralyzed as those of us witnessing those events on television. The thought crossed many of our minds, What if this had been a nuclear attack?

Equally disorienting was the fact that the prime suspect was not an unknown quantity. Even those having a passing acquaintance with foreign affairs knew the name Osama bin Laden. In 1998, his followers had simultaneously blown up two U.S. embassies in different African capitals. Two years later, what appeared to be a group under his sponsorship had hit a U.S. destroyer that had just been refueled in Yemen's Aden harbor. Bin Laden had vowed to attack America and had been indicted in federal court. The Clinton administration had tried to kill him by launching cruise missiles at a camp in Afghanistan where he was expected to be. Although President George W. Bush had never said anything publicly about bin Laden, it had to be assumed that this master terrorist had not completely fallen off the National Security Council's radar screen since the 2000 election.

After years of studying the intelligence and security world, I have come to believe less in the efficiency of conspiracies than I do in the inefficiency of government. Most of the supposed conspiracies of modern American history dissolve when one examines them closely. The Roosevelt administration would have had advance warning of the Japanese attack on Pearl Harbor had not interservice rivalry and overclassification of intelligence led to a decision to focus on the wrong Japanese communication channel. Japanese diplomats had not been told about the attack; Japanese admirals, on the other hand, had been. Unfortunately, U.S. intelligence had chosen to break the Japanese diplomatic cipher instead of that of the Japanese Admiralty.[1] In 1963, Lee Harvey Oswald exploited a last-minute change by the U.S. Secret Service in the route of the presidential motorcade through central Dallas. Oswald had delusions of grandeur and was looking to kill someone famous. A few weeks earlier, he had shot at Edwin Walker, a prominent right-wing extremist. Now he would have a chance to use his marksmanship against an even more famous man, John F. Kennedy. Certainly, there have been real conspiracies in U.S. history—Watergate and Iran–Contra come to mind—but our society is open enough that we eventually hear about them. Someone is bound to leak to Bob Woodward.

The surprise on September 11 almost immediately seemed to fall in the category of government ineffectiveness. In the days following the attack, newspapers reported the story of Zacarias Moussaoui, described as the missing twentieth hijacker. Three of the planes had been commandeered by teams of five. Flight 89, which through the heroism of its passengers was downed in a field in Pennsylvania, had been taken by four men. Moussaoui had entered the United States in February 2001 and then chosen traditional methods of evading detection. He tried to fit in. He paid his bills on time. He avoided traffic tickets. He also used untraceable modems and telephones to communicate with the leadership of Osama bin Laden's al Qaeda. In the language of espionage, Moussaoui was a sleeper. His mission was to blend into enemy territory until such time as his superiors had something specific for him to do.

But Moussaoui did engage in suspicious activity. Just after he arrived in the United States, Moussaoui took a flight course in Norman, Oklahoma. Three months later, he was told by his handlers to look into obtaining a crop-duster's license. In late summer of 2001 he was back at flight school, this time in Eagan, Minnesota. In what should have been a break for U.S. national security, Moussaoui made a mistake at this last assignment. He drew attention to himself. He was a poor student who didn't seem to show the slightest interest in becoming a better pilot. Plunking down nearly $19,000 to use the Boeing 747 simulator at the Pan Am International Flying school outside Minneapolis, he seemed to be doing it as an "ego thing," as one of the instructors later recalled.

It is dismaying to see how Moussaoui could have moved around
this country so easily and signed up as an improbable pilot without
anyone in Washington taking an interest. And then once he had
been noticed, the FBI was incapable of fully investigating him. Lacking probable cause in a criminal case—the standard then employed in
antiterrorism matters—the FBI did not request a special warrant to
look onto the hard drive of his computer. The Moussaoui case
seemed to be evidence that on September 11 there had been a break-
down not only in the military security of the country, but in whatever antiterrorism mechanisms the country was supposed to have.

American intelligence history is not, however, a litany of missed
opportunities and incompetence. The United States can be very
good at man-hunting. Sixty years before 9/11, a group of young men
and women had learned how to catch spies. In World War II, American counterespionage officers identified, captured, and turned most
of the German network in liberated France and Italy, using these
double agents to feed deception to Adolf Hitler. Countless lives were
saved in the final weeks of the war as German commanders made
decisions on the basis of what we wanted them to believe about the
size and location of Allied units. Ever since, the history of U.S. counterespionage has been characterized by peaks and valleys. Yes, there
were valleys, but there were peaks as well.

The talents required for effective counterterrorism are not dissim-
ilar from those for effective counterespionage. The government
needs to determine the structure of the enemy's organization, identify its assets, and prevent them from implementing their mission,
either by neutralizing or turning these agents. Although not an intelligence collector for a state, Moussaoui was a clandestine operative,
whose detection required many of the same man-hunting tools as
those used for traditional spies.

Moreover, terrorism was not a new problem. In the 1970s, Palestinians had hijacked airplanes and murdered Israeli athletes at the
Munich Olympics. In the 1980s, Ronald Reagan had declared war

on terrorism after hundreds of U.S. military and diplomatic personnel were killed in a series of explosions in Beirut. And a decade ago, the United States was targeted again in the Middle East and had experienced a terrorist massacre at home. What, if any, institutional wisdom had the U.S. government acquired after sixty years of tracking down enemy agents and saboteurs and a generation of having to worry about Middle Eastern terrorists? We seemed to be so good at this work in World War II, and I knew of a few successes at penetrating networks in the Cold War. What had gone wrong? Were we ever good at counterterrorism before the obvious surprise of September 11? Was there something about the nature of our society that prevents us from protecting ourselves from terror?

As a boy growing up in Montreal I had seen a country confront a terrorism problem. In the late 1960s, the Front de libération du Québec sent a number of letter bombs to prominent Montrealers, and in 1970 they kidnapped a British diplomat and a provincial cabinet minister. For some months in the fall of that year, civil rights were suspended in Montreal, and Canadian soldiers with machine guns manned major intersections in my hometown. Those were very turbulent times in Quebec, and even though the terrorist group was ultimately dismantled, the climate of political intimidation continued for years. For Canadians, the threat of a terrorist attack at home had been real. But for many in my adopted country this had apparently not been the case until 9/11.

This book is an effort to outline the history of the U.S. government's struggle with international terrorism. It begins with the very first efforts to combat terrorism in the waning months of World War II, when it appeared that renegade Nazis would use violence to disrupt the hard-fought peace of Europe; discusses the work against Palestinian, Lebanese, and European terrorists; and in its last chapters benefits from the superb work of the 9/11 Commission and staff to bring the story through the surprise of 9/11. The subtitle refers to counterterrorism: active operations to preempt, neutralize, or destroy terrorists and their organizations. This book will also examine the importance of antiterrorism, those defensive measures at borders, ports, and airports designed to detect or thwart terrorists. Success in the struggle against terrorism, it will be shown, requires that we be effective on defense as well as offense.

A stroke of luck enabled me to develop this study in ways I never could have imagined. When Philip Zelikow became executive director of the 9/11 Commission, he and Ernest May—who had joined Philip as senior advisor on the commission staff—talked with me about writing a history for the staff of the early period of U.S. counterterrorism activities. I was just then finishing up some chapters in an official report for the Nazi War Crimes and Japanese Imperial Government Records Interagency Working Group, which studied the use of war criminals as intelligence assets by the U.S. intelligence community, and had been awarded a sabbatical from the University of Virginia. The counterterrorism study was to be unclassified, and all interviews were to be voluntary. I was encouraged to interview as many former principals and counterespionage specialists as possible. I submitted that report in 2004, and this book draws upon it. I am grateful to the commission for partially funding the research for this book. The debt I owe to Zelikow and May extends beyond my work for the 9/11 Commission. Philip brought me to the Miller Center in 1998 and has supported my work ever since. I studied with Ernest May at Harvard, ultimately completing my dissertation on U.S. counterespionage for him in 1993. On the commission staff I worked closely with Michael Hurley, Team 3 leader, and Warren Bass, both of whom provided important encouragement and support. Warren also gave extremely useful editorial guidance, as did Hyon Kim, Yoel Tobin, and an anonymous reviewer from the staff's intelligence team. Lloyd Salvetti and Dan Byman were very helpful as I worked to turn the report into a book. John Poindexter, Oliver "Buck" Revell, and Fred Turco were also attentive readers. I greatly benefited from the professionalism of the staffs of the National Secu-

rity Archive, the Richard Nixon Library and Birthplace at Yorba
Linda, the Nixon Materials Project in Washington, D.C., and the
Lyndon Baines Johnson, Jimmy Carter, Ronald Reagan, and George
H. W. Bush Presidential Libraries. I would also like to single out
Tom Blanton and Peter Kornbluh at the National Security Archive,
and Regina Greenwell at the Lyndon Baines Johnson Library and
Sherrie Fletcher at the Ronald Reagan Library for their extraordi-
nary assistance. Two close friends, Ken Pollack and Gideon Rose,
kindly helped me get started on the research into the Clinton period,
which I had not covered for the commission. Other friends who at
various times provided encouragement and inspiration for this work
are Cicely Angleton, Bart Aronson, David Coleman, Felix Cowgill,
Robert Feldman, Gerry Haines, Fred Holborn, H. Montgomery
Hyde, Zachary Karabell, Fred Logevall, Anne Mark, Betsy Maurer,
Ewen Montagu, Laura Moranchek, Wistar Morris, James R. Murphy, Gloria Naftali, Leopoldo Nuti, Walter Pforzheimer, Lee Smith,
Brewer Stone, John Waller, Wesley Wark, Allen Weinstein, Robin
Winks, Pamela Yatzko, and Fareed Zakaria. Aleksandr Fursenko
and Drake McFeely kindly tolerated this project as a distraction
from my work on Khrushchev and the Cold War. I am grateful to
my friends and colleagues at the Miller Center's Presidential Record-
ings Program, who don't need me around to achieve great scholarship but make me feel wanted. My agent, John Hawkins, was a great
help, as were Susan Rabiner, who brought me to Basic Books; Don
Fehr, who allowed me to reshape this project; and Chip Rosetti, Lara
Heimert, and Christine Marra, who championed the manuscript
through its completion. As ever, I remember my late father and
thank my mother and sister, Debbie. For this book I am grateful to
be able to add thanks to my brother-in-law Serge Lacroix and my little niece Zoë Lacroix and godson Dylan Stone, who both make me
smile and will, I hope, grow up in a less fearful world.

CHAPTER ONE

The Plot to Kill General Eisenhower

"WHAT IS THE CAPITAL OF ILLINOIS, SIR?" A U.S. army jeep flying a gold-braided pennant with four stars had just driven up to the roadblock, and the young American sentry had the unenviable task of quizzing the man in the passenger seat wearing those stars. It was mid-December 1944, and as part of a major counteroffensive on the Western front, the Nazis had sent saboteurs across the lines dressed in U.S. Army uniforms. To separate friend from foe, the U.S. military in northwestern France had tightened security and started this game of trivial pursuit.

"Springfield," replied the general, who at that moment was probably not wearing the familiar grin captured frequently by *Life* magazine.

During the chaos of what became known as the Battle of the Bulge, General Omar Bradley would be asked questions ranging from detailed football tactics to the name of silver-screen star Betty Grable's latest boyfriend. These unusual precautions seemed necessary at the time because in its desperation, the Nazi leadership had chosen to violate the laws of war.[1]

Allied concerns about these new Nazi tactics reached an even higher level a few days later. On December 19, a German Air Force officer, wearing a U.S. Army uniform, had given himself up near Liège, in eastern Belgium. Stating that he was ashamed of his country's conduct in the war, he offered full cooperation. Along with seven other men who had been captured wearing the American blue serge, the officer presented a frightening picture of German ambitions to his interrogators at U.S. First Army headquarters. He told them that SS-Sturmbannführer Otto Skorzeny, the notorious Nazi special operations specialist, had personally led a contingent of between fifty-four and sixty men across the lines on December 13. The German officer warned that the Skorzeny team was planning to assassinate General Dwight Eisenhower, the supreme allied commander, at his headquarters outside Paris. The deed would take place that very day or on December 21. This information was passed up the chain of command and among Allied counterespionage specialists. "Their mission is to gun for Eisenhower," reported the counterespionage representative of the Office of Strategic Services (OSS) at the U.S. First Army to OSS headquarters in Paris.[2]

If there was any SS officer capable of this audacious scheme it was the blue-eyed, six-foot-five-inch Otto Skorzeny, disfigured by a menacing scar from his left ear to his chin. His daring airborne rescue of Italian dictator Benito Mussolini from Allied detention in September 1943 had received international press attention. Since then, through intercepted messages, Allied counterintelligence had been able to monitor the progress of the sabotage organization he had created for Heinrich Himmler. In liberated France, a joint Anglo-American team led by Lord Victor Rothschild, of the famous banking family, had already started turning up sabotage dumps left by Nazi intelligence for use against the Allied occupiers.[3]

Skorzeny represented a new kind of threat to the Allied war effort. As the German army continued to lose conventional battles on both fronts, evidence was accumulating that rather than surrender, the Nazis planned to launch a guerrilla war, led by Skorzeny and the other SS chiefs. The plot to kill Eisenhower turned out to be a false alarm. Nevertheless, by early 1945, a consensus developed among Allied intelligence officers that the liberation of Germany would unleash an unprecedented terrorist campaign. Led by Skorzeny, Nazi collaborators in liberated Europe were expected to "cause political upheaval by assassinations, terrorism, and acts of violence at political meetings, in such a manner as to make the blame appear to rest with Left-wing elements and Communists." The goal of this upheaval would be to inspire the liberated governments to choose authoritarian regimes that promised order. Within Germany, it was predicted, "these operations . . . will be directed toward the perpetuation of the Nazi terror with a view to dominating the German population and preventing collaboration with the Allies. The knowledge that there is still a Nazi headquarters and the possibility of a Nazi revival would keep alive Nazi doctrines and encourage the formation of autonomous underground movements throughout Germany."[4]

The origins of modern U.S. counterterrorism are to be found in the mobilization of a group of gifted amateurs to meet this threat in the last months of the war. Located in the counterespionage branch of the Office of Strategic Services—the so-called X-2 branch—these six hundred men and women participated in an international effort to track and neutralize an enemy terrorist organization. Sixty years before Osama bin Laden, Otto Skorzeny focused the collective mind of U.S. intelligence and inspired the actions of a nimble, centralized secret organization. Many of the techniques that would become useful in that later struggle were first learned in 1944–45.

The Channels Theory

The story of X-2 begins with an unusual offer from the British in 1942 to teach Americans their theory of counterespionage, the art and science of defeating foreign agents. The scale of the British empire, which spanned all five continents, was too great to permit man-to-man coverage of potential spies, saboteurs, and guerrillas. Instead, the British established a system of channels through which those who wished to move or communicate within the empire had to pass. Each time an enemy moves, is paid, or communicates to a headquarters, an opening is created in that agent's security system. The British sought to exploit that vulnerability by controlling the channels through which the agent could travel, receive money, or communicate. The technology of the 1930s and 1940s facilitated this mission. Although Charles Lindbergh had first flown a nonstop transatlantic flight in 1927, commercial nonstop air travel had not yet begun. Planes flying from New York to London stopped to refuel either at Gander, Newfoundland and Ireland, or in Bermuda and Lisbon. At each stop the plane's hold would be checked secretly by British intelligence.

By the late 1930s the British had become expert at rapidly steaming open letters and breaking and replacing the official seals on foreign governments' diplomatic bags, which carried official correspondence. At the Hamilton Princess hotel in Bermuda, for example, a censorship staff of over two hundred opened transiting mail using tools as rudimentary as a tea kettle.[5] The British used secret agents and private agreements to obtain passenger manifests on airplanes and cruise ships. Relationships were established with concierges at hotels in major cities to determine who was staying where and when. British intelligence also controlled transatlantic telegraph cables. The system was by no means foolproof, but it was an eye-opener for American investigators who had never conceived of an imperial system to control the movement of individuals into areas of special U.S. interest and, of course, into the American homeland itself.

A few months after Hitler invaded Western Europe, the British found that they could control a new channel used by spies: Intercepted radio messages quickly displaced opened letters as the principal source of intelligence on the movements and activities of enemy agents. In December 1940, British code breakers began attacking the hand cipher of the Abwehr, the German military intelligence service. Abwehr agents used this cipher to disguise radio messages sent from the field. A year later, the British cracked the Abwehr's machine cipher, which was used to protect communications between headquarters and their stations in neutral and occupied countries. The deciphered messages revealed the movement of German agents, and though the identities of these agents were usually hidden behind a code name, at least the intercepts revealed how many agents the Allies had to look for. With this powerful resource, British investigators acquired a new sense of self-confidence. It created the possibility not simply of capturing almost every enemy agent and saboteur but of making double agents out of many of them. In the words of Norman Holmes Pearson, who would lead the U.S. counterespionage effort in Western Europe, the British "were the ecologists of double agency: everything was interrelated, everything must be kept in balance."[6] By 1942, the British would be running double agents in Great Britain and Spain and using them to pass disinformation to the Nazi regime.[7]

The British decision to share this powerful and highly sensitive source of information forced a change in the structure of U.S. intelligence. A year after Pearl Harbor, the United States still lacked a counterespionage service that tracked spies in Europe and Asia. The Federal Bureau of Investigation (FBI) managed counterespionage in the United States and since 1940 had been responsible for all intelligence collection and man-hunting in Latin America. On the eve of joint military operations in North Africa, what would become known as the Torch invasion, the British approached the United States with a recommendation that a foreign counterespionage service be established. London was eager to share its signals intelligence with an American group, and they had some ideas on how that sharing might occur.

The British suggested that the most experienced FBI counterespionage officer be named to head this new organization.[8] Percy "Sam"

Foxworth was special agent in charge of the bureau's New York office. For three years he had been running some double agent operations against the Germans and the Japanese. The British had worked closely with him on a few of these cases and thought highly of his skills. The British proposal was that Foxworth be transferred to the newly created OSS, a U.S. overseas intelligence service that reported to the Joint Chiefs of Staff and was headed by the legendary World War I hero Colonel (later General) William J. Donovan. The British wanted this unit to be self-contained, with its own communications system. Any American officers cleared for using British signals intelligence would be vetted by the British and would be trained by them in London.[9]

Had J. Edgar Hoover accepted this offer, the FBI would have effectively controlled counterespionage throughout the world. However, the FBI chief did not trust the British. The bureau had evidence that the British had been breaking into the Italian and Spanish embassies in Washington. And Hoover had an additional reason to be suspicious of the British offer: Foxworth, while a gifted and professional intelligence officer, was in Hoover's eyes a bit of a disciplinary problem. Pudgy and a poor shot, Foxworth did not match the ideal picture of the model G-man, and despite a series of cautionary letters accumulating in his personnel file, Foxworth seemed unwilling to lose his excess weight and appear regularly at the FBI shooting range. Moreover, Hoover mistrusted Donovan and did not want to lose his agent to a rival.

When Hoover strongly discouraged Foxworth from leaving the bureau, U.S. foreign counterespionage and British liaison in such matters became the unchallenged responsibility of William J. Donovan. In 1943, the OSS created X-2, a counterespionage service that would use British signals intelligence to capture agents in the field, turn some of them, and feed deception to the Germans. The Americans came to London to study this new craft, and their British tutors found them very adept.[10]

Sam Foxworth died in a plane crash in South America in 1943, and his name was forgotten. But the legacy of Hoover's decision not to allow him to run U.S. foreign counterespionage in World War II would live on for the next sixty years. Had an FBI agent led Donovan's group, the active and occasionally debilitating rivalry between the OSS's and later the Central Intelligence Agency's counterespionage officers and the FBI might have been averted or at least would have been considerably muted. Instead, two separate services were created, and as each later undertook the counterterrorism mission, this divide would continue.

The War Room

In the months before the Battle of the Bulge, the X-2 branch of the OSS had organized a network of double agents in liberated France. In Cherbourg, the first port captured by the Allies, X-2 turned a German "stay-behind" agent named Juan Frutos. A pathetic Spanish national who had been bullied into working for the Nazis, Frutos became the first double agent ever run by the United States overseas. As agent Dragoman, he also became the first American deception channel in Europe to the German high command. In the south of France, X-2 also built a network of agents to support deception operation Jessica, designed to distract the Germans from the long supply line from the French Riviera to Switzerland. In Italy, X-2 ran other double agents, penetrating the new Italian intelligence services, launching operations that would prevail until the last of these men retired in the 1970s.[11] Finally, because of concern that German renegades could use stolen art to fund their activities after the war, X-2 also set up the Art Looting Investigation Unit (ORION Project). ORION enlisted American art historians to track down the masterpieces that the Nazi leadership—primarily Hitler and Luftwaffe chief Hermann Göring—had looted for their own collections.[12]

Uncertainty about the postwar plans of German intelligence drove the creation of even tighter cooperation between X-2 and its Allied counterparts. The idea of a central clearinghouse to make Allied counterintelligence information more readily available to field officers came from Dick Goldsmith White, a British intelligence officer who was the number-two counterespionage official in General Eisenhower's headquarters. "The War Room," he later recalled, "were the masters of detail."[13] Although White dismissed concerns in December 1944 that the Nazis were planning to kill the supreme allied commander, he agreed that the Nazis would not surrender without launching a terrorist campaign.

Called the SHAEF G-2 CI War Room, this central clearinghouse opened on March 1, 1945. Its director was British and its deputy came from X-2. The French secret service was also invited to join.[14] The goal of the War Room was to use signals intelligence, captured documents, and prisoner of war interrogation reports to destroy the Nazi intelligence system and prevent an outbreak of terrorism. To assist the work of Allied counterintelligence officers in the field, the War Room produced tactical information: target lists, analyses, and questions for interrogators. The War Room also issued tactical and strategic appreciations of the status and objectives of the German intelligence services (GIS). The Anglo-American leadership studied each subgroup within the Nazi services with care, as if each were a separate organism with unique characteristics. One of the War Room sections wrote assessments of cases and briefed interrogators who were going into the field, while another stepped back from ongoing operations with the task of "studying the GIS as a whole and appreciating its overall organization and development." The heart of the War Room was a card registry. In 1945, the Allies used computers to crack German ciphers, but not yet to organize intelligence data. The registry therefore consisted of shelves of three-by-five-inch index cards that pointed to relevant information in subject and personal files. Ultimately, the War Room registry contained information on one hundred thousand individuals in two thousand personal files and four hundred subject files.[15]

By the spring of 1945, Allied counterespionage's conclusion that a Nazi terrorist campaign would follow the collapse of the German army was impressing policymakers. In London, a decision was made at "a very high level" to use British commandos to assassinate leading members of the SS intelligence service. The British and American directors of the War Room argued against assassinating these potential terrorists, sensing that it was better to capture these individuals alive so that they could be turned or at least used as sources of intelligence. If the Churchill government insisted, then the War Room at least wanted to have a veto "before any action is taken against any of these individuals."[16] The assassination plan was ultimately dropped.

In Washington, President Franklin Roosevelt and his top military advisor, General George C. Marshall, also took the threat seriously. On March 23, the president received an X-2 report on the Nazi Party's preparations for guerrilla warfare following the collapse of the German military command.[17] In his cover letter, William Donovan emphasized evidence of extensive training of officers for a guerrilla army of thirty-five thousand to forty thousand men. The last six months had brought the eclipse of the Wehrmacht's own secret service, the Abwehr, by a more centralized and efficient intelligence apparatus answering only to Heinrich Himmler and the SS. It was assumed that this political service, the Reichssicherheitshauptamt (RSHA), would lead the expected German underground after the military defeat. A week later, General George C. Marshall, the chief of staff of the U.S. Army, cabled General Dwight Eisenhower, supreme commander of the Allied Expeditionary Force, requesting a statement on this anticipated guerrilla war that could be released to the public "with a view to conditioning its members for this possibility."[18] The same day, Eisenhower responded gloomily: "VE Day will come about only by a proclamation on our part rather than by any

definite and decisive collapse or surrender of German resistance
. . . Eventually all the areas in which fragments of the German
Army, particularly paratrooper, Panzer, and SS elements, may be lo-
cated will have to be taken by the application of or threat of force.
This will lead into a form of guerrilla warfare which would require
for its suppression a very large number of troops."[19]

Eisenhower's two fundamental decisions about ending the war
were made with this possibility in mind. On March 21, the
Rhineland campaign already a success and plans for the envelop-
ment of the Ruhr industrial area moving apace, Eisenhower looked
to the next phase of the Allied invasion of Germany and instructed
his planners to draft orders for a body blow across the German
midriff to cut the country in two.[20] He wished to make impossible a
southern movement of more troops and officials into the Bavarian
and Austrian alpine region, the most suitable area for a guerrilla war.
Three weeks later, having lost confidence in the Allied assumption
that the capture of the Ruhr and Berlin would compel a German surrender, Eisenhower decided to invade as much of Germany as possible with maximum force to deter resistance. On April 14, with two
of his army groups on the Elbe and one in Bavaria, Eisenhower ordered the bulk of his military force south to pacify the Alpine region
of Upper Bavaria and Austria.[21]

In an effort to magnify Allied anxieties, the Nazis spread propaganda about "werewolves," groups of members of the Hitler Youth
movement who had been trained in sabotage and assassination.
Some werewolves had indeed been trained, and others sprang up independently. But ultimately they were crushed under the weight of
the massive Allied advance. Skorzeny gave himself up on May 16,
having seen the writing on the wall. This notorious commando
turned out to be far more pragmatic than the Allies had assumed.
German preparations for postwar terrorism had never been serious.
Indeed, through interrogations of captured German intelligence officers, X-2 and the British learned that the Nazi leadership had viewed

post-hostilities planning as akin to defeatism. As for Skorzeny, he was not inclined to embark on a suicide mission.[22]

The centralized Allied system had not been flawless. In the weeks before the apprehension of most German intelligence officers, at a time when there were few intercepts to clarify Nazi postwar planning, the War Room had perpetuated an erroneous theory of how the war would end. But once U.S. intelligence officers were on the ground in occupied Germany, capturing important officials and tons of relevant documents, the War Room allowed for the efficient distribution of correct information. The effect of this new information could also be seen in War Room analyses of the possibilities of a Nazi revival. Thus this clearinghouse permitted the Allies to correct their error quickly and conclude with confidence by September 1945, less than four months after the end of the war, that the threat of Nazi postwar terrorism was gone.

The Postwar Legacy

The skills acquired by U.S. intelligence officers in the hunt for Skorzeny did not disappear with the threat. Several veterans of the wartime counterintelligence struggle stayed on in U.S. intelligence as the target shifted to the Soviet Union and its Socialist satellites. Formed in 1947, the Central Intelligence Agency(CIA) inherited the OSS's responsibility for overseas counterespionage and counterterrorism. However, a counterintelligence service established on the British model did not survive the transition to the CIA. What was known as the X-2 model had created jealousy inside the OSS, for it seemed to represent a threat to headquarters' control over U.S. agents and officers in the field. The British had insisted that because X-2 would have access to their signals intelligence, the branch had to be kept separate from the rest of the OSS, with its own communications system and reporting channels. In the new CIA, X-2's responsibilities were divided among three staffs, and CIA field officers reported through chiefs of stations, not directly to Washington, on matters relating to counterespionage and counterterrorism.

Despite the decentralization of X-2's work, the new CIA continued to apply aspects of the British channels approach to monitor subversive individuals. The U.S. government routinely received copies of passenger manifests from civilian airlines and had arrangements to receive telegraph communications. Through foreign services, the CIA acquired passport and visa information from various European, Latin American, and Asian countries. Initially, the only channel that did not receive blanket coverage was the U.S. postal system. The Korean War allowed U.S. intelligence to close that loophole. The Truman administration permitted the U.S. postmaster general to turn over letters addressed to the People's Republic of China, the Soviet Union, and the rest of the Eastern bloc to the FBI. This highly secret program, which circumvented the judicial system and was therefore unconstitutional, was known as HT/Lingual and would continue for the next twenty-four years.[23] Initially an FBI project, it would ultimately become the responsibility of the counterintelligence specialists at the CIA. These efforts to re-create the highly effective British imperial monitoring system hit a wall because Soviet espionage used an impregnable radio communications system. With the exception of about two thousand messages sent by Soviet intelligence between the United States, Great Britain, and Moscow in World War II, which were decrypted through the VENONA program because of an error in Soviet ciphering procedures, Soviet intelligence communications were impenetrable to Allied eyes for the entire Cold War.

James Angleton, who had cut his teeth as an X-2 officer in London and then as chief of X-2 operations in Italy, became the first chief of the CIA Counterintelligence (CI) Staff in 1954. In the language of Washington organizations, the CI Staff was not a line agency. It did not have field representatives, nor did it ordinarily run agents on its own. It was a supporting headquarters that could be called in whenever a CIA station encountered a counterespionage issue. Among its responsibilities, the CI Staff was to provide expertise on international organizations.[24] To the extent any work on independent terrorist organizations was done in the fledgling CIA, it was done by the CI Staff.

The KGB and Terrorism

Despite this inheritance, there was little perceived need for U.S. counterterrorism in the first half of the Cold War. Both of the superpowers were preparing sabotage teams to destroy civilian infrastructure in the event of war—the U.S. and the USSR trained agents to act in occupied territories—but neither side intended to start a war with an act of terrorism. Despite the mutual animosity and suspicion between East and West, the nuclear balance deterred a third world war.

The Soviet intelligence service, the KGB, did practice terrorism in peacetime, but not against U.S. targets. Continuing a tradition begun under Joseph Stalin, the Kremlin used its secret services to track down defectors or leaders of resistance organizations within the Soviet bloc. As a result of a few cases, the CIA learned something about how Moscow occasionally employed the tactics of assassination and sabotage. The first of these took place in Frankfurt, West Germany, in February 1954 and would involve a KGB terrorist who refused his mission.

On February 18, 1954, a fair-haired stranger knocked at the apartment door of Georgi Okolovich. "Georgi Sergeevich," the young Soviet agent Nikolai Khokhlov told the Russian nationalist, "I've come to you from Moscow. The Central Committee of the Communist Party of the Soviet Union has ordered your liquidation. The murder is entrusted to my group."[25]

The KGB's Department 13, its assassination and terrorism service, had issued Khokhlov a small gun with cyanide-laced bullets that could be concealed in a cigarette pack.[26] But he was not carrying it, because he had no intention of carrying out his mission. "I can't let this murder happen," he told Okolovich.[27] Khokhlov's target was chief of operations of a Russian dissident group known as the NTS.

Okolovich was also a CIA asset. After hearing the young man's startling admission in his front foyer, Okolovich called his American controller. The agency saw the advantage of taking charge of Okolovich's surprise visitor. A short while later, Khokhlov was detained at the U.S. consulate in Frankfurt. David Murphy, a young CIA officer, received a call in Paris, where he was on a short break. "I was told to get my tail back to Frankfurt," recalls Murphy.[28]

Once he met Khokhlov, Murphy hoped he could use him to penetrate the KGB's Department 13. In a few days, Khokhlov was supposed to meet with a Soviet illegal in the Soviet zone in Vienna to report on the assassination operation. An illegal was a KGB agent who operated without diplomatic immunity. Murphy suggested that the appointment be made with the illegal but with one change. He would go instead of Khokhlov.

This was the CIA's first opportunity to look inside the Soviet terrorism apparatus. Fluent in Russian, Murphy appeared at the meeting site in a car. He stepped out and approached the illegal. "Who are you," asked the surprised man, who had expected to see the assassin. "I'm from Moscow. Get in the car and I will explain." Murphy then drove the unsuspecting agent across the line into the American zone. At the U.S. embassy the CIA made the pitch: Will you work for us? "Ya gotov [I'm ready]," he responded.

Khokhlov and the illegal could tell U.S. authorities about only a small portion of Department 13's activities. Since 1951, Department 13 had been developing plans for sabotage against U.S. military installations in the event of war or a prolonged military crisis near the

Soviet Union. "By the beginning of the 1950s," recalled Pavel Su-
domplatov, who headed the department, "we had acquired agents
with access to military installations in Norway, France, Austria, Germany, the United States, and Canada."[29] Department 13 kept maps
annotated with the locations of "power-transmission lines, oil
pipelines, communications systems, and major industrial com-
plexes," all of which were considered potential targets.[30] When recip-
rocal visits commenced between the United States and the Soviet
Union, Soviet delegations were instructed to collect information to
update Department 13's database on U.S. critical infrastructure.[31]
The Soviets also penetrated the U.S. by recruiting agents who were
stationed in Mexico and could cross the U.S. border at a time of crisis dressed as migrant farm workers. The chief Soviet illegal in the
United States, Vilyam Fisher, alias Rudolf Abel, was in touch with
the leader of this migrant group. Another combat group was established in France, which planned for extensive port and airport sabotage. The members of that group formed a sleeper cell that could
spring into action at a moment's notice. Khokhlov did not know
about any of this.

For its sleeper terrorists, the Soviets were looking for people who
fit into the local population. They wanted professionals and citizens
of the country in which they would be working. They also had to
seem ordinary. A KGB report cautioned that "people who adhere
strictly to church dogma and rules are not suitable, nor are people
with a tendency toward alcohol, drug addiction, and sexual devia-
tions."[32] The Soviets also thought that these people should be well
off, owning two houses some distance apart. Travel should seem second nature to them and not be viewed as unusual to their neighbors
and acquaintances.

Although the Kremlin's interest in assassinations abroad faded after the defection in 1961 of another Department 13 assassin, Bogdan
Stashinsky, the Soviets continued active intelligence gathering for its
sabotage teams.[33] In the late 1950s, the KGB had stepped up prepa-

ration of arms caches throughout Western Europe. For most of the Cold War, the CIA and British intelligence were unaware of the extent of these plans.

In the latter half of the Cold War, the Soviet Union would turn to proxies to employ unconventional warfare to weaken the United States and its Western allies. In Canada, for example, a Soviet illegal code-named Paul opened lines of communication to the Front de libération du Québec (FLQ), a terrorist group that advocated the violent secession of the province of Quebec from the Canadian Confederation. In the Middle East and in Northern Ireland the Soviets would supply weapons to terrorist organizations. These relationships, while significant, were limited and represented assistance to autonomous movements. These groups did not become extensions of Soviet foreign policy.[34]

Fears of Terrorism at Home

Soviet terrorism was of even less concern to the FBI in the first decades of the Cold War. What little terrorism there was then in the United States was more the consequence of the Spanish-American War of 1898 than the confrontation with the Kremlin. In the 1950s, radical members of the Puerto Rican independence movement turned to violence and caused a few dramatic terrorist incidents in Washington, D.C. In 1950, two gunmen killed a guard in a failed assassination attempt on President Truman, and four years later some Puerto Rican terrorists opened fire in the House of Representatives from the visitors' gallery, wounding five congressmen. Neither incident caused the FBI or the interested public to treat terrorism as a threat to national security. The influential columnist Walter Lippmann spoke for many when he wrote in the wake of the attack on the House, "Things are different in some parts of the world, where assassination is a regular practice. But here these outbreaks of terrorism may be regarded as accidents—against which there are precautions but no absolute guarantees—rather than as symptoms of organic disease."[35]

In these years, the White House shared this lack of concern about Soviet use of terrorism. After the Cuban missile crisis, President Kennedy had some concern about the possibilities that nuclear devices and other weapons of mass destruction could be smuggled into the United States. On March 13, 1963, the Central Intelligence Agency reported that the United States was unprotected against the smuggling of these weapons into the country: "Nuclear weapons yielding up to 300 KT [kilotons] could be brought into the U.S. by a variety of means such as by ground or air transport across land borders or at points along U.S. seacoasts." And weapons with smaller payloads, between one hundred and three hundred kilotons, "could be designed to break down into a number of relatively simple and transportable components. Not much technical skill would be required to reassemble and maintain a low-yield device (10 KT or less)." The threat posed by chemical weapons was no less real. Although large quantities would be required to cause mass casualties, the CIA reported that "chemical agents could be used effectively on a small scale against personnel in key installations." These would not have to be brought into the country: "A supply of nerve gases ample for this purpose could be clandestinely produced without great difficulty or great risk of detection."

The fact that this report did not startle President Kennedy or cause him to set any antiterrorism measures in motion said a lot about how the Kennedy administration and the U.S. intelligence community viewed the threat of terrorism in the first half of the Cold War. The Soviets were believed to be the only adversaries who had the capability to exploit weak U.S. domestic security to attack with weapons of mass destruction. And the CIA concluded, and Kennedy evidently agreed, that the Soviets would not make this kind of trouble. "Although the Soviets are capable of introducing nu-

clear weapons clandestinely into the U.S.," the CIA asserted, "we believe that the limited advantages of this course of action, when
weighed against the consequences of possible detection, make it unlikely that the Soviets will do so." The U.S. government believed
that the Soviets did not want a nuclear war, and it was broadly assumed that Moscow understood that getting caught sneaking nuclear weapons into the United States was a sure way to start one.[36]

"I don't think we used the term terrorist," recalls former secretary
of defense Robert McNamara.[37] The Kennedy administration indeed used it, but as a synonym for insurgent or guerrilla. There
were no international terrorist organizations to worry about and no
regional insurgents who would have the will or capability to take advantage of the weaknesses in U.S. domestic security. As long as the
Soviets were deterred, there appeared to be no urgency to remedy-
ing the insufficiency of U.S. borders, even as it related to the movement of nuclear, chemical, and biological weapons.

Kennedy's successors, Lyndon B. Johnson and Richard Nixon,
would be the first American Cold-War presidents to have to contend
with the problem of international terrorism. As we shall see, the
threat involved neither weapons of mass destruction nor the Soviets.
Events in the Middle East would be responsible for grabbing Washington's attention and introducing this new threat to the American
people.

CHAPTER TWO

Hijacking

"I'M GOING TO KILL YOU; I am a sick man." The young man saying these words pointed a shiny, silver-plated .45 automatic at the white-haired gentleman he passed on his way to the front of the plane. Senator James O. Eastland, chairman of the Senate Judiciary Committee, had just left his seat to go to the lavatory when the gunman pushed past him. Eastland hurried back to his seat but did not think he was a target. "He wanted to get to the cockpit," the senator later told reporters, "and I just happened to be in his way." Once inside the cockpit, the hijacker, Oran Daniel Richard, ordered the plane to be flown to Havana.[1]

Eastland was not alone in staying calm. There was no panic as word spread among the other forty-seven passengers that their plane was being diverted. "Most people thought we were going to Havana just from the way the plane was turning and where the sun was," recalled Eastland, who had boarded the flight in Baltimore on July 12, 1968, for a trip to Houston. In the summer of 1968, passengers flying to destinations in the American South knew that there was a real possibility that their plane would be hijacked and diverted to Cuba. This Delta Airlines flight was the eighth commercial jetliner hijacked in the United States that year alone. Since 1961, the year the first U.S. commercial plane was hijacked, twenty-one planes had been commandeered in flight, and all but one had been taken to Havana.[2] Hijackings to Cuba were so frequent that U.S. pilots flying in the southern United States routinely carried maps of Havana's José Martí Airport. The Swiss embassy in Washington, D.C., which handled U.S. official messages to the Cuban government, had forms prepared for whenever Washington wished to formally request the return of a hijacked plane, its crew, and passengers. All the Swiss needed to do was to fill in the flight number and date the request.[3]

Even at the White House there was a sense that commercial hijackings had become routine. President Lyndon B. Johnson received a report from his National Security Council (NSC) staff whenever a U.S. commercial airliner was hijacked. In February 1968, when a Delta flight from Chicago to Miami was being hijacked to Cuba, an NSC staffer reported to Johnson that two U.S. Air Force 104s had taken off to escort the commercial jet out of U.S. airspace. "Recent Cuban practice," reported the staffer, "has been to allow the hijacked planes to return within a day or so."[4] The implication was that though the incident had to be monitored, it was not a cause for presidential concern.

The plane carrying Senator Eastland did not end up in Cuba. The pilots managed to talk the gunman out of the hijacking. Richard, who had once been institutionalized at the Columbus, Ohio, State Mental Hospital, gave himself up to the authorities when the plane landed in Miami.

In a different time, the attempted hijacking of a plane carrying a U.S. senator might well have created a groundswell in favor of new laws. Senator Eastland spoke for many in 1968, however, when he suggested there was no need for legislative remedies: "We've got all the laws that we need." Instead, Eastland blamed the Warren Court for the hijacking problem. "It's all the Supreme Court's affair—they make it possible for criminals to run wild." In Eastland's eyes, laws to improve air security would be an unnecessary restriction on personal liberty. "I don't think any laws Congress might pass would have anything to do with it . . . That's like these gun laws," he said.[5]

Since 1961, hijacking had been a federal crime punishable by at least twenty years in prison and possibly the death penalty. The Kennedy and Johnson administrations had been reluctant to treat hijacking as anything other than a domestic criminal matter. When the International Civil Aviation Organization (ICAO), an arm of the United Nations that oversees international regulations for air traffic, produced a convention in 1963 mandating that the country where a hijacked plane landed return the plane and passengers promptly, the United States signed the convention, but as of July 1968, the White House had not yet submitted the convention to the U.S. Senate for ratification. Neither the Kennedy nor the Johnson administration had chosen to expend any political capital on the problem.

After the first rash of hijackings, President Kennedy's Federal Aviation Administration (FAA) commissioner, Najeeb Halaby, recommended the arming of flight crews and the posting of undercover federal air marshals on flights. The FAA, however, chose neither to require compliance from the airlines nor to seek legislative remedies. Consequently, Halaby's proposals produced few results. The FAA initiated the training of federal marshals at an airfield in Texas, but reluctance from both the airlines and the Air Line Pilots Association (ALPA) stymied the development of any effective air marshal program. The pilots and the airlines feared the possibility of a shootout at 20,000 feet more than an increase in the rate of hijackings. In the popular 1964 movie *Goldfinger,* James Bond brought down a business jet by piercing the fuselage with a bullet. Despite the fact that a commercial jetliner could withstand many bullet holes without a structural collapse, pilots and even the FAA believed that this fantasy represented a real threat to airplanes. Pilots were instructed to obey hijackers, who were believed to be either mentally ill or admirers of Cuban leader Fidel Castro, or both.[6] No one had ever died in a domestic hijacking, and it was assumed that this trend would continue. Why tempt fate by placing additional armed men in the air?

The FAA was also unsuccessful in getting airlines to voluntarily comply with a program of installing bulletproof cockpit doors.

Airplane manufacturers intentionally constructed cockpit doors out of flimsy materials so that pilots could kick them down in the event that they needed to escape.[7] The pilots and the airlines opposed the FAA's recommendation in the belief that a hijacker could just as easily force his way into the cockpit by taking a flight attendant hostage, a scenario that had already occurred in some hijackings.[8]

Besides these failed efforts at voluntary compliance by the FAA, the federal government's effort to avert hijackings consisted in a Justice Department program instituted in 1962 to offer a $10,000 reward to anyone who provided a tip that prevented a hijacking.[9] This program also proved a failure—not one reward was ever paid in the 1960s.

These failures had no discernible political consequences. By the late 1960s, the FAA had concluded that there was little that could be done to prevent hijackings. "It's an impossible problem," said an FAA spokesman in the summer of 1968, "short of searching every passenger."[10] In 1968, "searching every passenger" seemed a fantastic overreaction to the apparent threat. There was as yet no screening at airports: no metal detectors, no checks on passengers or their luggage. The other key interest groups in commercial aviation agreed with the FAA. The pilots and the airlines argued that the only practicable solution was to reach an agreement with the Castro government that required the Cubans to return the hijackers as well as the plane.[11] Air travel was not yet a mass phenomenon in the United States. Only fifteen million Americans flew each year. The airlines feared competition from trains and worried about the added inconvenience and costs that would come from a mandatory screening program. The White House, the U.S. Congress, and the press all seemed to agree, or at least showed little interest in starting a screening program.

After the tenth U.S. commercial jetliner of 1968 was hijacked on July 19, the FAA began sending a very small number of armed plainclothes officers on board selected flights headed to Florida.[12] In retrospect, the July 19 hijacking brought evidence of another large gap in the federal approach to the problem: Although the Federal Bureau of Investigation (FBI) had jurisdiction over hijacking, since the first of these crimes in 1961, the bureau had not developed any special teams to manage these incidents. When the tenth hijacked plane of 1968 landed in New Orleans to refuel before continuing to Havana, FBI officers—lacking any training in airplane rescue operations—could only watch helplessly as the plane took off again.[13]

Besides prompting the FAA to put a few sky marshals aloft, the rash of domestic hijackings in 1968 provoked only minimal discussion within the Johnson administration over the problem of air piracy. On July 19, the Interagency Group on International Aviation, comprising representatives from the Departments of State, Defense, Justice, and Transportation, decided it was time that the United States ratified the ICAO convention on hijacking (known as the Tokyo convention) and drafted a presidential message for approval and submission to the Senate.[14]

As a charter member of ICAO, it was well past time for Washington to do this. As of mid-1968, hijacking was an almost entirely American problem that involved only one sanctuary for hijackers, and that was Cuba. Ratification of the ICAO convention would put a spotlight on Cuban misbehavior, without involving the administration in any diplomacy with the regime. The Johnson administration would make no effort to contact Cuba directly over this issue or to seek the assistance of allies, all of whom maintained diplomatic relations with Havana, to pressure the Castro government to alter its policy on sheltering hijackers. As we shall see, Washington had reasons related to terrorism but unrelated to the hijackings that complicated any dealings with the Cubans.

The El Al Hijacking

A recurrent theme throughout the history of U.S. counterterrorism strategy is that particular events have the power to change sharply

the ways U.S. policymakers and the interested public view the problem of terrorism. The first of these events came on July 23, 1968,
only four days after the Johnson administration began looking for
international support to solve its domestic hijacking problem. That
day, gunmen from the Popular Front for the Liberation of Palestine
(PFLP) took over a plane belonging to El Al, Israel's national airline,
en route to Tel Aviv from Rome. The hijackers forced El Al Flight
426 to land in Algeria. All non-Israeli passengers were allowed to
leave the plane, among whom were two U.S. citizens. The Israelis,
including the crew, were held prisoner. Although it was never proved
that the Algerian government had foreknowledge of the hijacking,
once the plane landed in Algiers, it became a full party to the crime.

Despite Israeli requests that Washington take a public stand
against the hijackers, the U.S. government chose to work quietly
through diplomatic channels to help Israel secure the release of the
plane and the hostages. On July 24, the State Department cabled
U.S. embassies in Rome, Paris, and Cairo with instructions to ask
the local governments there to apply pressure to the Algerian government. Since the end of the Six Day War of 1967, the United
States had not had diplomatic relations with Algeria. U.S. diplomats
were to convey to the leaders of Italy, France, and Egypt the concern
that it would be "a serious blow to international civil air transport
. . . if hijacking of El Al aircraft were permitted to stand."[15]

The El Al hijacking altered the way the Johnson administration
viewed the problem of air piracy. Hijacking moved from a largely
U.S.-Cuban matter to an issue of international concern. Not only
did this incident signify the exportation of the violent politics of the
Middle East, but this was the first time that hijackers had taken
hostages. Up to that point, hijacking could be dismissed as largely a
victimless crime, whose costs were inconvenience and financial loss.
Not any longer. The El Al incident brought the realization that the
crew and the passengers could themselves become the targets of
the crime.

This incident created a fissure in the coalition of complacency that had characterized the world aviation community. In its wake, a powerful interest group in the fight against terrorism first found its voice. Until July 23, 1968, airline pilots and their union had remained remarkably aloof from the discussion of hijacking. In the United States, the Air Line Pilots Association had largely agreed with the FAA's handling of the issue, including the reluctance to put armed marshals on board planes. Algeria's flagrant disregard for the civil rights of the El Al crew and its passengers had sent a shiver through the pilot community.

After the Israelis had spent a month in captivity, the International Federation of Airline Pilots threatened the government of Algeria with a strike. French and Italian pilots warned their national airlines that if the Israelis were not released they would refuse to fly to Algeria. The International Transport Workers Federation also announced it would no longer service Algerian planes at major international airports.[16] Fearful of the loss of air traffic, Algiers gave in and released the hostages on September 1.[17]

The victory in Algiers emboldened U.S. commercial pilots to seek federal assistance with the domestic problem of hijackings to Cuba. The pilots' ability to organize also drew the attention of the Cuban government, which had been ambivalent toward the string of unexpected hijackers that it had received. By late September, the Castro government was signaling that it wanted a deal with Washington on procedures to handle these hijackings.[18]

Terrorism as a Concept

Despite this new awareness of the vulnerability of airline passengers, the Johnson administration did not identify the El Al incident as the opening shot in an international struggle against terrorism. The terms *terrorist* and *terrorism* were in use in the administration well before July 1968, but they meant different things to different advisors. Walt Whitman Rostow, Johnson's special assistant for national security affairs, used the word *terrorist* interchangeably with *insurgent* and *guerrilla* in describing attacks on nonmilitary targets. In a September 1968 report to President Johnson, for example, he described the "terrorist incidents in Saigon" in reference to Vietcong attacks on civilians.[19] The CIA, which had the principal responsibility for collecting information on foreign organizations, used the term more precisely. In CIA reports to the Johnson White House, *terrorism* denoted certain kinds of tactics, the use of torture or the indiscriminate killing of civilians, more often than it did the character of those groups. The term was used to describe the actions of friendly governments as well as those of Communist insurgents or guerrillas.[20]

The concept of international terrorism had also not yet emerged. The Johnson administration tended to view terrorist actions as regional phenomena. In South Vietnam and Latin America, where U.S. personnel were targeted by those who adopted terrorist tactics, the U.S. response dating back to the Kennedy administration was to increase overt and covert support for what was known as regional counterinsurgency. In mid-1967, for example, the Johnson administration oversaw counterinsurgency programs in seven Latin American countries: Bolivia, Colombia, the Dominican Republic, Ecuador, Guatemala, Peru, and Venezuela.[21] Specialists from the Department of Defense and the U.S. Agency for International Development (US-AID) trained special counterinsurgency battalions in each state's army and rural police units.

The United States understood that these insurgent groups had state sponsors. In Southeast Asia, the Vietcong included members of the North Vietnamese army and received funding from the Soviet Union and the People's Republic of China, as well as from Hanoi. Soviet support for Latin American revolutionary movements was more circumscribed, but the significant assistance from Cuba was not. The Johnson administration viewed the deaths of U.S. citizens caused by these state-sponsored groups as the unavoidable casualties of the Cold War.

Washington's reaction to a wave of terrorism in Guatemala in 1967–68 illustrates this attitude well. With training assistance and helicopters from the United States, the Guatemalan government had launched a counteroffensive against the Cuban-backed insurgency in late 1966.[22] By early 1967, the government had eliminated the offensive capability of the rural Rebel Armed Forces (FAR) and had turned its attention to the movement's urban "nerve center." Within a few months, the government was enjoying similar success in the cities. Nevertheless, two hundred hard-core FAR guerrillas remained.[23]

The CIA acknowledged that the Guatemalan government's success came at a great cost to Guatemalan society. "There is little doubt," the agency noted in July 1967, "that the success of the urban campaign has been largely attributable to government-sanctioned police and military terrorism . . . The assassinations and terrorist bombings by the Special Commando Units of the Guatemalan army, coupled with the propaganda bombardment of threatened assassinations, has served to keep the community left in a strictly defensive posture."[24]

U.S. involvement in Guatemalan counterinsurgency appears to have led to a decision by the FAR to target Americans.[25] In January 1968, the FAR killed the commander of the U.S. military group, Colonel John Webber, and the chief of the military group's naval section, Lt. Commander Ernest Munro, and wounded two others. In March 1968, CIA sources reported that the head of the FAR threatened to kidnap Americans to gain the release of a high-level rebel held in government jails.[26]

CIA information on threats to U.S. officials in Guatemala City became quite specific in July. On July 18, a CIA report that the FAR was planning attempts on the lives of U.S. personnel, "perhaps including the ambassador," was widely disseminated to the intelligence community and to the U.S. embassy in Guatemala.[27] Nevertheless, there was no specific warning of when the attack might occur or whether the terrorists would use explosives or a sniper to kill Ambassador John Gordon Mein.

On August 28, 1968, FAR guerrillas killed Ambassador Mein. Mein was the first U.S. ambassador to be murdered in the nearly two hundred years of this country's foreign relations. President Johnson was informed immediately that the FAR were behind the killing, though the Guatemalan government quickly determined that the FAR had probably not planned to kill Mein. Initially, the rebels had hoped to hold him hostage until one of their guerrilla leaders was released from jail. The ambassador, however, had resisted capture and was killed in the struggle.[28]

Cuba's role as a state sponsor of the FAR was well known to U.S. intelligence and the Johnson White House at the time of Ambassador Mein's death. In March 1968, NSC staffer W. G. Bowdler warned National Security Advisor Walt Rostow that the Cubans were "fishing in troubled waters again" and that they were behind the recent increase in terrorist activity in the country.[29] CIA sources in the Guatemalan party reported in March 1968 that elements of the FAR were "bragging that they will carry out a campaign of sabotage and violence, including the assassination of U.S. personnel and Guatemalan army officers."[30]

Cuba was already considered an enemy of the United States, and there is no available evidence in the public domain that Mein's assassination led to increased covert activity against Cuba or to a more overt warning to the Cuban leadership about the consequences of their surrogates targeting U.S. personnel. By the summer of 1968, the Johnson administration had already communicated to the intelligence agencies its belief that the country's covert action "platter was full."[31] In the previous eighteen months, the 303 Committee, an NSC group that in the Johnson administration reviewed and approved "the most sensitive covert operations involving largely over-head reconnaissance and political action," had considered thirty-three operations in Latin America alone.[32] The Mein killing likely did not result in any covert response at all.[33]

In the Middle East, in contrast to Latin America, the Johnson administration did not view terrorism through the prism of the U.S.-Soviet Cold War struggle. Even before the El Al hijacking, U.S. national security officials and intelligence experts had noted the use of terrorism as a tool of Palestinian nationalists to undermine Israel.[34] In this region, however, these actions were not directed at the United States, nor were U.S. personnel, either in the region or at home, considered at risk. Although there was evidence of some Soviet and Chinese support for Palestinian militias, the NSC, the State Department, and the CIA assumed Soviet caution in the region and tended to look elsewhere to understand the motivations for Palestinian terrorism.[35] When the tempo of terrorist incidents increased in the fall of 1967, the NSC staff advised Walt Rostow that the Soviets "no doubt see the risks in renewed terrorism."[36]

Washington concluded that terrorism in the Middle East was a product of two different factors. The most important was a struggle between radical Arab regimes and more moderate regimes over the future direction of regional politics. Gamal Abdel Nasser's bid to unite the Arab world under Egyptian leadership had unsettled an already unstable region.[37]

The other factor was the Palestinian problem, which affected the stability of both Israel and neighboring Jordan. King Hussein's predecessor King Abdullah had annexed the West Bank in 1951 over the objections of both Israel and fellow Arab states. The four hundred thousand inhabitants of the West Bank were a mostly urban, literate population, some of whom had received administrative training under British colonial rule. In the original 1947 UN partition plan for Palestine, the West Bank was expected to become part of Arab Palestine. But Jordan, then called Transjordan, coveted the West Bank. A sparsely populated desert country, Jordan had half the number of people as the West Bank. King Abdullah's decision to annex the West Bank and its inhabitants in 1951 improved the Jordanian economy but created a Palestinian problem for Jordan as well as Israel.

The Six Day War in June 1967 had transformed the Arab-Israeli landscape, resulting in, among other things, the capture of the West Bank and East Jerusalem by Israel and an additional refugee flow into Jordan. Palestinian residents of the West Bank remained Jordanian citizens. By 1968, Jordan had a population of approximately two million people, two-thirds of whom were Palestinian. In its analyses of Jordan, the CIA termed Amman, the Jordanian capital, "a Palestinian city." Since the mid-1950s, it had been U.S. policy to support Abdullah's successor, King Hussein. By 1968, it was generally accepted that Hussein, whose regime received $45 million a year in U.S. grants and loans, remained in power because of this support. In late 1966, the U.S. intelligence community estimated that the United States had already invested half a billion dollars to secure Jordan as a bulwark against the twin challenges of Arab nationalism and international Communism.[38]

In 1964, Nasser decided to create the Palestine Liberation Organization (PLO), which Cairo could use to put pressure on both Israel and Jordan. The PLO was a loose coalition of Palestinian activists, from political moderates to radicals, who espoused armed struggle to defeat both Hussein and the Israelis. Yasir Arafat, a young former student of the University of Cairo, headed Al Fatah, or Fatah, the radical faction that soon seized control of the PLO. Arafat came to the attention of the CIA in mid-1964. "He was not thought of as much of a problem then," recalled James Critchfield, who served as chief of the CIA's Near East Division from 1960 to 1968.[39]

Fatah turned increasingly to the Syrians for training and material support for paramilitary operations against Israel and Jordan. In 1966, Arafat's men launched raids into Israel from Syria. The Syrians prohibited the Fatah guerrillas from entering Israel directly from

Syria, fearing a direct Israeli reprisal. Instead, Fatah used the largely unpoliced Jordanian desert as its route to Israeli villages.

By 1968, Fatah had grown to between three and five thousand guerrillas and was receiving assistance from across the Arab world and the Soviet bloc. Much of the money came from wealthy Palestinians in Kuwait and Saudi Arabia, supplemented by assistance arranged by both governments. The Saudis levied a 5 percent income tax on all Palestinians, with the proceeds going to Fatah, and Kuwait sent to the Palestinians the proceeds from a 2 percent tax on gasoline and theater tickets.[40] The Soviet bloc provided weapons and training. In July 1968, Arafat accompanied Nasser to Moscow. In addition to Soviet aid, Arafat received a little assistance from the Chinese. Beijing trained a few Fatah fighters.[41]

Fatah was not the only Palestinian faction to employ terrorism. In October 1967, a Marxist-Leninist named George Habash established the Popular Front for the Liberation of Palestine (PFLP). Having about five hundred men under his command, Habash decided to cooperate with Arafat, and PFLP training in 1968 took place at Fatah camps.[42] The hijackers of the El Al plane in July of that year were from the PFLP.

In 1966–68, the United States tried to help Israel and Jordan control Palestinian commandos. The United States took the lead in putting diplomatic pressure on Syria, which consistently denied its sponsorship of the guerrillas. The United States also sought to facilitate Israeli-Jordanian conversations. Although both countries had been holding secret meetings since the time of Abdullah, this relationship was complex and benefited from U.S. efforts.

Mideast experts in the Johnson White House and in the State Department believed that very little good could come from unilateral Israeli efforts to control the Palestinian border crossers. With Israel occupying the West Bank and the Golan Heights, Palestinian guerrillas had even more Israeli targets to hit, and these targets were now even closer to their training camps in Syria and their forward bases

in Jordan. Convinced that the Jordanians were either unable or unwilling to police their own borders, Israel regularly chose unilateral
military retaliation against the forward bases in Jordan. Such efforts
posed a direct threat to the stability of Jordan, one of the most moderate Arab regimes in the region.

In the wake of the El Al hijacking, the Israeli government cautioned the United States that this act of terrorism signified a troubling shift in Palestinian tactics. Israeli diplomat Shlomo Argov
warned the acting assistant secretary of state that "this was a new dimension of trouble for [the] Near East."[43] Two months later, the Israeli warning seemed to be coming true. A Lebanese source told an
embassy officer that "Arab commando groups were giving thought
to expanding their activities outside the Middle East into countries
that support Israel." This source warned in particular that Arab terrorists were considering "dispatching commandos on assassination
missions against high-level leaders 'who have adopted pro-Israeli positions' such as President Johnson, Vice President Humphrey, and
Richard Nixon."[44] Although the source did not link the assassination
of Robert F. Kennedy in June 1968 by a Palestinian named Sirhan
Sirhan to Fatah or any of the other groups, he warned that future
political assassinations were possible.

The information from Beirut was given by the NSC to the Secret
Service but did not occasion any White House policy review.[45] And
just as in the case of the Johnson administration's handling of
Cuba's involvement in the death of Ambassador Mein, it is unlikely
that there was a covert response to the increased radicalization of
this regional enemy of the United States. Covert action in the Middle East was considered very difficult, and the CIA's efforts there
were largely restricted to intelligence collection.[46] In the end, the
Johnson administration left office seeing the PLO as a regional actor
that could cause headaches but little else for Israel. It was not considered a mortal threat to that state, let alone to the United States.

President Johnson, who had extended the writ of the federal government in so many other areas of American life, did not use his re-

maining months in office to do battle with the airlines and conservatives on Capitol Hill on the issue of air safety. He also did not use these months to assign the United States a role in protecting Israel from Fatah or to step up the United States' covert struggle with Havana. The president chose instead to devote the waning energy of his administration to negotiating an end to the war in Vietnam, putting other foreign policy matters to one side. As a result, Lyndon Johnson would leave the new challenges of Mideast terrorism and air piracy to his successor, Richard Nixon.

Nixon and the Hijacking Problem

The Nixon administration would be the first in U.S. history to consider international terrorism a national problem. Over the Nixon years, the U.S. government's response would grow in intensity from a simple endorsement of the international community's first efforts to deter hijackings to the establishment of a permanent executive branch institution facilitating widespread counterterrorism cooperation and information sharing.

Initially, terrorism, domestic or international, was not on the administration's agenda. As it had been in the Johnson administration, the word *terrorist* was used interchangeably by the Nixon team with *insurgent, guerrilla,* or, in the Palestinian and Vietnamese cases, *fedayeen* and *Vietcong,* respectively. These regional bands, outside of Latin America and Southeast Asia, did not target Americans. Despite the taking of the El Al flight in July 1968, there still seemed to be nothing international or transnational about them.

Nixon's foreign policy program was focused on tangible threats to U.S. national security. Nixon and his advisors sought to build a better relationship with the Soviet Union based on an understanding that even these two adversaries shared an interest in avoiding nuclear war. Détente with Moscow, as this approach became known, was one of three interlocking achievements that would define the core of Nixon's foreign policy. The second was to be the establishment of relations with the People's Republic of China. Presidents before Nixon had viewed China as the most dangerous Communist power, less committed to international order than the Kremlin and a potential political problem at home, where Congress still recalled the "Who lost China?" debate of the early Cold War. Nixon was not naive in his expectations of what Mao Zedong would give the United States, but he decided that the time was right to recognize China. He saw through the ideological similarities of the Soviet and Chinese regimes to the traditional rivalry beneath, locating in those mutual suspicions the basis for a constructive relationship between Beijing and Washington. Détente and the opening to China were two pillars of a new foreign policy structure that would allow the United States to withdraw with its reputation intact from the unpopular war in Vietnam. Ending the U.S. dimension of the Vietnam War, which was the Nixon administration's third foreign policy objective, had been Nixon's most important campaign promise.

At the top of the second tier of his foreign policy goals, Nixon placed a renewed commitment to a process that would move Arabs and Israelis to reduce tensions in the Middle East. Not wholly divorced from the Cold War realities that shaped Nixon's top agenda items, the new administration's Mideast policy was also designed to improve the United States' standing in the region, where Washington had been doing less well than Moscow in the campaign for political influence. Seven Arab countries—including Egypt and Syria—had broken relations with the United States following the 1967 Six Day War, and the Nixon team hoped to restore those links as the peace process went forward.

Nixon's management of his foreign policy team reflected these priorities. He assigned the three core policy areas to Henry A. Kissinger, a Harvard professor of government and foreign policy entrepreneur who had been advising Democrats and Republicans alike for over a decade. As the presidential assistant for national security affairs (or national security advisor), Kissinger became Nixon's principal foreign policy advisor. Middle East policy, which Nixon considered less important, was farmed out to the Department of State. Nixon chose as his secretary of state his old friend and former law partner, William P. Rogers. Rogers, who had served as attorney general in the Eisenhower administration, had no foreign policy experience and did not bring any specific goals to his new post. Rogers and his concerns, despite his close personal relationship with the president, would take second place in the hierarchy of the new administration. Counterterrorism would eventually belong to Rogers's set of responsibilities.

TWA 840

Terrorists first grabbed the attention of the Nixon administration in late August 1969, when two Palestinian terrorists hijacked TWA Flight 840. This hijacking stirred immediate high-level concern as the first case of Palestinian violence being directed at a U.S. target. The flight, which originated in Los Angeles, was scheduled to end in Tel Aviv after stops in New York, Rome, and Athens. Instead, the plane was taken to Damascus. A man and a woman belonging to the Che Guevara Commando Unit of the Popular Front for the Liberation of Palestine (PFLP) had boarded the plane in Rome and initially instructed the pilot to fly to Beirut. The hijackers then changed their minds, and the plane headed for Tel Aviv, its original destination. Their reason for the attack also seemed to change as inexplicably as their destination. At first, the hijackers informed the passengers that they would be freed except for "a passenger responsible for death and misery of a number of Palestinians." Speculation later centered on Yitzhak Rabin as their principal target; Israel's ambassador to the United States had left for Israel on the same day but on a different flight. With Rabin not on their flight, the hijackers blamed the recent sale of U.S. Phantom jets to Israel as the motive for this act of piracy. As the plane was preparing to land in Tel Aviv, the hijackers panicked and forced the pilot to abort the landing and head for Syria.[47] The Syrians welcomed the hijackers, who managed to set off a bomb in the cockpit to create a final moment of panic as the crew and the passengers were filing out of the plane.

The State Department was designated the lead agency in responding to the incident, which involved an aircraft registered in the United States, an American crew, and several U.S. citizens among the ninety-eight passengers. There was no debate within the administration over who should manage the U.S. response to this event. In 1969, the Justice Department lacked jurisdiction over most crimes committed abroad, even on U.S. planes. It was also assumed that diplomacy was practically the only tool available for extracting a U.S. plane under hostile control on the ground in a foreign country. In 1969, the U.S. military had had no experience in rescuing civilians from commercial airplanes, nor did it have any small units trained for that particular kind of operation. The choice of the State Department over the National Security Council (NSC) seems to have reflected a tacit understanding that hijackings should be kept at arm's length from the president. "The supreme irony of this age of power," wrote James Reston, of the *New York Times,* "is its impotence to deal with determined or fanatical minorities."[48]

Secretary of State Rogers immediately issued a statement condemning "this act of international piracy" and calling on Syria to "take immediate steps to arrange the release of the aircraft, its crew, and its passengers."[49] A year earlier, during the El Al Flight 426 incident, the government of Algeria had decided to hold some passengers hostage to help publicize the Palestinian cause. The Nixon administration hoped for better behavior from Damascus.

Unfortunately, the Syrian government was no more prepared to show respect for the rights of Israeli passengers than the Algerian government had been. On August 30, Syria allowed the crew of twelve and the ninety-three passengers who were not Israeli citizens to leave. Three women, a fifteen-year-old girl, and two elderly gentlemen, one of whom was a professor at Hebrew University, were kept in Damascus as prisoners. Under international pressure, the Syrians released the three women and the girl two days later. But they refused to surrender the two remaining male hostages.

The taking of TWA 840 was major news in the United States and provoked widespread debate over the federal government's handling of hijackings. Although the thirtieth U.S. commercial plane hijacked in 1969, this was the first hijacking that year to involve foreign hijackers and the first not to involve a demand to fly to Cuba. Ninety percent of all hijackings since 1961 had been committed by U.S. citizens who wanted for one reason or another to go to Cuba. By a combination of signaling and trial and error, the United States and Cuba—which still did not have diplomatic relations—had established procedures to regularize these incidents and reduce the inconvenience to the passengers and crew.[50] As a result of this informal arrangement, the White House, the FAA, the airlines, and the public had come to view hijackings in the United States as a travel inconvenience more than a danger, something akin to bad weather in Chicago.

Even before the hijacking of TWA 840, airline pilots and some in the U.S. Congress had disagreed with this policy of tolerating hijacking. "It's a tragedy waiting to happen," warned James G. Brown, the captain of a National Airlines flight hijacked to Cuba earlier in the year, in testimony before Congress.[51] Congress had held hearings in response to the steep increase in hijackings in 1968, when twenty-two took place (there had never been more than five in any previous year). The hearings, however, had not led to any legislation, and the Air Line Pilots Association, which represented all of the country's commercial pilots and about half of the flight attendants, saw in the TWA 840 incident an opportunity to force the federal government,

U.S. airlines, and the international aviation community to take airplane security more seriously. As the Syrians continued to hold the Israeli passengers, the Air Line Pilots Association began gearing up for an international strike.

John H. Shaffer, the administrator of the FAA, agreed with the pilots that there was a problem. In his eyes, TWA 840 was a worrisome "new" kind of hijacking. "I'm afraid that this is a warning of things to come."[52] But Shaffer and the FAA were pessimistic that much could be done in the short term to solve it. Although careful never to admit this publicly, the FAA shared the view of the airlines that hijacking was a flaw in the system that just had to be managed. The FAA was also very sensitive to the argument of the airlines that their profit margins were so slender that only the most effective and most essential security systems should be required.

Following the congressional hearings on the hijacking problem in early 1969, the FAA set up a government–industry task force to look into cost-effective ways to increase security.[53] The task force, which involved psychologists, developed a system that profiled passengers according to the six behavioral traits believed to be associated with hijackers. Any passengers who fit that profile would then be screened by a metal detector, a so-called passive electromagnetic device. This system was still on the drawing board when TWA 840 was taken. In the wake of the public concern that followed that hijacking, the FAA decided to test the system on a trial basis. Eastern Airlines offered itself as the guinea pig. "It is not the final answer," admitted Shaffer, who was publicly pessimistic about the effectiveness of defensive measures at U.S. airports. Shaffer reminded the traveling public that some hijackings had occurred without a real weapon being present. In one case, the hijacker had bluffed with a can of shaving cream made up to look like a bomb. The FAA believed that the only real solution was for the State Department to use diplomacy to close down all the safe havens where planes were being diverted.[54] In the meantime, hijackings were inevitable.

The State Department shared the FAA's fatalism about dealing with the problem in the short term. "It's really frightening how damned vulnerable an airplane can be in a political situation like this [in the Middle East]," lamented one State Department official to the *New York Times*. "How do you protect the planes and the passengers? It's going to be awfully tough."[55] As for the long term, like the FAA and the airlines, the State Department believed that persistent multilateral diplomacy was the answer.[56]

The White House assigned itself a limited role in handling the hijacking of TWA 840. President Nixon approved U.S. efforts to increase diplomatic pressure on Syria to release the two remaining Israeli passengers and was kept briefed.[57]

Not all of the president's efforts occurred offstage. Nixon did make a very public statement to encourage an international response to the general problem of terrorism. At the suggestion of Labor Secretary George P. Shultz, Nixon included a reference to the problem of air piracy in his September 1969 speech before the General Assembly of the United Nations.[58] Shultz had relayed to the White House the pilots' union's impatience at the hijacking epidemic. "Sky piracy cannot be ended," Nixon said at the UN on September 18, "as long as the pirates receive asylum."[59] But Nixon did not publicly refer to Syria, nor did the White House establish any deadlines of its own for the release of the Israelis.

While the White House's patience seemed inexhaustible, that of the Israelis was not. In what would become a recurring pattern, the Israelis, in private conversations with the United States, threatened to take matters into their own hands if U.S. diplomatic efforts to secure the release of the two remaining Israeli hostages failed. The NSC staff, which believed that Israeli policy rested on a hair trigger, was particularly vulnerable to these pressures.[60] As the TWA hijacking entered its second month, for example, Henry Kissinger warned the president that in response to a diplomatic failure, "Israel may attack a prominent target like the Damascus airport."[61]

Ultimately, the two remaining Israeli prisoners were released before any Israeli retaliation occurred. U.S. diplomacy did play a role
in the successful conclusion of this affair, but not one that Washington would want to crow about. Despite a stream of messages to the
Syrians from the United States by way of the Italians, it was the fact
that Washington ultimately pressured Israel to release some captured Egyptian troops that brought the two Israelis home at the end
of October, nearly two months after their ordeal began. As the NSC
staff later concluded, "the 1969 TWA hijacking experience showed
that the U.S.—without even diplomatic relations—has no leverage to
use against Syria except for those pressures that can be generated
through the international forums associated with air travel."[62] Paying
the ransom was all that worked.

By his later actions, Nixon would eventually show that he did not
accept that hijacking or terrorism had to be a permanent feature of
American life. However, toleration of domestic hijacking initially remained the policy of the U.S. government despite the TWA affair.
The end of the crisis brought no thoroughgoing White House assessment of how to avoid similar events in the future. In part, this
could be explained by the enormous number of items on the president's schedule in late 1969. But it was also because the president
was misinformed by his advisors at the NSC and the Department of
State. In October, Kissinger mistakenly assured the president that
the FAA was working with the airlines on the "perfection of a system to detect hijackers in advance."[63] As of the fall of 1969, no one
at the airlines or the FAA believed that a perfect defensive system
was possible. The FAA was moving forward with only a limited test
of its profiling system that involved precisely one airline and appeared not to be in any hurry to try it out on an airportwide basis.[64]
The State Department had not made Kissinger's mistake in over-
selling the FAA's efforts, but the lead agency in managing the Syrian
incident did not attempt to explain to the president—or perhaps did
not itself understand—the trade-offs involved in the FAA and the air-

lines' approach to airport security. In the interest of lower overhead and passenger convenience, the FAA and the airlines accepted the risks implicit in a minimal security system.

A year later, when the PLO attempted the simultaneous hijackings of four aircraft, a feat not replicated by a terrorist organization until September 2001, Nixon became aware of the widespread weakness in U.S. airplane security and would try to get the federal government to do something about it.

The September 1970 Crises

Three simultaneous crises in September 1970, two in the Middle East and one in the Caribbean, were the Nixon administration's baptism of fire. The terrorist crisis was considered the least threatening of the three; nevertheless, it would establish the president as standing front and center in reshaping the federal government's handling of the hijacking problem and, by extension, the matter of terrorism.

On Sunday, September 6, the PFLP hijacked four airplanes flying from Europe to New York. Teams of two hijackers took control of Pan Am Flight 93, with 152 passengers and a crew of 17; TWA Flight 741, with 141 passengers and a crew of 10; and Swissair Flight 100, with 143 passengers and a crew of 12, and attempted to commandeer El Al Flight 219, which had originated in Tel Aviv. This fourth hijacking failed; the pilot sent the plane into a controlled dive while two plainclothes El Al security guards shot and killed the male hijacker and wounded his female accomplice, Leila Khaled. Khaled was a veteran in this deadly new game of terrorist hijacking. She had been the female member of the team that diverted TWA 840 to Damascus in 1969. Once the hijackers had been defeated, the pilot of El Al Flight 219 received permission from the British government for an emergency landing in London, where Khaled was taken into custody. The ordeal for the passengers on Pan Am 93 also did not last long. The hijackers diverted the 747 to Beirut and then Cairo, where, after freeing the passengers, they blew up the plane. The Swissair and TWA passengers were not that fortunate. Their planes were diverted to an abandoned British air base, Dawson Field, in the Jordanian desert, where the sun was hot and the planes' air-conditioning systems soon failed. These 306 people became hostages.[65]

This time, the hijackers made it clear that they were attacking the United States as much as Israel. Through the U.S. embassy in Amman, the PFLP sent word that it was "not operating against the American people in any way but rather against the policy of the U.S. government." Its spokesman, Abu Omar, said that "because of this attitude we are protecting passengers." The Palestinians provided a list of compatriots that they wanted released. For the safe return of the Swiss hostages, they requested the release of three Palestinians in Swiss jails; the British nationals would be set free when Leila Khaled was released. Similarly, the West German hostages would remain in captivity until three Palestinians in West German jails were freed. The United States held no Palestinian prisoners—and the PFLP did not request the release of Robert F. Kennedy's assassin, who seemed to have been moved more by madness than politics—so the American hostages would remain until all the PFLP's other demands were met. The terrorists' last demand was that Israel agree to an as yet unspecified "prisoner exchange" for the release of its citizens and any Israeli dual nationals.[66]

At the time, it was U.S. policy to negotiate with hostage takers.[67] This approach had brought the TWA 840 hijacking to a peaceful conclusion. In supporting negotiations with hijackers, the State Department was merely adapting U.S. domestic practices for its own use. The FBI and local police believed in paying ransoms and then going after the criminals.[68] In the first phase of the incident, the main objective was to ensure the safety of the hostages by separating them from the criminals. On September 7, the United States welcomed the mediation of the International Committee of the Red Cross, which represented the interests of all of the hostages in negotiations with the PFLP. On the first day of the crisis, the terrorists had moved 123 passengers, mainly women and children, to the Intercontinental Hotel in Amman, which was under PLO control, with the remaining passengers left aboard the two planes at Dawson Field, outside Amman. Besides the goal of the safe return of its hostages, the United States hoped to keep the Western side united so that the Western Europeans would not seek side deals that permitted their nationals to go home before the Israelis and U.S.-Israeli dual nationals.[69] Before the negotiations began, the Swiss and the West Germans had announced they would release the prisoners requested by the PFLP. Washington was able to convince the Swiss and the West Germans not to proceed with this side deal. On September 8, these two governments joined the British in offering to hand over the seven Palestinian terrorists in their jails only in return for the release of all of the hostages and the two planes.[70]

Nixon was at his western retreat in San Clemente when the hijackings took place. After releasing a statement condemning the hijackings through his press secretary, Ronald Ziegler, Nixon chose to remain almost invisible. Fearful that this crisis could come out badly, Kissinger had recommended a low-key approach to Nixon. Besides a general concern for the fate of the hostages, the national security advisor's great concern was still that the Western negotiating bloc would collapse before the Israeli passengers were freed. The British, the Germans, and the Swiss might deal for their nationals, leaving the Americans with Israeli passports stranded in Jordan, much as the two Israeli men had been a year earlier when TWA 840 was taken to Damascus.[71]

Although he adopted a quiet public stance, Nixon was impatient for action. On a status report from Kissinger he received the day after the planes were taken, he wrote, "I would like to see on a priority basis a recommendation by State (as the lead agency) and others as to what new steps we can take to deal with this type of activity in the future."[72] In the year since TWA 840 was taken, there had been an additional twenty-seven hijackings in the United States, a rate of more than two a month.

Nixon was the most interventionist high-level administration official on the terrorism issue. At the first crisis meeting on September 8, held without Nixon, in the secretary of state's office, Secretary of Transportation John Volpe, who oversaw the FAA, explained that "it would probably be impossible to develop any system that would give 100% certainty against conceivable sabotage threats."[73] Neither Volpe nor anyone else in the room—Secretary of State Rogers, Kissinger, or Secretary of Defense Melvin Laird—said anything about expanding the federal presence at airports or in the air.

In Nixon's eyes, his advisors were not working the problem hard enough. He wanted an immediate improvement in U.S. air security. He was impressed with the success of EL AL's onboard security in subduing the hijackers without hurting any of the passengers. Nixon instructed his administration on September 8 to begin preparing for the immediate implementation of a similar system on international flights by U.S. carriers that originated from U.S. airports. There were 2,300 such flights a day, and the FAA calculated it would need an average of 2.5 guards per flight.[74] As a first step, Nixon suggested hiring about four thousand armed airplane security officers as sky marshals. Airline industry officials and law enforcement experts were brought to the White House on September 9 to hammer out a workable plan. Within hours, the administration located 125 sky marshals, 100 from the Treasury Department and the FAA and 25 security officers from the CIA, who could be put on planes with little delay.[75] These numbers were still too low for Nixon. When he was told that it was going to take considerable time for the civilian agencies to train the remaining 3,875, he decided to turn to the U.S. armed services as a stopgap measure.

The first interagency struggle in the history of U.S. counterterrorism efforts erupted in response to the president's decision to involve the U.S. armed forces in air security. Defense Secretary Melvin Laird, a former congressman from Wisconsin, was ideologically opposed to the involvement of the federal government in air security. "The most preferable course by far," he counseled the White House, "is to provide training assistance to the airlines to establish their own guard service." The next-best solution, according to Laird, was to involve civilian law enforcement agencies. But he strongly opposed using military personnel, a proposal he admitted to viewing "with grave concern." He advised Nixon that the military was not trained for those types of conditions and that this duty would have a negative effect on morale while depleting the already insufficient number of military policemen.[76]

Laird also tried to rewrite the presidential announcement about the sky-marshal initiative that Nixon planned to give. Laird argued that the president should not identify himself with the hijacking problem. There was little the U.S. government could do to prevent these attacks, and it would be better to shield the White House from future blame. "If a statement is to be made," he wrote on September 10, "I believe it unwise for the president personally to do it. The tenor of the statement indicates that hijacking will be stopped. An additional hijacking or hijackings could occur within one hour or one day after the statement is made."[77] Laird took a page from history to warn the White House of any hubris: "A long history from the Barbary Pirates to the Pueblo argues strongly against the conclusion that effective means have been found [to deal with piracy]."[78]

Laird was not the only member of the Nixon administration who was uneasy with Nixon's desire to put the White House out front in the fight against hijackers. Nixon rejected the first draft prepared by NSC staffers for his antihijacking statement because he found that it watered down the role of the president. H. R. Haldeman, Nixon's chief of staff, noted in his diary, "[The president] wants to say 'I have directed that,' not 'I urge that.'" Nixon also encountered opposition at the State Department and in the NSC when he raised the idea of putting an embargo on states that protected hijackers. Secretary of State Rogers opposed the idea because it would complicate efforts to bring a diplomatic settlement to the Arab-Israeli conflict.[79] Kissinger and the NSC staff also considered an embargo unwise because U.S. trade was too small to provide any leverage with Syria, Algeria, and the other countries that had provided safe haven to terrorists in the past.

Despite these misgivings in his administration, Nixon announced an ambitious commitment to counterterrorism. Over the objections of his defense secretary, Nixon issued a statement on September 11, 1970, that ordered the creation of federal sky marshals and included military personnel to meet current requirements until civilian replacements could be found.[80] Over the concerns of his NSC staff and the State Department, Nixon also included a line in his public statement vowing to hold states where hijacked planes landed accountable for the protection of U.S. lives and property. Laird had been unable to prevent the creation of the sky marshals. However, Rogers and Kissinger, in one of their rare examples of cooperation, would make multilateral organizations the focus of U.S. efforts to apply economic sanctions to states that sponsored or condoned international terrorism.[81]

As the internal debate over how to deter future hijackings took place, the administration still had the problem of managing the hostage situation in Jordan. On September 9, the administration's crisis management team—the Washington Special Actions Group (WSAG)—held a wide-ranging discussion that involved consideration of a military operation to free the hostages. Before the meeting, Kissinger had arranged for six C-130 aircraft to be moved to Incirlik, Turkey, a ninety-minute flight from Jordan, "for evacuation purposes."[82] The national security advisor also arranged for the attack aircraft carrier USS *Independence* to move from a position southeast of Crete to the Lebanese coastline. Meanwhile, the U.S. military was instructed to review "appropriate contingency plans for Europe and the Middle East."[83] At the WSAG meeting, the principals, without the president, reviewed contingency plans for three different scenarios: "extricating" the hostages, evacuating all U.S. citizens from Jordan, or intervening to assist King Hussein should the PLO gain the upper hand in Jordan. The third scenario reflected a continuation of the long-standing U.S. policy of keeping King Hussein, a moderate Arab leader, in power.

The Pentagon advised the group that the U.S. military could be ready within forty-eight hours to initiate a military evacuation of all U.S. citizens using a brigade in Europe. The U.S. military, however, did not have a special capability available for extracting the hostages from a terrorist-held airfield. The Pentagon's assumption that it could employ the same plans for this kind of operation as it had ready for a military evacuation of U.S. citizens was unpersuasive.[84] Nixon's aides were unanimous in advising the president that a U.S. military operation to rescue the hostages would be inadvisable "except in the extreme case in which there is conclusive evidence that the hostages would otherwise be killed."[85] Nixon's national security team was also wary of encouraging the Israelis to try to free the hostages for fear that this would spark another Mideast war. As discussions continued in Washington, the PFLP placed additional pressure on the British government to release Leila Khaled by hijacking a British Airways flight from Bombay and diverting it to Dawson Field.

With reluctance hanging heavily over Washington, there was little actual preparation in Jordan for a hostage rescue mission. The CIA officer in Amman who was sent to Dawson Field to report on the planes was not tasked to acquire additional information to assist a military rescue. His mission through the crisis was to act as the principal line of communication between the embattled King Hussein and Washington.[86]

As the Nixon administration reviewed its contingency plans, rumors of a possible U.S. military intervention swept through Jordan.

Memories of the consequences of the U.S. and British military inter-
ventions in 1958 in support of the Lebanese government and the Jordanian monarchy caused the Palestinian leadership to reconsider its
tactics. A split developed between Yasir Arafat's Fatah movement,
which now controlled the PLO, and the PFLP, which controlled the
hostages. Since replacing Ahmed Shuqairi, the first chairman of the
PLO, in 1969, Arafat increasingly set the priorities of the entire
Palestinian movement. Seeking to avoid a Western or Israeli military
intervention in Jordan, which would upset PLO hopes to overthrow
King Hussein, the PLO suggested to the PFLP that all of the
hostages be moved from the three planes to Amman. All Israelis and
Israeli dual nationals would be segregated from the rest. The Western European and American hostages would be traded for the seven
Palestinian prisoners in Switzerland, West Germany, and Great
Britain. The PFLP disliked that approach and in a dramatic display
of its independence blew up the three airliners at Dawson Field after
evacuating the passengers. The PFLP took a group of over fifty
hostages, of whom forty were U.S. citizens and four were U.S. government employees, to an undisclosed location. The rest were permitted to go on buses procured by the PLO to Amman.[87]

The PLO intensified its pressure on King Hussein as it worked to
moderate the hostage issue. Yasir Arafat was playing for larger
stakes than the release of Palestinian prisoners. He hoped to overthrow the king and install himself as the leader of a Palestinian state
in Jordan. Understanding this, Washington advised Hussein to
mount a more effective defense of his position. The Jordanian army
had fifty thousand men, many of them well trained. The PLO, on
the other hand, had fewer than fifteen thousand troops, none of
whom was a match for a trained Jordanian. In the view of official
U.S. observers, the king's indecision was the greatest threat to the
Kingdom.[88]

On September 15, King Hussein informed the United States that
he would finally use his army against the PLO. The king's decision

posed a difficult trade-off for Washington. Washington recognized that the Jordanian counteroffensive would mean that the hostages, who were being held in a few homes in Amman, were about to enter a period of "grave danger." At the request of the administration, Hussein planned to include a warning to the Palestinians that there would "be severe consequences if they harmed the hostages." But the administration understood that "this may not be enough to stop them if they are desperate." The Nixon administration, however, concluded that the political survival of King Hussein was more important to U.S. national security than the survival of the estimated forty American hostages.[89]

The situation worsened in Jordan over the next few days. On September 19, in reaction to the king's decision to use his army against the PLO, Syria invaded northern Jordan. As the United States watched, Soviet advisors jumped off the tops of Syrians tanks as they crossed into Jordan. In all, Damascus sent a force of three hundred tanks plus artillery and infantry. Desperate to hold his position, the king requested emergency help from the United States. Meanwhile, the Israelis signaled to the United States that they wanted to intervene against the Syrians in Jordan.[90]

The Nixon administration preferred to let Israel intervene against the Syrians rather than undertake a U.S. military intervention in Jordan.[91] On September 21, the United States gave the Israelis the green light to bomb the Syrian army in northern Jordan. Alexander Haig, who was Kissinger's deputy at the time, recalls conveying the message to Israeli ambassador Yitzhak Rabin in a long conversation.[92] Although not its preferred option, the administration continued to consider direct U.S. intervention in the Jordanian conflict if the situation deteriorated further. Amphibious troops were moved into the region and plans were developed for the use of carrier-based aircraft.[93] Trapped in Amman, the hostages might be rescued, but this would be incidental to the main mission of keeping King Hussein in power.

As the administration tried to manage both the hostage incident and the military crisis in Jordan, the most dangerous challenge from Cuba since the 1962 missile crisis arose unexpectedly. In mid-September 1970, U.S. intelligence discovered evidence of a nuclear submarine base being built in Cienfuegos, Cuba. The Nixon administration subsequently concluded that the Soviets were violating the guarantees that Nikita Khrushchev had given John F. Kennedy and were again attempting to turn the island into an extension of its strategic striking force. The Cuban submarine base affair, which would ultimately be resolved to Washington's satisfaction, effectively ended discussion of U.S. military involvement in Jordan. The administration had no desire to fight wars on two fronts.

As it had in 1969, the granting of concessions to the PFLP brought the safe return of all of the Dawson Field hostages in late September. The Swiss, the West Germans, and the British released their Palestinian prisoners, and Israel staged a major prisoner release that, though timed to look voluntary, was understood to be part of the overall package.[94] It seemed to the essentially pragmatic Nixon foreign policy team that for a second-tier issue like terrorism, giving in to an adversary's demands was both prudent and effective. The negotiations with the Palestinian terrorists "was Vietnam-driven," recalls Haig.[95] The United States would resolve whatever it could diplomatically while so much of its focus remained on events in Southeast Asia.

Following the events at Dawson Field, the United States expanded its diplomatic efforts to deal with air piracy. Although President Nixon, in his statement of September 11, 1970, had conveyed a willingness to undertake unilateral measures to deal with states that showed a lack of cooperation on the terrorism issue, U.S. actions in the fall of 1970 reflected the NSC staff and the State Department's preference for a multilateral approach to this particular matter. "The United States is not sufficiently important as an external trading or financial partner of the above countries [deemed 'uncooperative' in hostage incidents]," concluded Kissinger's staff in October 1970, "to give us decisive influence through [unilateral economic measures]."[96]

Moreover, the NSC staff advised, "by using instruments outside the civil air field, we would be declaring ineffectual economic war; costing ourselves business to no end other than the marginal gains of a moral stance on the issue; and thus subordinating our entire foreign policy to the hijacking incident."[97]

Nixon's foreign policy advisors also had modest expectations for what could be achieved multilaterally. The NSC staff advocated, and the Department of State apparently agreed, that since there was little chance of getting multilateral support for broad economic sanctions against terrorist safe havens, it was best to work through the International Civil Aviation Organization (ICAO) to arrange boycotts in the area of civil aviation. A threat by Pan American Airways to boycott Beirut airport, for example, "had some effect, and there is no reason," the NSC staff concluded, "why similar sanctions should not be applied provided there is broad international support so that U.S. carriers will not be exploited by those of other flags."[98]

This effort at multilateral diplomacy brought some success. Thanks in part to pressure from the United States, the ICAO passed what became known as the Hague Convention, which required states to extradite or prosecute hijackers. In October 1970, U.S. representatives at the ICAO also introduced a resolution calling for sanctions against countries that assisted or abetted hijackings. Behind the scenes, the Nixon administration unsuccessfully tried to convince both the Soviets and the French—the two members of the ICAO whose Arab diplomacy made them most reluctant to support air piracy agreements—to ratify not only the Tokyo and Hague Conventions but also this new one that would impose sanctions. A year later, the United States did succeed in rallying enough support for an ICAO agreement, known as the Montreal Convention, which compelled signatories to extradite or punish individuals responsible for sabotage or the destruction of airplanes, but the effort at a multilateral sanctions regime in the civil air community failed.[99]

At the UN, where so many newly independent countries in the developing world were finding their political voice, the opportunities for helpful U.S. public diplomacy were less auspicious. Discussions in the General Assembly over what to do about terrorism quickly dissolved into debates over what constituted terrorism, as opposed to legitimate acts of anticolonialism.

Although the U.S. pilots' union, in particular, lobbied for a Security Council debate, the administration believed that the subject would inevitably get entangled with the politics of the Arab-Israeli conflict. "The veto," lamented an NSC staffer, "will preclude anything but the blandest of resolutions."[100] Meanwhile, the United States tried to encourage the Israelis not to take the lead on the issue at the United Nations. NSC staffers and State Department officials were concerned that any U.S. support for Israeli diplomacy on the hijacking problem would lead to countermeasures by Arab states directed at Washington.[101]

It appears that the Nixon administration also chose not to pursue any unilateral efforts to weaken Palestinian terrorist groups. Although the declassified record of CIA operations in the Middle East in this period is scanty, interviews suggest that the agency was not engaged in any covert operations directed at the PFLP in the 1970s.[102]

Administration documents still referred to members of the PFLP as "guerrillas" or the "fedayeen." The peaceful end to the Dawson Field incident did nothing to shake the assumption of intelligence and law enforcement professionals that even the most radical of the Palestinian groups, which at the time seemed to be the PFLP, used terrorist tactics solely to make political statements. In this view, hostages were useful as bargaining chips to secure the release of PFLP prisoners, but the PFLP saw no political value in killing them.

The terms *international terrorist* and *international terrorism* did not yet appear in high-level documents or in the national consciousness. In a little over two years, Palestinian terrorists had transformed hijacking from a domestic inconvenience associated in American minds with Cuba into terrifying political theater on the global stage. The Nixon

administration had reacted by mandating the first serious antiterrorism measures at U.S. airports and increasing protection on international flights by U.S. carriers. But since this theater had not yet taken
any innocent lives and for all its military efforts in Jordan, the PLO
had failed to take control of a state, Washington's concern was limited. Neither the Nixon administration nor the American people
viewed Palestinian terrorism as a significant threat. This would
change in September 1972.

CHAPTER THREE

The Lessons of Munich 1972

THE PALESTINIAN ASSAULT on the Israeli team at the 1972 Munich Olympics shocked the consciousness of the world and finally defined the new menace of international terrorism. Two athletes were killed in the initial attack on the Israeli quarters at the Olympic village, and the rest were held hostage. The unit, now known to be linked to the PLO, that staged this attack called itself Black September in commemoration of the events in Jordan of September 1970. The terrorists demanded the release of two hundred Palestinians from Israeli jails. In the course of a botched rescue attempt by the West German authorities on September 5, 1972, the remaining nine Israeli athletes and five of the eight terrorists died.[1]

Along with the millions of sports fans who unexpectedly found themselves witnesses while watching the drama unfold on live television, the U.S. administration had monitored the situation closely. A task force was set up at the State Department; the Executive Protective Service was asked to provide protection for Israeli, Arab, German, and Soviet delegations in the United States; and the administration instructed local police departments to protect sensitive areas.[2]

The massacre at the airport came as a complete surprise to the Nixon administration. The West Germans initially reported that the affair had been resolved peacefully, and staffers at the State Department prepared congratulatory messages for Nixon and Rogers to sign. Rogers decided to wait for word that the Israelis had been released. "Thank God we didn't [send the message]," Rogers recalled later.[3]

In the wake of the killings, both the State Department and the CIA instituted changes in how they handled Palestinian violence. The terms *counterterrorism* and *international terrorism* formally entered the Washington political lexicon as the U.S. government established its first groups to manage the problem. The State Department established two departmental committees to deal with terrorism: one to "stimulate and coordinate international action against terrorism," the other to "protect foreign persons and property in the United States."[4] And it set up an ad hoc interagency group to "coordinate intelligence data regarding terrorist organizations and their activities and to improve exchanges of such information with other governments."[5] Meanwhile, the CIA began systematic reporting on "international terrorism." The agency quickly created a team of midlevel analysts in the Directorate of Intelligence, who would pull together what they could on terrorist organizations around the world. Their first product, the so-called weekly summary on international terrorism, appeared on September 15. Specialized reports on Black September and the fedayeen movement followed.[6]

The White House, however, was initially less concerned about the new problem of the internationalization of Mideast violence than it was about how to contain Israeli anger. Israel wanted the United States to pressure the International Olympic Committee to cancel the remainder of the games. Over the course of the night of September 5, Kissinger and Haig tried to discourage the Israeli government from making this demand. They did not wake the president, whose opinion on the matter they already knew. Nixon believed that canceling the games would be handing the terrorists a public relations victory. "They want to make it appear that they've stopped the games," Nixon said the next morning to Kissinger. "It's like these assholes that tried to stop us running the government. . . . If we'd stopped like some of the softheads around here [wanted] or gone over and prayed at the Lincoln Memorial, that's what they want. So the thing to do is to do it the other way."[7]

Nixon also worried about the domestic political fallout of the Munich massacre. "The trouble with the Jews," he told Kissinger and Haig, "is that they've always played these things in terms of outrage. You've got the Jewish Defense League raising hell and saying we ought to kill every Arab diplomat." If the administration did not show that it cared about the massacre, Nixon feared it would come under stiff criticism from the American Jewish community. "You don't really know, Henry, what the Jewish community will do on this. It's going to be the goddamnest thing you've ever saw." On the other hand, Nixon had a sense that he should not do too much. Some Jewish community leaders were asking for a national day of mourning, a proposal that Secretary of State Rogers agreed with. Nixon thought this was grandstanding, as did Kissinger.

Kissinger's greater concerns were international. Drawing a parallel with the circumstances surrounding the beginning of World War I, he worried that the Israelis would start a war over the Munich attack. "My great fear," he told Nixon that morning, "is World War I started because the Austrians had been frustrated for fifteen years, had the archduke assassinated, the Germans and the whole world was outraged." Kissinger thought that Israel was contemplating an invasion of Lebanon to capture the leadership of the PLO, and he was concerned that they might take U.S. support for granted. "We've got an election campaign," argued Kissinger, ". . . and I don't want them to think that they've got you in their hip pocket." Following this conversation with the president, Kissinger warned the Israelis not to launch any military attacks.

However, Nixon understood better than Kissinger that there was indeed something precedent-setting about this new level of Palestinian violence. As soon as he returned from San Clemente, the president began in Oval Office conversations calling the PLO operatives "international outlaws." "They are unpredictable and all the rest. Egypt and Lebanon did not put them up to it," explained Nixon to his chief of staff, H. R. Haldeman, on September 7.[8] "We have to do something to deal with that threat," Haldeman chimed in. Nixon agreed but was at a loss what to do: "Rogers is consulting with people to see what the hell we can do, talking about the hijacking convention." Nixon was angry at the Lebanese for having provided a home to the PLO after Arafat was thrown out of Jordan in September 1970. "Why is Lebanon harboring those sons of bitches?"[9]

Despite U.S. warnings, on September 8, the Israeli air force attacked approximately ten PLO bases in Syria and Lebanon. Three Syrian jets were shot down in the course of the operation, and Israeli bombs destroyed the railway between Syria and Beirut. It was estimated that two hundred Arab civilians were also killed.[10] The administration was prepared to accept the attacks on PLO bases but worried that the Israelis would want to bomb much larger targets. A week later, three Israeli armored columns invaded southern Lebanon. Designed as a show of force, the tanks destroyed 130 homes of suspected PLO militants before withdrawing.[11]

President Nixon's interpretation of the Munich incident shifted dramatically on September 19, four days after the Israeli incursion into Lebanon. That morning, the president used a meeting with the U.S. permanent representative to the United Nations, George H. W. Bush, and Secretary Rogers to explain the significance of the Munich tragedy as a test of U.S.-Israeli relations. The administration had started picking up hints that Israel's friends in Congress were playing on public sympathies to raise objections to détente with the Soviet Union because of Brezhnev's unwillingness to allow the free emigration of Soviet Jews. Kissinger and Nixon believed that Israel might use the Munich massacre to force the administration to insist on emigration rights for Soviet Jews as part of détente with Moscow.

By the afternoon, however, some information came to the president that encouraged him to see the Munich incident as the harbinger of a new kind of threat, not to his plans for détente, but to U.S.

security itself. In one of the oddest moments in the history of U.S. counterterrorism, this information came from Jeanne Dixon, an alleged psychic syndicated in many U.S. newspapers. Nixon thought well of her prophesies and used his secretary, Rose Mary Woods, as a conduit for Dixon's predictions. Not long after Bush and Rogers left the Oval Office, Rose Mary Woods came in with Dixon's latest "information." The psychic predicted a major terrorist attack on either an Israeli official in the United States or an American political figure.[12]

On hearing this, Nixon unleashed a diatribe against Israel in the presence of Ms. Woods. "What the hell do we care about that [Soviet exit permits to the Jews]? Why should the Jews get out and not the Ukrainians? Why should the Jews get out and not the Poles?" He blamed the Israelis for creating the conditions that were now making a terrorist attack in the United States possible. And he resented how the Israelis seemed to be using the Munich tragedy to push their anti-détente agenda in Washington. Once he calmed down, Nixon decided that however angry he might be at the Israelis, he had an obligation to take measures to protect Americans and foreign diplomats assigned to the United States. Nixon later called Kissinger's deputy, Haig, to see that the FBI had contingency plans for dealing with a terrorist incident in Washington, D.C., or New York.

Kissinger, who was in New York, at the United Nations, still believed that the principal threat posed by the Munich massacre was an Israeli overreaction. In addition to decrying international terrorism at the UN, Kissinger believed that the United States could slow the Israelis down by showing that it was gearing up institutionally to fight international terrorism. His idea was the formation of a meaningless but nonetheless impressive-sounding Cabinet Committee to Combat Terrorism. In broaching the idea to Nixon once he returned from New York, Kissinger was candid about this being little more than a gesture. He nevertheless believed that it might encourage the American Jewish community to lessen its attacks on détente.

Nixon liked the idea of forming a cabinet-level committee, but he envisioned it as more than a gesture. "Rose talks to this soothsayer, Jeanne Dixon, all the time," said Nixon, confessing to Kissinger on September 21 the intelligence on which he was basing his new threat assessment. "She was in," he continued; ". . . they are desperate that they will kidnap somebody. They may shoot somebody . . . We have got to have a plan. Suppose they kidnap Rabin, Henry, and demand that we release all blacks who are prisoners around the United States, and we didn't and they shoot him? . . . What, the Christ, do we do? We are not going to give in to it . . . We have got to have contingency plans for hijacking, for kidnapping, for all sorts of things that [could] happen around here."[13]

In subsequent days, as Kissinger pulled the plan for the cabinet committee together, Nixon insisted that it be more than window dressing for the benefit of the Israelis and the American Jews. Nixon wanted both acting FBI director L. Patrick Gray, who had replaced the late J. Edgar Hoover in May 1972, and Director of Central Intelligence Richard Helms as members of the committee, so that intelligence about possible terrorist attacks would be coordinated at the highest level. "I don't want a bunch of . . . jerks from State," he told Kissinger. "No, no," assured the national security advisor in an effort to placate his boss, "this is a cabinet-level committee . . . lots of prestige."[14]

Kissinger and the NSC staff never accepted Nixon's view of the cabinet committee. Haig later recalled the committee as "a charade."[15] In a contemporary memorandum to Nixon's chief domestic advisor, John Ehrlichman, Haig stressed that the "reasons for this [establishing the committee] involve the Soviet Jewry issue and our need to keep the Israelis cooperative on this issue. This vehicle will serve that purpose."[16]

The committee would meet only once, in early October 1972, before it was replaced by a different executive counterterrorism organization in 1977. But it did spawn an active working group, chaired by the State Department's new coordinator of combating terrorism and attended by representatives of nine other agencies, including the CIA and the FBI. The working group, as it became known, gathered only midlevel officials. The chairman himself was outranked by deputy assistant secretaries of state, and the rest of the working group carried little more clout. Nevertheless, it constituted the first interagency study group to be thinking about terrorism on a regular basis. Initially, the group, which would grow beyond the original ten members, met every two weeks.

The difference of opinion between Kissinger and Nixon on the importance of the working group was evident in the choice of the White House representative. Probably on the advice of John Ehrlichman, the White House selected David Young to be its representative. Young, who was codirector with Ehrlichman of the White House "plumbers" unit, reported through Ehrlichman to Nixon. In late 1971, Young had investigated leaks from the White House to the Joint Chiefs of Staff.[17] Indeed, on September 16, only nine days before the formation of the working group, at the instruction of the president, Haldeman had asked Young to check out the source of the leaking of two CIA documents to Dan Rather, of CBS News.[18] Young's assignment to the working group signaled the importance that the president and his inner staff gave to it.[19]

In the fall of 1972, the newly established working group received some alarming reports on PLO activity in the United States. On October 18, Young reported back to Ehrlichman some intelligence that the PLO was plotting to kidnap Rabin and Sargent Shriver, George McGovern's vice presidential running mate. The FBI wanted presidential authorization to be able to move quickly in the event of an attempted assassination. Ehrlichman brought this to the president because of his concern that with Nixon leaving on another campaign swing, he might be out of touch in the critical early moments of an incident. Ehrlichman wanted to distance the president from any government counterterrorism operation. He wanted to set up an automatic mechanism so that the FBI could respond to any terrorist incident. "It gets it away from here," said Ehrlichman, "if something goes wrong."[20]

As he did in 1970 when pushing for a greater federal commitment to airline security, Nixon saw efforts to shield him from the terrorism issue as an abandonment of his presidential responsibilities. He wanted the FBI to assume responsibility for responding to terrorist incidents. "But I will back him . . . [Gray] can say he had orders from the President," Nixon told Ehrlichman.

Solving the Hijacking Problem?

U.S. commercial pilots had been predicting for at least three years that a domestic hijacking would turn violent because of the ease with which hijackers could bring guns onto airplanes. On Saturday, November 11, 1972, the Nixon administration witnessed what was then the most chilling domestic hijacking in U.S. history.[21] Although not an act of international terrorism, the incident would have a major effect on the nation's ability to deal with that challenge. Three men, all with criminal records, boarded Southern Airlines Flight 49, a twin-engine DC-9, in Birmingham, Alabama, for an evening flight to Memphis. Lewis D. Moore and Henry D. Jackson were running from rape charges in Detroit, and Melvin Cale was a fugitive from a prison in Nashville. Southern Airlines had adopted the FAA's voluntary hijacker profiling system, which apparently these three men triggered. They were nevertheless allowed to board their flight, and an airline employee quickly passed a metal-detecting wand over them in their seats. The perfunctory search missed the arsenal of guns, ammunition, and grenades the men had brought with them.

Soon after the plane took off, the three criminals broke into the cockpit and demanded $10 million to release the plane, the largest ransom in the history of U.S. hijackings. They diverted the plane to

Detroit, where they demanded that the money be paid. When the FBI offered only $500,000, the men ordered the pilots to fly to Toronto, Canada, thus turning this into an international incident. It was now the early morning of November 12, and desperate to prove to the U.S. government that they were serious, the gunmen devised an ingenious plan. One of them had worked at the Oak Ridge National Laboratory, in Oak Ridge, Tennessee, a major nuclear research center. After the plane was refueled, the hijackers ordered the pilots to fly in a holding pattern around Oak Ridge, twenty-five miles from Knoxville, Tennessee. The hijackers then let the air traffic controllers know that if their ransom demand was not met, they would force the pilots to fly the plane into the Oak Ridge facility, causing the nation's first nuclear disaster. "It was a very, very scary situation," recalls Jim Alexander, who was a public relations officer at the Atomic Energy Commission (AEC) facility in Oak Ridge. Weekend staff at the Oak Ridge National Laboratory could see the plane circling overhead.

Air-to-ground communications from the cockpit found their way to the local media, which began broadcasting the hijackers' threats against the nuclear facility. Officials at the AEC, which oversaw both the country's civilian and its military uses of nuclear energy, decided after receiving news of these threats to shut down Oak Ridge's high-flux isotope reactor. The hijackers had identified it as one of their targets, as well as two other smaller nuclear reactors in the immediate area.[22] In response to media questions, the AEC explained that the main facility would be severely damaged if hit by an airplane but that because the reactor core was underground, only a limited amount of radioactivity would be released.[23]

With President Nixon in Key Biscayne, relaxing following his recent reelection, the incident was handled in Washington by the Justice Department in collaboration with the FBI and the White House. In their desperation to gain the attention of the White House, the hijackers demanded to speak with President Nixon. White House officials refused to involve the president directly, but the hijackers were offered the chance to speak with other White House personnel, which they quickly rejected.

The federal government's offer to pay the ransom convinced the hijackers to allow the plane to land at a nearby airfield. In Chattanooga, the local FBI office forged a document "signed" by John Ehrlichman and "witnessed" by John Dean granting the hijackers $10 million.[24] A truck then delivered between $2 and $2.5 million in ten- and twenty-dollar bills. The hijackers, who assumed they had received $10 million, piled the money in the last rows of the aircraft.

Assuming they had the entire ransom, the hijackers next ordered the pilot to fly to Havana. The Cuban government, however, no longer had any interest in providing safe haven to extortionists. Two weeks earlier, Castro's government had arrested two bank robbers from Virginia who had hijacked a Delta Airlines plane. When the Cubans refused to admit the hijackers after they had landed, the gunmen ordered the pilot to take off for Europe. The crew, however, convinced them that they needed oil for the engine and additional fuel before attempting to fly across the ocean. The DC-9 jet could not fly nonstop from Cuba to Europe and would have to puddle jump to Iceland and then to Ireland.

Throughout the crisis, the FBI had looked for ways to disable the plane. In recent years, the FBI had reached an agreement with the airlines and the pilots association that in a hijacking situation the bureau would not attempt to disable the plane without the approval of the captain on board. The Southern Airlines hijacking revealed the flaws in the arrangement. How could the FBI seek the pilot's approval without tipping off the hijackers? The incident revealed other flaws in the federal government's standard procedure for responding to hijackings. The FBI had few undercover assets for use in terrorist emergencies. Instead, it had to rely on the airlines for this dangerous work. The FBI had requested that Southern Airlines approach Delta Airlines to get one of its mechanics to disable the plane's engines when it was on the ground for refueling in Chattanooga. Fearing a future lawsuit for damages from its competitor Southern Airlines, Delta had initially refused. Ultimately, Delta ordered one of its mechanics to approach the plane to disable the engine. Having no crisis training, the mechanic panicked and ran from the task.

That scheme having failed, the FBI had no resources to fall back on other than its sharpshooters when the plane later landed in Orlando again to refuel. The FBI had very little experience in ending hijackings, but in August 1961, the FBI had forced a father-and-son hijacking team to surrender in El Paso after shooting out the tires on the plane.[25] When the hijackers of Southern Airlines Flight 49 requested charts for Europe at this stop in Orlando, acting FBI director L. Patrick Gray, in consultation with the airline and the FAA, decided to try a second time what had worked in El Paso. In this case, Gray approved a plan calling for FBI officers, once they had immobilized the plane, to enter through the emergency exit at the back of the plane and kill the three hijackers. Fortunately for the passengers, some of whom would surely have been killed in the melee, the FBI's effort to immobilize the plane by shooting out the tires failed. Despite the assurances of the FAA and the airline, it turned out that a DC-9 could take off with flat tires. With a revolver at his head, the captain managed to get the plane off the ground.

The foiled FBI operation enraged and frightened the hijackers. "That drove them into a frenzy," recalled a passenger later. "They were raving maniacs after that. Before, they were just docile maniacs."[26] Once the plane was aloft again, the hijackers took the copilot outside the cockpit and told the passengers that he would be sacrificed. One of the terrorists shot at the copilot as he tried to duck behind the first two rows of seats, shattering his right arm.[27] The insistence of the captain that he needed his copilot to fly the plane stopped the hijackers from killing the wounded man.

The hijackers tried for a second time to escape to Cuba, and they directed to pilot to fly again to Havana. This time the Cuban government, in a humanitarian gesture, accepted the hijackers. A foamy flame retardant was sprayed on the runway at José Martí Airport, the plane landed safely despite its flat tires, and twenty-nine hours after it had begun, the ordeal of Southern Airlines Flight 49 ended.

This one incident altered the domestic politics of hijacking. "How many more airline passengers must fly with terror, how many more airline employees face death or serious injury before the United States Government, the international community, and the airlines put safety before politics or profit and take decisive action to curb aerial hijackers?" asked the *New York Times* editorial page the day after this hijacking ended.[28] Media coverage of the drama, which was carried live by radio and television, remarkable for an era before twenty-four-hour news, broke the back of public, industry, and government complacency that had prevented strong antihijacking measures. The ordeal of Southern Airlines Flight 49 also enraged the Airline Pilots Association (ALPA) and the Transport Workers Association—representing between them the nation's thirty-one thousand pilots and twenty-nine thousand flight attendants—which criticized the FBI for its inept handling of the case. "This incident was the closest to the total loss of a plane and its passengers we've had from hijacking," commented the president of ALPA, John J. O'Donnell.[29] ALPA asked President Nixon to restore the principle of "pilot in command": "Our experience has shown," argued the interest group, "that without prior knowledge and complete cooperation of the captain and his crew, any action by outside forces could end in total disaster."[30] ALPA also requested the posting of federal marshals to supervise boarding on commercial airlines and encouraged the Nixon administration to "directly negotiate an accord" with the Castro regime so that Cuba was no longer a magnet for skyjackers.[31] The pilots union let it be known that it would organize a worldwide strike of airline pilots in January 1973 if its demands for greater airline security were not met.

In the days that followed, even the political taboo of dealing with Fidel Castro was temporarily suspended. After the Castro regime

arrested the hijackers and sent word that they were interested in negotiating an antihijacking pact with Washington, the Nixon administration initiated indirect negotiations through the Swiss. Members of
Nixon's own party advocated the end to the twelve-year embargo on
Cuba. Three months later, the United States and Cuba initialed the
first agreement ever between the two countries since Castro had
come to power. Both countries agreed either to try hijackers or to return them and to provide safe passage for the aircraft or ship and its
passengers. In a concession to the Cuban government, which had
concerns about the activities of Cuban-exile groups in the United
States, the two countries agreed to prosecute terrorists who used the
territory of one signatory to attack the other. Havana and Washington also agreed to retain the right to grant political asylum to each
other's dissidents.

The other consequence of the hijacking of Southern Airlines
Flight 49 was the beginning of serious antiterrorist security measures
at the nation's airports.[32] Before this incident, the Nixon administration and the House of Representatives had allied themselves with
the airlines in resisting an antihijacking measure that would have
dramatically expanded the federal role in airport security. The bill,
which went down to defeat in the House after passing in the Senate,
would have created "enlarged Federal airport security forces, with
security responsibility centered in the Federal Aviation Administration," appropriated federal money to purchase screening devices,
and mandated 100 percent screening of passengers and carry-on
baggage.[33] In light of new public concerns about hijacking, the
Nixon administration dropped its opposition to 100 percent screening of passengers and carry-on luggage but maintained its opposition
to the creation of a federal airport security service, leaving the implementation of these security measures to the airlines.

On December 5, the U.S. Department of Transportation announced that 100 percent screening of passengers and hand luggage
would begin January 5, 1973. To prevent a recurrence of the "Key-

stone Cops" routine in Orlando, the Department of Justice signed an agreement with the Department of Defense on November 22 to make military assistance available to the FBI in a terrorist emergency.

In a quiet response to the hijackers' threat to destroy the nuclear reactor at Oak Ridge, the U.S. government took the possibility of nuclear terrorism seriously for the first time. A decade earlier, the CIA, the White House, the AEC, and the Department of Defense hardly imagined that a group of individuals not linked to a government could acquire fissionable materials. But on November 25, 1973, an aide to the national security advisor, Henry Kissinger, wrote that "The AEC is developing better procedures for protecting nuclear raw materials which, if captured by terrorists, can be made into crude atomic bombs or exploded to cause contamination." Expecting his boss to see this as alarmist, the staffer added, "This is a real threat, not science fiction."[34] The hijackers' threat to Oak Ridge raised general awareness of the vulnerability of the country's nuclear facilities and materials. In background briefings to reporters, the AEC was now admitting that there was enough nuclear technology in the public domain for a terrorist to build a nuclear device.[35] The AEC instituted new procedures for the transportation of radioactive materials in the United States. For the first time, armed guards were to accompany the shipments.[36]

Not all of the U.S. government's serious antiterrorism measures in the fall of 1972 came in response to the Southern Airlines case. The Munich massacre brought a change in how the State Department handled foreign visitors. The U.S. government ended a program that allowed up to six hundred thousand visitors a year to remain in the United States for ten days without prior approval or screening if they said that they were in transit.[37] As of September 27, 1972, all foreign travelers, with the exception of Canadians, had to have visas to enter the United States. At the same time, the State Department launched Operation Boulder to establish safeguards against the entry into the country of foreign terrorists or terrorist sympathizers.

Under this program, there was a five-day waiting period for Arab
nationals seeking visas as well as for nationals of other countries
with active terrorist organizations. Visa applicants were to be
screened by the FBI and the CIA, as well as the Immigration and
Naturalization Service (INS), and a special teletype system was installed at the INS to facilitate information sharing.[38]

For the U.S. government, despite a new awareness of the lethality
of Palestinian radicalism and the possibility of nuclear terrorism, terrorism remained the annoying little gnat that buzzed around the superpower while it was trying to handle truly dangerous matters.
Policymakers were quick to see improved statistics as a sign that the
problem was going away. In 1973, it appeared that the antiterrorism
steps taken by the Nixon administration had finally solved the country's twelve-year air security problem. Hijackings dropped from
twenty-one in the first seven months of 1972 to only one, which was
unsuccessful, for the same period in 1973. It was impossible to know
how many hijackings had been prevented by the Department of
Transportation's screening program or the State Department's Operation Boulder, but what was immediately clear was that the FAA and
the airlines had seriously underestimated or even misrepresented the
value of the available screening technology in the early 1970s. In just
the first three months of the program, screeners intercepted 4,916
weapons, which led to 573 arrests at the nation's airports.[39] The pact
with Cuba had also played an important role in the improvement of
the situation. Even the conservative editorial page of the *Wall Street
Journal* singled out the memorandum of agreement with Cuba as
"the biggest breakthrough yet in the campaign to cut down international air and sea piracy."[40]

The "No Concessions" Policy

Unfortunately, as the country seemed to become less vulnerable to
hijacking, foreign terrorists were adopting a new set of weapons to

send their message to Washington. On March 1, 1973, as a reception for the departing U.S. chargé d'affaires George Curtis Moore was winding down at the Saudi embassy in Khartoum, Sudan, four Palestinian gunmen jumped out of a Land Rover and began shooting at the diplomats. They took five hostages, including three Westerners: Moore; the U.S. ambassador Cleo Noel; and a Belgian diplomat, Guy Eid. The Palestinian Black September faction took responsibility and demanded the release of several hundred Palestinians in foreign jails, including Sirhan Sirhan, the assassin of Robert F. Kennedy. The Sudanese government denounced the attack and ordered soldiers to form a ring around the occupied embassy.

Palestinian radicals had targeted the U.S. mission in Khartoum because of the warming of U.S.-Sudanese relations. Starting in early 1972, the Sudanese had shown increasing interest in helping the United States bring key Arab states like Egypt and Libya into the Western fold. Sudanese president Gaafar Nimeiri told the U.S. ambassador to the UN, George H. W. Bush, who went on a special mission to Sudan in February 1972, that "the Sudan could assist any initiative which the U.S. might undertake, provided he [Nimeiri] felt it serious and genuine and provided that any action he was called on to take would not embarrass or weaken Egypt."[41] Nimeiri had also offered to arrange a meeting between Bush and Libya's leader, Muammar Gadhafi. Bush had been prepared to go, as he told Rogers: "I feel I could thread my way through this particular minefield if you believe President Nimeiri's suggestion worth trying."[42] But Washington had rejected that suggestion. Nevertheless, formal diplomatic relations between Sudan and the United States resumed in August.

Initially, the State Department shaped the U.S. response to the Khartoum hostage incident. The State Department expected to negotiate the release of Moore as it had negotiated the release of the hostages in Damascus in 1969 and at Dawson Field in 1970. Rogers dispatched Undersecretary of State William Macomber to Sudan to lead these negotiations. The terrorists' demand that Sirhan Sirhan be released, a concession no U.S. leader could agree to, meant that some sort of compromise would have to be arranged. During the Dawson Field incident, the administration heard rumors that the release of Sirhan Sirhan would be one of the PFLP's demands, and there had been widespread relief when the PFLP did not make this demand.

Washington's next move was completely unscripted. During a press conference on March 2, as Macomber was on his way to Sudan, a reporter asked President Nixon to comment on the Palestinian demand that Sirhan Sirhan be released. Outraged by the idea, Nixon instantly created a new policy for the United States in terrorist incidents. "We will do everything we can to get them released," said Nixon, "but we will not pay blackmail." Nixon was blowing off steam. There appears to have been no discussion or staff work prior to his uttering this pledge.

Some uncertainty remains as to whether the counterterrorism working group, which continued to meet regularly, and the NSC staff had already started moving toward a "no concessions" policy even before the Khartoum incident.[43] Armin Meyer, who as the State Department's coordinator for combating terrorism chaired the midlevel working group in 1973, later recalled that the working group had advocated this new policy but that until Khartoum, Secretary Rogers considered it "too callous" to accept.[44] These internal debates, in any case, had not bubbled to the surface before March 1973.

Indeed, to that point, the five-year-old negotiating approach had never come under public scrutiny. But once the president had endorsed the morally transparent and rhetorically simple statement that the United States did not reward blackmail, an open and unambiguous return to the policy of negotiating with terrorists became politically untenable. Thus was born what future administrations would enshrine as the United States' "no-concessions policy."[45]

Nixon's statement doomed Noel and Moore. After King Hussein's victory in the Jordanian civil war in September 1970, the Palestinian guerrillas had left Jordan, and PLO chairman Yasir Arafat had moved his headquarters to Beirut. The terrorist operation in Khartoum was under the control of PLO headquarters in Beirut, which supervised the hostage drama through telephone calls to the PLO office in Khartoum. When the Beirut headquarters learned of Nixon's rejection of its terms, the PLO immediately changed tactics. In communications intercepted by the United States, the PLO sent the order "Cold River" to the terrorists in the Saudi embassy. This was a codeword instruction to execute the three Western envoys. Noel, Moore, and the Belgian Eid were then led to the basement of the Saudi embassy and riddled with bullets, as each terrorist was allowed to take his turn at the trigger. PLO chairman Yasir Arafat participated in the supervision of the operation, and the U.S. government later concluded that he had given the order to kill the diplomats.[46]

The murders left Washington in a quandary as to what to do next. Harold Saunders, the NSC staffer responsible for the Middle East who had held the same position under Lyndon Johnson, proposed the strategy that Kissinger and Nixon ultimately approved: On the theory that any unilateral reaction by the United States would upset moderate Arab countries and kill any hope of Arab-Israeli negotiations, Saunders suggested quiet encouragement of the Arabs to deal with Black September. Nevertheless, Washington had known for years that the moderate Arab states, such as Saudi Arabia and Kuwait, were funding Fatah, which controlled Black September.[47] Saunders suggested and Kissinger agreed that they should be told privately that such activities were not helpful to the peace process. Saunders, however, warned against making counterterrorist actions a precondition of U.S. engagement with any Arab states. Such a policy, he advised Kissinger, "would play into Black September's hands because they would like to prevent a negotiated solution."[48]

Help soon arrived from an unlikely quarter. Sudanese president Nimeiri asked his minister of national reform, Abdel Rahman Abdullah, to accompany the bodies of Noel and Moore to the United States. Minister Abdullah carried with him a request for President Nixon. In the Oval Office on March 6, Abdullah explained that the Sudanese government planned to "see that justice was done and to brook no interference from outside." The terrorists, who had given themselves up to the Sudanese authorities on March 4, were to stand trial. The Sudanese also believed that Black September, which claimed responsibility for the attack, was merely a cover for a covert operational unit within Arafat's Fatah.[49] Sudan would be the first Arab country to bring charges against a Palestinian terrorist. The NSC could not have asked for a better outcome.

Worried about a backlash from Arafat and his terrorist organization, Nimeiri had Abdullah request emergency security assistance from Nixon. The Sudanese wanted U.S. intelligence training for their Public Security Department and National Security Organization. They also requested assistance in improving the security at the Khartoum airport, including the provision of metal detectors. Nixon approved the requests. The United States had given Sudan's security requirements "a high priority" in the year since Ambassador Bush's productive visit to Khartoum. But with Nimeiri's helpful response to the murders of Noel and Moore, Washington decided to step up these efforts.[50]

Washington left to the Sudanese the investigation of the murders. On March 6, President Nimeiri announced on radio and television that he was closing the Khartoum office of Fatah and accused its director, Fawaz Yassin, of complicity in the murder of the Western diplomats.[51] Yassin had fled to Libya hours before the attack. Although Washington was persuaded that responsibility for the actions in the Saudi embassy could be traced back to Arafat and Fatah, the Nixon administration almost certainly did not undertake any covert operations to destroy Arafat or the Black September faction. "That was not part of the ethos," recalls Robert Oakley, who was in the embassy in Beirut before taking over the NSC Middle East portfolio in 1974.[52] "We did not go after them," agrees Oakley's predecessor at the NSC, Harold Saunders. It was assumed, he recalled, that the Israelis would go after them. This was not something the Nixon administration wanted the CIA to do.[53]

The Sudanese would ultimately disappoint the Nixon administration. After charging eight members of Black September with murdering the three Western diplomats, the Nimeiri government delayed the trial sixteen months. In Khartoum, U.S. reporters and officials were told that Israeli attacks in Lebanon, particularly one that claimed the lives of three Palestinian leaders in April 1973, were to blame for the Sudanese government's growing reluctance to be the first Arab regime to put Palestinian terrorists on trial. The trial ultimately took place in June 1974. The eight men confessed, were sentenced to life imprisonment, and Nimeiri immediately intervened. He reduced their sentences to seven years less time served and announced that the men would be turned over to the PLO, which could detain them for the remainder of their sentences. On June 25, 1974, the eight were flown to Cairo. The U.S. government strongly condemned Nimeiri's decision but did not break relations with Sudan.[54]

Morocco and Beirut

Any inclination on the part of the Nixon administration to seek retribution for the murders of Noel and Moore had dissipated in the wake of the Yom Kippur War. In October 1973, audacious attacks by the Egyptians and the Syrians caught Israel by surprise. However, the Israeli Defense Force regrouped within a few days and launched a successful counterattack. On the Sinai front, the Egyptians were pushed back across the Suez Canal. Israeli forces followed, and as the capture of Cairo became increasingly likely, the superpowers intervened to restore the status quo and a tenuous balance of power.

Egypt's leader, Anwar al-Sadat, who had succeeded Nasser after his sudden death in September 1970, had launched the attack in the hope of reshuffling the playing cards of Middle East politics. As Nimeiri had hinted in early 1972, the Egyptians were ultimately looking for a way to build better relations with the West. In the wake of the Arab defeat, regional negotiations acquired renewed vigor.

Among those who now wished to speak to the United States was Yasir Arafat, who approached the United States the day after a UN-backed ceasefire went into effect. The moderate Arab states all wanted Washington to accept Arafat, despite the recent murder of the two U.S. diplomats, as the political spokesman for the Palestinian people.[55] "Talk to him," was their refrain. When Arafat signaled his interest in back-channel communications, Nixon approved discussions in Morocco and assigned the deputy director of the CIA, General Vernon Walters, to represent him. Walters was instructed not to begin negotiations, but just to convey a U.S. message and listen. The principal message he was to bring with him was that "there are no objective reasons for antagonism between the United States and the Palestinians." The PLO was also to be praised for the "responsible positions" its leaders had taken during the Yom Kippur War. There was to be no mention of the killings in Khartoum.[56]

Walters's opposite number was Arafat's chief of intelligence, Ali Hassan Salameh. Salameh had blood on his hands as the chief organizer of Black September's attack on the Israeli athletes at Munich.[57] Arafat's decision to send him to meet the Americans suggested that he had no fears that Fatah's terrorist past would disqualify the PLO from discussions with the United States.

The discussions continued in Beirut in December 1973. Robert Oakley, the political officer in the U.S. embassy, passed messages from Kissinger to Arafat through Walid Khalidi, an "advisor on the political side, not on the operational side, to Arafat." The notes from Kissinger had no address and no signature, but the PLO knew whom they were coming from. "There was little of substance; this was just an attempt to start a dialogue," recalls Oakley.[58] Arafat, however, treated these contacts differently. In April 1974, he sent word to the Nixon administration through this back channel that he needed "very early indication" of U.S. reaction to his position that the PLO should be the representatives of the Palestinian people at any peace talks. Arafat, who referred to himself as a "moderate Fedayeen leader," now agreed to recognize King Hussein as the ruler of Jordan as long as the world agreed to recognize him as the eventual leader of the "Palestinian National Authority" in the West Bank and Gaza.[59] Eventually, Kissinger raised the PLO's use of terrorism in the exchanges. The United States let Arafat know that for him to be accepted as a party in any negotiation, he would have to renounce the use of terror.[60]

These early discussions introduced a new complication into U.S. thinking on terrorism. Arafat now presented himself as a foe of terrorism. In laying out his concerns, he warned the Americans that if they chose not to deal with him, they faced only worse alternatives. He complained that the governments of Iraq and Libya, as well as the PFLP faction in the Palestinian movement, had been "working hard and spending lots of money to swing Fatah away from [his] moderate position." The PLO chairman was also blaming recent terrorist attacks on these hard-liners. Washing his hands of those events, he lamented that the "sharp upsurge in fedayeen terrorism could destroy hope of ever reaching the negotiating stage."[61] Khalidi stressed that Arafat and his circle had "come very far, indeed, on the road to realism and moderation" and they now feared assassination by the radicals.[62] Arafat said that he was working hard to convince George Habash, the leader of the PFLP, to accept something less than the return of the entire UN mandate of Palestine and the destruction of Israel.[63]

Arafat also continued to use the channel established between Salameh and the CIA to reinforce the image of his change of heart. After the meeting with Walters, Salameh started meeting with a CIA case officer named Robert Ames. Ames and Salameh apparently had established contact in the late 1960s, when Ames was in Beirut.[64] Their discussions were broken off before Munich, but now Arafat wanted them resumed. For the next four years, Arafat used Salameh to pass intelligence to the CIA on the world of Arab terrorism and the interests and aspirations of the PLO. "They were constantly trying to recruit each other," recalls a longtime CIA officer in Jordan, Jack O'Connell.[65] The information from Salameh, which was raw and voluminous, reached the NSC staff and gained for Ames a reputation as the CIA's main expert on the PLO.[66] The contact remained unbroken until 1978, when the Mossad killed Salameh, whom they had dubbed the Red Prince, in retaliation for Munich.

Arafat's signaling was seductive. But could he be believed? What tests would be sufficient to prove that a terrorist had transformed himself into a responsible leader of a peaceful national liberation movement? By his actions after the Yom Kippur War, Arafat provoked a policy debate in Washington over his true political identity that continued until Arafat's death three decades later.[67]

In its last months, the Nixon administration decided to discourage Arafat from thinking that he was in direct contact because of a concern that these contacts were bound to complicate U.S. negotiations with Israel and Jordan.[68] Despite receiving this message, the PLO continued to use Khalidi to send messages to the Americans. Following a terrorist attack at Ma'alot, where some Israeli children were taken prisoner and killed, Arafat used Khalidi to deplore the act because it involved children. Arafat implied that those responsible had crossed a line, though he added that in principle "neither he nor any other Palestinian leader could oppose operations inside Israel."[69] Arafat's ambiguous dance with the United States would continue into the next administration.

The discussions with Arafat did not mean that future Khartoums were impossible. Nixon remained concerned about terrorism and did not want the federal government to slip into the old pattern of complacency. Although the cabinet committee never met for a second time, the secretary of state reported to Nixon every six months on the government's achievements in combating terrorism. In mid-1973, Rogers had reported that despite Khartoum, the decrease in hijackings and in letter bombs, a terrorist tactic used by the extremist Jewish defense league in the United States, showed that Washington was winning on at least two fronts. After receiving a summary of this report prepared by Kissinger, Nixon wrote that though he wanted this good news to get out to the public, he also wanted "some admonition for additional action and sense of urgency."[70]

Despite Nixon's wishes, there was little, if any, additional action by the U.S. government and no sense of urgency. Even in the wake of the assassinations in Khartoum, Nixon's foreign policy team continued to view terrorism as at most a secondary problem. The PLO's decision to dabble in the Mideast political process had not caused any kind of lull in international terrorism; yet what little the administration had done against terrorism seemed to have satisfied the public and prevented international terrorist incidents at home. With Watergate about to engulf the Nixon presidency, the U.S. position in South Vietnam collapsing, and fruitful negotiations with the Soviets still proceeding, the NSC had more important challenges to manage.

CHAPTER FOUR

"There's Very Little We Can Do"

RICHARD NIXON'S RESIGNATION on August 8, 1974, thrust Vice President Gerald R. Ford instantly into the presidency. Most top-level members of Nixon's domestic staff had already left, charged with Watergate crimes. Some of his foreign policy team had also gone. Secretary of State Rogers had resigned in 1973, disgusted with Watergate and tired of the ceaseless battles with Henry Kissinger. But Kissinger, who had replaced Rogers and now carried both the title of secretary of state and that of national security advisor, remained to serve the new president and to carry on Nixon's foreign policy initiatives.

U.S. policy toward international terrorism initially remained the same. The Ford administration continued the effort to form an international coalition against terrorism and was committed to sustaining the Middle East peace process, including the back-channel relationship with the PLO. With one important exception, the Ford administration saw no reason to move beyond the domestic security measures initiated by the Nixon administration in reaction to the spate of hijackings between 1968 and 1972. The one exception was a Ford initiative in November 1974 to create the capability to deal with "lost or stolen nuclear weapons and special nuclear materials, nuclear bomb threats, and radiation dispersal threats."[1] The Cabinet Committee to Combat Terrorism's midlevel working group would continue to convene every two weeks to discuss terrorism trends and review federal antiterrorist activities.

By 1975, Ford had placed his stamp on his national security team. He kept Kissinger at the State Department but gave the national security position to General Brent Scowcroft, who had served as Kissinger's deputy. At the Defense Department, Ford placed Donald Rumsfeld, who had served Nixon in a number of domestic advisory positions and had became Ford's first chief of staff. Richard "Dick" Cheney succeeded Rumsfeld as Ford's chief of staff. From his vice presidential staff, Ford tapped former Democratic congressman John O. Marsh, Jr., to be his counselor to the president for national security affairs.

As the Ford administration settled in, a sharp divergence was developing between the growing counterterrorism community, consisting of midlevel officials at the Departments of State, Treasury, Justice, and Defense as well as at the CIA and FBI, who continued to be concerned about terrorism, and their principals, who believed that this threat had waned. The principals, for the most part, continued to associate terrorism with the hijacking problem and the activity of the PLO. In November 1974, as diplomatic relations were restored with Algeria, a country that had once offered itself as a haven to the world's skyjackers, a State Department spokesman explained that hijacking "is no longer the problem it once was."[2] Meanwhile, PLO terrorist activity continued the steady decline that had started after the Yom Kippur War.[3] Indeed, in early December 1974, PLO leader Yasir Arafat was reported as having launched a purge of extremist Palestinian elements in part to curb international terrorist attacks against "neutral parties."[4]

Thinking that international terrorism was yesterday's news, the Ford White House was already predisposed to taking a hard look at

Nixon's limited counterterrorism system when doing so became a matter of political necessity. A dramatic and almost immediate shift in public perception of the CIA set the stage for this review. "Huge CIA Operation Reported in U.S. Against Anti-War Forces, Other Dissidents in Nixon Years," blared the headline of the *New York Times* on December 22, 1974. Seymour Hersh had scored a journalistic coup by gaining access to an internal CIA review of its most questionable operations, involving domestic wiretaps, break-ins, and mail opening. The agency, which was prohibited by the National Security Act of 1947 from operating within the United States, had, according to Hersh, maintained "files on at least 10,000 American citizens," all in the name of counterintelligence.[5] Hersh did not use the words *counterterrorism* or *antiterrorism* in his exposé. Still, Richard Ober, the official on the CIA's counterintelligence staff who apparently oversaw these files, came to be described as the agency's "antiterrorist expert."[6]

What had happened was the discovery of the vestiges of the X-2 system of managing channels through which enemy subversives might communicate or travel. Hersh discovered the HT/Lingual mail-opening program, which had started in the Korean War but whose inspiration was the bumper crop of intelligence from opening the U.S. mail in World War II. This approach to counterespionage, and by extension counterterrorism, had never been compatible with U.S. law in peacetime. But rather than seek legal authority or public approval, a series of administrations had chosen to implement this approach in secrecy. With the political climate already poisoned by Vietnam and Watergate, these revelations raised public suspicions about the objectives of U.S. intelligence and would produce a dramatic backlash with long-lasting effects on the U.S. government's ability to carry out counterterrorism at home.

Ford, who was on his way to Vail, Colorado, for a Christmas skiing vacation when the story broke, instructed his aides to prepare an immediate assessment of the reporter's allegations. In follow-up reports, both CIA director William Colby and Henry Kissinger explained that the allegation of illegal domestic activity by the CIA was accurate. Kissinger added that there was even more political dynamite to be discovered in the CIA's closet. "There are other activities 'in the history of the Agency,'" wrote Kissinger on Christmas Day, "which though unconnected with the *New York Times* article, are also open to question . . . Some few of them clearly were illegal, while others—though not technically illegal—raise profound moral questions."[7] That same day, Ford vowed to establish a commission to investigate CIA wrongdoing. On January 4, he announced that Vice President Nelson Rockefeller would head the commission investigating questionable CIA activity.

Eager to distance the president from any institution that might be suspected of domestic espionage, Ford's advisors Philip W. Buchen and John O. Marsh advocated dismantling the modest counterterrorism structures established by Nixon, including the Cabinet Committee to Combat Terrorism and its working group.[8]

The national security advisor chose not to follow through on this suggestion, and the idea died. Perhaps Scowcroft decided not to bother because he, like Kissinger before him, saw these organizations as harmless and inexpensive. Perhaps he assumed that they were doing a creditable job and would not prove politically embarrassing in the investigations to come. The available record is incomplete. What is certain is that this would be a Pyrrhic victory for the working group, which would never earn the confidence of key Ford advisors. Marsh soon became counselor to the president for national security affairs, essentially the White House's point man for the congressional investigative committees of CIA activities that formed a few weeks later. For the remainder of the Ford presidency, the working group remained for him a source of suspicion.

The Hersh revelations also inspired a congressional response that would have an influence on the country's approach to counterterrorism extending beyond the life of the Ford administration. On January

21, 1975, the Senate launched an investigation of U.S. foreign and domestic intelligence activities. Known as the Church Committee, after
its chairman Frank Church, this Senate investigating body took testimony and fifteen months later issued its report on subjects ranging
from CIA attempts to kill Fidel Castro to the FBI's political intelligence activities, including its pursuit of Martin Luther King, Jr.

The Church Committee's investigations of FBI political intelligence activities would be the most influential in shaping U.S. counterterrorism in the future. According to James B. Adams, a high-ranking FBI officer at the time, Attorney General Edward Levi had
worried that Congress was in a mood to pass highly restrictive laws
that would have "severely impaired the effectiveness of the FBI."[9]
The FBI was very vulnerable. A number of its agents, sometimes at
the request of J. Edgar Hoover or his top deputies, had for decades
committed acts of harassment and entrapment against members of
racial and ethnic minorities and political dissidents. Some of these
abuses occurred within the context of the so-called COINTELPRO
(an acronym for "counterintelligence programs") investigations of alleged political subversion. In an attempt to head off any crippling legislation, Levi drafted a set of guidelines in 1975 that restricted the
FBI's ability to collect political intelligence outside of a criminal investigation.[10] What would become known as the Levi Guidelines established the principle that a file could not be opened on a U.S. citizen
without a criminal predicate, in other words, evidence of the commission of a crime or a crime in progress. These guidelines curbed
Hoover-era abuses but also had a chilling effect on information gathering. Collection on all domestic political targets was affected. Adams
recalled being admonished by Assistant Attorney General Laurence
Silberman, who informed the bureau that the FBI would have to
drop all of its Ku Klux Klan informants in klaverns who had not
committed crimes. A few years later, the FBI was told to drop an investigation of a group of seventy activists in Wisconsin who were
preaching the violent overthrow of the U.S. government but who

were careful not to advocate putting this philosophy into practice. Under the Levi Guidelines and the Privacy Act that Congress passed at roughly the same time, FBI officers could not even clip newspaper articles on these groups unless there was an official file, and they could not open such a file unless there was a criminal predicate. The FBI's counterintelligence division was spared these restrictions, so that if there was evidence that a citizen had connections with a foreign government, an investigation could begin. But in the case of a homegrown terrorist or an individual who had contact with a nongovernmental foreign terrorist organization, the FBI was not allowed to investigate the individual before a crime was committed.[11]

Undeterred by this new political climate in Washington, the government's midlevel counterterrorism experts were becoming increasingly worried about the growing activity of international terrorists. In October 1975, for example, the Defense Intelligence Agency reported that the PLO and the Irish Republican Army possessed Soviet-made SA-7s, a "man-portable, shoulder-fired, heat-seeking, surface-to-air missile with a maximum effective range of 3 nautical miles." Also widely available was the Soviet army's standard light antitank weapon, the RPG-7. In January 1975, a group of Palestinian terrorists under the command of the Venezuelan terrorist Ilych Ramirez Sanchez, alias Carlos the Jackal, had used RPG-7 rocket launchers to attack an El Al plane at Orly airport, outside Paris. They launched two rockets, both of which missed the plane, which was preparing for takeoff.[12] Not all of these weapons came from the Soviet bloc. The French, the West Germans, and the Swedes produced portable guided missiles that could be purchased openly as well as on the black market. A direct hit from one of these missiles could bring down a low-flying commercial airliner.[13] Although such a rocket attack had occurred only abroad, there was no reason to believe that these attacks could not occur on U.S. soil.

The perceived threat to U.S. security did not just come from a new generation of conventional weapons. In the mid-1970s, law

enforcement and intelligence specialists began to worry about nuclear terrorism. In 1974, an extortionist had threatened to explode a
nuclear device in Boston unless the FBI left $200,000 at a drop site
in the city. The threat turned out to be a hoax, but in the course of
responding, the FBI and the Atomic Energy Commission (AEC)
concluded that the federal government was woefully unprepared to
deal with the real thing. "If they were counting on us to save the
good folk of Boston," recalled a bomb recovery expert at the AEC,
"well, it was bye-bye Boston."[14] It took forty-eight hours for the AEC
to assemble appropriate detection devices and then discovered that it
had no way of flying them to Boston.[15] This experience led the AEC
in late 1974 to create a response capability to nuclear threats. Earlier
in the year, the AEC had conducted an audit of the security of the
nation's nuclear arsenal and found alarming flaws in the system.
Some of the twenty-six factories licensed to handle plutonium and
uranium were obsolete and lacked adequate security.[16] The use of
armed guards to protect the materials, a practice begun in the early
1970s, helped when they were in transit; but fissionable materials
had disappeared from factories and research facilities. In 1965, for
example, about two hundred pounds of enriched uranium went
missing from a uranium plant in Apollo, Pennsylvania.[17]

It was not long before the AEC's new Nuclear Emergency Search
Team (NEST)—a group of two hundred specialists in nuclear detection, recovery, and protection—had its first major deployment.[18] In
July 1975, NEST responded to a threat to detonate a nuclear device
in New York City. The extortionists or terrorists—they were never
caught, and their motives could never be determined—seemed to
have a sophisticated understanding of nuclear physics. "We have
successfully designed and built an atomic bomb," they claimed, and
provided a drawing of the device to underscore this threat. "It is
somewhere on Manhattan Island," they asserted. Asking for $30 mil-
lion in small bills, they gave the government until 6:00 P.M., July 10,
to comply. After the FBI left a "dummy ransom packet" at the drop

site in Northampton, Massachusetts, the mischief-makers disappeared. However, as far as the nation's newly minted counterterrorist experts were concerned, the threat had not.[19]

As U.S. counterterrorism experts catalogued new ways in which
terrorists could wreak havoc, they were also noticing a troubling radicalization within the Palestinian movement. Arafat's decision to
seek international recognition for the PLO as the political representative of the Palestinian people had begun to pay off in 1974. The
PLO received the endorsement of the Arab world at the Arab Summit in Rabat in October 1974, and a month later the United Nations
awarded the PLO observer status. But these diplomatic gains had
come at a price. They fractured the Palestinian leadership, causing
deep rifts within the PLO.

The so-called rejectionists wanted no part in negotiations that
might lead to the recognition of Israel. In late 1974, Sabri al-Banna,
who fought under the nom de guerre Abu Nidal, split from the PLO
and gained the patronage of the Libyan government.[20] In November
of that year, terrorists under his command hijacked a British Airways flight leaving Dubai in what seemed to be the beginning of a
campaign against Western commercial jetliners. Meanwhile, there
was a surge in attacks by the PFLP. Although these were restricted
to Israel, the PFLP had been the first of the Palestinian groups to
target Western assets, and it might do so again.

After reporting a steady decline in Palestinian terrorist activity
from the Yom Kippur War through 1974, the CIA warned the counterterrorism community that since July 1975, the trend had moved
decidedly in the opposite direction.[21] The splintering of the PLO
spawned a discussion of "transnational terrorism," a new category of
political violence that relied less on state sponsorship. "The wave of
the future," the CIA concluded in 1976, "seems to be toward the development of a complex support base for transnational terrorist activity that is largely independent of—and quite resistant to control
by—the state-centered international system." The CIA, however, did

not assume that this new problem implied an ever-increasing cycle of violence and destruction. While noting that "individual terrorist groups already have the capability of manufacturing or otherwise acquiring a variety of weapons or agents of mass destruction," the CIA thought that the risk was low that terrorists would seek to use these weapons. "Basically," the CIA concluded, "terrorists are in business to influence people, not exterminate them."[22]

In a switch from the early days of U.S. monitoring of Mideast terrorism, some of the intelligence on the plans of Arafat's rivals apparently was the product of the CIA's ongoing liaison with Fatah's intelligence chief, Ali Hassan Salameh.[23] These tips helped Western governments take preventive measures, but by increasing awareness of the anger and perhaps exaggerating the capability of PLO rejectionists, they also had the effect of increasing the insecurity of those who watched terrorism for a living.

In one instance, however, the tips were not sufficient to prevent the killing of two more U.S. diplomats. In Beirut on June 16, 1976, gunmen abducted and killed U.S. ambassador Francis E. Meloy, Jr.; the embassy's economic counselor, Robert O. Waring; and their chauffeur. Meloy had just arrived in Lebanon and was headed for his first official appointment. "Meloy's assassination triggered a crisis over those Americans remaining in Beirut," Kissinger would later write.[24] The Ford administration responded by evacuating Americans by sea from Lebanon, and the U.S. Congress passed an international convention "for the prevention and punishment of crimes against internationally protected persons."[25] There was no retaliation against the terrorists, however. The identities of the murderers could not be determined at the time, though it was assumed that they were part of a terrorist organization.[26] It was later concluded that a "Palestinian terrorist splinter group" had killed the men.[27]

The working group found itself lobbying the rest of the government to pay attention to these worrisome trends in Mideast terror and the ease with which terrorists seemed able to acquire ever deadlier weapons. In October 1975, at the same time that it received information on the proliferation of conventional "man-portable" missiles, the working group distributed to all agencies and the White House a top-secret report by its Task Force on Mass Destruction Terrorism, chaired by Robert Kupperman, the chief scientist at the Arms Control and Disarmament Agency. The report examined "the trends in terrorism, the physical effects of various terrorist weapons, and the domestic and international crisis management problems" involved.[28] The working group did not assign a high probability to a mass casualty event happening, saying simply that one "could arise at any moment, although this is not likely."[29] Nevertheless, it expressed concern that the U.S. government had never prepared any coordinated planning for this kind of event. With its report completed, the working group believed it could go no further and hoped to interest John O. Marsh, then counselor to the president on national security affairs, in proceeding with higher-level consideration of the problem.

The working group discovered that the Ford White House was extremely reluctant to discuss terrorism, even nuclear terrorism. The White House put off a meeting with Kupperman and the interagency task force. Indeed, Marsh had been on the verge of granting Kupperman a ten-minute briefing when his staff dissuaded him. "I have serious reservations," wrote staffer Mike Duval, "concerning the degree with which top White House officials, such as yourself, should be involved in [counter]terrorism." Duval, who worked the intelligence beat with Marsh, added, "As you know, there's very little we can do (that hasn't already been done) without incurring far more negatives than pluses. Any presidential involvement in this subject invites terrorists to target the United States and latent domestic dissidents to move into action."[30] The meeting apparently did not take place.

A president can be shielded from the terrorist problem only so long as an incident does not happen on U.S. soil. A month after the

White House turned down the working group's request for ten minutes of its time, a mysterious explosion at LaGuardia Airport forced the issue of terrorism to the top of President Ford's agenda.

At 6:33 P.M., December 29, 1975, a bomb exploded in a baggage claim area used by TWA and Delta, killing twelve people and injuring seventy-four. The FAA closed the airport for twenty-four hours while they began their investigation. The bomb, estimated to contain between twenty and twenty-five sticks of dynamite, had been placed in one of the rentable lockers. The explosion was so powerful that it blew a four-by-six-foot hole in the reinforced concrete above the locker area and damaged the ceiling of the departures area - upstairs.[31]

This had the look and feel of a terrorist act. Anonymous callers to two press services claimed responsibility on behalf of the PLO. "TWA flies to Israel," said one. "Death and destruction shall be the penalty for those who deal with the Zionist state."[32] The PLO, however, immediately denied responsibility, and none of Arafat's rivals stepped up to claim responsibility. The CIA, meanwhile, concluded that Palestinian extremists were probably not responsible. PLO representatives were just about to participate in the UN General Assembly session and had no motive for an attack in New York City. If the rejectionists had wanted to undermine Arafat's diplomat efforts, the CIA believed they would have attacked Kennedy International Airport, not a U.S. airport that handled primarily domestic flights.[33]

The day after the explosion, Ford chaired a meeting on the incident in the Cabinet Room. In attendance were Secretary William Coleman of the Department of Transportation, John McLucas of the FAA, the deputy attorney general, the assistant to the director of the FBI, and Ford's senior White House staff, including Dick Cheney and Marsh. The White House wanted to know whether the airport security measures implemented by the Nixon administration in 1973 were sufficient. Since 1973, there had been 100 percent screening of passengers and carry-on luggage for bombs and firearms.

The LaGuardia explosion was the latest in a series of incidents that raised concerns about U.S. transportation security. This was the tenth bombing in three years to have occurred at a U.S. airport, five of which involved public lockers, and recently airline employees had discovered two explosive devices in checked bags on board an Allegheny Airlines flight.[34] "The facts available concerning the La-Guardia incident," FAA administrator McLucas wrote in a memorandum available within hours of the event, "do not indicate any weakness in the existing civil aviation security procedures . . ."[35] But the FAA's conclusion failed to address the question whether a new wave of terrorism required the adoption of additional security procedures, specifically the screening of all checked baggage.

President Ford, like Nixon before him, was more seized by the problem of terrorism than were his senior staff. He considered the bombing an opportunity to push ahead on increasing airline security. "[Let's] seize [the] opportunity for public support," he told the gathering, "[to] get things done [we] couldn't do in normal times." If the FBI determined that the explosion was an act of terrorism, Ford indicated that he wanted the issue "kick[ed] up for 'new direction' decision."[36]

As it turned out, the FBI was not able to conclude one way or the other whether terrorists had been involved, and the White House's interest in terrorism soon faded. Ford did, however, put pressure on the FAA to undertake "a maximum federal effort to prevent the recurrence of [similar kinds of] bombings."[37] Public lockers located outside the screening area at U.S. airports—estimated at thirty thousand to thirty-five thousand—were all systematically removed. The FAA ordered consideration of "instituting at least a random physical or x-ray inspection of checked luggage" and set up a task force to assess a policy of 100 percent screening of checked luggage.[38]

The FBI assigned five hundred agents to the investigation of the LaGuardia bombing and by mid-January had interviewed over 1,150 witnesses. The bureau could not develop a theory "strong

enough to back a guess" as to who or what organization might have
been responsible. At a meeting of the working group, an FBI representative explained that "it could have been a terrorist, or a lunatic
acting alone . . . It could have been an act of retribution, such as a
murder of a narcotics peddler picking up drugs at the locker."[39]

Besides advocating that all coin-operated lockers be removed
from airports, the Department of Transportation's security task force
offered few major suggestions. The process had been tilted in favor
of inaction. The Air Line Pilots Association, which was by this time
a well-known advocate of baggage screening, had not been invited to
participate in the task force. Instead, President Ford received a
stream of information from the FAA and the airlines showing that
100 percent screening of checked luggage would clip the airline industry, causing small airports to shut down and many airlines to suffer huge losses.[40] In the task force's report, these estimates of
economic hardship outweighed any potential threat from concealed
explosives.

As the White House turned to more pressing matters, the counterterrorism working group continued to observe disturbing trends
overseas. A week before the LaGuardia bombing came a reminder
of the ingenuity of the Palestinian groups that had rejected Arafat's
diplomatic initiative. On December 21, an international terrorist
team of six took hostage the eleven oil ministers and fifty-one staff
members attending the Organization of Petroleum Exporting Countries (OPEC) meeting in Vienna. The terrorists wanted money from
Saudi Arabia and Iran. The figure has never been disclosed, but
somewhere between $20 and $50 million was transferred to a bank
account in Aden controlled by PFLP leader George Habash's
deputy Wadi Haddad on December 23, 1975. The oil ministers and
their staff were released shortly thereafter.[41]

The CIA had predicted that "extremist groups, most likely with
Libyan support, would try to upset any movement toward an Arab-
Israeli settlement."[42] Libyan support for the OPEC hostage-taking

could not be confirmed, but the fingerprints of the PFLP were all over the case. The commander of this operation was the elusive Carlos the Jackal, the Venezuelan terrorist who had worked for the PFLP in the past. An added cause for concern was that Carlos's team included two members of the West German Baader-Meinhof organization. This was one more piece of evidence that suggested a coalition of terrorist forces against Western interests in the Middle East. In May 1972, Japanese Red Army (JRA) terrorists had attacked Lod airport in Israel on behalf of the PFLP, and in late 1974, a large JRA network was discovered in Paris.[43]

These factors—the changes in terrorist capabilities and the sense that international terrorists were taking greater risks and working together—produced the first ever official concerns that a spectacular terrorist attack on the U.S. homeland could be imminent.[44] In the eyes of many federal counterterrorism experts, the approach of the bicentennial celebrations across the United States and the two major party conventions presented excellent opportunities for international terrorists to grab the world stage. Given the experience in Munich four years earlier, the working group also worried about the vulnerability of U.S. citizens at the upcoming Montreal Olympics.

In January 1976, the chair of the counterterrorism working group, Robert Fearey, initiated a report on what he called intermediate terrorism, "a level of terrorist violence lying between mass destruction and the types of assassinations or abduction of medium-grade USG [U.S. government] officials or private citizens with which U.S. terrorism policy and the working group have been primarily concerned."[45] The working group assembled a task force with midlevel officials from the State Department, the FBI, the CIA, the Departments of Defense and Transportation, and the other departments and agencies with an interest in counterterrorism.

Overseen by Robert Kupperman, the chief scientist at the Arms Control and Disarmament Agency, the task force developed a report that looked at the likelihood of a "spectacular" terrorist attack.

Kupperman, who had written the working group's study on nuclear terrorism in 1975, had an equally difficult time in getting the attention of the White House or any of Ford's key advisors once this new report was completed. Even the President's Foreign Intelligence Advisory Board (PFIAB), which was responsible for giving an outside opinion on the priorities and practices of the U.S. intelligence community, showed little interest in the Kupperman study. Having received it on May 19, the chairman of the PFIAB, Leo Cherne, acknowledged it only two months later, after the bicentennial was over and the Montreal games were well under way.[46]

Nonetheless, the working group did its best to disseminate the conclusions on intermediate terrorism. Its chairman, Fearey, convinced Kissinger to convene an unusual meeting at the assistant secretary or deputy assistant secretary level to discuss "the current, increased danger of major terrorist attacks in the United States requiring urgent preventive and preparatory action."[47] This would be the highest-level meeting on terrorism since the first and only cabinet committee meeting on October 2, 1972. Although he was able to get the secretary of state to sign the letter, Fearey was unable to lure any assistant secretaries to the meeting. In fact, only two with the rank of deputy assistant secretary, one from the Transportation Department and one from the Justice Department, turned up. Associate Deputy Attorney General Rudolph W. Giuliani represented the Justice Department.

Giuliani was the most active participant at this meeting, which took place on May 27, 1976. Praising Kupperman's report for making "Justice aware that it must take a more active position in combating terrorism," Giuliani said that his department was reactivating the Civil Disturbance Unit in preparation for the possibility of attacks at official bicentennial events or the two major party conventions. Giuliani also made an observation about the flow of intelligence about terrorism that would in retrospect appear farsighted. Kupperman had advocated an "antiterrorism management information system."

Giuliani warned the working group that the new Privacy Act and Attorney General Edward Levi's guidelines on domestic security investigations would complicate terrorism reporting. "Under the new guidelines," explained Giuliani, "there [is] difficulty in collecting domestic intelligence unless there was some indication that there had been a violation of law." Although the CIA said it believed it would have no trouble collecting what it needed abroad and disseminating that information to the appropriate U.S. agencies, it was clear that the FBI would face obstacles in any participation in a central terrorist information center.[48]

Giuliani encouraged the working group to use its clout to make intelligence collection and sharing by the FBI easier. "If the guidelines on intelligence collection are too stringent and were hampering the U.S. government in keeping track of terrorists," he explained, "they could be amended." All he requested was that the counterterrorism experts submit specific examples "indicating areas in which the guidelines should be relaxed." Giuliani was cautiously optimistic that if this were done, "such a change might be accomplished."[49] Available evidence suggests that the FBI was too cowed by its recent public thrashing to request any amendments to the guidelines in the Ford period and later obtained only marginal changes in the guidelines under Presidents Carter and Reagan.[50]

Election-year politics forced the White House to reconsider its opposition to involving the president in making terrorism policy. In the spring of 1976, Ford was criticized in the media and from the Right for lacking an interest in fighting terrorism. C. L. Sulzberger of the *New York Times* unfavorably compared U.S. efforts in the antiterrorist field to those of the West Germans, the French, and the British. "The three European security partners," he wrote, "eagerly await the day when the American services are less flabby and can join in the covert antiterrorist war."[51] The challenge on this issue that mattered most to Ford came from former California governor Ronald Reagan, who was giving the incumbent president a race for the Republican nomination. In May, Reagan criticized the administration for allowing a deterioration in the U.S. intelligence community's ability to collect intelligence on terrorists. "Piously claiming defense of civil liberties and prodded by a variety of bleeding hearts of the society," he said to a group of policemen in California, "we have dismantled much of the intelligence operations of law enforcement that we must have if we are to protect society from [political terrorism]."[52] The terrorists Reagan was likely referring to were domestic radicals such as the Symbionese Liberation Army, who had kidnapped and then converted the newspaper heiress Patricia Hearst and had been in the news in the mid-1970s. These charges of softness on terrorism increased Ford's political vulnerability to a terrorist event of any kind, foreign or domestic.

It is unlikely that new intelligence information about possible threats played any significant role in this shift. As of June, the FBI's "threat cards," on which it listed threats to bicentennial events, "were coming in at a much faster rate than earlier in the year." But some were of "limited credibility," and none were reported to the working group as particularly threatening. By mid-June, the CIA was discounting the possibility of an attack at home and suggested that the more likely scenario was an attack on a U.S. installation abroad. Regarding the homeland threat, the CIA representative to the working group reported that "there is no firm indication, thus far, that any incidents of the latter type were being planned."[53] The CIA offered that Iranian students opposed to the shah who were studying in the United States might organize a few demonstrations.

Despite the lack of intelligence inside the administration on any specific threats, there was a sense in the press that these threats existed. Frustrated by the inattention of the White House, someone in the working group probably played a role in fanning those fears. Leaks of information from working group meetings started appearing in Jack Anderson's syndicated columns in mid-May 1976.[54] Anderson learned of the discussion that had occurred in October 1975 of the availability of portable missile launchers to terrorists. He also caught wind of concerns about a possible domestic terrorist attack. By June, the White House was noticing "a rash of news reports on the terrorist potential," which were immediately blamed on the working group.[55]

A year earlier, Ford's advisors had believed it politically hazardous for the president to associate himself with antiterrorism activities; now the political winds had shifted enough for it to be potentially a greater problem to seem aloof from them. Some NSC staffers started discussing having the NSC replace the State Department as the lead agency in managing the counterterrorism community, such as it was. One staffer suggested the formation of a Terrorist Special Action Group (TSAG). Chaired by the national security advisor, the TSAG would be a deputies committee, a membership two ranks higher than that on the existing counterterrorism working group. The goal was to have something powerful in place, on paper at least, before a major terrorist attack, to show that the White House was prepared.

In late June, Marsh's assistant Mike Duval, who had argued against White House involvement in antiterrorism, wrote to Ford's chief of staff, Dick Cheney, about the need to revisit this question. "It is impossible to rule out the possibility of a major terrorist attack in the United States," warned Duval. "The current Executive Branch organization (which was set up by former President Nixon) to combat terrorism, i.e., the Cabinet Committee and Working Group, is not adequate . . . I think the President should move very quietly to strengthen Executive Branch efforts to combat terrorism. I think he should take caution now before a major incident turns this latent problem into a major public issue."[56]

Although the NSC staff produced a draft National Security Decision Memorandum (NSDM) creating the TSAG, in the waning months of the Ford administration the White House never took charge of the terrorism problem. The only NSDM remotely related to the problem of security signed by the president in the fall of 1976 involved enhanced port security against foreign espionage and sabotage.[57] The only sign that counterterrorism was gaining any clout in Washington had come in the summer of 1976, when the State Department assigned the rank of ambassador to the post of chairman of the working group.[58]

Fortunately, there were no terrorist acts at the Montreal Olympic Games or the bicentennial celebrations. This fact seemed to weaken the arguments of what the White House called the "doomsday-type papers" of the working group.[59] So, too, did the next terrorist act on U.S. soil, which fell only marginally outside the parameters of those that had come before. Not long after the closing ceremonies in Montreal, a terrorist hijacking took place that resulted in the death of one New York Police Department officer.[60] The perpetrators were not Arabs. On September 10, 1976, two Croatian nationalists commandeered TWA Flight 355 over New York City and demanded that a political manifesto calling for an independent Croatia be published in a major newspaper. To demonstrate their seriousness, the terrorists informed the U.S. government that they had planted a bomb at Grand Central Terminal and provided a detailed description of the location and apparently of how to defuse the device. Sadly, though the New York bomb squad found the bomb where the Croats had left it, the police were not able to detonate the bomb safely, and one policeman died. The FBI negotiated with the hijackers and agreed to let them issue their statement as long as they promised to release the hostages unharmed. In France, after a two-day ordeal, the incident ended peacefully. The hijackers surrendered and were extradited to the United States.

Unlike the hijacking cases of the early 1970s, this one apparently had little effect on America's antiterrorism stance. The decision to allow the manifesto to be published revealed a disagreement between the FBI and the Department of State on how to apply Nixon's "no concessions" doctrine. After the incident had ended, two State Department officers visited the FBI to reprimand the bureau for "violating" U.S. terrorism policy. James Adams, the third-ranking official in the bureau, who had made the decision, refused to accept the criticism. "Where were you when we had one policeman killed [and] we had a planeload of people with hijackers who claimed to have explosives?" he asked.[61]

It is unclear from available records what role, if any, the national security team in the Ford administration played in the handling of the TWA hijacking. The key decision seems to have been made by the FBI. The principals and their senior advisors, it appears, were keeping their distance from the increasingly restive counterterrorism community. When higher-ranking members of the State Department were briefed that the military dictatorships of the Southern Cone states in Latin America (the countries from Paraguay south to Chile) had formed a terrorist international of their own, under the code name Operation Condor, to kill dissidents as well as guerrillas, the working group was not informed.[62] On September 21, 1976, in Washington, D.C., a Chilean hit squad used a car bomb to kill dissident Orlando Letelier and his American assistant, Ronni Moffit. Working group discussions in the wake of that attack, the first successful political assassination in the capital since 1865, betrayed an unwillingness of both the State Department and the CIA to share with the working group or the FBI what it knew about Operation Condor.[63] After liaison on this issue proved unproductive, the FBI made a direct appeal to CIA director George H. W. Bush for cooperation from the CIA. Bush agreed, and apparently at that point material flowed to the bureau that helped FBI officers solve the case.[64]

The Ford administration was the first in history to consider the likelihood of a major terrorist attack on U.S. soil. This was, however, a low-level discussion, and with the White House deeply skeptical about the threat of terrorism, key policymakers did not participate in any systematic way. Whatever concerns President Ford may have had peaked with the LaGuardia bombing. And when the period of greatest perceived danger passed uneventfully in 1976, those who had resisted a serious assessment of the terrorism problem had no reason for self-doubt. Despite evidence to the contrary—the ongoing investigations of the LaGuardia bombing, the Letelier assassination, and evidence of increased Palestinian rejectionist activity—the Ford administration left office confident that the United States had the counterterrorism system that it needed.

CHAPTER FIVE

The Lull Before the Storm

IN THE MIDST OF THE 1976 presidential election campaign, both Jimmy Carter and his running mate, Walter Mondale, suggested that counterterrorism would be an important concern of their administration. "Peace is not the mere absence of war," said Carter at the Democratic convention. "Peace is action to stamp out international terrorism." Walter Mondale compared modern hijackers to the Barbary pirates who had challenged Thomas Jefferson in the early days of the republic. The nation must "defeat the new breed of pirates," promised Mondale, "and guarantee freedom of the skies."[1]

These strong words brought no action by the incoming Carter administration until an obscure domestic Black Muslim sect terrorized Washington, D.C., for two days in March 1977. On Wednesday, March 9, Hanafi Muslim extremists took control of the B'nai B'rith headquarters, the Islamic Cultural Center, and the Washington, D.C., city government offices. The takeover of the offices of the D.C. city government was especially violent. A young reporter from Howard University's student radio station was shot dead by the terrorists, and city councilman Marion Barry was wounded in the chest. The twelve Hanafi gunmen held 134 people hostage in the three buildings for thirty-nine hours. The standoff ended through the intervention of three Middle Eastern ambassadors, who offered

their services to talk the ringleader of the Hanafis, Hamaas Abdul
Khaalis, into surrendering. Khaalis's family had been murdered by a
rival Black Muslim group in his Washington, D.C., home in 1973.
Some of the assailants had gotten off with light sentences, and one of
Khaalis's demands was that he be able to meet and then kill the individuals who had killed his family. Khaalis also wished to stop screen-
ings of *Mohammed, Messenger of God,* a commercial movie on the life of
the prophet Mohammed, which he considered blasphemous. His final demand was for the reimbursement of a $750 fine that he had
once paid in a D.C. court.[2]

Under existing procedures, the incident was managed by the D.C.
police. It was the police who called in the Working Group on Combating Terrorism when it became clear that Khaalis was interested in
speaking with some Arab and Muslim representatives. The White
House remained informed, but it was Douglas Heck, the State Department's new antiterrorism expert and chairman of the working
group, who worked with the Egyptian, Pakistani, and Iranian ambassadors, who were acting as mediators. The one symbolic act by
the White House in the crisis was a decision to cancel the traditional
nineteen-gun salute for a visiting head of government, in this case
British prime minister James Callaghan, on the second day of the
standoff for fear that this would upset the seven terrorists in the District Building nearby. Otherwise, President Carter himself made no
public statements, leaving this task to the local authorities.

Late on the evening of the second day of the incident, after a
three-hour meeting with the ambassadors, Khaalis gave himself up,
and the hostages were released. Khaalis had by this time dropped all
of his demands and requested only that he be released after arraign-
ment on his own recognizance. His request was granted, and Khaalis
later turned himself in.[3]

Following the Hanafi hostage incident, the Carter administration
undertook a review of U.S. counterterrorism policy. Initially, under
the guidance of Jessica Tuchman, an NSC staffer, the process did not
draw the full attention of the president's national security advisor,

Zbigniew Brzezinski. "Brzezinski did not believe that terrorism was a strategic issue," recalls William Odom, who replaced Tuchman in the summer of 1977, after she lost Brzezinski's support.[4] Brzezinski considered the Soviet Union the greatest threat to U.S. interests and saw anything else as secondary at best. Called by wags "the Polish Kissinger," Brzezinski had a powerful mind that sized up the international system in terms of power and interests. Terrorists were not among his principal concerns.

Odom completed the review, which resulted in Presidential Security Memorandum 30 (PSM-30), signed by President Carter on September 16, 1977. Odom reinforced Brzezinski's views on counterterrorism. From his own study of the problem, Odom concluded that as a phenomenon terrorism did not exist. "When it happens here, it is a crime," he argued. "When it happens abroad, it is war." Terrorism was a tactic, not an end in itself. It was the group or individual who used that instrument who was the enemy. The United States did not need a general counterterrorism organization or strategy to deal with these different enemies, Odom argued.[5]

The fact that they did not believe in creating something elaborate did not mean that Brzezinski and Odom were satisfied with the interagency system bequeathed to them by the Ford administration. PSM-30 gave the NSC an active role in counterterrorism. The State Department remained the lead agency in overseas incidents, and the Justice Department remained the lead agency in domestic terrorist incidents. The FAA would serve as lead agency whenever the incident involved a U.S.-registered airplane. But the interagency process would be lodged in the NSC. The Nixon-era cabinet committee was abolished. PSM-30 also created a new Working Group on Terrorism. The membership of this new working group was the same as the old interagency working group. The difference was that the new working group would report to an executive committee of the NSC—a new Executive Committee on Combating Terrorism—that would meet to determine counterterrorism policy.[6]

PSM-30 also included a provision to improve the flow of intelligence on terrorist groups to the NSC. It created a Terrorism Intelligence Subcommittee of the director of central intelligence's Critical Collection Problems Committee. This was the first time since 1972 that the White House had shown a formal interest in terrorism's place in the intelligence community's agenda.[7] Nevertheless, as Carter's director of central intelligence, Admiral Stansfield Turner, later explained, terrorism "was not a great deal of a concern."[8] Although the CIA collected intelligence on it, even with PSM-30, terrorism was still thought of by the intelligence community to be more of a foreign problem than an American one.[9] Turner's deputy, Frank C. Carlucci, cannot recall any particular reason why the community had believed this at that time. "It was more of an intuitive feeling," says Carlucci.[10]

As the policy review leading up to PSM-30 was taking place at the NSC, terrorism was increasingly becoming a public issue. New York's long, hot summer of 1977 was remembered for more than the "Son of Sam" murders and a major blackout. On August 3, two bombs went off, causing a citywide bomb scare. The twin towers of the World Trade Center, which had opened only a year earlier, were evacuated for the first time, as were other buildings in Manhattan. The bombs, which were placed near the U.S. Defense Department's office at 342 Madison Avenue and in front of the world headquarters of Mobil Oil Corporation at 150 East Forty-second Street, killed one and injured eight. The bombings, described by New York City mayor Abraham Beame as "an outrageous act of terrorism," were the fiftieth and fifty-first in the city claimed by the Fuerzas Armadas de Liberación Nacional Puertorriqueña (the Puerto Rican National Liberation Armed Forces, or FALN) since October 1974.[11] In thirty years of terrorism in support of Puerto Rican independence, the FALN had already tried to kill one president, Harry S. Truman, in 1950, gunning down in the process a Washington, D.C., policeman and injuring five congressmen in an armed attack on the Capitol in 1954. Having reemerged after years of relative quiet, the FALN had gone on a three-year bombing spree, which, besides the attacks on Manhattan, included nearly a dozen incidents in Newark and Chicago. The bloodiest attack had killed four and injured sixty diners at the historic Fraunces Tavern in the Wall Street area in January 1975.

The bombings in August 1977 sharpened concerns that after three years, law enforcement was still incapable of doing anything about the FALN. Press reports criticized the New York Police Department for having "little more than an inkling of how large FALN is, where it is headquartered, or how it originated."[12] The FBI knew more, thanks to the discovery of a bomb factory by Chicago police in November 1976, but the FALN's principal bomb maker remained at large. The impression created in the aftermath of the New York bombings was that the FALN threat was out of control.[13]

The apparent helplessness of local authorities to contain the Puerto Rican terrorists had its counterpart in unsettling revelations that same summer that the federal government did not actually have control of the nuclear materials in its care. On August 4, the Energy Research and Development Administration (the successor to the AEC) and the Nuclear Regulatory Commission revealed that more than four tons of bomb-grade uranium and plutonium could not be accounted for in the country's nuclear research and development facilities. A government scientist estimated that it would take only forty pounds of the enriched uranium or twenty pounds of the plutonium to make a bomb. The *New York Times* explained that the government provided this information because of concerns that "some sophisticated group might steal a small amount of special nuclear material, make a homemade bomb, and use it against some important target such as the United States Capitol or the World Trade Center."[14] Although it was assumed that these four tons had not been stolen, the actual amount of this special material that had disappeared was believed by the U.S. government to be much higher. For national security purposes, the government did not include in this number materials missing from the nation's two principal bomb-making facilities, at Rocky Flats, Colorado, and Oak Ridge, Tennessee, believed to be another four tons.[15]

Meanwhile, in late August and early September, the residents of San Francisco faced a wave of bombings by a group calling itself the New World Liberation Front (NWLF). Over a period of eight days, the group claimed responsibility for four different bomb attacks against "symbols of San Francisco's wealth." Claiming "decent housing for all" as its goal, the group also claimed responsibility for six bombs that had been left at Adolf Coors beer distributorships since July.[16] A week later, anti-Castro Cubans set off two midnight explosions in downtown Washington, D.C. No one was killed or hurt, but U.S. authorities were concerned that anti-Castro Cubans belonging to the United Revolutionary Organization Command (CORU), which was headquartered in Miami's Little Havana, would step up their efforts to deter the Carter administration from developing diplomatic relations with the embargoed regime.[17]

Fortunately, the Hanafis, the FALN, the NWLF, and CORU were not in the same class as the PLO rejectionists or the Marxist-Leninist groups of Latin America and Western Europe, all of whom used terror more effectively as a political weapon. Even so, against these B-team terrorists the nation's internal security system was admittedly not doing well. What if the world's most talented terrorists decided to target the United States? As the Europeans increased their vigilance and their ability to respond, was it not reasonable to assume that the United States would become a more welcome target for terrorists who sought to strike at the West? The Washington, D.C., police's response to the Hanafi hostage situation had been particularly dismaying. The police deployed to attack the building if the negotiations failed had never trained with the M-16 machine guns they were issued during the crisis. Policemen ordered onto helicopters to land on the roof of the building had never jumped from helicopters before. But they would have never received an order to jump anyway. The radios in the helicopters were not integrated into the D.C. police's radio system.[18]

Nothing illustrated the apparent gulf between the efforts of the United States in counterterrorism and those of its European allies better than the actions of the West German government in rescuing a planeload of hostages in Mogadishu, Somalia, on October 18, 1977. The daring raid was the work of Bonn's GSG-9, a counterterrorism unit developed in the aftermath of the disastrous West German effort to rescue the Israeli Olympians in 1972.[19] The German operation came at a high cost. West Germany's leading domestic menace, the leftist Baader-Meinhof Gang, had enlisted the help of Wadi Haddad and the PFLP to pull off the hijacking. A month earlier, the West German terrorists had abducted a prominent banker, Hanns-Martin Schleyer, and they wanted the PFLP to help them to increase the pressure on Bonn to release their jailed leader, Andreas Baader, and other terrorists. After GSG-9 rescued the passengers, the Baader-Meinhof Gang murdered Schleyer. The West Germans swallowed hard but pressed on in their determination to weaken their domestic terrorists.

The previous summer, the Israelis had pulled off a similar rescue of hijacked passengers at the Entebbe airport in Uganda. Israeli commandos carried off this feat with little loss of life. The West Germans, too, had shown considerable daring in the same class as the Israelis. But where were the Americans?

Javits and Ribicoff

Some key lawmakers, from both parties, were more impressed with Mogadishu and Entebbe than with the NSC's reorganization of the U.S. counterterrorism system. Senator Jacob Javits, Republican of New York, denigrated PSM-30 as "little more than a reshuffling of the already existing bureaucracy."[20] Describing the new Working

Group on Terrorism as "little more than a group where various agencies share information, discuss policy on a relatively low level, and guard their bureaucratic jurisdictions," Javits said that given the existing threat from terrorism, the federal government needed a stronger mechanism. "I am becoming increasingly apprehensive," added Javits, "that the Carter administration has been relinquishing the lead expected of the United States in this struggle."[21] He joined Senator Abraham Ribicoff, the chairman of the Senate Government Affairs Committee and a Democrat from Connecticut, in introducing legislation to upgrade U.S. counterterrorism organizations. The proposed Omnibus Antiterrorism Act would have created a council to combat terrorism, chaired by the national security advisor, "to oversee and coordinate a comprehensive national antiterrorism program."[22] Ribicoff and Javits wanted the State Department to elevate its Office on Combating Terrorism to the level of a bureau. Bureaus at the State Department comprised at least forty-five people, whereas the counterterrorism office traditionally had fewer than ten. In recognition of the importance of alerting domestic agencies to the fight against terrorism, the bill placed the president's domestic policy advisor on the proposed counterterrorism principals committee and required that the Department of Justice create a new position at the assistant attorney general level to head a new office for combating terrorism.[23]

With the president of the Air Line Pilots Association sitting next to him, Senator Ribicoff outlined the new bill on October 24, 1977. A product of the congressional activism that followed Watergate and Vietnam, the bill not only forced a new set of institutions on the executive branch but mandated sanctions against countries that "aid and abet terrorism."[24] Under the bill, Congress could veto any attempt by the president to add or subtract a country from that list. The sanctions ranged from canceling air service between those countries and the United States to preventing baggage coming from one of the listed countries from entering the United States unless it had first been checked in a neutral country. All arms sales to those countries would be banned. The bill also required the president to list countries with airports that did not meet certain security standards and imposed mandatory sanctions against them.

In the press, a debate developed between those who believed that PSM-30 was adequate and those who felt, as one insider told the *Washington Post,* that it was "nothing but hot air."[25] The argument over adequacy was based on whether one was more impressed with the actual terrorist threat or with the potential threat of terrorism. Although terrorist attacks had been increasing in number and lethality since 1968, when the U.S. government started keeping such statistics, they had resulted in fewer than seventy-five deaths.[26] Most of the bombings in the United States targeted property and not people. The Americans who were most at risk were businessmen working abroad and diplomats. And as yet, there had been no mass murders in either category. In terms of violence, despite the fact that terrorist events in the Middle East tended to be the more spectacular, and therefore tended to get wide media attention, most of the terrorism directed at Americans took place in Latin America and Western Europe.[27] In both places, Washington still viewed such violence as a regional problem.

The NSC believed that the chance of a terrorist attack against the United States was actually decreasing. The end of the Vietnam War had sucked the energy from the violent fringe of the New Left domestically. And in mid-1977, the PLO seemed ready to accept United Nations Resolution 242, thus implicitly recognizing the state of Israel, and to forswear its support of international terrorism.[28] The NSC under Carter shared with its predecessor the belief that at heart terrorists sought attention, and the more presidential attention you gave them, the more they would want.[29]

The pessimists, on the other hand, spoke in terms of the potential threat of terrorism. For every positive development, they predicted an even more lethal counterreaction. With every step the PLO took toward recognizing Israel, the greater the activism of rejectionists like George Habash and Abu Nidal. And in spite of the détente between the superpowers, European Marxist-Leninist terrorists had continued their kidnapping and killing. There was no reason to believe that terrorists who lived closer would not adopt such tactics against the largest capitalist state of them all.

Delta Force

Despite their unwillingness to be alarmed at the prospect of future terrorist attacks, Brzezinski and his staffer Bill Odom became firm supporters of developing a U.S. paramilitary capability in counterterrorism. After the West Germans staged the rescue in Mogadishu, the NSC undertook an investigation of the U.S. military's hostage rescue capabilities. For two years before Mogadishu, the army had been studying the possibility of setting up a special unit to rescue hostages. Colonel Charles Beckwith had already set in motion a training program for what would become the Special Forces Operational Detachment-DELTA, or Delta Force. Since the formal training of the first Delta Force was expected to take two years, the army had initiated Operation Blue Light to recruit a special unit from within the existing Special Forces as a stopgap measure. Blue Light and Delta Force would coexist until early 1978, when Delta Force received official blessing and Blue Light was eliminated as duplication.

The Carter NSC had known nothing about Delta or Blue Light before Brzezinski started asking questions after Mogadishu. Blue Light had already started training in late 1977 when Brzezinski visited their facility for the first time and came away impressed with what he saw. He learned that members of the Blue Light team had not only been in touch with the GSG-9 in West Germany but had trained with them. Odom accompanied Brzezinski to see the Blue Light group and then traveled to Europe to visit with British paramilitary experts at Whitehall in London and to see the West German GSG-9 himself.[30]

A New System?

Unlike the Hanafi extremists who attacked in Washington, D.C., Libyan leader Muammar Gadhafi liked the movie *Mohammed, Messenger of God*. The Libyan government had helped finance the $18 million film with the Kuwaitis and, after the film crew encountered some difficulties with clerics in Morocco, allowed the film to be shot in Libya.[31] Gadhafi, who acted as an evangelist for both Mohammed and the film, took the movie on the road to show leaders whom he hoped to convert to Islam. In late 1977 or early 1978, Gadhafi visited Bangui, the capital of the Central African Republic. "Gadhafi had paid one million dollars to [Jean-Bedel] Bokassa to get him to convert," recalls Anthony Quainton, who as U.S. ambassador was invited by the self-proclaimed and now Islamic emperor Bokassa to the screening with Gadhafi.[32] What followed was almost surreal. The movie was in English, and the only Western language spoken by Bokassa was French. Gadhafi's English was rudimentary, consisting of what he had learned as a cadet at a police academy in Great Britain. As the film ran and Gadhafi added a running commentary in broken English, a harried female translator tried to follow in French on a microphone for the emperor. What was ultimately understood by anyone in the room is unknown.

The scene with Gadhafi, who already in 1977 was known to be a supporter of not only the PLO but the rejectionists as well, was Anthony Quainton's only brush with the terrorism problem before Washington recalled him to become the new director of the State Department's Office on Combating Terrorism and chair of its working group. Why was Quainton chosen to head the U.S. government's counterterrorism efforts? "There was a sense that we were

Renaissance men," he recalls with a smile. Quainton readily admits that this is a guess on his part. Indeed, the job required competence and was probably not considered important enough to require any special preparation.[33]

When Quainton assumed his new duties in 1978, he had a staff of six officers and reported to Deputy Secretary of State Warren Christopher. "The principals had little interest in the counterterrorism shop," Quainton recalls. In the event of a crisis, they knew where to go to be briefed; but in advance of a crisis, they provided no further policy guidance. "The policy of no concessions, no negotiations had already been established."[34]

The State Department continued to chair the working group, which now reported to the NSC executive committee. The working group met less regularly than before and remained a clearinghouse of information on what the various agencies were up to. In earlier years, the FBI and the CIA had given presentations on how they saw the terrorist threat. Quainton recalls a much higher level of mutual suspicion in the late 1970s, and he found no way to bridge the gap between the FBI and the CIA: "The FBI had a law enforcement mentality and CIA, of course, had an intelligence approach and these people disliked sharing information." Quainton, however, tried to use "table-top exercises" and actual field exercises to improve interagency cooperation.[35] One table-top exercise involved thinking through the federal response to a biological terrorist attack. The Centers for Disease Control explained that if a spoonful of anthrax were left on the marble stoop at the C Street entrance of the State Department, it would be quickly spread on the bottom of shoes and then get picked up by the building's air-conditioning system. Within two weeks, it was estimated, two hundred people would be dead. In the late 1970s, the U.S. government did not even have enough anthrax vaccine for everyone at Foggy Bottom. Despite this chilling thought experiment, Quainton could recall no follow-through. The working group lacked executive authority. It was up to the various participants to take the message back to their principals for action, but no action followed.

In the second half of 1978, the Carter administration reviewed its policy toward Libya. This was a time of tectonic shifts in Mideast politics. In November 1977, Anwar al-Sadat made his courageous visit to Jerusalem; less than a year later came the Camp David Accords that established the framework for an Israeli-Egyptian peace treaty in 1979. Amidst these changes, the U.S. government looked for possible defections from Sadat's hard-line opponents in the Arab world. The Carter administration decided to tie the sale of two Boeing 727 passenger jets to "Libyan behavior in the wake of the Camp David Accords."[36] Tripoli was told that if the United States observed this helpful shift, then this sale "could lead to substantial follow-on sales of civilian aircraft by U.S. companies."[37]

The initial responses from Gadhafi were hopeful. In the fall of 1978, he told Bonn that a group of German terrorists that had been released by the Yugoslavs would not be allowed into Libya. Then his government communicated directly to Washington that Libya was reconsidering its position on international terrorism and welcomed a U.S. envoy for this purpose. In December 1978, Secretary of State Cyrus Vance picked Quainton to represent the United States in this discussion.[38] Quainton went to Tripoli and met with the Libyan foreign minister, who with a straight face pledged Libyan assistance in aviation security.[39] Libya subsequently signed the ICAO conventions on hijacking.[40] Though he had expected to see Gadhafi, Quainton ultimately did not meet with the Libyan leader. The bizarre movie night in Bokassa's palace would remain the only meeting that the State Department's terrorism expert had with the man who would soon become the focus of U.S. counterterrorism strategy.[41]

Meanwhile, congressional efforts to alter the federal government's approach to terrorism stalled. Ribicoff and Javits introduced their Omnibus Antiterrorism Act in early 1978, delaying the measure because of a heavy congressional schedule in late 1977. The bill was reported out of Ribicoff's committee in May 1978 but failed to pass in the Senate.[42] Although Javits and Ribicoff would try again in 1979, the measure was doomed. The White House opposed it, not so much because of the implied executive reorganization—though Brzezinski and Odom strongly disliked that—but because Ribicoff and Javits wanted Congress to be able to dictate to the president which states were sponsors of terror and which, therefore, would have to be punished. It was assumed, for example, that the list would immediately complicate U.S. efforts to facilitate the Arab-Israeli peace process. The two senators had made no secret of their intention to sanction four Arab countries that sponsored Palestinian terrorism.[43]

The Carter White House tried to avert a clash with the Democratic-controlled Congress. In late December or early January 1978, Brzezinski, Vice President Mondale, Secretary of State Vance, Energy Secretary James Schlesinger, and Transportation Secretary Brock Adams met to discuss how to handle the bill.[44] After their staffs prepared a list of required amendments, the principals sent a delegation headed by the NSC to Ribicoff. Described as constructive, the meeting nonetheless brought "no compromise." "The basic problem for the administration," observed White House staffer Annie M. Gutierrez in a memorandum to Stuart Eizenstat, the president's domestic policy czar, following the failed meeting, "is how to appear nonnegative on antiterrorism without endorsing a bad bill. The bill has the support of a large number of senators, and the topic of terrorism is a very popular topic on the Hill."[45] Mondale, a former senator, was a leading voice within the administration arguing that the White House not be seen in Congress as openly opposing the antiterrorism bill.[46] The Carter White House encouraged the Senate to get bogged down in a definitional dispute on terrorism. "It became a 'my terrorist is your freedom fighter' debate," says Odom, who participated in executive committee discussions over how to respond to this legislative initiative.[47] This definitional dispute killed the bill in 1978.

But Ribicoff and Javits's efforts to give counterterrorism a higher profile in the executive branch were not wholly in vain. At the initiative of New Jersey's congresswoman Millicent Fenwick, Congress attached an amendment to an appropriations bill in 1979 that gave the State Department the duty to create a list of state sponsors of terrorism. Any state on that list would be subject to sanctions. For over a decade, the U.S. government had been monitoring the role of states in assisting terrorist organizations. Now Congress was requiring far more than monitoring.

The Iran Hostage Crisis

On Sunday, November 4, 1979, Zbigniew Brzezinski was the first to tell President Carter that Iranian militants had overrun the U.S. embassy in Teheran and were holding between fifty and sixty people hostage.[48] That same day, Anthony Quainton was attending the inaugural ceremonies for the U.S. Army's new Delta Force, at Fort Bragg, North Carolina, when he heard the news. Upon his return, Quainton set up a crisis center at the State Department.

Washington initially assumed that this hostage incident would not last long.[49] Within a few days, however, it became clear that this incident would be more challenging than anyone had imagined. Both the Iranian prime minister and the Iranian foreign minister resigned; meanwhile, Ayatollah Khomeini and other clerics publicly supported the militants and their seizure of the U.S. embassy. In Washington, Quainton's counterterrorism team was firmly but politely pushed to one side.[50] Quainton unsuccessfully protested this decision to Deputy Secretary of State Warren Christopher, arguing that the interagency cooperation that had been developed at this lower level would have to be created anew at the level of the principals or their deputies. But the principals believed that this was a matter beyond the pay grade of the working group. "The hostage-takers were no longer considered terrorists; this had become an international and political issue," recalls Quainton.[51]

Although the U.S. government's interagency counterterrorism apparatus played no further role in the Iran hostage crisis, the new Delta Force would play a tragic part in the drama. In April 1980, Delta Force, under the command of Colonel Beckwith, made its international debut in a failed attempt to rescue the hostages. Eight U.S. servicemen died in the operation, proving that the United States still lacked the ability to pull off an Entebbe or a Mogadishu.

In the last year of the Carter administration, the world reeled from crisis to crisis. In December 1979, the Soviets invaded Afghanistan, which led to a covert U.S. commitment to the Afghan resistance. Although he retained responsibility for the counterterrorism portfolio, Odom's attention was diverted elsewhere. In mid-1980, he was tapped to help redraft the U.S. strategy for nuclear war. Approved by President Carter in late July, Presidential Directive 59 replaced the previous targeting of Soviet cities with a targeting that emphasized Soviet missile and strategic weapons sites.[52]

Despite these distractions, Odom believed that the counterterrorism system that he and Brzezinski had formulated contained a surge capability that could have been employed if needed. And it was flexible enough to have been transformed into an active instrument to target foreign terrorist organizations. "It could have been used for preemptive or active defense, but that was not the policy then."[53] As had been the case since 1972, however, the U.S. policy remained active diplomacy in regions where terrorists dwelled. The decision to use Delta Force to rescue the hostages in Iran had been a departure from this traditional policy. Meanwhile, U.S. defenses against terrorism partly returned to the levels at which they had been before the PLO started hijacking U.S. carriers at the start of the decade. Metal detectors remained at airports, but there were fewer air marshals in the air. With the death of the antiterrorism bill in 1978, discussion of further security measures ended.

The self-confidence of the Carter NSC belied a strong feeling among the American public that U.S. power was slipping, which the Iran hostage incident only magnified. The nation had not shaken its collective uneasiness after the defeat in Vietnam before it had to confront a series of apparent Soviet gains in other regions of the Third World, particularly in Africa and Central America. The Kremlin's brazen invasion of Kabul had then come as the ultimate expression of contempt for U.S. leadership. For many of those who went to the polls in November 1980, international terrorism, though not the cause of American troubles, was an annoying symptom of a world that no longer respected the United States.

CHAPTER SIX

False Start

"ABOVE ALL, WE MUST REALIZE that no arsenal, or no weapon in the arsenals of the world, is so formidable as the will and moral courage of free men and women. It is a weapon our adversaries in today's world do not have. It is a weapon that we as Americans do have. Let that be understood by those who practice terrorism and prey upon their neighbors."[1]

On a crisp, sunny day in January 1981, Ronald Reagan delivered the first inaugural address to mention terrorism. Terrorism was already very much in the minds of ordinary Americans. In many towns, yellow ribbons had appeared around trees, symbolizing the hope for the safe return of the hostages held in Iran. As the new president spoke, the last of the Iranian hostages was released after 444 days in captivity.

In Washington, some Reagan appointees hinted that the president intended to use the terrorism issue to establish a stark contrast with Jimmy Carter. Throughout the campaign, Reagan had hammered away at the theme that the Carter administration was weak, that a nation's resolve was a wasting asset and had to be used. Citing unnamed sources, conservative columnists Rowland Evans and Robert Novak wrote on the day of the inauguration that "Reagan's top national security officials are moving against a global curse. They have quietly sworn to start an immediate international effort to reduce the use of terror as an international political weapon."[2]

The quotations in the Evans and Novak piece suggested that they had spoken to at least one member of the incoming administration's foreign policy team. Secretary of State–designate Alexander M. Haig, Jr., had unusual policy experience with counterterrorism. In the Nixon administration, as deputy national security advisor, he had been responsible for monitoring the Middle East and had briefed the president on hijackings and bombings in the region. At that time, he had not rated terrorism as a major challenge. But his personal experience in surviving a terrorist attack five years after Nixon's resignation made Haig's commitment to a policy of counterterrorism visceral.

Just a week before he was to retire from the post of supreme allied commander in Europe, in 1979, Haig had been the target of an unsuccessful assassination attempt. His attackers placed a bomb along a route that he normally took to work. It went off seconds after his car went by. A few days after the incident, he had called the director of central intelligence (DCI), Stansfield Turner, to ask for the CIA's assessment of which group had been behind the attack. Turner's response surprised him. "Belgian nihilists were responsible," explained the DCI. "Belgian nihilists?" Haig replied incredulously. "There aren't any." "I don't know," said Turner, "but we think it was Belgian nihilists."[3]

Dissatisfied with what the CIA had to offer, Haig contacted the West German intelligence service, the Bundesnachrichtendienst (BND), which within a matter of weeks came back with strong evidence from an informant in the East German secret police that the Baader-Meinhof Gang had planned the attack in a KGB safe house in Belgrade, Yugoslavia. The West Germans believed that Baader-Meinhof benefited from substantial Eastern bloc assistance. From this information, Haig concluded that the Soviets had tried to have him killed.

Haig's personal brush with Soviet-backed terrorism left him convinced of both the real threat that it posed to U.S. personnel and the inability of the U.S. government to understand or take action against it. Within days of Reagan's inauguration, Haig worked to put counterterrorism at the top of the Reagan administration's foreign policy agenda. He arranged for terrorism to be featured at the first NSC meeting of the new administration, scheduled for Saturday, January 24, 1981.

To give the main briefing, he called on one of the few holdovers from the Carter administration, Ambassador Anthony Quainton, the head of the State Department's Office on Combating Terrorism and the chair of the interagency Working Group on Terrorism. "I was quite surprised when Haig called," Quainton recalls. Quainton was at home doing some chores outside his home in northwest Washington. "Haig asked me whether I could be ready to give a presentation to the NSC about our counterterrorism capabilities." [4]

Besides the members of the NSC, key figures of the intelligence community attended Quainton's presentation.[5] If Haig's goal was to give the president an opportunity to signal to his national security team that counterterrorism would be a priority in the first year, the presentation was a failure. "Reagan was fast asleep within fifteen minutes," Quainton remembers. Edwin Meese III, however, who was the president's coordinator for both foreign and domestic policy, was very alert and asked what Quainton recalls as good questions. This cheered Quainton but would ultimately mean very little to Haig, who viewed Meese as a rival.[6]

On paper, Meese, the counselor to the president, had enormous power in the early days of the Reagan administration. Reagan's transition team had decided to deemphasize the national security advisor and the NSC staff in the new government. Richard Allen, the incoming national security advisor, reported directly to Meese, making him the first assistant to the president for national security affairs not to have direct access to the president.[7]

Like Haig, Meese brought some personal experience to the issue of terrorism. In California, he had managed Governor Reagan's handling of the Weather Underground and Patty Hearst (Symbionese Liberation Army) cases.[8] Also like Haig, he tended to view terrorism as a by-product of the Cold War, with Moscow the heart and soul of this international menace. Although most of Carter's NSC was dismissed, Meese intended to keep Zbigniew Brzezinski's counterterrorism advisor, Colonel William Odom, who was known to be a hard-line anticommunist.

At a meeting with Odom in the first days of the new administration, Meese laid out for him what he felt the U.S. government needed to do to combat terrorism. "He wanted to launch covert operations all over the world," Odom recalls.[9] Odom was as anti-Soviet as one could be, but he was appalled by what Meese seemed to have in mind. Odom refused to accept the theory that Moscow was the cause of all terrorism everywhere. Odom had not seen evidence that the Soviet Union or its allies made much use of terrorism as an instrument to damage U.S. interests. For this reason, he and his Carter-era boss, Brzezinski, had consciously played down the threat of terrorism, which they did not view as a strategic problem. Not long after the meeting with Meese, Odom called up the chain of the army command to see whether he could get out of the Reagan NSC. Within a few weeks, Odom was back at West Point teaching.

There was one office in the new administration that had not signed on to the idea that the terrorism issue was linked to the superpower conflict. Initially, the national security team surrounding Vice President George H. W. Bush tended to see counterterrorism much as the Ford administration had. Skeptical that international terrorism was Soviet sponsored and a strategic threat to U.S. interests, the Bush team reflected the collective judgment of the CIA veterans who served as sometime advisors to Bush, a former DCI.[10] The vice president's principal national security aide, Donald P. Gregg, a former CIA station chief with years of experience countering the Chinese and the Soviets in Asia, provided a point of contact for these advisors.

In preparation for the January 1981 meeting on counterterrorism, Vice President Bush's staff suggested three areas of possible discussion: (1) What are the "rules of engagement" at embassies under attack? Should the Marine guards be allowed to shoot? (2) Is there a central clearinghouse for intelligence on terrorism? Such a clearinghouse is needed both for the United States and for exchange with other governments. (3) How can we make more progress on the adoption of international antiterrorist conventions, such as penalties for particular acts, special extradition procedures, and the exchange of techniques?[11] None of these questions suggested going on the offensive. Besides the novel suggestion of coordinating all U.S. intelligence on terrorism, the ideas represented a continuation of the multilateral approach favored by every administration since Lyndon Johnson left office.

There were no shades of gray in Ronald Reagan's opinion of Moscow's role in propagating terrorism. In the nationally syndicated daily radio addresses he gave after leaving Sacramento in January 1975, Reagan had drawn attention to the scourge of terrorism and singled out the Soviet Union and international communism as its main sponsors.[12] For Reagan, the threat from terrorism was not just overseas. He believed that thousands of terrorists were hidden in the United States and credited a newspaper story that Black September cells "posed a serious threat" in Northern Virginia and Washington, D.C.[13] Reagan criticized both the Ford and Carter administrations for being too passive in the face of terrorism. Not only were they wrong in negotiating agreements with the Soviets that seemed to reward the Kremlin's misbehavior, but Reagan asserted that the Justice Departments of these administrations had undermined the FBI's ability to conduct counterterrorism. "I don't hold with unwarranted prying by government in the lives of any of us," he said in November 1976, "but note the qualifying word 'unwarranted.'"[14] In the campaign, in a speech that decried isolationism and the so-called Vietnam syndrome before the Veterans of Foreign Wars in Chicago, Reagan vowed to "take a stand against terrorism."[15]

What was unclear as Reagan took office was how he intended the U.S. government to take this stand. Neither in the campaign nor during the transition did Reagan outline how the struggle against terrorism would fit into his foreign policy. Behind the scenes, his thoughts on antiterrorism or counterterrorism seemed just as vague. Reagan, for example, did not assign any particular priority to overturning the Levi guidelines at the Department of Justice, restrictions he had once criticized in a radio address for weakening the FBI in the fight against terrorists.[16]

When presidential rhetoric on terrorism became even tougher after the inaugural address, it suggested that Reagan was ready to undertake some kind of struggle against terrorism. He used a meeting with the returned hostages and their families on January 27, 1981, to announce that his administration would handle the terrorism problem energetically. "Let terrorists beware," he vowed, "that when the rules of international behavior are violated, our policy will be one of swift and effective retribution." In a critical reference to Jimmy Carter, the new president added, "We hear it said that we live in an era of limit to our powers. Well, let it also be understood there are limits to our patience."[17]

Reagan's words suggested a willingness to use force to retaliate against terrorists, implying a dramatic shift in U.S. counterterrorism doctrine. The United States had never directly retaliated for the loss of its citizens at the hands of terrorists, though Reagan's recent predecessors had been given opportunities. The deaths of U.S. ambassador John Gordon Mein in Guatemala in 1968, U.S. ambassador Cleo Noel and chargé d'affaires George Curtis Moore in Sudan in 1973, and U.S. ambassador Francis E. Melloy, Jr., in Beirut in 1976 had not resulted in "swift and effective retribution," even though in all but one case there had been agreement on the guilty party. Observers who believed that this tougher language meant that the new administration was prepared to act, however, were soon to be disappointed.

Emboldened by the presidential rhetoric, Secretary of State Alexander Haig used his first press conference on January 28, 1981, to announce that "international terrorism will take the place of human rights in our concern." Reagan's secretary of state then put the blame squarely on the Soviet Union for "training, funding, and equipping" the world's main terrorist groups, a charge that none of his predecessors had ever made.[18] Haig's point was clear: Far from being a regional phenomenon, international terrorism was, he believed, actually a coordinated global threat sponsored by the Soviet Union.

Although the *Wall Street Journal* editorial page applauded Haig's remarks, rumblings were heard elsewhere in the press about the implication of this direct challenge to Moscow.[19] Haig's statement also surprised and angered some in the Reagan White House. In one press event, he had managed to achieve two undesirable things: upstage the president as the communicator of U.S. strategy and signal the Soviet Union that it might be held accountable for any future acts of terrorism committed anywhere.

Just after the press conference, Haig received a tough telephone call from James Baker, Vice President Bush's former campaign manager and now chief of staff to the president. It would be the beginning of a difficult relationship between the two men. Haig recalls Baker telling him that the president did not want him to talk about international terrorism. Apparently, Baker then added that the administration would not focus on any foreign policy issues for the first year. Everyone was expected to stay on message, and that message was the economy. "But foreign problems are not proposed," Haig remembers explaining to Baker, "they just happen." Haig defended himself on the implied charge of disloyalty by mentioning the campaign speech that Reagan had given to the Veterans of Foreign Wars in August 1980. Baker did not bend.[20]

Baker's call confused Haig, who had assumed that he understood the president's mind on international terrorism. Haig arranged a private meeting with Reagan to ask the president whether he shared his belief that international terrorism was a significant challenge to the United States. Haig recalled the VFW speech for Reagan. Reagan then said he agreed with Haig. At the time, Haig thought he had scored an important victory. Only later would he realize that Reagan had not given him what he needed to carry on his crusade against allegedly Soviet-sponsored terror. "He disliked confrontations," Haig later explained.[21] Having the president agree in a one-on-one meeting sometimes meant very little in the Reagan administration.

Although he shared a similar view of the terrorist threat, Ed Meese did not rally to Haig's side. Haig's main ally in trying to focus the administration's attention on Soviet-sponsored terrorism in the first year of Reagan's presidency was William J. Casey, the incoming DCI. Casey, a hugely successful businessman who had run Ronald Reagan's presidential campaign, had learned about intelligence in World War II as a young section chief assigned to London in the Office of Strategic Services. Following Haig's press conference, Casey directed the CIA to begin working on a Special National Intelligence Estimate on Soviet sponsorship of international terrorism. Unfortunately for both Haig and Casey, they soon discovered that the resident Soviet analysts at the CIA did not believe in the existence of a strong link.

In the spring of 1981, Washington witnessed a sharp public debate over Soviet involvement in international terrorism that the administration did not want and for which it was not particularly well prepared.[22] Critics identified counterterrorism as neo-McCarthyism. Columnists friendly to the administration began quoting from the work of Claire Sterling, a journalist whose new book, *The Terror Network: The Secret War of International Terrorism,* argued that the Soviet Union was using terrorists to fight a proxy war in Europe and the Middle East. Sterling and those who made the Soviet argument were anathema to the terrorism experts in the CIA. Signs that the Reagan administration was losing control of this story came in the form of leaks to the *Washington Post* and the *New York Times* from disgruntled CIA analysts who said that there was no evidence to sustain Haig's conspiracy theories. The more Casey tried to get his analysts to revisit their analyses, the more they talked about their "ideological boss." With each passing week, the secretary of state's charges became less credible.

With the advantage of hindsight, the terrorism debate of 1981 reveals that the alarmists were not as far off the mark as their detractors assumed. The Soviet Union was not the fount of international terrorism that Haig and Casey believed, but neither was it an innocent bystander. After the fall of the Berlin Wall, Soviet archives revealed startling details about Soviet intelligence's patronage of one of the terrorism masters of the 1970s, Wadi Haddad. The KGB had recruited Wadi Haddad, George Habash's deputy in the PFLP, in May 1970. The Soviet leadership considered this a major recruitment. "The nature of our relations with W. Haddad," wrote KGB chief Yuri Andropov to Leonid Brezhnev, "enables us to control the external operations of the PFLP to a certain degree, to exert influence in a manner favorable to the Soviet Union, and also to carry out active measures in support of our interests through the organization's assets while observing the necessary conspiratorial secrecy."[23] From 1970, the KGB was a major supplier of money and weaponry to the PFLP, the most active Palestinian rejectionist group before the rise of Abu Nidal in 1974. Fortunately for the West, Haddad died of natural causes in 1978, and he seems not to have been replaced by the KGB. In the Soviet document rush of the 1990s, no one could produce evidence that the Soviet Union had been behind all international terrorism or that the use of terrorist organizations had been a central part of Soviet efforts in the Third World. What evidence there was, however, left no doubt that even in the era of détente, the Soviets were helping some of the world's most violent terrorists.

Haig's inability to focus the U.S. government on the problem of terrorism was symptomatic of larger organizational problems within the Reagan administration. The new team had come into office expecting to be able to govern according to the model of Reagan's decision-making system in Sacramento. In practice, this would prove much more difficult to achieve. Ordinarily, one of the first presidential decisions is a charter, a National Security Decision Directive (NSDD), laying out the responsibilities of the various institutions and departments in formulating foreign policy, but Reagan's people could not agree on how to graft the California experience onto the existing executive foreign policy structure. "It was a zoo," recalls an understandably bitter Haig, who would leave the administration under a cloud in 1982.[24]

Admiral John Poindexter, who was brought in to analyze the operations of the White House Situation Room, recalls that competition among Meese, Haig, and Secretary of Defense Caspar Weinberger prevented any institution-building until 1982.[25] The change started in January 1982, when Assistant Secretary of State William Clark, who had served Reagan in Sacramento, replaced Richard Allen. Clark, who brought Robert McFarlane with him to the NSC, insisted on having direct access to the president. Reagan agreed, and Meese subsequently lost his responsibility for foreign affairs. Half a year later, Haig resigned, and the new secretary of state, George Shultz, established a close working relationship with William Clark. With the White House and the Department of State finally cooperating, the NSC started issuing NSDDs.

The Reagan administration developed a two-tier foreign-policy-making system. The president's key advisors sat on the National Security Policy Group (NSPG), which was staffed by a deputies-level committee known as the Crisis Pre-Planning Group (CPPG). The vice president, the national security advisor, the secretary of state, the secretary of defense, the chairman of the Joint Chiefs of Staff, the White House chief of staff, and the DCI were regular members of the NSPG, which was chaired by the president.

William Clark's appearance on the scene also brought a new order to policymaking on counterterrorism. In its first year, the administration had eliminated the NSC's Executive Committee on Combating Terrorism. Quainton, however, was kept on, and his working group was renamed the Interdepartmental Group on Terrorism (IG/T).[26] In April 1982, President Reagan signed NSDD 30, formalizing the State Department's role as "lead agency" for terrorism incidents overseas and granting formal status to Quainton's terrorism committee.[27] The IG/T, as it was known, had eleven permanent members and remained under the chairmanship of the State Department, though Quainton himself left for Nicaragua to become U.S. ambassador there. It was made responsible "for the development of overall U.S. policy on terrorism, including . . . policy directives, organizational issues, legislative initiatives, and interagency training program."[28] Although NSDD 30 did not draw any distinction between foreign and domestic terrorism, the NSC and the Department of State assumed that the role of the IG/T applied *only* to international terrorism.[29]

Reflecting the role that the Carter White House had played in the Iran hostage crisis, NSDD 30 also reaffirmed the NSC's leading role in the management of terrorist incidents. It established a Terrorism Incident Working Group (TIWG) to be chaired by an NSC staffer.[30] Although not a principal or a deputy, that staffer could at least lay some claim to the authority of the Office of the President.

There was also some change in how the CIA managed counterterrorism, though the effect of this change was minor. William Casey named David Whipple the first national intelligence officer for terrorism. This was largely an analytic position that did not provide Whipple with the clout to coordinate operational information on terrorism. This change at the CIA, like those at the NSC, was a modest step and reflected a sense that the existing counterterrorism system was sufficient for U.S. requirements.

Even before these institutional steps were taken, the Reagan administration did undertake some actions against states that sponsored terrorism. However, the target was Libya and not the Soviet Union. The Reagan administration established a Senior Interdepartmental Group on Libya chaired by Under Secretary of State Walter J. Stoessel in March 1981.[31] Initially, the principal concerns were the military and political threats that Gadhafi posed to his neighbors, especially Sudan and Egypt, and the possibility that Libya might acquire nuclear weapons.[32] In May 1981 the president approved an assistance plan for Libya's neighbors. Evidence that Gadhafi was using intelligence officers under diplomatic cover to arrange attacks on Libyan dissidents in the United States also led to a decision that spring to close the Libyan People's Bureau in Washington, D.C., and in the fall to sever all diplomatic relations with Tripoli. An investigation by U.S. law enforcement had determined that the former Green Beret who shot and wounded a Libyan student in Colorado in November 1980 had been hired by the Libyan government. In 1981, eleven other Libyan dissidents were less lucky: All were assassinated in Western Europe or the Middle East by Libyan hit squads. Although Gadhafi had not yet threatened any U.S. citizens, in the fall of 1981, security was tightened around federal buildings in Washington, D.C., in case of any Libyan effort at reprisal.

At the end of 1981, the NSC met to consider additional measures against Tripoli. Earlier, Raymond Tanter, an NSC staffer, had circulated a paper as part of a staff review of the policy that laid out the reasons for additional activity: "There is general consensus about the volatile threat represented by Libyan capabilities for sowing subversion, intimidation, the overt use of military force, terrorism, and other forms of attack on vulnerable governments throughout North Africa and the Middle East."[33] The NSC staff then examined three contingencies—the status quo, an increase in Libyan terrorism or subversion, and a Libyan conventional military attack on its neighbors—and concluded that Libyan support for terrorism was not in itself a reason to deploy U.S. military force. "In the event that Libya intensifies terrorism or subversion," Tanter summarized for National Security Advisor Allen, "economic sanctions are relevant."[34] Pressure for considering military action came from Secretary Haig and the State Department, but at its meeting on December 7, 1981, the

NSC seemed to accept the NSC staff's approach to the Gadhafi problem.[35] President Reagan approved sending a private warning to Gadhafi, and the U.S. government subsequently imposed economic sanctions on Tripoli, ending all trade in oil and high technology in 1982.[36] These decisions were not as yet part of a coordinated policy against states that engaged in terrorism or even the overt component of a sustained campaign against Gadhafi. The Reagan administration would not coalesce around the need for an aggressive counter-terrorism strategy until after a series of shocking events took place in another Middle Eastern country.

Lebanon

One of the few foreign policy initiatives of the early Reagan administration took place in Lebanon. After years of fighting with Palestinian militiamen in southern Lebanon, the Israeli government launched a full-scale invasion of Lebanon in June 1982. Ultimately, no member of the U.S. administration was pleased with the Israeli action, which further complicated Lebanon's ongoing civil war.[37]

By the 1970s, Lebanon's complex power-sharing agreement among the principal interest groups in the country had collapsed. The Lebanese Shia population, whose birthrate was higher than that of their Christian compatriots, began to demand more power to reflect their greater numbers. Complicating this power struggle was the appearance of the PLO in Lebanon after Jordan expelled Palestinian leaders following Black September. Civil war erupted in 1975. Israel and the Lebanese Christians united over a shared mistrust of the PLO. Meanwhile, the PLO relied on the military support of Syria, which deployed some of its troops to Lebanon's Bekaa Valley, just over its border, and the financial support of the Gulf states. A tenuous cease-fire had taken effect in 1976.

Ayatollah Khomeini's revolution in Iran in 1979, which radicalized Shia throughout the Middle East, increased the temperature in the Lebanese pressure cooker. In Lebanon, a series of shadowy Shia groups sprang up, most of whom drew local inspiration from clerics who had studied with Khomeini in the 1960s and 1970s at the seminaries in Najaf and Karbala in southern Iraq. Their goal of an Islamic Republic of Lebanon pitted these groups against Amal, the existing party for mobilized Shia. At the time of the Israeli invasion of June 1982, Amal split, and a faction calling itself Islamic Amal fused with the independent radical Shia militias to form the Hezbollah, or the "Party of God." Besides inspiration, the Khomeini regime supplied weapons to Hezbollah, which also received training from Iran's newly indoctrinated Islamic army.[38]

Fearful that a complete collapse of the Lebanese state might open the region to further penetration by the Soviet Union, the Reagan administration negotiated a cease-fire that involved the removal of the PLO from Lebanon. The cease-fire did not hold. In mid-September 1982, a bomb killed the Lebanese leader backed by the Israelis, and in retaliation, a Lebanese Christian militia entered a Palestinian refugee camp in a part of West Beirut controlled by Israeli troops and slaughtered innocent men, women, and children. In an attempt to end the cycle of violence, President Reagan decided to deploy U.S. Marines to Beirut as part of a multinational force that included troops from France and Italy. The incoming secretary of state, George Shultz, argued for the necessity of using U.S. troops to support the Lebanese government and of encouraging the withdrawal of Israeli and Syrian troops from the country.

Hopes that the United States would be viewed as an honest broker were soon dashed. In April 1983, a suicide bomb exploded outside the U.S. embassy in Beirut, killing sixty-three, including seventeen Americans. A group calling itself Islamic Jihad claimed responsibility.

The bombing confronted the Reagan administration with its first terrorist challenge. This was not the terrorism problem that the Reagan team had expected to face. This was not a Palestinian attack, nor was it the act of a local Marxist-Leninist group. Instead, it immediately became clear that Islamic extremists were responsible. No one in the Reagan administration believed that the Kremlin was behind the radical Shia, who were ferocious anticommunists. If there was any state sponsor, it was Iran.[39]

"Lord forgive me for the hatred I feel for the humans who can do such a cruel but cowardly deed," Reagan confided in his diary the night he learned of the attack on the U.S. embassy in Beirut.[40] In his public remarks, however, Reagan pointedly avoided mentioning the need for retaliation. After calling the bombing a "vicious . . . cowardly act," Reagan emphasized instead that terrorism could not deter the United States from playing the role of mediator in the Middle East.[41] There were twelve hundred Marines in the multinational force, and the administration vowed to keep those U.S. troops in Beirut as long as they were needed. Only one authoritative voice publicly suggested a response. "Let us rededicate ourselves to the battle against terrorism . . . It is long past time for peace and security to prevail," said Shultz, who was on a visit to Mexico when the attack occurred.[42]

Reagan's public statements mirrored the administration's private response to the attack. There is no evidence that his chief foreign policy advisors, even George Shultz, seriously considered any military retaliation. As of early 1983, it seemed that the Reagan administration was no more prepared than any of its predecessors to use military force as a tool of counterterrorism. The administration, however, did press forward on the diplomatic front to send a message to Iran. It initiated an international effort, called Operation Staunch, to coax allies not to sell weapons to Tehran.[43] But if the message was supposed to deter Tehran from continuing to sponsor terrorism, it failed.

The Bombing of the Marine Barracks

At two o'clock in the morning on Sunday, October 23, 1983, President Reagan, who was in Augusta, Georgia, was awakened by Robert

McFarlane, who had just replaced William Clark as national security advisor. A suicide bomber had driven a truckload of dynamite
into the Marine barracks in Beirut. The first report was that one
hundred men had been killed. Although the grim toll would more
than double, this was already the bloodiest terrorist incident in U.S.
history. "There was to be no more sleep for us that night," Reagan
later recalled.[44]

The president quickly returned to Washington, arriving in time to
chair a 9:00 A.M. meeting of the NSPG. Over the course of two
meetings that day, the president indicated his intention to retaliate
with military force against the perpetrators of the attack and to coordinate this U.S. action with the French, who had lost fifty-eight men
in a nearly simultaneous suicide attack in West Beirut. But his advisors were not united in support of a military reprisal. Shultz, McFarlane, and Vice President Bush all supported taking action. The
Pentagon, however, had its doubts that this was the right choice of
instrument. Richard Armitage, then assistant secretary of defense for
international security affairs, later recalled that "many of us felt that
that kind of retaliation was a sort of 'feel good' exercise rather than a
sharp, tight, military response."[45] General John W. Vessey, the chairman of the Joint Chiefs of Staff, found the idea morally unacceptable. It was "beneath" the U.S. military to strike back at terrorists
for a cowardly bombing. The laws of war prohibit retribution.
Vessey and the commandant of the Marine Corps, General P. X.
Kelley, were also concerned that any U.S. action would make the remaining Marines in Lebanon even more vulnerable.[46]

If the military strike had gone forward, it would have been the
first time that the United States had ever retaliated with military
force against a terrorist attack. There had been no discussion of a
military response to the attack on the U.S. embassy in April, and
even now, it became clear that the administration had not thought
through the implications of striking back at terrorists. Information
revealed at a trial in U.S. district court in 2003 suggests that the administration had "24-karat proof" of the group involved in the

bombing. According to Admiral James Lyons, who at the time was the deputy chief of naval operations, the National Security Agency had intercepted a September 26, 1983, message from Tehran to the Iranian ambassador in Damascus instructing him to see Hussein Mussawi, the leader of Islamic Amal, a pro-Iranian splinter group from the pro-Syrian Amal Shia militia and part of the Hezbollah movement.[47] The Iranian ambassador was to order Mussawi to attack the U.S. Marines in Beirut.

Before the day was out, the president felt confident that he knew the identity of the United States' attackers. He signed NSDD 109 on October 23, which held Iran and the Iranian-sponsored Hezbollah responsible for the barracks bombing and authorized countermeasures against them. Marine Corps commandant General P. X. Kelley was sent to the region to "convey to the leadership of the Lebanese Armed Forces the urgent need to tighten security in the south Beirut area including closer collaboration with Lebanese security agencies and those confessional militias able to assist in controlling the movement of hostile terrorist factions."[48] Meanwhile, the U.S. ambassador would request the Lebanese government to cut its ties with Iran. Back in Washington, the administration undertook a review of its policy in the Iran-Iraq War. In September 1980, Iraq had invaded Iran to gain control of the oil-rich province of Khuzestan, and to that point, the U.S. government had been a neutral bystander.

The president also considered military action. The military component of NSDD 109, entitled "Responding to the Attacks on the USMNF Contingents," remains classified.[49] However, there is available evidence to conclude that within hours of the attack on the Marine barracks, the Reagan administration prepared to launch a military strike against the terrorists. "We wanted to put a cruise missile into the window of the Iranian ambassador in Damascus," recalled Richard Armitage of one target that the Pentagon supported.[50] Ultimately, the administration decided not to use its new cruise missiles, the Tomahawks. Secretary of Defense Weinberger feared that if one misfired, the Syrians would hand it over to the Soviets, who could reverse engineer it.[51] And to limit potential collateral damage in the populated areas of the Bekaa Valley, U.S. aircraft would strike only at the Sheikh Abdullah barracks in Baalbek, northeast of Beirut, a known training facility for Hezbollah.[52] Reagan was planning to leave on a five-day trip to the Far East in the second week of November. The attack was to occur when he returned.

Before leaving for Asia, Reagan went on television to assure the American people that the United States would respond. "Those who directed this atrocity must be dealt justice, and they will be," he said.[53] In early November, the U.S. Navy increased its deployment in the eastern Mediterranean to three aircraft carrier task forces: the USS *Eisenhower,* the USS *Independence,* and the USS *John F. Kennedy,* and their over three hundred attack aircraft.[54] Meanwhile, given France's losses, discussions proceeded with the French, through Deputy National Security Advisor Admiral Poindexter and Mitterrand's military advisor François Saulnier.[55]

Upon his return on November 14, Reagan approved the air attack plan at a meeting of the NSPG. The chairman of the Joint Chiefs of Staff, after reporting that U.S. forces were ready, reiterated his concerns that an attack could make the situation more dangerous for U.S. troops in the region. Reagan was unfazed by the dissent. After the NSPG meeting, McFarlane and Poindexter communicated to the French that the operation was approved for November 17. Despite the president's apparent decisiveness, the NSC staff worried that the Pentagon would find some way to abort the mission.

On November 16, French defense minister Charles Hernu called Defense Secretary Caspar Weinberger for one last conversation before the combined operation was to begin. Accounts differ on what happened next, although there is no doubt of the outcome. Weinberger claimed to Hernu, with whom he was not thought to have a good relationship, that he knew nothing about the operation. "I had received no orders," Weinberger later recalled, "or notifications from the President or anyone prior to that phone call from Paris." When Hernu reported that the attack would be occurring in a few hours, Weinberger told him, "Unfortunately it is a bit too late for us to join you in this one."[56] The French went ahead on their own.

What happened between November 14 and November 16 remains a matter of dispute. McFarlane and Poindexter believe that Weinberger intentionally overruled a presidential directive. "Cap got away with murder," Poindexter later recalled.[57] The unclassified paper trail is still too fragmentary to know how formal the order was. Most military operations require a series of orders prior to the final order to execute. At the top of the pyramid is the president, who as commander in chief orders a military attack through the secretary of defense, who then transmits that order to the chairman of the Joint Chiefs of Staff. In this instance, the chairman would have transmitted the presidential directive to the commander in chief of the European Command (CINCEUR), then General Bernard Rogers, who would then have ordered the commander of U.S. Forces in Europe (CINCUSNAVEUR) to instruct the commander of the Sixth Fleet (COMSIXTHFLT) to proceed. On November 15, according to Admiral Poindexter, the commander of the major carrier task force in the Mediterranean, Rear Admiral Tuttle, reported that he had received the strike plan and was awaiting the execute order to proceed.[58]

In his memoirs, President Reagan says that he changed his mind at the last moment and called off the attack.[59] If he did, then he told only Weinberger and left McFarlane and Poindexter in the dark. Poindexter recalls the president's showing surprise when McFarlane told him that the secretary of defense "had canceled the air strike."[60]

McFarlane and his deputy Poindexter were frustrated by the inaction. And Reagan himself was at the very least unhappy at the disunity among his advisors revealed by the incident. On November 21, 1983, the NSC staff forwarded to Shultz, Weinberger, Casey, and General Vessey a set of decisions that the president had made on his own to prevent a recurrence of this inaction.[61]

Whatever these decisions were—and the details remain classified—they did create some momentum for military action against the next challenge to the U.S. position in Lebanon. After Syrian antiaircraft batteries launched some surface-to-air missiles (SAMs) against U.S. photoreconnaissance planes in early December 1983, President Reagan ordered a small retaliatory strike against Syrian positions. The attack failed. Two airplanes were lost, a pilot was killed, and his bombardier-navigator was captured and later released by the Syrians. Meanwhile, the U.S. Air Force hit little of consequence.[62] The NSC blamed the chairman of the Joint Chiefs of Staff for the outcome. "Vessey screwed it up," recalls Poindexter. "He micromanaged the task force."[63] Having received incorrect orders from the Pentagon, the task force commander launched the strike too early, at a time when the planes were especially visible to the Syrian defenders. The U.S. Air Force also failed to maintain radio silence.[64]

The December air strike and President Reagan's November initiative had done little to strengthen the vulnerable U.S. position in Lebanon. In 1984, Hezbollah would exploit that vulnerability for its own ends.

William Buckley

Hezbollah's bombing of the U.S. embassy in Beirut in April 1983 had dealt a body blow to the CIA's counterterrorism work in the Middle East. Among the seventeen Americans killed in the attack were seven CIA employees, including the chief of station Ken Hass, his deputy James Lewis, and the CIA's chief expert on the PLO, Robert Ames, who had been visiting the Beirut station. At the memorial ceremony held at CIA headquarters, in Langley, Virginia, a few days later, Casey described Ames as "the closest thing to an irreplaceable man."[65]

Over the course of the 1970s, Ames had transferred from the Directorate of Operations to the Directorate of Intelligence.[66] This meant he was running fewer agents and writing more analyses. Although Ames had lost one of his best sources in 1978, when the Israelis killed Ali Hassan Salameh in retribution for the Munich massacre, he remained the most knowledgeable CIA officer on the ways of Yasir Arafat and the Palestinian movement.[67]

With the loss of Ames and the entire leadership of the Beirut station, Casey knew he needed a player in the world of terrorists and counterterrorists to reconstitute what was left of the agency's local networks in Lebanon. William Buckley, a thirty-year CIA veteran, had the personal courage—he had won a Silver Star in combat in Korea—and the regional knowledge to fit the bill. The only problem was that Buckley's cover had already been blown in the Middle East. Four years earlier he had been forced to leave Damascus when the Syrians figured out who he was. It was CIA policy to wait at least five years before trying to reinsert a blown agent. But Casey believed he needed an emergency replacement for his team in Beirut. Buckley was also wary about going back to the region so soon. The Syrians would know who he was immediately, and then so would every other adversary or foreign intelligence service that mattered. Would he be useful as a marked man? Casey did not pressure Buckley, but he wanted him to go, and Buckley went.[68]

Less than a year later, on March 16, 1984, members of Hezbollah took Buckley hostage. A handful of Americans had been taken hostage during the Lebanese civil war in the mid-1970s, but they had all been released within a few weeks at most. When the attacks resumed on U.S. citizens in Lebanon in 1984, they were deadlier, and the terrorists more determined. Hezbollah wanted to force the release of a group of radical Shia terrorists who had been arrested in Kuwait in December 1983 after a series of car bombings against the U.S. and French embassies. The so-called Dawa ("the Call") terrorists were from the same families as some of the key officials in Hezbollah.[69] In January 1984, terrorists killed the president of the American University of Beirut, Malcolm Kerr. After the Shia militias took over West Beirut in early February, they began kidnapping Westerners. Buckley was the third American abducted since February 10. Frank Regier and CNN journalist Jeremy Levin were the first to be taken. Kerr's murder and the three kidnappings would set policy wheels in motion in Washington.

More traditional terrorist challenges were rather quiet in 1983. Although Abu Nidal continued to attack moderate Arabs, the PLO seemed to be holding to Arafat's 1974 promise to restrict Fatah's terrorism to Israel and the occupied territories. The newer threat, Libya's Muammar Gadhafi, also seemed to have climbed into a box after the U.S. diplomatic initiatives of 1981–82. By the end of 1983, the Department of State concluded that the policy of diplomatic and economic sanctions against Tripoli seemed to be working.[70] No one believed, however, that Hezbollah could be deterred through diplomatic and economic sanctions.

Secretary of State Shultz pushed the administration to coordinate its approach to the terrorism problem. On January 20, 1984, days after Kerr's murder, Shultz officially designated Iran a sponsor of international terrorism. This was followed by an announcement that like the other countries designated as state sponsors of terrorism, Iran would be prohibited from receiving U.S. military assistance.[71] Meanwhile, Operation Staunch, an effort begun in 1983 to discourage other countries from selling weapons to Iran, continued to be a priority for the Department of State.

A week after William Buckley was taken in March, Shultz had his staff organize an all-day seminar on terrorism at the State Department. Shultz intended to use the March 24 seminar to send a signal to the department that terrorism was an issue to which more creative energy had to be devoted.[72] He also invited officials from other parts of the government to listen to the experts among whom was Brian M. Jenkins.

CIA director William Casey also had a hand in the shake-up that was about to occur in how the United States dealt with terrorists.

The disappearance of his top man in Beirut only a year after losing an entire station was tough to swallow.

On April 3, 1984, President Reagan approved the most ambitious U.S. counterterrorism policy yet, one that would not be matched until the mid-1990s, under Bill Clinton. This directive, NSDD 138, was designed to "shift policy focus from passive to active defense measures and to require that resources be reprogrammed and/or obtained to support that policy focus." To implement this new policy, the Department of State was instructed "to intensify efforts to achieve cooperation of other governments." The White House ordered the DCI to "intensify use of liaison and other intelligence capabilities and also to develop plans and capability to preempt groups and individuals planning strikes against U.S. interests." Meanwhile, the Department of Defense was expected to "maintain and further develop capabilities to deal with the spectrum of threat options." [73]

As part of this initiative, the Reagan administration submitted a package of four antiterrorism bills to Congress. Two of the bills provided for the full implementation of the ICAO's Hague and Montreal conventions on the disposition of hijackers and the problem of airplane sabotage, both of which had been signed by Richard Nixon. This implementing legislation had been included in the Javits and Ribicoff antiterrorism measure that had died in Congress in 1979. A third bill would allow the payment of rewards to individuals who provided useful information in the struggle against terrorism. Finally, this antiterrorism package included a measure making it a federal crime to provide training or support to groups or states that engaged in international terrorism.

With these bills headed to Congress, the administration undertook a public awareness campaign about terrorism. Secretary Shultz launched the campaign in late April with a muscular speech in which he vowed that the administration would be taking the fight to the terrorists.

Despite the clarity of both the secret NSDD 138 and the public comments of the secretary of state, the Reagan administration acted as though it were not fully committed to an offensive policy against terrorism. The White House did little more than watch as its antiterrorism package got bogged down in Congress. Similarly, the administration allowed the intelligence community to choose the pace at which it would or would not implement the new policy. The CIA was due to report to the NSPG on May 31, 1984, on how it would go on "active defense" against international terrorism: It may well have reported, but there were no structural changes implemented at Langley or in the field to improve the collection and flow of information on terrorism either within headquarters or between the CIA and other U.S. intelligence agencies.[74] Terrorism remained a secondary matter at the CIA.

In 1981, FBI director William Webster had promoted counterterrorism to one of the main missions of the bureau. But NSDD 138 did not improve the way in which information flowed to the bureau; nor did it provide the bureau with greater investigative powers or effect new border or visa controls that would have helped the FBI do its job better. "There was nothing revolutionary in it," recalls Buck Revell, who as the assistant director for criminal investigations was the FBI's point man for counterterrorism in the Reagan years.[75] There is no evidence that the Justice Department was concerned about the bureau's ability to manage the president's terrorism concerns.

The administration also sent mixed messages abroad. After weeks of assuring the American people that the United States would steadfastly support the mission of the multinational force in Lebanon, on February 7, 1984, Admiral Poindexter read a statement from the president indicating that U.S. Marines were to be "redeployed" out of Beirut.[76] To even neutral observers it seemed that Hezbollah's use of terrorism had achieved at least one of the organization's political goals.

The terrorist attacks against U.S. civilians in Beirut continued after the U.S. pullout. Frank Regier managed to escape his captors in April 1984. But in May 1984, he was replaced in captivity by Reverend Benjamin Weir. Weir joined CNN journalist Jeremy Levin and CIA official William Buckley as a prisoner of Hezbollah.

A Third Beirut Bombing

A third suicide bombing in seventeen months against a major U.S. target in Beirut further revealed the ineffectiveness of the administration's approach to Hezbollah. On September 11, 1984, the Security Section of the Department of State sent an alert to all Near Eastern and South Asian diplomatic posts. Three days earlier, an anonymous caller had told a Western press service in Beirut that Islamic Jihad would "strike very shortly at a key American interest in the Middle East" in retaliation for a U.S. veto at the United Nations of a resolution criticizing Israel for violating civil rights in southern Lebanon. The caller hinted at a suicide attack, saying that Islamic Jihad members were ready "to sacrifice their lives to destroy an American or Zionist institution, even of secondary importance."[77]

The State Department had little precise information to provide its diplomats. "The shadowy nature of this umbrella organization," Washington explained, "does not lend itself to much post-specific analysis." The CIA could add very little. In its alert, which it sent on September 20 as part of a longer report on terrorism, the agency reported that Islamic Jihad was "a cover name for a variety of radical pro-Iranian groups and individuals. Although the authenticity of this latest threat is difficult to assess, it is an undoubtedly accurate reflection of the sentiment generated by the U.S. veto."[78]

The bombing took place later that day. In an attack reminiscent of what had occurred in October 1983, a truck filled with explosives rammed into the U.S. embassy annex in West Beirut, killing two

U.S. citizens, seven Lebanese employees, and about fourteen Lebanese bystanders.[79]

The NSC staff convened a meeting of the Terrorist Incident Working Group at 10:00 A.M. on September 21 to review the intelligence and discuss U.S. options. The group was disheartened. It was the third time that a U.S. installation had been bombed in Lebanon in less than a year. Referring to weapons carried by Marine guards at the entrances to U.S. residences abroad, one member lamented, "M-16s should not be our first and last line of defense." The group was equally dismayed at the ineffectiveness of the Lebanese army, which was supposed to protect diplomatic residences in Beirut.[80]

Details on what had happened came in slowly. It was not certain who was responsible. Given the assumption of U.S. intelligence that Islamic Jihad was not "a distinct organization with identifiable leaders," the fact that Islamic Jihad took responsibility did not provide much information about the identities of the bombers.[81] The explosive used was the equivalent of two hundred kilograms of TNT, but its composition, which would provide a signature of sorts for the investigators, had not yet been determined.

Even without a clear idea of who was responsible, the administration proceeded on the diplomatic front on the assumption that Hezbollah was guilty. Assistant Secretary of State for Near Eastern and South Asian Affairs Richard Murphy was already prepared to raise the issue of the bombing with the Syrians. Syrian forces controlled the Bekaa Valley, a sanctuary used by Hezbollah. The State Department was also thinking of sending longtime troubleshooter and now UN ambassador Vernon Walters to Syria to address the issue of Hezbollah with Damascus.

The fact that Hezbollah continued to hold three American hostages complicated the situation. McFarlane's deputy, Admiral John Poindexter, worried about the risks to the hostages of launching a retaliatory strike: "If we can determine who, and if [the] decision is taken to respond, what [would be the] effect on the hostages?" The U.S. intelligence community had lost track of Buckley, Levin, and Weir. Oliver North, who attended the meeting, noted, "No precise info on Buckley et al. within last 2 weeks."[82]

This diplomacy involved carrots as well as sticks for the Lebanese Islamists. The Algerians were gently exploring with the Kuwaitis, under the eye of the United States, the possibility that Kuwait would exchange the Dawa prisoners that it had jailed for the December 1983 bombings for the three U.S. hostages. The CIA representative at the meeting agreed that it was hard to predict how Hezbollah would respond to U.S. signaling, saying, "[They] are not known for logic." The only general conclusion came in the form of a comment from one participant: "Life [just became] more difficult."[83]

Within a day or so of the incident, U.S. Marine Corps Lt. Colonel Oliver North, of the NSC staff, brought some disquieting news to Admiral Poindexter about an intelligence failure.[84] A contact of his at the CIA, Charles Allen, had discovered that before the attack—at a time when the State Department was already primed for an attack against a facility in the Middle East—imagery analysts at the CIA were in possession of very suggestive satellite photographs of the Sheikh Abdullah barracks. The photographs, which apparently had not been sent up the chain of command, showed an array of oil drums that mimicked the layout of the streets and the concrete barriers in front of the U.S. embassy annex.[85] Still discernible in the sand were the tire tracks evidently from dry runs that the suicide bombers had taken in preparation for the attack. The barracks was the site that the United States had intended to strike in November 1983. The French had hit it when they launched their own strike in November, but in the intervening months the Iranians or Hezbollah had reconstructed it. It had remained a U.S. intelligence target.

The bombing of the U.S. embassy annex had occurred as President Reagan was running for reelection. He was on a campaign swing through the Midwest and had not been told of this imagery from the Bekaa Valley. In Milwaukee, in answer to a question from a college student, Reagan blamed the lack of warning before the most recent suicide bombing in Beirut on the "near destruction of our intelligence capability" in the Carter years. He characterized the view of the CIA under Carter's appointee Admiral Stansfield Turner as, "Well, spying is somehow dishonest and let's get rid of our intelligence agents and . . . We're feeling the effects today."[86] Under Turner, the CIA had contracted. Though few officers were actually fired, a large number had retired and not been replaced.[87] Turner was also not popular at CIA headquarters, because he seemed to be more interested in satellites than spies. "Stan did place a lot of emphasis on intelligence derived from technical means," recalls Frank Carlucci, who had been Turner's deputy at the CIA and would be national security advisor and secretary of defense in Reagan's second term, "but he did not disparage human intelligence."[88]

When President Reagan returned from this campaign trip, he headed into meetings to discuss what to do about Hezbollah's latest attack. McFarlane and the State Department's coordinator for combating terrorism, Robert Oakley, outlined a new kind of enemy who was fanatical and could not be deterred by the threat of death. Oakley was just back from a quick survey trip to Beirut. Behind these terrorists stood Iran, which financed the Lebanese Shia militias. Iranian Republican Guard units trained the groups known as Islamic Jihad at camps in the Syrian-controlled Bekaa Valley.[89] "Why the hell can't we tell the Syrians to send the Iranians home?" asked an annoyed Reagan. Oakley, reporting on Murphy's work in Damascus, tried to reassure the president that the bombing represented "a good chance to split" the Syrians and the Iranians.

Given the imagery intelligence, the NSC staff recognized that it had been a mistake for Reagan to criticize the Carter administration for the lack of warning before this bombing. After all, in this instance, even without human sources of intelligence, the U.S. government had had what it needed to prevent a terrorist attack. On September 28, the NSC put together a summary for President Reagan of all intelligence that pointed to Hezbollah's "complicity" in the embassy bombing.[90] This is when Reagan probably saw the overhead photographs of the mock-up at the terrorist training barracks in the Bekaa Valley for the first time.

After receiving the NSC report, President Reagan called former president Carter at his home in Plains, Georgia, "to explain his remarks." Carter had already publicly described Reagan's statement as "personally insulting and . . . gross." "I certainly did not suggest that your administration was the cause of that happening at the embassy in Beirut," said Reagan to Carter.[91] Reagan did not tell Carter that in fact, the U.S. government had possessed enough intelligence to have thwarted the attack.

This particular intelligence failure had nothing to do with mistakes made in the Carter era. According to George Shultz, neither the NSC staff nor the CIA had adequately warned the State Department. There are no declassified documents available on what, if any, measures William Casey took to determine why the U.S. intelligence community had failed its customers in this instance. Twenty years later, upon hearing that this information had been available to some in the U.S. government *before* the bombing, Shultz replied, "This comes as a shock to me."[92]

Despite the administration's public commitment to an aggressive policy and the frustration of all of the principals with Islamic Jihad, there was a disagreement over whether it made sense to retaliate. The more Robert McFarlane learned about Hezbollah, the less confident he was that a military strike against them made sense. "If we respond against Hezbollah," he argued, "our actions could very well drive the Shias into more of a frenzy." Believing that the diplomatic track with Syria might prove useful, McFarlane also warned that "a response could very [well] slow down . . . [Syrian] efforts to restrain Iranians in Lebanon."[93]

McFarlane made these comments at a meeting of the NSPG on October 3, 1984, to discuss possible military action against Hezbollah. George Shultz, who knew about the imagery intelligence implicating Hezbollah—though he apparently did not know when the U.S. government had received it—did not have these concerns.

While agreeing that a reprisal might increase the threat of future attacks, the secretary of state believed that "there is a net plus to taking action against Hezbollah."

"Pure retaliation is not our objective," Reagan told his advisors. The president explained that he was more interested in preventing future attacks than in revenge. "We believe they are planning new attacks. [And] the question is whether a strike will deter future attacks." Reagan also wondered about the political cost both at home and abroad from an attack. "There will be a big outcry of criticism from many quarters." First of all, it was now three weeks since the bombing. The president had to assume that some U.S. planes and pilots would be lost in the attack. Finally, Reagan was also thinking about the possibility that the terrorists would retaliate by killing one or more of the three American hostages in Beirut.

Reagan kept his mind open to a military strike, if someone could persuade him that it would lead to a decrease in future terrorism. When the secretary of defense offered that he could not see how an attack would have "a major impact on Hezbollah," Reagan played devil's advocate to force his advisors to think harder. Reagan agreed that "he did not see an attack as having much impact on the suicide drivers." But, he asked, "would it affect the thinking of the leadership: Wouldn't an attack slow things down?"

Shultz told the president that he was sure that it would deter the leadership, but Weinberger said that there was really no way of knowing. When McFarlane tried to wrap up the meeting with a presidential directive that "we should be prepared and ready if there is another attack," Shultz noted angrily, "This is what we said after the last attack." Reagan reminded his secretary of state that the goal of U.S. policy was to "reduce the capability of Hezbollah and not in revenge." Reagan said that "his overriding interest [was] in securing the release of the hostages."

Shultz left that meeting disappointed at the direction in which the administration was heading. As time passed, the possibility of a military response would fade. Three weeks later, Shultz decided to take the debate outside the confines of the NSPG. On October 25, he said in a speech at the Park Avenue Synagogue in New York City that the United States should not become "the Hamlet of Nations, worrying endlessly over whether and how to respond."[94]

Shultz knew that the White House would not be happy with the Park Avenue Synagogue speech. "The draft had been circulated around the government in Washington," Shultz recalled later. And the response was almost uniformly negative. "Calls began coming in complaining that I was going too far." The most important arrived just before he was to speak, as he was finishing dinner at the home of his host, Rabbi Judith Nadich. It was from the vice president's office. Shultz was told that Bush was "unhappy" with the speech. It was too belligerent. The caller complained on behalf of the vice president that Shultz was presenting his policy preference as if this were the policy of the U.S. government. Bush's aide reminded Shultz that this was not what had been decided at the NSPG earlier in the month. Shultz dismissed these criticisms. He believed that there was nothing in his speech that contradicted the spirit of NSDD 138, which was the charter of the new U.S. approach to counterterrorism. So he gave the speech anyway.[95]

President Reagan did not comment publicly on Shultz's speech the next day. Instead, while he was campaigning in Cincinnati, Vice President Bush took issue with Shultz's characterization of U.S. counterterrorism strategy. "I think you have got to pinpoint the source of the attack," said Bush; "we are not going to go out and bomb innocent civilians or something of that nature." It is unclear whether he was acting at the request of the president, although Bush's words accurately reflected Reagan's own thinking on the problem. When asked whether the administration had come to an agreement on when to retaliate, Bush added, "Not to terrorism, generally." The government, he said, "has great difficulty in fine tuning retaliation."[96]

The disagreement between Shultz and the White House gave the secretary of defense an opening to set the ground rules for the use of military force in counterterrorism. He used a speech at the National Press Club that fall to introduce the so-called Weinberger Doctrine, which established six conditions governing the use of military force in combat overseas that could also be applied to the use of force in counterterrorism: (1) The challenge should be vital to our national interest. (2) Forces should only be committed overwhelmingly and "with the clear intention of winning." (3) Forces should be used in support of "clearly defined political and military objectives." Only forces sufficient to achieve those objectives should be sent. (4) The relationship between U.S. objectives and the forces deployed should be constantly reassessed. (5) Before the United States commits forces overseas, "there must be some reasonable assurance we will have the support of the American people." (6) The use of U.S. forces "should be a last resort."[97]

Shultz's public challenge revealed the chasm between Reagan's public remarks against foreign terrorists and his private qualms about retaliation. It also illustrated the limited creative thinking of the entire administration concerning their options. Admiral Arthur Moreau, General Vessey's assistant at the Joint Chiefs of Staff, called Oliver North to complain that the NSPG meeting on October 30 was "a disaster." "McFarlane," he said, "was losing [his] grip on [the] process."[98]

The October 30 meeting was apparently the low point in the administration's response to the September bombing. The next day, McFarlane tried to restore order to the process. He wanted the agencies and departments to cooperate in crafting a policy that would reflect the president's priorities. U.S. counterterrorism in Lebanon would have two objectives: (1) reducing the capabilities of Hezbollah to prevent future attacks and (2) securing the release of the hostages. The solution to the disagreement over using overt means was to choose covert action instead.

On October 31, 1984, the deputies committee (the Crisis Pre-Planning Group, CPPG) discussed funding and training the

Lebanese army, so that it could go after Hezbollah. Following the meeting, the NSC staff drafted an NSDD for President Reagan's signature that authorized military and intelligence assistance to the Lebanese government.[99] The NSDD also authorized covert action. The next morning, McFarlane, Shultz, Weinberger, Vessey, and Casey participated in a secure conference call to discuss the NSDD. After reading over the NSDD, McFarlane asked for and received the approval of the other principals before forwarding it to the president.[100] While they disagreed on the role that overt military action would play, Shultz and Weinberger agreed on the need to explore the use of covert means to achieve these goals. On November 2, President Reagan signed NSDD 149.[101]

As part of its program of supporting the Lebanese government, the United States would train and equip Lebanese "hit men" who would be responsible for tracking down the people responsible for the terrorist attacks on U.S. facilities and the abduction of the three U.S. citizens. The State Department and the CIA expressed some concern about this plan, which originated with the NSC staff.[102] Robert Oakley and Clair George, the CIA's deputy director for operations, wanted greater assurances that the United States would be able to control what use these men made of their training and equipment. At their suggestion, the Pentagon agreed to send members of the Joint Special Operations command to Lebanon to review this operation. Despite the concerns raised by the State Department and the CIA, Reagan signed a "finding" for this operation on November 10.[103] Under the Intelligence Oversight Act of 1980, the president was required to approve covert action in writing in the form of a finding and to communicate this finding, which included a description of the operation, to the congressional intelligence oversight committees "in a timely fashion."[104] It appears that this finding was shared with Congress, although the timing is not known.

In general, U.S. counterterrorism was taking a turn toward the covert. Since the bombing of the Marine barracks, the Reagan administration had been embroiled in a debate over whether military retaliation was the most effective response to international terrorism. The U.S. military's reluctance to use force as a tool in counterterrorism and the president's own reasonable doubts had prevented any real test of the military option. In now opting to use spies, hit men, and saboteurs, the administration finally seemed unified in its approach to terrorism.

CHAPTER SEVEN

Striking Back

EVEN IF THEY HAVE BEEN OUT of office for a decade, former directors of central intelligence (DCIs) stay very well plugged in. Not long after President Reagan signed the November 1984 Lebanon finding, Richard Helms, who had served as DCI from 1966 to 1973, apparently picked up something about the administration's plans for more aggressive counterterrorism operations and had concerns. Helms, the legendary director of central intelligence whose career spanned World War II and most of the Cold War, bore scars from the years when the CIA was ordered to kill Fidel Castro. He had little time for assassination plots and covert operations. His distaste for this form of counterterrorism also reflected the feelings of many in the CIA's old guard.

The former DCI got in touch with Donald Gregg, Vice President Bush's national security aide, who had also once worked for Helms at the CIA. "[Helms believes] that we cannot and should not go as far as the Israelis have in fighting terrorism with terrorism," Gregg wrote to Bush in early December.[1] The intelligence veteran had wanted a meeting with the vice president as a way of discouraging the administration from going too far along the path of violent counterterrorism. Israel believed that its very existence was threatened by terrorism. The United States, however, was a superpower whose existence did not appear to be threatened by terrorism. U.S. global leadership in the nuclear age was more often exercised using the tools of soft power—persuasion, economic and public diplomacy, credibility—than by using military force. Helms did not want U.S. efforts in counterterrorism to undermine those tools. Gregg agreed with Helms's worries about the direction in which U.S. counterterrorism might be going and encouraged Bush to meet with him.[2]

George Bush had known Helms a long time and thought highly of him.[3] In September 1972, when UN ambassador Bush had received intelligence that Arab terrorists might attempt to kill him, he had turned to Helms for an evaluation of the information.[4] Bush agreed to meet Helms over breakfast on December 20, 1984.[5]

By early 1985, despite Helms's fears, the covert action against terrorists in Lebanon suggested by the NSC staff as a stopgap measure was already stalling. The CIA's top civil servants, starting with Casey's deputy, John McMahon, were very uncomfortable with the Lebanese surrogates being trained by the CIA. "Do you know what intelligence means to these people?" McMahon reportedly said to Casey. "It's tossing a bomb. It's blowing up people."[6] McMahon also worried that if these Lebanese teams succeeded in killing any Hezbollah leaders, the CIA would be blamed for unilaterally violating the executive order banning assassination that had been issued by Gerald Ford and reaffirmed by every president since him. "To the rest of the world," McMahon warned, "it's not administration policy, it's not an NSC idea—it's those crazy bastards at CIA."[7] Casey's representative in the Crisis Pre-Planning Group (CPPG), the deputies-level committee that oversaw all U.S. covert action, also did his part to throw up roadblocks. Clair George, who knew something about Beirut, having served as chief of station there in the mid-1970s, did not like the covert action plan of November 1984. Together with the State Department's Robert Oakley, he pressed for more and better information about the Lebanese hit teams and their accountability. At his and Oakley's request, the military's Joint Special Operations

Command (JSOC) sent two different survey teams to Lebanon to assess these groups and each time returned with a negative opinion of them. As a result, recalls Robert Oakley, "not one U.S. cent or one bullet ultimately went to them."[8]

Frustrated, Casey may have decided to press on with the help of Saudi Arabia.[9] The Saudis shared Casey's dislike for Sheikh Mohamed Fadlallah, the spiritual leader of Hezbollah. According to the journalist Bob Woodward, Casey transferred $3 million to the Saudi government in early 1985 to pay for the assassination of Fadlallah by foreign mercenaries. There is no available evidence in the public domain to corroborate the Woodward claim. But on March 8, 1985, a car bomb exploded outside Fadlallah's residence in Beirut, killing eighty civilians and wounding two hundred, though not Fadlallah himself. Oakley, the State Department's representative on the CPPG, assumed that uncontrollable elements of the Lebanese intelligence service were responsible. "This is what we were concerned would happen," he later recalled. Whether Casey had a hand in the affair remains a matter of conjecture. When Casey heard about the bombing, he called McMahon into his office. "I'll have to call the president," said Casey, "and tell him we have to rescind the finding and shut down the operation. In the meantime, let's find out what the hell happened."[10] The finding was subsequently canceled.

Whatever his role in the assassination attempt on Fadlallah, Casey was busy on the counterterrorism account in early 1985. He replaced David Whipple as national intelligence officer (NIO) for counterterrorism with a man who was much closer to the NSC staff, Charles "Charlie" Allen. It was Allen who had told Oliver North that the U.S. embassy annex bombing in September 1984 could have been averted. Once he became NIO, Allen instituted a virtual counterterrorism fusion center so that a similar intelligence failure could not happen again. He arranged for a secure telephone line to link the CIA's National Photographic Intelligence Center (NPIC), at that time the source of imagery intelligence for the intelligence community, to the rest of the CIA, the State Department, the Defense Intelligence Agency (DIA), the NSC, and the National Security Agency (NSA), which was responsible for intercepting and decrypting foreign communications. The NSC staff appreciated Allen's choice of a system that allowed specialists in terrorism to remain in their own agencies while ensuring that they were able to keep abreast of the most important developments.[11]

Although there was disagreement within the administration over the role that assassination should play in aggressive counterterrorism, a threat from Hezbollah in early 1985 forced the White House to take a second look at the use of overt military power as a weapon against terrorists. On January 14, 1985, a spokesman for Islamic Jihad, a cover name routinely used by Hezbollah, called the Reuters news agency to warn Washington that the U.S. hostages in Lebanon would be tried as spies and receive "the punishment that they deserve."[12] There were now five of them. Peter Kilburn, a librarian at the American University of Beirut, had been abducted in November 1984, and in January, just six days before making this threat, Iran's Lebanese clients had taken Father Lawrence Martin Jenco, the director of Catholic Relief Services in Beirut.

Hezbollah's threat spurred the State Department into action. A year earlier, Secretary of State George Shultz had placed Iran on the list of state sponsors of terrorism. Now he wanted Iran to feel some heat for continuing to assist Hezbollah. The United States routinely intercepted Iranian communications that showed Tehran's complicity in Hezbollah's terrorist activities. Based on this intelligence, the State Department concluded that "elements in the government of Iran are directly guiding the activities of Lebanon-based terrorists, including terrorists operating under the name of Islamic Jihad."[13]

Concerned that the lives of the five men were hanging in the balance, the State Department wanted Iran to know that it would be held responsible for the hostages' safety. The State Department also wanted U.S. allies to be prepared in the event military action was taken. A strong warning was prepared for delivery to Tehran. The State Department also drafted a démarche to send to key allies.[14] U.S. diplomats in Ankara, Islamabad, Tokyo, Bonn, London, and Paris were to approach the local government both to ask that it "make a drive against Iran's sponsorship of terrorism" and to alert it that if any harm came to the five Americans, "there will be very serious consequences."[15]

The State Department expected "a mixed reaction" from its allies and general surliness from Iran.[16] But if a diplomatic coalition could be forged against Iranian sponsorship of terrorism, the Iranians might just avert "any irrevocable action by the terrorists."[17] As part of this diplomatic initiative, the United States also sent a strong démarche to Damascus in the vain hope that Syria would apply some pressure on Hezbollah, whose principal training facilities were in the Syrian-controlled Bekaa Valley.

As these messages were going abroad, Shultz reasoned that he also needed to build a coalition at home for this tough policy. The secretary of state had seen in 1983 and 1984 how effectively Weinberger and Vessey—and even at times Ronald Reagan himself—could throw up obstacles to military action against terrorists. This time he wanted to neutralize possible opposition ahead of time by locking the White House into an aggressive posture from which it could not back down without serious consequences to President Reagan's credibility. "Before sending these messages [to U.S. ambassadors and to Tehran]," the State Department explained to Robert McFarlane on January 15, 1985, "we request presidential confirmation that the U.S. is prepared to take action against Iran if Iran does not assure the safety of the hostages."[18]

President Reagan approved the strong démarches the same day.[19] By siding with Shultz, the president signaled his willingness to put the word of the United States on the line to protect American lives abroad. McFarlane meanwhile alerted members of the National Security Policy Group (NSPG) that they should prepare to meet on January 18 to discuss possible military action. Despite his reluctance to use U.S. military force to respond to terrorist acts, Weinberger nevertheless informed the White House that he agreed with sending the démarches and "ensuring that we have the military options to back them up."[20] McFarlane's deputy, Rear Admiral John Poindexter, prepared briefing notes for President Reagan. At the end of the memorandum, Poindexter wrote, "I believe it is important that you get general agreement on [contingencies if the terrorists carry out their threats]. If the hostages are put on trial, we should already have decided upon a pre-planned response which needs only your final approval in order to move. We should also have similar decisions if the terrorists execute one, several, or all of the hostages."[21] Vice President Bush and Edwin Meese, who had become attorney general in Reagan's second term, also received copies of this briefing memorandum.

The NSC staff designed the hour-long meeting so that most of the discussion focused on the military options. Casey and Shultz were told to keep their briefings short, and the Pentagon was ordered to bring contingencies for action against both Hezbollah and Iran. The president needed to know "closure times and the availability of forces in the region." The NSC staff already believed that the United States could easily position the military strike capability that it needed in the Mediterranean.[22]

In the fall, Reagan had hesitated to use military force as a tool of counterterrorism because of his concern that retaliation for the bombing of the U.S. embassy annex might lead to the deaths of the U.S. hostages. Now he was being asked to use force to avenge them. Reagan identified with the fate of these five individuals. He knew their names. In some cases, he had met their families. He was not prepared to let them die on his watch.

There was no mistaking the fact that an important change in domestic politics since the fall had also made this tough decision easier. In October 1984, the president had talked about the effect on public opinion if a U.S. pilot or two were lost in the retaliatory attack. Four months later, after having won reelection in a landslide, Reagan could afford to be less concerned about public reaction to the costs of an air strike.

The Pentagon assured the president that U.S. forces were currently "well positioned to execute any strike." There were two aircraft carrier battle groups in the Indian Ocean and one in the eastern Mediterranean. Weinberger's team then offered four different options, two of which probably involved hitting targets in Iran or Iranian targets in Lebanon. Among the Iranian targets in Lebanon were the 1,500 members of the Iranian Revolutionary Guard Corps (also known as the Pasdaran) stationed with Hezbollah in the Bekaa Valley.[23] The Pentagon preferred the two options that involved going after Hezbollah itself. The options involving Iranian targets "would require more assets, would affect allies or friendly nations, and would be difficult to stop once we had set them in progress."[24] Hitting Iran might also cause an overreaction by the Soviets.[25]

President Reagan approved retaliation against Hezbollah targets in Lebanon. "If they harm just one or two of the hostages," the president ordered, "we should go with the two strikes as planned."[26] Although there were to be no attacks on Iranian targets, the president was not about to let Iran off the hook. Should some of the hostages be harmed and the initial air strikes not lead to the release of the remaining hostages, Iran was to be threatened with having its harbors mined.

No one had promised Reagan any magic bullets. During a discussion of hitting Hezbollah, CIA director Casey explained that there were between 100 and 150 terrorists at Hezbollah's main facility in the Bekaa Valley who "leave during the day but return at night." "Smashing that," Casey added, "would set them back, but this would only be temporary." No other advisor suggested that a military attack would end the threat from Shia terrorism. What Reagan was told with confidence, however, was that the link between Hezbollah and Iran was clear. "We do know," said Casey, "that the

Iranians supply, direct, train, and work with the terrorists through the Iranian Revolutionary Guard."27

Weinberger appeared to support the president's decision. However, to prevent a repeat of what had happened in October 1983, Poindexter, who was at the meeting in place of McFarlane, asked Reagan for confirmation that the NSPG would not have to meet again to approve the strikes formally. "We've now agreed," said Poindexter, "that if the hostages are harmed, we will conduct the strikes."28 "Like that," interjected Reagan, snapping his fingers. Reagan then repeated in detail the precise military action he expected should "any" hostage be harmed. Military retaliation for Iran-sponsored terrorism was now, for the first time, the firm policy of the United States.29

When Hezbollah did not follow through on its January 1985 threat to try the Americans, the threat of U.S. military action subsided. In the wake of the minicrisis, the White House indicated to the CIA that the U.S. government needed better intelligence on the location of the hostages.30 At the January 18 NSPG meeting on Lebanon, Casey had admitted that the CIA did not know where they were. A friendly foreign service asserted to the CIA that it knew the exact location of the hostages but also said that they were moved frequently. The importance of knowing the location of the hostages became dramatically obvious after Jeremy Levin, the CNN producer who had been taken in February 1984, managed to elude his captors in mid-February 1985. Levin reported to the U.S. government that all of the hostages were held in the area of the Sheikh Abdullah barracks in the Bekaa Valley. Levin had escaped from the adjoining married officers' quarters, but it was reported that some of the hostages were in the barracks themselves. As members of the NSPG knew well, these barracks had figured prominently on U.S. Air Force target lists.31

In February 1985, Casey set up a DCI Hostage Locating Task Force (HLTF) and made Charlie Allen its chairman. Although anchored at the CIA, the HLTF comprised "intelligence, diplomatic, forensic, and criminal experts" who were to conduct "a detailed analysis of all available information in broadening our search for the hostages."[32] The Terrorist Incident Working Group (TIWG), which was chaired by Deputy National Security Advisor Admiral Poindexter, supervised this new task force. It was understood that the HLTF was to stay in business "until such time that the hostages have been released/rescued or the TIWG agrees that it is no longer productive."[33]

Washington would get only a month to catch its breath before the threat of terrorism against U.S. interests in Lebanon again attracted its attention. Hezbollah publicly blamed the Fadlallah bombing on the United States, as it did a second large bombing that also took place in a Shia neighborhood in March 1985. Yet another reason to worry that Hezbollah might be preparing to lash out soon was that Washington had just vetoed a Lebanese-sponsored UN Security Council resolution condemning Israeli actions in Lebanon. Hezbollah bombed the U.S. embassy annex after the United States had vetoed a similar resolution in early September 1984.[34]

A third attack on the U.S. embassy compound in Beirut was the scenario that most worried the administration. U.S. intelligence satellites had again picked up images of a "mock-up at the Sheikh Abdullah Barracks for use in training car-bomb drivers." The CIA explained that it appeared "to simulate the approach to the Porfin facility."[35] The Porfin facility was not the U.S. embassy. It was a "largely unoccupied" U.S. facility that was being used by a "contract security force."[36] Nevertheless, it looked as if a U.S. target would be hit.

In anticipation of trouble, the State Department decided in mid-March 1985 to "thin out" its official delegation in Beirut. Fourteen more people would leave for Cyprus, with only thirty foreign service officers and military advisors remaining.[37] More hostage-taking was also a possibility. But the U.S. government was resigned to the fact that it could do little to enhance the security of the American civilians still in the city. There were two hundred left, clustered at the American University of Beirut. The United States had the capability to evacuate all of them by helicopter or naval units, as it had done when fighting in the city became fierce in February 1984. However, Washington believed that "few, if any, of these would choose to be evacuated."[38]

The deputies committee met on March 13 to go over U.S. readiness. The USS *Vinson* and the USS *Eisenhower* carrier battle groups were already on a ninety-six-hour response time, and the chairman of the Joint Chiefs of Staff was instructed to be prepared to move even faster after a strike order.[39]

In preparing for the expected Iranian-sponsored terrorist attack, the Reagan administration gave no serious consideration to its happening in the United States. The U.S. intelligence community had apparently not received any solid intelligence pointing to that kind of reaction by Hezbollah, and the Lebanese group had not yet attacked anywhere in the Western Hemisphere. Moreover, the U.S. counterterrorism community, the intelligence professionals who studied terrorist organizations, and the policymakers who took an interest in terrorist incidents considered it unlikely that a major terrorist attack would take place in the United States. It was assumed both that overseas targets were easier to hit and therefore more attractive to international terrorists and that U.S. domestic safeguards, while not perfect, were adequate.[40] The members of the CPPG seemed to share the assumption of the CIA that the attack by Islamic radicals, if it came, would happen abroad and there was no need to plan for any domestic alternative.[41]

But had there been some piece of contradictory information, showing radical Islamist activity in the United States, it is unlikely that anyone at the CPPG meeting would have known about it. No representative of a domestic policymaking agency, including the Department of Justice, was invited to the March 13 meeting to discuss the impending terrorist attack on a U.S. target. The entire intelligence community was represented by Casey's deputy, Robert Gates, and there was no one from the U.S. law enforcement community.

The Shia radicals did retaliate in March 1985 for U.S. actions at the United Nations, but not by bombing any of the four U.S. facilities in Beirut. On March 14, 15, and 16, Hezbollah took three additional hostages, two British and one American. The American was Terry Anderson, the chief Middle East correspondent of the Associated Press. Since Jeremy Levin had recently escaped, Anderson became the fifth U.S. citizen in captivity. On March 18, Hezbollah, again using the cover name Islamic Jihad, announced that the three men had been taken as "part of a campaign to rid Muslim regions of foreign spies."[42] "Islamic Jihad" said that it had delayed two days in claiming responsibility because it wanted to get the three captives safely out of Beirut. It seemed that there were now even more Westerners at the Sheikh Abdullah barracks.

Fortunately, no one had died in Hezbollah's riposte, but the kidnappings nonetheless painfully revealed the continuing ineffectiveness of the U.S. government's approach to this terrorist organization. By the summer of 1985, Hezbollah would add two more hostages, David Jacobsen and Thomas Sutherland, raising the total number of Americans in captivity to seven. Meanwhile, the Reagan administration's goals remained the same: gaining the release of the hostages and reducing the power of Hezbollah. The military option was still on the table, but with Hezbollah having decided to bring the hostages into its nest in the Bekaa Valley, there were not many useful targets that could be safely attacked. The assumed concentration of the hostages made a rescue more feasible; yet in discussions in March, the deputies believed that their location at the terrorist training barracks also meant that an assault would be especially bloody, because Hezbollah was believed to be well armed there.[43] Meanwhile, the Lebanese had not turned out to be trustworthy surrogates, and the authority of the Lebanese government, never great, seemed to be ebbing. Diplomacy with the Syrians had been tried, but it seemed that they either lacked influence with Hezbollah or were unwilling to use it. Syria occupied most of Lebanon, including the Bekaa. The Iranians and their Shia allies operated there with the approval of Damascus, which should have given Syria leverage with Hezbollah. However, Iran had paid in real coin for Syrian acquiescence. In late 1982, the two countries agreed that Iran would supply Syria with nine million tons of discounted crude oil per year.[44] But since early March 1984, because of the internal struggle in Lebanon between the Syrian client Amal and Hezbollah, the Syrians had begun to show a little independence from Iran.[45] There was even talk in Washington of somehow involving them in a hostage rescue attempt. But this kind of joint planning with the suspicious Assad regime would be unprecedented and likely fruitless.[46] That left the Iranians.

Within the U.S. government, a small but influential knot of people believed that the future of U.S. policy in the region depended on finding a way back into the good graces of Iran. In the 1970s, Iran had been one of the two pillars of U.S. policy in the Persian Gulf, the other being Saudi Arabia. The overthrow of the shah had brought that relationship to an end. But now the leader of that revolution was eighty-five years old, and there were rumors that his health was not very good. The other immediate threat to Iranian stability was the war raging between Tehran and Baghdad, which had begun in September 1980. The United States had been happy to see Iraq bleed Iran, but U.S. officials feared the consequence of an Iranian defeat by Saddam Hussein, who seemed to have widespread regional ambitions.

Charlie Allen was one of those who believed that this was the time for the United States to make its move into Iranian politics.[47] He saw the hostage problem as a means by which to look around for potential allies in whatever successor government emerged in Tehran. Casey, Allen's boss at the CIA, as well as McFarlane, his deputy Poindexter, and some regional specialists at the NSC, also viewed the situation in the same way.[48]

In the spring of 1985, Robert McFarlane requested a CIA assessment of Iran and then instructed the NSC staff to prepare a draft NSDD on a policy of seeking an opening to Tehran. In January, the U.S. government had considered using a stick to compel Iran to contain Hezbollah. Now some seemed to want to use a carrot.

Shultz and Weinberger strongly opposed the idea. For Shultz, this initiative represented the negation of everything he had been advocating on Iran. He had pushed for sanctions in 1984 and then through Operation Staunch had invested U.S. prestige in cajoling allies to respect the embargo on selling arms to Tehran. In 1985, he had led the charge for direct military action against Iran. Iran was a prime supporter of international terrorism, and Shultz refused to push that reality to one side for some possible future geopolitical gain. Weinberger, who did not often find himself on the same side as Shultz, used particularly colorful language to make his point: "This is almost too absurd to comment on . . . It's like asking Gadhafi to Washington."[49] As the Departments of State and Defense were trying to kill this shift in policy, a dramatic terrorist incident in the Middle East would provide evidence that paying ransom to the Iranians might be a successful counterterrorism strategy.

TWA Flight 847

On June 14, 1985, two Hezbollah operatives hijacked TWA Flight 847 en route from Athens to Rome and diverted it to Beirut. The hijackers were seeking the release of 766 Palestinian prisoners in Israeli jails and had hoped to find many Israelis on the flight. As it turned out, there were none, so the hijackers singled out U.S. citizens with what they described as Jewish-sounding names and any Americans carrying military identification. The hijackers then released seventeen women and two children.

Once he learned of the hijacking, Poindexter convened a meeting of the TIWG. The Pentagon recommended the use of Delta Force to free the passengers. As the administration was considering its options, the terrorists directed the pilot to fly to Algiers. The Algerian government persuaded the terrorists to release more women and children but could not get them to release the entire group. Despite U.S. efforts to prevent it, the terrorists forced the plane to return to Beirut, where they wanted to meet the leader of Amal, Nabih Berri.

While the plane sat on the tarmac in Beirut, the terrorists became impatient. To get Amal's attention, they murdered one of the U.S. military personnel aboard, U.S. seaman Robert Stethem, and threw his body out of the plane. Once Amal's representatives reached the aircraft, the hijacking became a combined effort of Hezbollah and Amal. Although the two terrorist organizations were competitors in Lebanon, they both saw an advantage in sharing the hostages. Amal subsequently took some of the hostages off the plane to acquire some bargaining power of their own in discussions with the United States.

Although it flirted with using Delta Force, the Reagan administration approached the settlement of the incident much as the Nixon administration had managed the Dawson Field crisis in September 1970. Despite its stated policy of "no negotiations with terrorists," the administration wanted a swap of Israeli prisoners for the Western hostages. Through back channels and via the International Committee of the Red Cross, Washington put pressure on the Israelis to release the 766 prisoners demanded by the hijackers. The Reagan administration explained that Israel could dress up the release so that it appeared to be independent of the hostage drama. Initially, Israeli prime minister Shimon Peres and his defense minister, Yitzhak Rabin, resisted. But as the ordeal dragged into its third week, Peres relented. Once the Syrians were told that three hundred of the prisoners would be released after the passengers had been set free, Amal was prepared to allow the hostages under its control to go.[50]

This was not the first time that the Reagan administration had advocated concessions by an ally for the release of its citizens. In 1984, the CIA had tried to arrange for a release of the seventeen Dawa prisoners held by Kuwait through an intermediary after Hezbollah had cited their release as one of its conditions for releasing the American hostages in Lebanon. The Dawa group was in a Kuwaiti jail for trying to bomb the U.S. and French embassies in December 1983. But the Kuwaitis refused, and Washington eventually stopped asking.[51] Admiral Poindexter recalls that President Reagan was unwilling to rigidly apply the U.S. public position of "no concessions, no deals" to hostage situations. "If you study Israel's handling of hostages," he said, "they do not always go in with guns blazing." Poindexter added, "it is the same with us. . . It would not please all of his supporters, but Reagan was pragmatic."[52]

Iran played an intriguing part in the negotiated end of the TWA drama. Syria lacked the influence with Hezbollah to get that terrorist organization to release the passengers that it held. Without those passengers, the deal was off, for the United States demanded the release of all of the passengers. No one wanted to see a repeat of the TWA incident in 1969, when two Jewish passengers were kept for an additional two months after everyone else on the plane had been freed. On June 29, the NSC staff sent a message to the speaker of the Iranian parliament, Hashemi Rafsanjani, requesting that he intervene to bring about the release of the TWA passengers under Hezbollah's control. The next day, Rafsanjani traveled to Damascus to participate in resolving the crisis. Through Rafsanjani's mediation, Hezbollah agreed to release its TWA hostages. On June 30, the remaining passengers and crew left for the West via Damascus, and the Syrians and the Lebanese allowed the hijackers, despite having killed Stethem, to disappear into the anarchy that was Beirut. On July 1, Israel announced the release of three hundred Lebanese prisoners, and President Reagan suspended U.S. landing rights for two Lebanese air carriers and ordered U.S. carriers to end cargo flights to Beirut. With Weinberger and Vessey opposed to any military reprisal, the administration rejected a military response to Hezbollah. Although Reagan was also furious with the Syrian government, which had a great deal of influence in Lebanon, for letting the hijackers go, the administration did not penalize Syria in any way.

Operations Tulip and Rose

The TWA incident was heartbreaking for the Reagan administration. A U.S. serviceman had been killed, and there would once again be no retribution. On July 3, Reagan attended what he described in his diary as a "frustrating NSPG meeting *re* the seven kidnap victims and the matter of Lebanon generally."[53] The discussion appears to have degenerated into a painful rehash of the arguments for and against military action that Reagan had heard back in October 1984. "Some feel we must retaliate," Reagan noted. "I feel to do so would definitely risk the lives of the 7."[54] Reagan saw a linkage between U.S. policy toward Hezbollah and the fate of the hostages. So long as the hostages were unharmed, Washington should do nothing to provoke a violent reaction in Beirut.

The Lebanese situation exposed a tension between Reagan's belief in the importance of defending U.S. lives abroad and his desire that on his watch U.S. international prestige be increased. On July 8, the president gave a widely covered speech to the American Bar Association. Ronald Reagan named Iran, Libya, Cuba, North Korea, and Nicaragua "a confederation of terrorist states." "Most of the terrorists who are kidnapping and murdering American citizens and attacking American installations," Reagan said, "are being trained, financed, and directly or indirectly controlled by a core group of radical and totalitarian governments, a new international version of Murder, Inc." Reagan described state sponsorship of terror as "an act of war" to which the United States had the right to respond. Reagan also threatened the individual terrorist, vowing to apprehend anyone guilty of terrorism, wherever it was committed. "There can be no place on Earth left where it is safe for these monsters to rest, or train, or practice their cruel and deadly skills. We must act together, or unilaterally, if necessary, to ensure that terrorists have no sanctuary—anywhere."[55]

However eloquent the words and brilliant the delivery, Reagan was using rhetoric for which there was not yet supporting policy direction. NSDD 138 was still on the books, but in a year there had been only one attempt at aggressive counterterrorism, the covert action against Hezbollah in Lebanon, and it had collapsed.

The Iran-Contra scandal, which very nearly brought down the Reagan administration, emerged from the frustration of those summer days in 1985. In his diary, Reagan noted during the TWA incident that "Gadhafi is talking to Iran and Syria about a joint terrorist war against us."[56] Reagan agreed with Shultz that to defeat terrorists, one had to deal with the states that supported them. Everything else was secondary. In the wake of TWA 847, the president let it be known that he wanted policies that could do this. Over the course of the rest of that summer, Reagan would choose two different kinds of policies to achieve this same goal.

Although Reagan called Muammar Gadhafi the "mad clown of Tripoli," he took Libya's capacity to cause harm to the United States very seriously.[57] For some time, the Libyan leader had been fishing in troubled waters, but in 1985 Gadhafi seemed to have made a conscious decision to step up his harassment of the U.S. government. Unlike other state sponsors of terrorism, Libya was willing and able to meddle in U.S. domestic matters. The Libyans had forged an alliance with the American Nation of Islam, led by Louis Farrakhan. In February, Gadhafi addressed the Nation of Islam's national convention by televised hookup and promised weapons to African Americans to fight "your racist oppressors."[58] Two months later, Farrakhan announced that he had received a $5 million interest-free loan from his Libyan "fellow struggler."[59] Meanwhile, the FBI was also monitoring the activities of suspected members of Libyan hit squads in the United States. In May, FBI agents served subpoenas on between fifteen and eighteen pro-Gadhafi Libyans in Virginia, Colorado, Michigan, and North Carolina.[60] A federal grand jury had been impaneled to hear testimony on their activities on behalf of the Libyan regime. In early June, the United States expelled a diplomat from Libya's UN mission for activities "incompatible with his status and illegal."[61]

Overseas, Libya seemed to be scoring diplomatic successes. In mid-1984, the longtime U.S. ally Morocco had shocked Washington by signing a "treaty of union" with Tripoli. By March 1985, the Reagan administration was convinced that Morocco had done this to settle its struggle with the separatist Polisario Front in the Western Sahara, but Libya's leverage in North Africa remained worrisome. This regional authority grew in April when the U.S. ally Gaafar Nimeiri was overthrown in Sudan. Gleeful over the defeat of his enemy Nimeiri and Washington's subsequent disappointment, Gadhafi threatened that Reagan's "nose would be cut" if the United States somehow attempted to reverse the outcome in Sudan.[62]

Gadhafi's apparent successes did nothing to solve some troubles he was having at home.[63] These foreign adventures were eating away at Libya's foreign exchange reserves at a time when oil revenues were down due to problems in Libya's oil industry. Gadhafi's woes were magnified by his deteriorating relationship with Libya's professional army, which saw a growing threat in Gadhafi's revolutionary militia and East German–trained personal security force. In April, Gadhafi survived an assassination attempt by the National Front for the Salvation of Libya (NFSL), a group directed by disgruntled army officers.

After this attack, Gadhafi lashed out at the United States and Egypt, which he blamed for assisting his domestic opponents. Libyan intelligence agents organized a suicide truck bombing of the

U.S. embassy in Cairo. Fortunately, due to good police work by the Egyptians, the attack was detected in its planning stages and prevented. Sensing a growing coalition against him, Gadhafi sought improved relations with Iran.

At an NSPG meeting in mid-July 1986, Robert McFarlane argued that diplomatic and economic measures had so far not succeeded in tempering Gadhafi's behavior. He advocated stronger measures. The NSC staff had worked up two plans: Operation Tulip and Operation Rose.[64] Tulip was a plan to "assist Algerian and Egyptian training and direction of paramilitary operations within Libya."[65] The goal was to make the NFSL a "viable paramilitary force." Washington intended to leave to the Algerians and the Egyptians responsibility for guiding the NFSL in its war against Gadhafi. Rose was a plan for an overt military campaign against Libya, led by Egypt but supported by the U.S. Air Force.[66]

Reagan signed the Tulip finding and may also have signed the Rose finding.[67] At the very least, he indicated that he wanted the NSC to flesh out how the latter might be organized and to feel out the Egyptians on their interest.[68]

With the start of a covert war against Tripoli, the Gadhafi government became the first and only state sponsor of terrorism in the Middle East that the Reagan administration would attempt to overthrow. "Libya was low-hanging fruit," recalls John Poindexter, who helped design the Libyan findings.[69] It would be much more difficult to punish the other two state sponsors in the region, Syria and Iran. Libya was militarily weak and lacked any major sponsors. The Soviet Union was a strong supporter of Syria, and though Soviet-Iranian relations were tense, Moscow would view U.S. military action against a neighbor with great concern. The NSC assumed that Moscow would care little about Gadhafi's fate, even if a few Soviet technicians were killed in a Western or Egyptian action.[70] Another factor arguing in favor of making an example of Libya was the assumption that the United States could take action against Tripoli without endangering the U.S. hostages in Lebanon.

Soon after Reagan signed the Tulip finding, Poindexter went to Cairo to gain high-level Egyptian support for the initiative. Poindexter took Donald Fortier with him. Fortier was the staffer at the NSC who had pushed hardest to make an example out of Libya, using terms like *preemption* to explain the need to "get the sponsors of terrorism before the terrorists get you."[71]

When they learned of the Poindexter mission, the Middle East experts at the State Department considered the mission a fool's errand.[72] Poindexter thought he had reason to expect otherwise from the Egyptians. In August 1985, Libya had expelled thirty thousand Tunisian and ten thousand Egyptian workers. The move reflected Libyan economic concerns but was also an effort by the Libyan leader to penalize the Tunisians and the Egyptians for their moderate views on the United States and the Arab-Israeli peace process. The effort backfired, leading to greater cooperation among Tunis, Cairo, and even Baghdad and Algiers.[73] As the foreign service had expected, Poindexter returned with nothing to show for the trip. Without even allowing the deputy national security advisor to finish his presentation, Hosni Mubarak terminated the meeting. "When we decide to invade Libya," said the Egyptian president, "it will be our decision and on our timetable."[74]

As Poindexter continued to work toward regime change in Libya, McFarlane and the CIA were pursuing counterterrorism in Lebanon using a different set of tools. Given Reagan's reluctance to use force against Iran to compel the release of the hostages, there seemed no better option that trying to buy off Iran. The policy was couched in terms of establishing good credit with the successor generation to Khomeini in Tehran. But what caught the president's attention was the possibility that these Iranian "friends" of better relations would persuade Hezbollah to release the seven hostages.

Reagan was recovering from colon cancer surgery at Bethesda Naval Hospital when his national security advisor outlined the Iran initiative to him. "Some strange soundings are coming from some Iranians," Reagan noted in his diary on July 18, 1985. "It could be a breakthrough on getting our seven kidnap victims back," he added, suggesting that the return of the American hostages was his principal concern.[75] McFarlane explained that the Israeli government was passing on information from a group of Iranians that claimed to be in touch with "moderates" around Khomeini.[76] To curry favor with these men, Israel wanted permission to sell one hundred TOW anti-tank missiles to Tehran that it had purchased from the United States. Israel needed U.S. permission because under U.S. law, Israel could not resell the weapons it had purchased from U.S. manufacturers. The Israelis reported that the Iranians were "very confident that in the short term, they could achieve the release of the seven Americans held hostage in Lebanon. But in exchange, they would need to show some gain."[77]

It was a cynical ploy by a group of Iranian and Saudi arms merchants, who were looking to make money, and the Khomeini regime, which needed U.S. weapons. Israel's participation was what sealed the deal for Reagan. "We had great respect for Israel's intelligence capabilities relating to matters in the Middle East," Reagan later wrote, "and, as a result, we gave their assertions a great deal of credence. I was told that Israeli prime minister Shimon Peres was behind the proposal."[78] "Israel is not noted for dealing with fools and charlatans," McFarlane wrote to Shultz, whom he knew to be skeptical of approaching Iran.[79] Shultz, however, reminded McFarlane of the "complications arising from our 'blessing' an Israel-Iran relationship where Israel's interests and ours are not necessarily the same."[80]

Once he had left Bethesda Naval Hospital and was back at the White House, the president chaired a meeting of the NSPG on August 6, 1985, to decide whether to use the proposed carrot to induce Iran to secure the release of the Americans in Lebanon. The president was not yet fully convinced, or at least he was not willing to go against the wishes of his secretaries of state and defense, who opposed the deal. But within a few days, Reagan was ready. "The truth is," Reagan recalled, "once we had information from Israel that we could trust the people in Iran, I didn't have to think thirty seconds about saying yes to their proposal."[81] Reagan telephoned McFarlane a few days later with his approval.[82]

Even after the Iranian Revolution, Israel had maintained contacts with Iran to protect the Jewish population there.[83] Tens of thousands of Jews had left Iran following the revolution, but some had stayed. Israel was interested in obtaining U.S. assistance to widen its leverage in Iran. The hostage issue provided an ideal opening. Frustrated by years of paralysis over counterterrorism in Lebanon, eager to stake a claim on the future of Iranian politics, and seemingly oblivious to any Israeli ulterior motives, the NSC staff endorsed the Israeli offer.

The *Achille Lauro* Incident

A misstep by Palestinian terrorists loyal to Yasir Arafat in October 1985 would strengthen the NSC staff's role in overseeing U.S. counterterrorism.[84] In 1974, the PLO chairman had promised the United States that the PLO would restrict its terrorist activities to Israeli targets. This pledge did not please Israel, but it was enough for the United States to consider handling Arafat as yet another troublesome foreign political leader. The unexpected turn of events in October 1985 would test this U.S. approach to Arafat and the mainline PLO.

The *Achille Lauro* was an Italian cruise ship that in the first week of October was on a tour of the Mediterranean. On October 7, the 750 passengers were given the option of a tour of the Pyramids followed by a bus trip to Port Said or a leisurely cruise from Alexandria to Port Said. Only ninety-seven passengers, twelve of whom were U.S. citizens, opted to stay on the ship.

Among those who decided to stay were four young Arab men, who had earlier drawn the attention of one of the ship's stewards as the cruise set off from Genoa, Italy. As it turned out, the four carried fake passports and were members of the Palestinian Liberation Front (PLF), a splinter group headed by Abu Abbas, who had pledged his allegiance to Arafat in 1982. They were using the cruise ship to slip into the Israeli port of Ashdod, one of the destinations on the cruise.

Their plan was upset when the curious steward walked into their room as they were cleaning their guns. Alarmed at being discovered, the PLF terrorists decided to take the crew and the remaining passengers hostage. The terrorists then demanded the release of fifty-one Palestinians in Israeli jails.

At a TIWG meeting convened a few hours after news of the hijacking reached Washington, Reagan's chief counterterrorism specialists recommended sending Joint Special Operations Command (JSOC) forces to the region to prepare for a possible rescue attempt. As these special forces—which included U.S. Navy SEAL (Sea, Air, Land) Team Six and Delta Force—were deploying, the White House instructed the Department of State to discourage the governments of Cyprus, Lebanon, and Syria from allowing the cruise ship to dock at their ports. If a rescue were to be attempted, the United States wanted it to occur in international waters.

Syria decided to cooperate with Washington. When the hijackers learned that Syria would not allow them to land, they killed a wheelchair-bound American passenger, Leon Klinghoffer. Washington was not officially notified that an American had died. As the cruise ship left the Syrian coast, Reagan ordered the SEAL team to attempt a rescue if the ship entered international waters again and if the operation seemed feasible.

The ship returned to Egypt before a U.S. rescue could be mounted. Once the *Achille Lauro* was in Egyptian waters, Reagan ordered the U.S. special forces to stand down. "It is Egypt's call," said the president.[85] If they wanted U.S. assistance, they could have it; otherwise, it was their responsibility to end the incident.

One especially concerned bystander was Arafat. He announced that the PLO would mediate an end to the crisis and then sent his ally Abu Abbas to Cairo. The Egyptians were also eager to bring the incident to an end peacefully. President Mubarak had an interest in promoting the PLO as a legitimate partner in the Arab-Israeli peace process, and this incident had the potential of reminding the world of Arafat's continuing links to international terrorism.

The Egyptians allowed Abu Abbas into the country and with him negotiated the release of the hostages. In return, the four PLF operatives were allowed to go free. The Egyptians, who had by this time learned that an American had been murdered, misled the Reagan administration to get the Americans to accept a "no harm, no foul" outcome to the mishap.

When the U.S. ambassador to Egypt, Nicholas Veliotis, boarded the ship to make his own inspection, he learned that Klinghoffer had been killed and that Egypt had let four murderers and the leader of the operation go free. The White House asked Mubarak to hold the hijackers and Abu Abbas. The Egyptian leader told Washington that the plane carrying the four hijackers and Abbas had already left Cairo.

From the Israelis, the U.S. government learned that the getaway plane had not yet taken off. This information reached Admiral Poindexter. At the time, McFarlane was in Illinois with the president. Sensing a golden opportunity to make good on the president's recent statements on international terrorism, Poindexter called Vice Admiral Art Moreau, assistant to Admiral William Crowe, who had just replaced Vessey as chairman of the Joint Chiefs of Staff. Poindexter told Moreau he had reason to believe the hijackers were still in Egypt and asked Moreau to begin considering how to take action against the plane. As the Joint Chiefs of Staff were thinking through the logistics of diverting the plane, Poindexter called McFarlane and outlined the new intelligence and planning actions he had initiated. McFarlane reported this information to the president, and then Mc-

Farlane called Poindexter back to report that Reagan had agreed that the planning should proceed. Later in the day, when the president was back in the White House, he convened an NSPG conference call. After hearing the plan, deciding on the rules of engagement, and discussing the diplomatic implications, he ordered the execution of the intercept plan.[86]

The plane could have been brought down in Israel, but this would have magnified the embarrassment for Mubarak, so it was decided to force the Egyptian pilot to land at the NATO base at Sigonella, Sicily. Originally, the United States assumed that it would obtain the permission of the Italian government to arrest the hijackers. But when the Egyptian airliner landed at Sigonella, the JSOC forces surrounded the aircraft, and the Carabinieri (the Italian police) surrounded the JSOC forces. The Italians insisted that their judicial system would deal with the matter. In the end, the Italians did try the hijackers, but to the annoyance of the Reagan administration, they allowed Abu Abbas to go free.

Despite Abbas's escape, the handling of the *Achille Lauro* incident was deemed a great success by the administration. For Poindexter, who had managed this crisis for the president, the lesson was clear: "If the White House and the NSC wanted to, we could move fast." Poindexter opposed the NSC's becoming an operating agency. But with the incessant warring between the Departments of State and Defense, it seemed that the NSC was needed to fill the gap. "The worst thing would be," recalls Poindexter, "if nobody's in charge."[87]

Reagan was very happy with the outcome of his staff's activism. "Americans as well as friends abroad are standing six inches taller," he confided in his diary after the U.S. fighter jets forced the Egyptian plane to land.[88] The NSC staff would quickly employ this dynamism to pursue the administration's two-track policy on counterterrorism even more vigorously.

In November and December 1985, the NSC worked to further both the Iranian and Libyan initiatives with the president's support.

In November, President Reagan approved a shipment of HAWK surface-to-air missiles by the Israelis to Tehran. The operation was beset by difficulties, which ultimately required the intervention of the CIA. Duane "Dewey" Clarridge, of the CIA, arranged for an airplane owned by a CIA proprietary company to fly eighteen missiles to Iran. Reagan was informed of the operation before it took place.[89]

As the United States was moving closer to Iran, the Reagan administration continued its efforts against Libya. In spite of Poindexter's ill-fated trip to Cairo in the late summer of 1985, the administration was determined to pressure the regime in the hope it would crack. Mubarak's opposition to Operation Rose, however, was not the only snag that the administration's covert efforts encountered. In October, the leadership of the Senate Select Committee on Intelligence raised some objections to the Tulip plan. Once the administration explained that the goal was not to assassinate Gadhafi, a majority on that committee came around to supporting at least Tulip.[90] But the administration's headaches with covert action against Gadhafi did not end there. The congressional concern and the very existence of the covert action had in the meantime been leaked to the journalist Bob Woodward. On November 3, the *Washington Post* published his story disclosing the presidential finding for a covert operation to "undermine the Libyan regime."[91]

The administration and Gadhafi both reacted negatively to the *Post* story. The White House refused to rescind the finding and immediately initiated an investigation to determine who had leaked the story to Woodward.[92] In Tripoli, Gadhafi denounced the now no longer covert operation as "open blackmail and muscular thuggery."[93] The Tulip plan may not have succeeded anyway, but its public disclosure hurt the prospects that either the Egyptians or the Algerians would energetically do their part. The NSC staff noticed a marked decline in Algerian support after the Woodward leak. As the year came to a close, the option of using the Libyan dissidents did not seem to be the solution to Reagan's Gadhafi problem.[94]

The Vice President's Task Force

By the end of 1985, Robert McFarlane was tired of the bureaucratic struggles. Though he could see some solutions in a resurgent NSC, he thought it was time to resign. He recommended Admiral John Poindexter as his successor. Reagan had developed a rapport with Poindexter and announced the change on December 4, 1985. Poindexter shifted a few people around but essentially left the NSC team alone. He elevated Donald Fortier to the deputy position and made Oliver North the chair of the TIWG. North, who was director of the catchall Office of Politico-Military affairs at the NSC, retained that post.

Poindexter thought that a highly operational NSC was not a long-term solution to the sharp disagreements over counterterrorism. Both he and McFarlane had supported making some widespread changes in the community of agencies responsible for aspects of counterterrorism. In the first days of the TWA 847 incident in the summer of 1985, the NSPG had discussed measures to tighten U.S. aviation security. On June 20, the administration sent some suggested language to Congress, which was considering legislation similar to the provisions in the Ribicoff-Javits bill proposed back in 1977 dealing with sanctions against foreign countries that maintained unsafe airports.[95] President Reagan later signed NSDD 180, which expanded the FAA's federal air marshal program to cover, within two weeks, all flights "serving cities where the threat of hijacking is most severe." As in 1970, under Nixon, the FAA was permitted to draw an emergency supply of marshals from other federal agencies. The presidential directive also mandated increased research and development in detection devices and regular FAA inspections of foreign airports to determine the adequacy of security measures.[96]

To some in the administration, these seemed like Band-Aid solutions to deeper problems in the U.S. counterterrorism system. CIA director Casey had talked to Secretary Weinberger about forming a blue-ribbon government committee on counterterrorism. Weinberger signed on, as did McFarlane when he was approached. The NSPG subsequently recommended to Reagan the formation of a Task Force on Combating Terrorism to examine how the country identified, managed, and averted these threats.[97] In 1979, twenty-nine agencies had some piece of the counterterrorism mission.[98] By 1985, there were even more, and the U.S. government was spending between $2.5 and $3 billion a year on programs associated with counterterrorism.[99]

President Reagan assigned the task of chairing the task force to his vice president. "It was a vice presidential thing to do," recalls George Shultz.[100] "Bush was not viewed as having any institutional stake," recalls Poindexter. For executive director, Poindexter suggested to McFarlane his old boss, the former chief of naval operations, Admiral James Holloway. Holloway and Bush already knew each other.[101]

This was to be the most searching study of U.S. counterterrorism strategy attempted to date. Between 1972 and 1985, the interagency working group on counterterrorism had met frequently to discuss the U.S. government's readiness to meet various terrorist contingencies. The working group had allowed a cross-fertilization of ideas that led to some improvements in procedures among middle-level staffers. But it attracted little high-level attention. Vice President Bush's group assembled a Senior Review Group of counterterrorism professionals who were assistant secretaries or their equivalents from across the government.[102]

The vice president's relationship with President Reagan also ensured that whatever this group determined would be taken seriously. The president hosted Bush for a private lunch every week, at which the vice president could express his concerns openly. The vice president was also chair of the administration's Special Situations Group, a crisis management committee set up in the first year of the administration. As a charter member of the NSPG, Bush was given all of the principal policy documents and was consulted on the administration's covert operations. Indeed, his representative, Donald Gregg, sat on the CPPG, which drafted many of the covert plans.

The task force comprised a staff of professionals, partly from the Office of the Vice President and partly from the non-profit Institute of Defense Analysis, which produced fifty draft recommendations. The recommendations were then sent to the Senior Review Group.

The draft recommendations covered issues as disparate as the policy on dealing with hostage families to future deployment guidelines for the JSOC. The staff's overarching proposal was the creation of a counterterrorism coordinator, or "czar," who would operate out of the NSC. Lacking support from even the NSC, this proposal would never reach the president. Admiral Poindexter opposed the creation of a czar because of a belief that Congress would insist that the position be given a legislative foundation, in which case the position would have to be confirmed by Congress, and the occupant would be required to testify before Congress.[103] He preferred to keep North, the director of the NSC's Office of Politico-Military Affairs, as his point man on counterterrorism. The State Department, which also opposed the appointment of a counterterrorism czar, wanted the task force to reiterate the importance of the lead-agency approach that recognized the State Department's preeminence in all overseas terrorist incidents.

To assist the proposed czar, the staff hoped to create a counterterrorism "fusion center," where intelligence from all the agencies could be assembled and analyzed. This recommendation flew in the face of the standard practice of compartmentalizing information not only between agencies but even within them. The senior reviewers would ultimately accept this recommendation.

The staff also hoped to force the training of counterterrorism professionals across the government. This proposal encountered stiff opposition from the FBI and the CIA. The bureaucratic opposition was so intense that Admiral Holloway later commented that the task force "worked hard to pound those recommendations out of a bureaucracy reluctant to change or to move forward. The recommendations were the consensus of the government and 'were signed in blood.'"104

The vice president presented his report to President Reagan on January 6, 1986, with the forty-four recommendations on which the task force had finally agreed. These recommendations—which included an intelligence fusion center, tighter border control, enhanced FBI investigative powers, and a call for better human intelligence—were incorporated into NSDD 207, which the president signed the next day. The president also signed a covert action finding that enhanced the CIA's ability to "counteract terrorism" overseas.105 The recommendations also brought some institutional changes. Bureaucratically, the Senior Review Group, which had involved members of the TIWG as well as higher-ranking counterterrorism professionals, was given permanent status and renamed the Operational Sub-Group (OSG).106 For the remainder of the Reagan administration, this group of assistant secretaries would relieve the CPPG and the lower-level TIWG of being clearinghouses for the discussion of counterterrorism planning and implementation.107

Although there had been discussion of managing terrorist threats to the U.S. homeland, most of the task force's attention had gone to threats outside the United States. The consensus among the counterterrorism agencies remained that the U.S. government was managing the threat of international terrorist attacks at home quite well. "The potential threat inside the United States is real," Robert B. Oakley, of the Department of State, had stated in May 1985, "but our current efforts appear likely to keep it to a minimum."108 Noting that the number of terrorist attacks in the United States had decreased "dramatically," from fifty-one acts in 1982 to seven in 1985, the task force report agreed that U.S. law enforcement and intelligence efforts deserved some of the credit. "This can be attributed in part," stated the task force in its final report, "to the success of the

Department of Justice and Federal Bureau of Investigation (FBI) in their counterterrorist activities."[109] The task force identified twenty-three instances in which the FBI or other law enforcement agencies had foiled terrorist incidents that would have occurred in the United States in 1985. But the task force also singled out the intentions of the terrorists as another reason for the low threat environment at home. "It appears that international terrorist groups find it easier and safer to target Americans overseas rather than within the United States."[110] For this reason, the report stressed, the real and increasing U.S. vulnerability to terrorism lay abroad.

Meanwhile, a bureaucratic revolution was taking place independently in the CIA that would have dramatic implications for how the United States fought terrorism in the future. For all his concern about Soviet subversion, in his five years heading the CIA, William Casey had not thought systematically about how to deal with Arab terrorism. He had recognized this failing in the first half of 1985 by organizing the Hostage Locating Task Force around Charlie Allen and then advocating the formation of the vice presidential task force. But at the CIA, Casey had largely left things as they were. Despite the fact that President Reagan spoke as if the United States were at war with terrorism, at the CIA counterterrorism was largely a staff matter and a backwater. The CIA studied it but did little about it.

On December 27, 1985, terrorists from the Abu Nidal Organization (ANO) fired machine guns at the El Al ticket counters at the Vienna and Rome airports. Sixteen people were killed and more than 110 injured. Among the dead was an eleven-year-old American girl, Natasha Simpson. This was the second outrage from the ANO in two months. In early November, the ANO had hijacked an Egypt Air plane. Fifty-nine passengers, including one American, died when Egyptian commandos attempted to retake control of the plane. "Casey had hoped that these incidents would go away," recalls Fred Turco, who would eventually become the CIA's counterterrorism chief. The airport attacks destroyed that hope.[111] Duane "Dewey"

Clarridge, who had overseen Casey's Contra war against Nicaragua before becoming chief of the CIA's European operations, believed that it was essential to create a unit within the CIA's Directorate of Operations that focused solely on counterterrorism. "We thought it was time to go on the offensive against terrorism," says Turco, Clarridge's deputy in the European division, who would follow him as deputy into counterterrorism.[112]

"CIA was an amalgamation of baronial directorates," William Webster, who became DCI in 1987, would later recall.[113] Webster's predecessor Casey had been exceptionally good at building coalitions across these directorates. His greatest success, however, came within one of these baronies, the Directorate of Operations (DO). The DO was the inheritor of two fabled CIA services, the Office of Special Operations, led by Richard Helms in the early years of his Cold War career, and the Office of Policy Coordination, personified by its first and only leader, Frank Wisner. The DO is arguably the most secretive organization in the U.S. government. Responsible for CIA human intelligence collection, it protects the covers of CIA officers abroad as well as the identities of over fifty years' worth of CIA agents. The DO's computerized archive is likely the most compartmentalized database in the world.

Casey gained instant credibility with the DO. He was a throwback to the legendary period of the Office of Strategic Services, the World War II service. When Clarridge suggested a Counterterrorist Center (CTC) to Casey, he leapt at the idea.[114] Casey authorized a new special unit with unusual powers and placed it directly under him in the intelligence community structure. From the formation of the CIA in 1947 until the creation of an office of director of national intelligence in 2004, the DCI had two related but distinct functions. The DCI was both the director of the CIA and the manager of the U.S. intelligence community for the president. Casey made the CTC a creature of the larger intelligence community, though it was staffed and controlled by the CIA.

Clarridge, a longtime DO officer, provided suggestions for giving the CTC immediate credibility at CIA headquarters. To discourage second-guessing of the new center's analytic product, he suggested that terrorism reports continue to be issued by the Directorate of Intelligence (DI) and that the forty-two DI officers absorbed into CTC stay on the DI's payroll. One of the main criticisms of the Bay of Pigs operation of 1961, the biggest CIA fiasco of the Cold War, was that policymakers were given skewed analyses because CIA enthusiasts of the plan had cut all professional analysts out of the operation. Clarridge wanted to avoid such criticisms.[115]

Having the DI personnel in the CTC allowed Clarridge to give them unprecedented access to DO secrets. In the fourteen years of the Weekly Terrorism Review, the analysts working on it had never been given access to DO operational cables. Operational cables contain a large number of housekeeping details—the care and feeding of overseas assets—but they also reveal much about the nature of the sources providing the inside information on foreign terror groups. Clarridge's analysts were now getting to see this as they compiled their studies of the inner workings of foreign terrorist networks.

Casey also agreed to move the entire antiterrorist unit in the CIA's Special Operations Group (SOG) to the CTC. The SOG comprised the CIA's paramilitary specialists. They worked with the Joint Special Operations Command: Delta Force and the Navy SEALs. The SOG had become an expert in "sifting through the ashes" after a terrorist incident had occurred and determining the type and construction of any device used in a bombing.

Finally, Casey blessed the most difficult requirement. He gave Clarridge and his deputy, Turco, a hunting license to hire fifteen of the most capable case officers from anywhere in the DO, regardless of regional specialty. The two men estimated that their new task force would have to become expert on terrorists from over two hundred different organizations in every region of the globe. It therefore made sense that they would need people from every one of the

CIA's geographical desks. They recruited without regard for seniority, and they did so over the objections of the various DO geographical desk chiefs. Nevertheless, respect for Clarridge in the DO coupled with Casey's clout allowed the CTC to get between eight and ten of its fifteen first-round picks in the initial draft. The result was a strange hybrid organization that had both an analytic and an operational capability with a staff of about 250. The CTC began operations in February 1986.

When Clarridge and Turco built the CTC, they discovered that there were no ongoing offensive covert operations against international terrorist organizations.[116] The tide in the U.S. struggle with terrorism was about to turn.

The changes at the CIA put the U.S. government in a position to be able to run a sustained covert counteroffensive against international terrorism. With Operation Tulip and the Iran initiative, the NSC staff had interposed itself as a controlling operational authority for covert action. But this would not be a sustainable approach to handling the day in, day out challenge of deterring and preempting terrorist acts.

As these changes were taking place at the CIA, the White House was preparing for an overt confrontation with Gadhafi. By the end of December 1985, the administration had established a link between the Abu Nidal Organization's attack on the El Al ticket counters and the Libyan government. The terrorists had been carrying Tunisian passports that were among those that the Libyans had seized when they deported thirty thousand Tunisians in August. "I felt we couldn't ignore the mad clown of Tripoli any longer," wrote Reagan about his state of mind once Libyan involvement had been determined.[117]

On January 6, 1986, the NSPG met to discuss possible military options. Although he wanted to do something against Gadhafi, Reagan was persuaded by Secretary Weinberger to hold off on a military strike. Reagan was particularly concerned about the safety of the 1,000 to 1,500 American oil-service workers who were still in Libya.[118]

Poindexter argued for an attack on Libya. When Weinberger complained about the risks to U.S. airplanes and pilots, Poindexter suggested the use of cruise missiles. Weinberger objected with the same argument he had made against a military response to the bombing of the U.S. Marine barracks in 1983: "What if one misfires and it is captured and can be reverse engineered?" he asked. When Poindexter felt he had settled the question of taking that risk, Weinberger raised yet another problem with the cruise missiles: The attack could not be carried out by cruise missiles because the digital mapping for a precision strike had not been done.[119]

The president watched with increasing annoyance and, according to Poindexter, was determined to have real options. "OK. Enough is enough," Poindexter recalls Reagan saying. "I want planning to start now for a strike against Libya. Next time we have a smoking gun, I will execute the plan."[120] On January 8, Reagan signed NSDD 205, which determined that Libya posed "an unusual and extraordinary threat" to the United States because of its support for international terrorism. Pursuant to this decision, the U.S. ended all travel to and trade with Libya. Americans in Libya were given until February 1 to leave the country, and a second aircraft carrier battle group was sent to the Mediterranean.[121]

Also in response to the president's decision, the NSC and the Department of Defense planned a Freedom of Navigation exercise in the Gulf of Sidra.[122] Libya claimed the Gulf of Sidra as its territorial waters. The U.S. government did not respect this claim, and for years the U.S. Navy had sent ships into the gulf beyond the recognized twelve-nautical-mile limit to defend its international character. In March 1986, this exercise had the additional goal of provoking some kind of attack from the mercurial Gadhafi.

As hoped, Gadhafi launched surface-to-air missiles at U.S. fighters and dispatched boats close to the U.S. fleet in reaction to the exercise. All of Gadhafi's missiles missed their targets; the Reagan administration then sank a few Libyan ships. The Pentagon effectively argued against any stronger action.

The "smoking gun" that Reagan and the NSC wanted arrived in the form of signals intelligence. In March 1986, the NSA intercepted a Libyan order to dispatch twelve special teams to Western European capitals and Ankara to plan attacks on U.S. facilities. The U.S. government then shared this information with its allies. Acting on this intelligence, the French and the Turks arrested Libyans and found additional incriminating information. Not all of these preventive efforts were enough, however. A Libyan team in East Berlin was able to perpetrate a bombing at a nightspot popular with U.S. military personnel stationed in West Berlin. The blast at the La Belle discotheque on April 5 killed one U.S. soldier and wounded a hundred people.

The U.S. air raid, Operation El Dorado Canyon, took place on April 14 (April 15 in Tripoli). It had taken nearly three years, but for the first time, the administration was using an overt military attack as a tool of counterterrorism. Reagan felt that the risk to Americans was acceptably low.[123] All of the oil-service workers had left Libya. Gadhafi's residence and his military headquarters were included among the targets because they were command-and-control centers. No one in the administration, however, would have mourned Gadhafi's passing if one of the bombs had killed him. In retrospect, it appears that there was some divergence of opinion as to the goal of the attack. The CIA and elements of the NSC staff were convinced that the bombing could lead to Gadhafi's overthrow. President Reagan later wrote that "the attack was not intended to kill Qaddafi . . . The objective was to let him know that we weren't going to accept his terrorism anymore, and that if he did it again he could expect to hear from us again."[124]

While the administration was selecting the targets for the April 14 air strike, a separate drama was unfolding in Lebanon. Among the Counterterrorist Center's most important objectives in its first months was to back up Charlie Allen's hostage task force. In the spring of 1986, the CIA was negotiating with a group that held Peter Kilburn, the American University of Beirut librarian who had been abducted in 1984. This particular group seemed to be more mercenary than the other elements of Hezbollah and professed keen interest in trading Kilburn for $2 million. Kilburn's captors had been found thanks to two informants in Montreal, Canada, who had been referred to the FBI by the Royal Canadian Mounted Police. The CIA obtained the $2 million from the Federal Reserve, which had slated the bills for destruction. The bills were chemically treated to self-destruct two hours after being "brought out of a chemically suspended state."[125] The CIA was ready to make the trade when the entire region was transfixed by the U.S. air strike on Libya.

Dewey Clarridge's deputy, Fred Turco, had not been a fan of the air attack. "We should have gone in with a hammer," he would say later. Turco shared the views of the terrorism specialists at the CIA that dropping a few bombs on the Libyan leader would only make him mad. If it was serious about ending Libyan support for terrorism, the United States had to get Gadhafi, invade his country, or both. When he and Clarridge were told that the Reagan administration was planning to hit back at Gadhafi, Turco shared with Casey his blunt assessment of the consequences of the planned air strike. Casey listened and appeared to be sympathetic. The CIA director explained that the American people would not accept anything more dramatic than the air attack. It was the best of several imperfect solutions. When Turco continued to argue his point, as he later recalled, Casey asked him to leave.[126]

Two days after the air attack, the CTC received disheartening news from Beirut. Peter Kilburn was dead. In retaliation for the air strike, the Libyans had outbid the CIA for Kilburn and had also managed to buy two British hostages in Lebanon as well. Then, on April 17, they killed the three men. The CTC had not expected this kind of retaliation from the Libyans, but it confirmed the CTC's concerns about the dangers posed by wounding a terrorist regime without destroying it. In the next few days, the Libyans killed a U.S. embassy communicator in Khartoum, and two Libyans were picked up in Turkey as they tried to attack the U.S. officer's club in Ankara with hand grenades brought into the country by the Libyan diplomatic bag. Libya may also have been responsible for the shooting of a U.S. embassy employee in Yemen.[127]

Faced with this evidence of the apparent failure of the April 14 attack to cow Gadhafi, the Reagan administration considered a second air strike on Libya.[128] Donald Fortier, Poindexter's deputy at the NSC and the godfather of the Libyan policy, was a strong advocate of a second strike. He had seen the reports of Gadhafi's revenge killings in Sudan and Lebanon. In addition, on April 16, the United States detected a rebellion of a Libyan army battalion south of Tripoli, and there was civil unrest in the capital. This internal weakness, Fortier argued, "presents an opportunity we can exploit." Fortier suggested as a "maximum option" a strike on Gadhafi's desert retreat at Sebha, where photographic and human intelligence had placed him.[129] A lesser option would be a strike on the Libyan air force to give rebellious Libyan army units a chance to enter Tripoli.

Ultimately, the principals decided not to go forward with more attacks. It is not clear from the documents available today whether a major debate preceded this decision. Gadhafi then fell silent, and a lull in terrorism set in, affecting not only Libyan terrorist activity but also that of the Abu Nidal Organization (ANO). But the lull soon ended. In July 1986, the CTC reported that "true to form, Libya returned to terrorist activity."[130] Gadhafi was loudly vowing revenge against the United States and Great Britain for the air attacks. Two months later, in early September 1986, four ANO terrorists attacked a Pan Am airliner in Karachi, killing twenty-one and wounding 120 before the nightmare ended.

Again, the Reagan administration chose not to retaliate. Despite the president's pledge to keep sending messages to Gadhafi until he had learned his lesson, the Pan Am incident was met with nothing more than condemnation. As it turned out, the April 14 attack was the last time the Reagan administration would resort to overt military retaliation as a means of counterterrorism. Consensus on air strikes on state sponsors of terrorism proved elusive.

Libya was not the only state sponsor in 1986 whose actions tested administration policy. The Syrians were found to be behind an attempted bombing of an Israeli aircraft in London. In the fall of 1986, the CPPG discussed forms of retaliation against Damascus.[131] In November 1986, Reagan chose to impose economic sanctions on Syria and nothing more. As it turned out, this would be the administration's last major public act in its war on terrorism. Very soon, President Reagan and his administration would be overcome by the consequences of the other major counterterrorism initiative begun back in the summer of 1985.

Despite the demands of its active Libyan policy, the administration had continued the Iran initiative through the winter and spring of 1986. Indeed, U.S. involvement had gotten deeper. In January, President Reagan agreed to permit his administration to have direct contact with the Iranian "moderates." Former national security advisor Robert McFarlane headed a secret U.S. mission to Tehran to continue the dialogue. Meanwhile, additional shipments of U.S. weapons were sent to the Iranians. During the dealings, Hezbollah maintained a freeze on further abductions of U.S. citizens and released three U.S. hostages.

The Iran initiative warped the U.S. counterterrorism community. The NSC began cutting Shultz out of some of the NSA's intelligence reports.[132] In the intercepted traffic, Iranians were heard discussing the U.S. arms deal. The NSC made other fateful decisions. With the approval of the attorney general, the FBI was cut out of the Iran operation until July 1986.[133] As a law enforcement agency, the FBI might have felt compelled to investigate the Pentagon's activity in furnishing weapons to a country in violation of U.S. sanctions. The

Joint Chiefs of Staff were also not informed of the arms transfers to
Iran until late June or early July 1986.[134] Finally, the Reagan administration decided not to inform Congress immediately of the covert
action finding, despite a requirement to report all presidential findings within a reasonable amount of time. "The President did it because of a fear of leaks," Poindexter later explained, citing the leak
that had hurt the Libyan covert operation in November 1985. The
president thought he had some leeway in the timing of the notification, and Attorney General Meese agreed.[135]

The leak that the president, Poindexter, and the NSC feared did
occur later in 1986. It was Hezbollah, however, that disclosed the secret Iran initiative to the world.[136] The Lebanese Shia were increasingly uncomfortable with their patron's dealings with the West and
wanted to put a stop to them. In August 1986, Hezbollah unilaterally resumed its program of abducting Americans, replacing all of
those it had been forced to release by the Iranians. Then, on November 3, an obscure Shia magazine in Baalbek, Lebanon, published the first revelation of the arms-for-hostages program. After
that, the covert details of the Iran initiative unraveled in the U.S.
press. On November 13, 1986, Reagan addressed the nation on the
Iran operation. Behind the scenes, an investigation by the Justice Department disclosed that Colonel Oliver North, who oversaw the
NSC staff's controlling role in both the Iran initiative and the program of supplying the U.S.-backed Nicaraguan counterrevolutionar-
ies (Contras), had overcharged the Iranians for the TOW and
HAWK missiles and had used the excess to fund the Nicaraguan
Contras, contrary to a congressional ban. On November 25, Attorney General Meese and the president held a press conference to dis-
close this new twist. The next day, the president announced the
appointment of a commission headed by Senator John Tower to investigate the intermingling of the Iran arms sales and the Contra
program, which became known as the Iran-Contra scandal. The
Iran initiative was dead.

A Quieter Struggle

The Iran-Contra scandal shook the Reagan administration to its core. In response to the scandal, nearly two-thirds of the NSC staff was replaced.[137] Poindexter was reassigned and North fired. Frank Carlucci, who had been deputy director of central intelligence under Stansfield Turner and had served Reagan for two years as assistant secretary of defense, became national security advisor. Lt. General Colin Powell, who had been military assistant to Secretary Weinberger, became Carlucci's deputy.

Carlucci believed that the NSC should be a coordinating body, not an operational agency that competed with the Departments of State and Defense. In that spirit, he renamed and reorganized parts of the NSC to remove the symbols of activism and streamline the interagency policy process. The Crisis Pre-Planning Group, the interagency team that recommended foreign policy to the NSC, became the Policy Review Group. The Operational Sub-Group (OSG), which consisted of counterterrorism specialists at the assistant secretary level from around the U.S. government, was renamed the Coordination Sub-Group (CSG). Within the NSC, Carlucci chose not to fill Oliver North's position. He did not like the idea of having an Office of Politico-Military Affairs. "The entire NSC worked on politico-military affairs," Carlucci later explained. "That was abandoned as duplication."[138] Instead, he created an Office of Counterterrorism and Narcotics and put Thomas McNamara, a very low profile staffer, in charge of it.

Carlucci and Powell leaned toward a much quieter counterterrorism strategy. Powell had helped Weinberger draft the six preconditions for the use of military force in 1984. Carlucci had never gone on record in support of quieter counterterrorism, but he took little time in establishing new guidelines for how the Reagan administration talked about international terrorism. He believed that strident rhetoric raised expectations that the United States could never realistically meet. "It was counterproductive," he later recalled. Carlucci was dismayed not to discover any "game plan" behind the rhetoric that Reagan had been using. Moreover, Carlucci had a more modest view of what a superpower with its many international responsibilities could do against terrorists. "You could not just go out and hit them," he recalled.[139]

A change occurred in the president's rhetoric in 1987. Publicly, the administration seemed to be backing away from Reagan's pledges in 1981 and those made more recently in the summer of 1985 to deal with "Murder, Inc." In January 1987, three more Americans were taken hostage in Beirut—Robert Polhill, Alan Steen, and Jesse Turner—without any additional public warnings coming from the White House. Carlucci recalls sitting down with the president to explain his reasoning and the president agreeing. "But Shultz was a different story," Carlucci explained.[140] Getting the secretary of state to tone down the rhetoric was much harder, but eventually the entire administration was saying less.

The change in public strategy did not mean that the new team at the NSC was about to abandon the Reagan administration's struggle with terrorism. For the new national security advisor, however, "terrorism was a problem, it was not a war."[141] Carlucci and Powell wanted it to be fought below the radar screen, primarily by the CIA. As a result, the CTC did not receive any orders to slow down its clandestine offensive.[142]

Terrorism continued to challenge the Reagan administration. In March, Robert Oakley, a Princeton classmate of Carlucci's whom the new national security advisor had brought into the NSC to work on the Middle East, reported to Carlucci that "intelligence has revealed a much closer, more direct relationship between Hezbollah and authorities in Tehran than had previously been understood by the intelligence community. There is agreement by all agencies that Iran believes it has a command relationship with Hezbollah, although some disagreement persists upon how tight a control actually exists."[143] Rather than resorting to military threats, the new team reacted to these signs of Iranian aggression by trying to use regional actors, especially Syria, to see what kinds of pressure could be placed on Iran.

The president, however, remained a captive of the old Iran policy. Reagan could not let go of the idea that moderates in Tehran could help secure the release of the American hostages. In the winter of 1987, after the three additional Americans were taken, he asked Carlucci and Powell, "Why don't we talk to our friends, the Iranians" to see what they could do.[144] Despite the Iran-Contra scandal, Reagan still hoped for a deal. The new team explained to President Reagan that the U.S. policy was "no concessions" and that this was a good policy for the nation.[145]

As for the attempted reforms to the counterterrorism system in 1985–86, the Office of the Vice President acted as a strong lobby. Vice President Bush's staff saw the task force as a powerful symbol of the vice president's commitment to improving national security. As the Iran-Contra scandal closed in on the administration, Bush's aides pushed for a reconvening of the task force to assess compliance with NSDD 207. In early 1987, Carlucci agreed to let Holloway report to him on how well the agencies and departments had done.

The review indicated widespread complacency and an aversion to further reforms. The CIA explained that it had tried to set up a special training program for counterterrorism and decided it was not feasible, but the agency did mention that "relations with the FBI are excellent."[146] The FBI was a little more forthcoming about flaws in the system. Buck Revell had much good to say about the CIA and other agencies, but he told Holloway that there were still problems with border control. We "need to do more here," said Revell, who worried about the country's ability to "exclude people who are members of terrorist groups."[147] Besides these concerns, the FBI saw the situation as improving and did not signal the need for any urgent changes despite not having seen any enhancement of its domestic counterterrorism investigative capabilities. FBI director William Webster, who was about to become DCI, outlined to Holloway the four reasons the FBI had been as successful as it had been in deterring Arab terrorism at home: (1) good intelligence and police work, (2) "integration possibilities for ethnics," (3) distance, and (4) the fact that it is easier to hit U.S. targets overseas.[148]

Because of these advantages, Webster believed that terrorism did not pose much of a threat to domestic security. Instead, because of what he called the "fear factor," he saw terrorism as primarily a political problem for the U.S. government, which had to show that it took these fears seriously.

Holloway had an opportunity to speak with Attorney General Meese, who generally echoed the optimism of the FBI. He told Holloway that he agreed with the administration's new, quieter public stance on terrorism. It permitted the White House to "lower [the] value of hostages."[149] Meese's concerns stemmed from the possibility that if more terrorists were tried in the United States, there would be more terrorist attacks against U.S. targets to gain their release.

Holloway heard a no less upbeat report from the Department of Transportation (DOT), which oversaw the FAA and port security.[150] But the details that the DOT presented were disturbing. The U.S. Congress had refused to give the FAA access to the information it needed to warn the airlines about the backgrounds of their passengers, and efforts to design cockpits to make hijacking more difficult had been turned down by the airlines. Although there was an improvement in airport security, the DOT admitted that the fact that security issues had to be coordinated with so many airlines undermined the entire effort. Even more worrisome in retrospect were the facts that the DOT offered on port security. "Vulnerability is high," explained the representatives of the DOT, although the problem was not considered urgent.[151] A year earlier, the DOT's deputy assistant secretary for policy and international affairs had written to the NSC that "although the general lack of [port] security appears to be alarming, it must be viewed in the context of relatively low threat levels."[152] Nothing had changed in a year. The DOT was also straightforward in admitting that it had not figured out a way to use U.S. intelligence to alert ports, airports, or airlines as effectively as possible. "Communications problems," noted Holloway's team, "[exist] because of incompatible secure systems in Washington."[153]

Vice President Bush briefed the president on Holloway's findings on June 2, 1987. Bush told Reagan that the "task force has reaffirmed [that] our current policy for combating terrorism is sound, effective, and fully in accord with our democratic principles and national ideals." Bush suggested using the completion of the review to remind both the government and the American people that "the mistakes involved in our contacts with Iran resulted from not following the policy." Either Holloway did not raise the inadequacies he found with the vice president or Bush opted not to mention them to Reagan. "Overall," Bush told Reagan, "we found progress has been excellent and improvement in our counterterrorism capability has been evident in the results . . . Our nation is well served by our terrorism policy and program." [154] That would be the last word on counterterrorism or antiterrorism reform until 1995.

Despite evidence of significant weaknesses in the country's ability to protect itself from terrorism, the vice president's task force had declared victory in 1987. A major reason for this was the difficulty of getting federal agencies and the private sector to institute greater airline and port security. To do so would be costly, both in terms of the expense of purchasing new safeguards and the effect of such measures on the flow of goods. In the absence of any evidence that terrorists were planning to exploit these domestic loopholes, the risks of doing nothing seemed acceptable. On the other hand, the potential for political and economic harm if the administration tried to force through a package of antiterrorism measures appeared to be great.

The other reason for the apparent complacency was that the tide was beginning to turn in the war on terrorism. The U.S. government, especially the CIA's new CTC, was scoring unprecedented gains against its principal target, the Abu Nidal Organization. Since the mid-1970s, the ANO had been considered by the United States to be the most dangerous terrorist organization in the world. With an estimated membership of 500 people, the ANO had offices in Libya and Syria, and Abu Nidal himself was thought to be living in Syria. Shifts in the Cold War with the Soviet bloc provided an unexpected and significant boost to U.S. efforts. Soviet economic weaknesses and Soviet leader Mikhail Gorbachev's desire to achieve détente with the West put pressure on the Syrians to improve relations with the United States. Among the Eastern bloc countries, there was also increasing interest in better relations, even with the CIA.

There was a surprising amount of useful information in Eastern Europe about Abu Nidal. In 1979, the ANO had signed an agreement with the Poles: In return for promising not to sponsor any terrorism in Poland or against Polish interests, the ANO received safe haven in Warsaw and training for its cadres. The ANO reached a similar arrangement with the East Germans in 1983.[155]

Fred Turco, who had replaced Dewey Clarridge as head of the CTC in 1987, and L. Paul Bremer, who had replaced Robert Oakley when the latter went to the NSC, worked to encourage cooperation from Eastern bloc countries against Abu Nidal. Although real official cooperation would become possible only after the Berlin Wall fell in November 1989, some good information started coming out in 1987. The CIA developed intelligence on Samir-Adnan-Shakir (SAS), a trading company headquartered in Warsaw that was led by Samir Najm al-Din, Adnan Zayit, and Shakir Farnan, three men identified as members of the ANO economic section. SAS arranged the sale of embargoed Polish weapons to Iran, Iraq, and Zimbabwe, with some of the profits going into the coffers of the ANO.[156] The CTC was surprised at the level of Soviet bloc involvement with the ANO. "This was the time when the right-wing conspiracy theorists were saying that the Soviet Union was behind everything," recalls Turco, "so we had to be very sure of what we knew before we wrote of this connection."[157] Ultimately, the CTC would determine that the East German intelligence service had indeed been behind the 1979 assassination attempt on the then NATO commander, Alexander M. Haig, Jr.

The CIA recognized that the ANO's commercial dealings represented a useful back door into the organization. Unlike Hezbollah, which was clannish and highly secretive, the ANO was an easier target. The commercial needs of ANO affiliates provided opportunities for penetration and countermeasures. "It is the ANO's policy to isolate its commercial endeavors from its terrorist infrastructure," the U.S. government reported in 1987, "but the ANO businessmen are occasionally asked to provide operational support such as delivering messages or temporarily storing weapons."[158]

The CIA followed one of these businessmen, Mufid Tawfiq Musa Hamadeh, into the United States. Musa, who joined the ANO in the 1970s, had been sent to Europe in 1984 to do clandestine work.[159] By 1987, he was working in the United States.[160] Musa, who would at some point begin cooperating with the United States, was a fundraiser for the ANO.[161] The CIA cooperated with the FBI on the ANO case, and besides Musa, the bureau would develop information on a group of "sleeper agents" working for Abu Nidal in Missouri and Wisconsin. These cells were not planning terrorist attacks against U.S. targets.[162] Like the "provisional wing" of the Irish Republican Army, the ANO came to the United States to build bank accounts—to raise money from sympathizers—not to destroy bank buildings.

As the CTC developed information on the ANO's international connections, the NSC and a former U.S. president worked to convince Syria that it should be more helpful in dealing with the ANO. In early 1987, the Pakistani government informed Robert Oakley on one of his trips to the region that it had "irrefutable" evidence that Syria was behind the Abu Nidal team that had attacked the Pan Am plane in Karachi in September. The Pakistanis had sent a formal protest to the Syrian prime minister, who had denied the accusation. Former president Carter was slated to go to Syria in March 1987 to talk to Hafiz al-Assad on behalf of the Reagan administration. Oakley had the Pakistani story included among Carter's briefing material.

Carter, in the course of a meeting with the Syrian president, raised the question of Syrian sponsorship of terrorism. When Assad denied any links, according to one account, Carter asked about the Karachi plane incident. Assad specifically denied that. Apparently, the former president then asked about a message that the Pakistani government had given to Assad's prime minister. Assad denied that there had been such a message. Carter then left. Later, at a dinner with the Syrian prime minister, Carter was told that President Assad wanted to see him again before he left the country.[163]

The Syrian leader had a surprising admission to make to Carter. When they were alone, Assad explained that he had never heard of the letter before Carter mentioned it to him. Since their first meeting, he had demanded that his subordinates show him the letter and had just read it. "They kept it from me," he explained. The Reagan administration subsequently concluded that Assad was telling the truth about being out of the loop on the Karachi terrorist attack. He subsequently purged several high-ranking members of his intelligence community, including the chief of air force intelligence. More important for the United States, shortly after Carter's visit, the Syrian government told Abu Nidal to leave.

It was an important achievement for U.S. counterterrorism experts. The expulsion disoriented the ANO, which had to relocate its personnel to Libya and Lebanon. But the more important accomplishments would come later in 1987. The PLO had an interest in undermining Abu Nidal and helped the CIA. So, too, did the Jordanians and the Israelis.[164] Working with these allies, the CTC developed a strategy of undermining the ANO from within. Abu Nidal suffered from paranoia, a weakness that could be magnified and exploited. In the 1930s, Joseph Stalin had killed or sidelined his most talented lieutenants out of fear; perhaps Abu Nidal could be made to do the same thing. Salah Kahlaf, alias Abu Iyad, who was Arafat's chief of intelligence, provided information to the CIA on the progress of these efforts as the PLO collected defectors from the ANO. Soon Abu Iyad would be saying that there were "scores of defectors from the Nidal group."[165]

More dramatic than the defections were the assassinations of Abu Nidal lieutenants by Abu Nidal himself or his henchmen. In November 1987, Jasir al-Disi (alias Abu Ma'mun) and Ayish Badran (Abu Umar), reputedly the best officers in the ANO's "People's Army," were killed in Lebanon on Abu Nidal's orders. The two men were accused of being Jordanian spies, and once they were arrested, tortured, and killed, Abu Nidal then purged their supposed allies in the army. Dozens of other officers were subsequently shot and buried in a mass grave in Bqasta Faouqa, Lebanon.[166] Also murdered in 1987 were Ibrahim al-Abd, from the Finance Directorate; Mujahid al-Bayyari, from the Intelligence Directorate; and Muhammed Khair (Nur Muharib) and Mustafa Umran, from the ANO's Political Directorate.[167] In October 1988, Abu Nidal killed his former deputy, Abu Nizar.[168]

The CTC was involved in more than this struggle with the ANO in the last two years of the Reagan administration. "We put the pedal to the floor," recalls Turco. In that period, cooperation between the FBI and the CIA reached a new level. In 1987, the agencies worked together to achieve the first capture or forced extradition of a terrorist. In the busy terrorism year of 1985, Fawaz Younis, a member of Amal, had hijacked a Jordanian Airlines flight as it prepared to leave Beirut. Among the passengers were three U.S. citizens. Earlier, Younis had played a role in holding some of the hostages of TWA 847 when that plane landed in Beirut. In 1984, the U.S. Congress had passed the Hostage Taking Act, making the abduction of an American overseas a federal crime. In creating this extraterritorial offense, the act also expanded the FBI's jurisdiction overseas. The Younis capture was the first test of how well the FBI and the CIA could manage their overlapping overseas responsibilities.

Younis had first been spotted in Sudan. But the incoming DCI, William Webster, had vetoed the idea of grabbing him there. Webster recalled the fallout after Israel snatched the Nazi mass murderer Adolf Eichmann off the streets of Buenos Aires in 1960 and did not want to cause a similar international stir. Moreover, Sudan was moving away from Gadhafi and closer to the West, and he did not want to upset those helpful developments.[169] Then Younis gave Webster and the United States a second chance. When a Drug Enforcement Agency informant placed Younis in Lebanon, where he was also dabbling in drug dealing, Webster approved the attempt at capture. The CIA subsequently used a spurious drug deal to lure him to Cyprus and then onto a yacht in international waters piloted by FBI agents.[170] On September 13, 1987, the FBI agents arrested a surprised Younis.[171]

The CTC also made headway in working the Lebanese hostage problem, though Turco was frustrated to find that he could never provide enough information to get the Reagan administration to act. How to rescue the hostages was a standard agenda item at meetings of the CSG, the NSC's interagency group that oversaw U.S. counterterrorism. Delta Force was kept on alert throughout this period in case there was enough hard information to support a rescue attempt. The CTC found Hezbollah much harder to penetrate than the ANO. The organization was decentralized, and the cells were often based on family ties.[172] Hezbollah was, if anything, more vicious than the ANO. The CIA lost quite a few agents who crossed into the sections of Beirut controlled by Hezbollah.[173] Yet on two occasions in 1988, Turco brought information that he believed was good enough to trigger a Delta Force rescue operation. In each case, the JSOC agreed with him and wanted a green light to go ahead. In February 1988, Lt. Colonel William Higgins, the chief of the U.S. section of the United Nations force in Beirut, had been added to the list of Americans in captivity. Turco believed that "it was messaging time." Although the CTC could not develop information on the location of all of the hostages, Turco believed that rescuing even one would send a warning to Hezbollah not to take any more hostages.

On both occasions, however, the principals shot down the idea of a partial rescue. "The wheels had fallen off for Reagan by then," Turco recalls with regret.[174] It seemed to Turco that Carlucci and his deputy and successor Colin Powell were not inclined to risk a partial rescue, and the aging president did not make this tough call on his own.

Apparent Victory

In the fall of 1988, the U.S. intelligence community concluded that the threat from terrorism had subsided significantly and that the administration's counterterrorist actions deserved much of the credit. "Most regimes that sponsor or otherwise support terrorism have become less active or more discreet since 1986," wrote the CIA's terrorism experts in October, "largely in response to Western counterterrorist measures and regional political development."[175] Citing Western démarches, economic sanctions, and diplomatic expulsions, the CIA observed that "a number of state sponsors of terrorism had lowered their profile." The agency was most impressed with the change in Syria's and Iran's policies toward terrorism. The CIA assumed that both countries had political interests that outweighed gains that they might receive from continued sponsorship of terrorism. "Syria almost certainly will continue to back terrorist and guerrilla attacks against Israel but is unlikely to jeopardize its improved Western ties by sponsoring attacks elsewhere."[176] Similarly, Iran had an interest in maintaining international support for its efforts to negotiate an end to the eight-year Iran-Iraq War. The agency had even noticed a softening in the rhetoric of Hezbollah, despite the kidnapping of Lt. Colonel Higgins. The new moderation was attributed to the transformation of Hezbollah from a terrorist organization to a political movement with an active militia that was fighting for dominance in southern Lebanon. "We believe," argued the CIA, as it once had about the PLO, "that the group's reliance on terrorism will decline if it makes progress toward becoming a legitimate political actor."[177] The CIA noted Sheikh Fadlallah's visit to Syria in the summer and his restrained rhetoric following the unintentional downing of an Iran Air 747 by the USS *Vincennes* in August. Fadlallah, the spiritual leader of Hezbollah, had decreed that the U.S. hostages should not be punished for the incident.[178]

The one exception to the rosier picture was Libya, which, despite the economic sanctions and the military reprisal of April 1986, had not altered its support for international terrorism. "Although Libyan-backed groups have not hit U.S. interests since several bombings on the second anniversary of the US air strike," reported the CIA, "Tripoli continues to host the virulently anti-Western Abu Nidal Organization and other terrorist groups." The CIA noted that Gadhafi continued "to build links to terrorist groups around the world." Despite the terrorist actions attributed to Libya after April 1986, there was widespread belief in the press and among the principals in the Reagan administration that the air attack had succeeded in putting Gadhafi in a box. The CIA disagreed. "Libya continues to pose the greatest threat to U.S. interests," warned the agency in October 1988.[179]

The CIA's concerns were well founded. The Reagan administration had mistaken correlation for causation. Its use of military force against terrorist installations had been half-hearted, and the regimes that sponsored terrorism—not only Libya but also Iran and Syria—remained in power and could at any time resort to that weapon again. Only in its covert successes against the largely independent Abu Nidal Organization had the administration demonstrated that Americans were capable of effective counterterrorism.

CHAPTER EIGHT

The Silent Struggle

ON DECEMBER 21, 1988, Pan Am flight 103, on its way to New York from London, exploded over Scotland. All 259 passengers and crew members perished, and as pieces of the shattered plane fell on the town of Lockerbie, eleven more people died on the ground. The news dismayed but did not shock the U.S. government, which immediately assumed that these 270 people were victims of a terrorist attack. For two months, there had been warnings of a coming airline tragedy. In October, the West German police had arrested a Palestinian rejectionist cell in Hamburg. Among those taken was a bomb maker who was working on devices that could be concealed in portable tape players. The cooperation between the West Germans and the CIA had not been exemplary in this case.[1] But by November, the CIA's Counterterrorist Center (CTC) learned from the West Germans that these terrorists belonged to the Popular Front for the Liberation of Palestine–General Command (PFLP-GC), a PFLP splinter group sponsored primarily by Syria, and had been in the midst of planning to bomb a U.S. international air carrier when they were arrested.

The West German information was disseminated widely and quickly in Washington. The CTC sent warnings to all agencies in the counterterrorism community that the PFLP-GC had targeted

U.S. overseas air carriers. The FAA, which was included, subsequently passed on this alert to the airline industry in November and early December as a series of warnings of threats to U.S. civilian carriers.[2] Fred Turco, the chief of the CTC, followed up with private meetings with security personnel from the three most vulnerable U.S. international carriers, Trans World Airlines, Pan Am Airways, and Delta, to discuss the threat posed by the PFLP-GC.[3] The information was not specific as to when an attack might occur, but it was believed that the plane would originate in Germany and be flying to the United States. The information did not specify the motive, although the CTC wondered whether the Syrians had let the Iranians use their Palestinian clients to avenge the *Vincennes* incident.[4]

Tragically, the U.S. airlines and the FAA proved unable to use this information effectively. The airport security system had not fundamentally changed since 1973, when the Nixon administration had mandated 100 percent screening of passengers and their carry-on luggage. Checked bags were still stowed in the hold of the aircraft without any screening, and the airlines were still responsible for their own security. In spite of the FAA warnings and the meeting with the CIA, the three carriers primarily affected did not consider the threat specific enough to warrant instituting special screening of bags on international flights to the United States originating from or passing through West Germany. As investigators would later discover, the luggage containing an explosive device that found its way into the hold of Pan Am 103 had passed through Frankfurt airport.

This act of terrorism caught Washington in transition between the Reagan and Bush administrations. The CTC faced high-level pressure to solve the puzzle of who was responsible. "They did not pressure us to come up with a specific answer," recalls Turco, "but they wanted an answer."[5] At the meeting of the Coordination Sub-Group (CSG, the renamed Operational Sub-Group) in late December 1988, Donald Gregg, Vice President Bush's representative, informed the group that the president-elect had told President Reagan that he would support an attack on Syria or Iran or any other state sponsor if indeed it turned out that they were responsible.[6] On December 29, 1988, George H. W. Bush announced publicly his intention to "seek hard" and "punish severely" the guilty parties.[7]

The U.S. intelligence community immediately had a prime suspect. The bomb and the nature of the attack seemed to have the earmarks of the PFLP-GC. Marwan Kreeshat, the bomb maker of the cell arrested in Hamburg, had been a West German agent. Under West German control, Kreeshat had constructed bombs that were supposed to be duds. He seemed reliable, but the West Germans could not account for all of his incendiary devices.[8] Bombs have specific characteristics that make it possible for experts to identify the bomb makers. Pan Am 103 seemed to have been brought down by a bomb made either by Kreeshat or by someone trained by him or the PFLP-GC.

As the West Germans tried to sort out the location of Kreeshat's bombs, evidence continued to come in that pointed to the PFLP-GC as the culprit. Sixteen men arrested in Hamburg had ties to another Palestinian terrorist cell in Sweden. Those terrorists, who had already been linked to bombings in Denmark, had a habit of buying clothes in one particular shop in Malta, which they later resold to Palestinians living in Scandinavia. Forensic experts examining the bomb that had brought down Pan Am 103 reported to the CTC that the bomb had been wrapped in clothing that had come from the very same store in Malta.[9] Nevertheless, as the Reagan administration left office, the government's counterterrorism professionals were not yet prepared to make the call. It would be up to President George H. W. Bush to decide how and against whom the U.S. would retaliate.

The president-elect had named James A. Baker III as Shultz's replacement in November 1988, while the Reagan administration was still very active on a number of foreign policy fronts, especially in its relationship with the disintegrating Soviet Union. The incoming team disliked the Soviet policy that Reagan and Shultz had crafted with Mikhail Gorbachev and was eager to differentiate themselves from the Reaganites. "They were determined to make sure this was Bush I and not Reagan III," recalls the former secretary of state.[10]

General Brent Scowcroft returned to the job of national security advisor that he had held under President Ford. Dick Cheney, who had been Ford's chief of staff, was the new secretary of defense. The president himself had been Ford's director of central intelligence (DCI). As it had been after Ford replaced Nixon in 1974, terrorism was again downplayed as a national security concern. "The dominant security challenge," Scowcroft later explained, "was still the Soviet Union." As a result, "things that were not related somehow to the Soviet Union, sort of, ipso facto, were not given quite as much attention."[11]

Scowcroft established the Deputies Committee—enlarging and renaming what had been known as the CPPG and later the Policy Review Group in the Reagan administration—as the main interagency group for the development of policy options. By the fall of 1989, following a failed coup against General Manuel Noriega, the Deputies Committee added crisis management to its responsibilities.[12] On occasion, the Deputies Committee would discuss counterterrorism matters, but the principal forum for that was one step lower, the CSG, the interagency committee that was a holdover from the Reagan administration. Ambassador David Miller, who replaced Thomas McNamara as the director of the NSC's Office of Counterterrorism and Narcotics, was named the NSC representative on the CSG.

His short stint as DCI in the mid-1970s had left George Bush with a profound respect for the CIA and its professionals. In this administration, the president was intimately aware of what intelligence could do.[13] Bush inherited a group of very aggressive counterterrorism professionals from the Reagan period, and though the counterterrorism struggle would not be one of his foreign policy priorities, the president gave them whatever support they needed.[14] The CIA's Counterterrorist Center (CTC) would be as active and effective—

arguably more active and effective—in the Bush administration as it had been under Reagan.

The Pan Am Investigation

The U.S. intelligence community took much longer to solve the central puzzle of Pan Am 103 than anyone could have predicted in December 1988. For President Bush and his chief advisors, 1989 was the year that the world turned upside down. China seemed on the verge of a democratic revolution, the Poles stared down their secret police, Hungary threw off its socialist chains, the Berlin Wall fell, the Czechs and Slovaks staged their "velvet revolution," and the Romanians killed their dictator and his wife. For U.S. counterterrorism professionals, however, it was primarily a year of competing theories over who destroyed Pan Am 103.

The FBI was assigned responsibility as the lead agency in the investigation of the case. The CIA was to provide intelligence support. Oliver "Buck" Revell and Fred Turco each created task forces in their respective agencies to investigate the case and worked hard to ensure good cooperation between the FBI and the CIA. The bureau and the agency also worked very closely with MI5, the British security service, and the Scottish police, which had local jurisdiction. Both governments invested huge resources in the investigation. The Scots arranged for hundreds of policemen to walk shoulder to shoulder through miles of fields to recover every piece of the downed plane so that transatlantic forensic specialists could figure out who the perpetrators were.

Despite the temptation to blame Syria, the CTC refused to issue any reports in the first months of the investigation that unequivocally blamed the bombing on Damascus. Turco later recalled blocking three finished intelligence reports that would have made that claim.[15] The FBI shared the belief that the PFLP-GC had been involved but assumed that a different country had paid for the attack.

"From the start, we thought that the Iranians were guilty," recalls Revell.[16] In July 1988, U.S. fighter jets from the USS *Vincennes* had accidentally shot down an Iran Air jumbo jet, killing all aboard. The FBI believed that Tehran had brought down Pan Am 103 as an act of revenge.

The FBI and the CIA informed the rest of the U.S. government that a theory linking the PFLP-GC to the crime was the direction that the evidence was taking them. Turco presented briefings to the national security principals with the use of large presentation boards that showed the links of the various players. Bush, Baker, and Scowcroft were intensely interested in the progress of the case.[17]

In the early going, President Bush was quite prepared to blame Damascus. "Wasn't it the Syrians?" he asked the chief of the CTC. "No, Mr. President," Turco felt he had to respond. "We cannot be sure yet."[18] Pressure was also coming from the government of Israel and Israeli friends in Washington. Israel had its own reasons to want the United States to punish Syria. The message from Tel Aviv was that Syria had to be behind the bombing of Pan Am 103.

By mid-1989, Iran had displaced Syria in CIA briefings as the most likely state sponsor of the attack. There was information from Germany that Iran had paid the PFLP-GC perhaps as much as $10 million to bring down a U.S. airliner in retaliation for the USS *Vincennes* incident. "We believe that Iran's support for radical Palestinian groups, particularly the Popular Front for the Liberation of Palestine–General Command," the CIA reported in June, "poses a serious threat to U.S. and West European interests."[19] By December 1989, the CTC was all but convinced that the "Iran plus PFLP-GC" theory explained what had happened.[20]

The Hostage Issue

The turn taken by the Pan Am investigation dovetailed with evidence that the counterterrorism experts studying Hezbollah were picking up in Lebanon. There were nine Americans held prisoner by Hezbollah at the start of the Bush administration. By the fall of 1989, there would be only eight. In retribution for Israel's kidnapping in July 1989 of a powerful Shia cleric and Hezbollah military commander, Sheikh Abd al-Karim Obeid, Hezbollah killed Lt. Colonel William Higgins and released a gruesome videotape of his execution. "The emotional impact of that in the country was severe," recalled Scowcroft.[21]

The CSG met frequently to discuss the hostage issue. Delta Force remained on high alert to perform a rescue operation if the necessary intelligence were received. Revell recalls the commander of Delta Force attending CSG meetings about once a month to describe his level of readiness.[22] It was understood that once the intelligence community could provide the force with information on the location of the hostages, the special forces team would be ready to go. The one substantive difference was that the CTC did not have the intelligence to offer that it once had. "Hezbollah got better," Turco explains. The always secretive organization had managed to become even more difficult to penetrate. It appeared that they had scattered the hostages. As a result, in the Bush period, the CSG never found itself able to recommend a rescue to the Deputies Committee.[23] Only later would the explanation for Hezbollah's increased secrecy emerge. Hezbollah, which was in the midst of a struggle with both Iran and Syria, had more than Delta Force to protect itself against. The two countries wanted Hezbollah to turn over the hostages, but the Islamist terrorists in Lebanon intended to keep them as a guarantee that in any future political settlement the radical Shia community would be a participant.[24]

The limits on what U.S. intelligence could do frustrated the principals. "I was frustrated at the lack of HUMINT (human intelligence) to help with the hostage problem," Scowcroft later recalled. "We simply could not find out enough about the hostages, who precisely was holding them, where they were held, and so on, to make any attempt at rescue feasible, because we stood the chance of having more of them killed in an attempt to rescue one or two."[25]

Despite this frustration, the Bush administration believed that letting the hostage situation shape U.S. policy in the Middle East was akin to letting the tail wag the dog. The Deputies Committee put little if any pressure on the counterterrorism community to produce better information. This left the CTC convinced that "the Bush administration deemphasized the hostage issue in the hope it would go away."[26] The NSC director for counterterrorism recalls the matter differently. "Bush and Scowcroft did not need to put pressure on us. I was forward-leaning, so was Fred Turco at CIA, Bill Baker at FBI [Revell's replacement], General Pete Schoomaker [now chief of staff of the U.S. Army] and his aide Jerry Boykin at Delta Force [JSOC]."[27] One important shift in U.S. policy was that the NSC worked hard to spare President Bush the "emotional damage" that Reagan had clearly suffered by getting too close to the hostage issue and especially to the families. Miller was designated to speak to the families, especially to the tireless Peggy Say, Terry Anderson's devoted sister. "I must have talked to Peggy Say every day. I spoke to her when she was gardening; I spoke to her when she was at home," Miller later recalled.[28]

The Bush foreign policy team, unlike that of Reagan and Shultz, did not view the hostage issue as a test of U.S. credibility, but as an unfortunate by-product of the vicious politics of the region.[29] If the various parties could be brought to the table, then the value of the hostages would vanish for the Iranians and the Syrians. After Hashemi Rafsanjani became president of Iran in August 1989, a low-level dialogue began between the United States and Iran.[30] The Iranians sent messages to Washington through the Swiss embassy, which formally represented U.S. interests in Iran, and privately through the Japanese embassy. The point of these messages was that Tehran wanted to end its Cold War with Washington.[31] The United States was now on better diplomatic, though not particularly good, terms with Syria, the other major player in the hostage drama in

Lebanon. In the winter of 1990, global and regional events coalesced to put Iran, Syria, and the United States on the same side in discussing the hostages.

The ebbing of Soviet power left Syria increasingly exposed. The number of Soviet military advisors in Syria slipped from four thousand in 1988 to three thousand in 1989 and was due to be cut again in mid-1990. Part of what Moscow and Damascus called their thirty-year special relationship was the Kremlin's promise to supply whatever weapons Syria needed to maintain "strategic parity" with Israel. In early 1990, the Soviets informed the Syrians that they could no longer provide this level of support. The Kremlin added that were Israel and Syria to go to war, President Assad could no longer assume Soviet assistance.[32] The Syrian leader reacted by sending signals to Washington that he was prepared to participate in the peace process and to help the Americans recover their citizens from Beirut. In mid-March he again welcomed former president Jimmy Carter, who had previously visited in 1987 to convince Assad to expel Abu Nidal from Damascus. During this visit, Assad made clear from the start that he was prepared to help the United States with its terrorist problem in Lebanon. He and his foreign minister promised "to both locate the hostages and convince those who might be holding them they should be protected and released."[33]

The Iranians also felt that helping with the release of the remaining eight American hostages could send a useful signal to the Bush administration. Changes in Iran, rather than the tectonic shifts at the end of the Cold War, provoked Tehran's interest in better relations with Washington. The country was still trying to recover from its costly eight-year war with Iraq. As he consolidated his power, President Rafsanjani sought to assure his people of economic improvements.

In late February, the Iranian leader used the *Teheran Times,* an English-language newspaper under his control, to signal that Iran would use its influence to bring about the unconditional release of the hostages.[34] In the past, Iran had expected some kind of trade, whether for arms or for the $12 billion in Iranian assets that the Carter administration had frozen during the Iran hostage crisis in 1979.[35] A week later, Rafsanjani underscored his seriousness by sending his brother, Mahmoud Hashemi, to Beirut to persuade senior Hezbollah leaders to give up the hostages. On his way back to Teheran, Hashemi stopped in Damascus to brief the Syrians and coordinate their efforts on releasing the hostages.[36]

The White House had been waiting five years for Rafsanjani to act in this manner. President Bush took a "personal call" from President Rafsanjani in the first week of March that turned out to be an elaborate crank call. The story leaked, and the Bush administration had to make the embarrassing announcement that the president had been the victim of a hoax. At the very least, the taking of the call had been poorly staffed by the Bush White House. Seasoned Iran watchers argued that it was unlikely in the extreme that the Iranian president would call his U.S. counterpart out of the blue.[37]

Despite this blip, the Bush administration was careful in its dealings with Iran. Administration policy, as set out in NSD 26 of October 1989, was that "a process of normalization must begin with Iranian action to cease its support for international terrorism and help obtain the release of all American hostages, which will not be a matter for bargaining or blackmail."[38] President Bush and the NSC were aware that according to the best evidence available in late 1989, Iran seemed the likely culprit behind the Pan Am 103 bombing.[39]

Washington learned in April 1990 the limits of the control that both Iran and Syria might have over the Shia terrorists in Lebanon. In mid-March, Iran's first deputy foreign minister had publicly predicted in Beirut that all Western hostages would be freed by January 1991.[40] A month later, the Syrians and the Iranians were talking only about getting a handful released soon. The United States was told by the Syrians, who were working increasingly closely with U.S. ambassador Edward Djerejian in Damascus, to expect the release of a hostage on April 20. On the eve of this modest release, Hezbollah unexpectedly asked that Bush send Assistant Secretary of State John

Kelly to Damascus to receive the hostage and then to discuss with them the terms for the release of the remaining hostages.

The president himself publicly refused. "The United States does not knuckle under to demands," he said at a news conference in Florida, where he was meeting with French president François Mitterrand.[41] Privately, however, the U.S. government was prepared to send Kelly if the terrorists insisted. "The president's and secretary's statements," said Undersecretary of State for Political Affairs Robert Kimmitt at the meeting, "give us the flexibility on Kelly going if the Syrians don't have any other way around this and ask us to send him."[42] The Syrians did not think it was necessary. They were confident the hostage would be released in a few days.[43] "The prestige of Syria is involved," a Syrian official told the *New York Times* on April 21.[44] The Iranians also wanted the release to happen. An unsigned article appeared in the *Teheran Times* on April 21 stating, "Hurdles there may be on the way, but it is our hope that despite all, the freedom of the hostages can become a reality materializing soon."[45]

As the Syrians had predicted, an American hostage, Robert Polhill, was released on April 22. The Bush administration subsequently exchanged messages with both Damascus and Tehran. To show its appreciation to Rafsanjani, the United States offered to help the Iranians determine the whereabouts of three Iranian diplomats who had gone missing in Lebanon in 1982.[46] Other than that, no promises were made by the Bush administration to Iran or Hezbollah. A week later, Hezbollah released a second American, Frank Reed. In a message to Bush the day before Reed's release, National Security Advisor Scowcroft reiterated the logic of the administration's approach: "For now . . . there is a consensus here and at State that we ought to avoid going beyond where we are lest we find ourselves negotiating and accepting conditions despite our many assertions to the contrary."[47]

At that point, the releases stopped for sixteen months. Even before convincing Hezbollah to release Reed, Iran indicated that it was returning to its earlier position that the United States could not expect to get all of its citizens back without something in return.[48] It had taken a much greater effort to get the two Americans released than Iran had expected. There were rumors that Rafsanjani had had to promise arms shipments to Iran's Lebanese allies to guarantee their acquiescence.[49]

Rafsanjani's hostage policy also faced challenges at home. His chief political rival, Ali Akbar Mohtashemi, hoped to use the hostage releases against him. As Iranian ambassador to Syria in the early 1980s, Mohtashemi had helped build Hezbollah. It was Tehran's message to Mohtashemi instructing him to order Hezbollah to hit the United States that Washington had intercepted before the attack on the Marine barracks in October 1983. As one of his first official acts as president in August 1989, Rafsanjani had removed Mohtashemi from the position of minister of the interior. Despite this demotion, Mohtashemi had retained close links to Hezbollah and used them to stymie Rafsanjani's efforts to improve relations with the West.[50]

Given what had happened to Reagan, the Bush administration was not inclined to do much to help Rafsanjani out of his bind at home. Fragmentary evidence suggests that the Bush administration made few, if any, attempts to use the intelligence community to disrupt Hezbollah or moderate its policy on the hostages. If it did, then whatever the CIA tried had no significant effect. The eventual release of the hostages in late 1991 would be the result of events outside the control of the U.S. government.

Triumph over Abu Nidal

The U.S. government's continuing difficulties with Hezbollah contrasted sharply with the CIA's increasing success against Abu Nidal. The struggle with the Abu Nidal Organization (ANO) had by no means ended in 1988. In May 1989, the CIA and the PLO achieved a major victory with the defection of Atif Abu Bakr, one of Abu Nidal's closest associates. Besides the killings in Lebanon in 1987, there were rumors that Abu Nidal had ordered the deaths of 150 of his fighters in Libya, where he kept his personal residence. When Abu Nidal tried to lure Abu Bakr back to his organization in October 1989, Bakr managed to talk Abu Nidal's personal emissary, Abd al-Rahman Isa, into defecting as well. In June 1990, forces loyal to Abu Bakr attacked and overran Abu Nidal's headquarters in Lebanon, killing eighty of the ANO in the process.[51]

As internecine warfare continued within the ANO, U.S. intelligence gained additional information on the location of the remaining Abu Nidal loyalists from his former allies in Eastern Europe. In 1990–91, Turco went to Eastern Europe to tell the Eastern European secret services that they had a choice: They could hand over what they knew about terrorist organizations or suffer the consequences of angering the U.S. government. He subsequently learned a great deal about East German and Czech support for the Palestinians and the Marxist terrorist groups in Western Europe.[52]

The search for Abu Nidal cells hit a tragic note in the United States. In the late 1980s, the FBI was observing Abu Nidal sympathizers or operatives in sixteen U.S. cities from New York to Los Angeles.[53] The FBI received permission under the Foreign Intelligence Surveillance Act to place taps on the telephone of Zein al-Abdeen Hassan Isa, the chief ANO fund-raiser in the Western Hemisphere, who had brought his family to St. Louis from the West Bank in 1984. The wiretaps revealed growing domestic tension between Isa and his teenage daughter, Tina. The young woman was infatuated with a boy at school despite her father's stipulation that she would have an arranged marriage with a fellow Palestinian. In Isa's eyes, his daughter's rebellion was made worse by the fact that her boyfriend was black.

As caught on tape, Isa repeatedly threatened the life of his daughter while she was out of the house. Around midnight on November

6, 1989, he stabbed Tina to death with the help of his wife, Maria Matias Isa.[54] Surveillance of the Isa family, though continuous, had been passive. The conversations were recorded and then translated by FBI technicians. The FBI learned of Tina's death only the next day.

The bureau had no choice but to turn the Isas over to local police. "It was a decision made by the facts," recalls Revell.[55] A murder had been committed in St. Louis, and the State of Missouri would have jurisdiction. The FBI went to the FISA court with the surveillance tape and secured permission to share it with the local authorities.[56]

Over the objections of the CIA, the FBI felt that not only should the Isas be arrested, but their network had to be shut down.[57] The precise decision-making by law enforcement in this case, and whether any foreign-policy makers were aware of the dispute with the CIA, remain obscure. On January 28, 1991, 107 police and federal agents entered eight Arab-owned convenience stores in St. Louis City and County and discovered unreported income presumably destined for ANO coffers.[58] In February 1991, the Isas were brought to trial, and the local prosecutor received permission to introduce the wiretaps as evidence.

The Isa case was a sad chapter in what was otherwise the story of the greatest U.S. counterterrorism triumph since 1945. These detections, defections, and deaths did not destroy the ANO, but after 1991, it would never again pose a significant threat to U.S. interests. It had been neutralized, and its leader broken. Abu Nidal later died of natural causes in Baghdad. Since the collapse of the SS, the U.S. had not scored so complete a victory against a terrorist foe.

The dispute between the CIA and the FBI over how to handle the Abu Nidal cells in the United States coincided with a particularly difficult moment for the Bush administration. On August 2, 1990, Iraq had invaded Kuwait. Bush soon announced that "this would not stand" and demanded that Iraq withdraw. As it became increasingly unlikely that Saddam would abandon Kuwait without a fight, the counterterrorism community concluded that he would likely resort to unorthodox warfare, especially terrorism, to undermine the coalition arrayed against him. "Iraqi intelligence services and client Palestinian groups are capable of launching terrorist attacks against U.S., other Western, and moderate Arab targets at any time," concluded the CIA on January 10, 1991, five days before the end of the UN deadline for an Iraqi pullout. In the weeks following the deployment of U.S. troops to Saudi Arabia in the fall, the Iraqis had orchestrated a campaign of threatening letters and phone calls to U.S. diplomatic and military facilities around the world. Saddam himself had called for a holy war against the United States, and the CIA speculated that he was "keeping the terrorist option in reserve while he attempts to take advantage of international diplomatic initiatives." The CIA assumed that Iraqi intelligence and its Palestinian allies would "link implementation of their terrorist plans to hostilities in the Gulf." But the agency could not rule out the possibility of an attack designed to accelerate the onset of war. Although Abu Nidal had been thrown out of Iraq in 1983, there was concern that the ANO had an interest in jumping the gun. "The ANO, for example, which is dedicated to the destruction of Israel," the CIA warned, "might stage a major terrorist incident in order to light the fuse of a Middle Eastern war that almost certainly would include Israel."[59]

The U.S. intelligence community had little doubt that a rash of terrorist attacks would accompany a war with Iraq. "If war erupts, Saddam almost certainly will unleash a major terrorist campaign against Western—particularly U.S.—interests. Multiple, simultaneous attacks are likely to occur in several geographic regions—possibly including the United States—in an effort to capture maximum publicity and sow widespread panic." The CIA had evidence that European as well as Latin American groups had prepared, independently of Iraq and of each other, to hit U.S. targets once war started.[60]

In late 1990 and early 1991, the CSG discussed measures to protect key infrastructure. Certain places received additional protection.

The Ambassador Bridge between Canada and the United States received special attention because of the proximity of the large Arab population in Detroit. Concerned that Arab radicals would target Arab moderates, at Miller's recommendation the Islamic Center in Washington was added to the protected list.[61] The FBI was watching many groups that appeared to be planning terrorist incidents, and members of the CSG had to weigh the costs and benefits of treating terrorism as an intelligence problem rather than a crime. "What if [we know] the terrorists are seven-eighths ready and an outside event—like the start of a war—triggers the operation [before we have decided to pick them up]?" Miller recalled as the logic behind the concern.[62] Indeed, this may have been the reason that the FBI rolled up the Isa network after the expiration of the UN deadline.

FBI director William Sessions was very concerned about the possibility of an Iraqi-sponsored attack within the United States. He recalled Saddam Hussein saying three times that he would "take the fight to the enemy." Sessions worried about security for Super Bowl XXV, which was scheduled for January 27 in Tampa, Florida. Ultimately, FBI sharpshooters would be deployed at the game. To prepare for possible domestic attacks, Sessions called Scowcroft to ask that the FBI be given some warning before the air war began. As a result, the bureau received a three-hour notice: "That was enough."[63] The air war started on January 16, 1991, and the ground war followed five weeks later. Saddam was defeated within a hundred hours of the start of the invasion. The predicted wave of terrorist attacks did not happen. Although Washington now believed that it did not need to worry about the Iraqi intelligence service in the short run, the successful conclusion of the war did not bring an end to U.S. concerns about Palestinian extremists. "The threat to U.S. interests from Middle East terrorists has declined since the suspension of hostilities," reported the CIA on April 4, 1991, "but efforts to resolve regional problems and the militant agendas of extremist groups make terrorist acts against Israeli, moderate Arab, and U.S.

targets possible at any time. The Palestinian Islamic Jihad (PIJ), Hezbollah, and the Abu Nidal organization (ANO) pose the most serious threat to U.S. interests over the next several months."[64] The CIA, however, believed that the jockeying for position in the postwar negotiations would discourage state sponsors from provoking any action from those terrorist organizations.

There is no record available of any postmortems prepared within the U.S. intelligence community as to why it had exaggerated the terrorism capabilities of the Iraqi secret service, especially within the United States. The CTC's chief recalled the Iraqis as "hoodlums," not professional intelligence officers. "They either had no cells in [the] U.S. or did not activate them during the Gulf War," Turco remembers.[65] The FBI found that Iraq lacked the kind of network that the Libyans or the Iranians had in the United States and tried to get the PLO rejectionists to commit acts of terror on Saddam's behalf. The bureau did take some action against Iraqi sympathizers in the United States, "but it was never clear whether these would have become incidents," recalls Revell.[66] The most dangerous domestic case appears to have involved an American scientist who offered his services to the Iraqi embassy just before Bush delivered his State of the Union address on January 29, 1991. The scientist, who was later captured, told the Iraqis that he could launch a sarin gas attack on Congress.[67] There was some Iraqi terrorist planning abroad, and U.S. and allied services apparently proved very effective in shutting down all of these operations. The Iraqi military intelligence service dispatched "several" teams of undercover officers in Asia and the Middle East to attack U.S. targets, both governmental and commercial. Using signals intelligence and other means, U.S. intelligence followed these teams, and through cooperation with local services captured all of them.[68]

Cooperation between the CIA and the U.S. military was very good. The Joint Chiefs of Staff provided an airplane to the CIA so that at least one of the members of the Iraqi sabotage teams captured overseas could be brought to the United States for questioning. In return for this assistance, the CIA permitted the U.S. military to interrogate this man. The CTC was invited to suggest targets for U.S. bombing. The CIA counterterrorism experts argued that in light of the threat posed by these Iraqi attack teams, coalition air forces should destroy the command and control of both the Iraqi military and civilian intelligence services. Over the objections of the National Security Agency, which had penetrated Iraqi communications and did not want to lose this source of information, the military included these targets in the first wave of the air war. "We just did not want to give the Iraqis the chance," recalls Turco, "to send an attack order."[69]

The CIA shared information with the military about a very precise threat to the hotel in Riyadh where General Norman Schwarzkopf had his headquarters. U.S. military police never caught the Iraqi operatives, but the CIA remained convinced the operation had been planned but was called off when Schwarzkopf relocated his headquarters. "When you receive information as specific as this," argued Turco, "it is usually good."[70]

Solving the Pan Am Puzzle

While Iraq was developing as a terrorist threat, another state sponsor from the 1980s became a renewed concern because of a major break in the Pan Am investigation in 1990. In combing the scene of the disaster, the Scots picked up a fragment of a circuit board the size of a fingernail. The British thought it might belong to the timing device of the bomb on the plane but could not be sure. When the chief British investigator arrived in Washington, D.C., for a conference, the FBI requested permission to share the fragment with another agency.[71]

The CIA's Special Operations Group (SOG), which was now lodged within the CTC, catalogued photographs of various timing devices found around the world. The handiwork of a bomb maker was as individual as a fingerprint. When the SOG experts were shown the electronic fragment, one of the technicians said, "I know that one," and turned around to pull out a manual of photographs. Within a few moments, he pointed to a picture of a bomb timing device found in Africa that had been built by the Libyan intelligence service.[72]

Although the intelligence community shifted quickly to seeing Libya as the country that had organized this terrorist attack, it would take the Bush administration until well into 1991 to respond. Theories abound at the working level as to why the principals did not react aggressively to the evidence of Gadhafi's guilt. The Lockerbie attack poked a hole in the logic of the April 1986 strike, which was supposed to have deterred the Libyan leader from ever targeting U.S. interests again. Revell, the FBI's representative on the CSG, recalls being told that U.S. policymakers had ruled out a military response because of the long gap between the crime and the determination of Libyan involvement.[73] At the time the new theory reached the principals, Gadhafi also seemed to be attempting to change course. In the spring of 1990, he organized a summit of the leaders of Egypt, Syria, and Sudan in Libya, ending the twelve-year estrangement from Cairo. He also added his voice to calls for Islamic groups to stop taking hostages and apparently pressured Abu Nidal, who still lived in Tripoli, to release some French citizens whom he had taken hostage in the late 1980s. Gadhafi used U.S. oil executives to send messages to the Bush administration about his willingness to seek some accommodation.[74]

For whatever reason, the administration chose to regard the Lockerbie incident as a crime and not an act of war, as Ronald Reagan had done in reaction to the Libyan attack on the La Belle discotheque. The Bush Justice Department, Assistant Attorney General Robert S. Mueller III in particular, successfully argued for indicting the two Libyan intelligence officers who could be linked to the crime. David Miller, at the NSC, disagreed with Mueller. He asked Mueller why these two men should be brought to trial as if they had acted independently of their government. Mueller dismissed the argument, joking with Miller that in wanting to go after Gadhafi himself, he was "further right than Genghis Khan."[75] The CIA and the British MI5 also disagreed with turning the bombing into a criminal case.[76] The decision, however, had been made by the president and his closest advisors, at a much higher level than the CSG or its British equivalent.

"They Had Not Rung Our Bell Yet"

The Abu Nidal case in St. Louis had created some tension between the CIA and the FBI. The two agencies viewed cases involving sleeper agents very differently. Fred Turco did not blame his colleagues Revell or Bill Baker, but he wondered whether the essential problem for the FBI was that its principal customers were not in Washington but were an army of U.S. attorneys spread across the country whose job was to score prosecutions.[77] Although relations were good between the two organizations, legal restrictions and institutional differences complicated cooperation. The fact that the FBI was a domestic law enforcement agency meant that there were certain things it could not share with the CIA. For example, under Rule 6(e) of the Federal Rules of Criminal Procedure, the FBI could not share grand jury information with the CIA. There were similar restrictions on sharing information derived from criminal wiretaps. In any case, FBI information was difficult to use unless you knew what you were looking for. It was case specific, and the bureau employed few analysts to produce status reports on terrorist organizations in the United States.[78] It was these limitations on the FBI's ability to disseminate what it knew, as much as the institutional secrecy of the CIA's Directorate of Operations, that prevented the CTC from becoming the "counterterrorism fusion center" that the Bush task force had recommended in 1986. "We had a dysfunctional relationship with the FBI," explains Turco, "but it seemed to be good enough."[79]

Before Turco, Revell, and Bill Baker left the scene, a case occurred that might have alerted them to the tremendous danger posed by these institutional obstacles. On November 5, 1990, El-Sayyid Nosair killed a Jewish extremist, Rabbi Meir Kahane, in the Marriott East Side Hotel in Manhattan.[80] Nosair was an Islamic radical, who believed in holy war against the United States and had troubling international connections. Earlier that year he had helped find a U.S. home for Sheikh Omar Abdel Rahman, a spiritual leader of a violent offshoot of the Muslim Brotherhood in Egypt who had inspired Islamists to kill Egyptian president Anwar al-Sadat in 1981. At the time of the Kahane killing, Rahman was preaching jihad at the Farouq mosque in Brooklyn.

The CIA knew who Sheikh Abdel Rahman was but did not know he had entered the United States.[81] In April 1987, CIA analysts had described Abdel Rahman as "Egypt's most militant Sunni cleric and a close associate of the Egyptian Jihad organization."[82] That year, the CIA had also noted that Hezbollah was quoting approvingly from Abdel Rahman's anti-Western articles. But the CIA did not see Abdel Rahman's reach extending into the United States.[83] "The Kahane murder and the Nosair case never came on my radar screen," recalls Fred Turco.[84] Nosair was arrested and successfully prosecuted for the killing of Kahane without the CIA's counterterrorism specialists taking any notice. In any case, the CTC lacked the personnel to do much work on the Muslim Brotherhood. "The Muslim Brotherhood had a long history of terrorism," explains Turco, "but they had not rung our bell yet."[85] With a staff of only about four hundred, the CTC had to engage in some triage. The fact that the Greek revolutionary organization November 17 had killed a CIA officer and some U.S. military personnel meant that it received analytic and operational resources, whereas the Muslim Brotherhood did not.

In assessing the threat posed by hostile groups, U.S. experts were unable to predict when an unfriendly organization would choose terrorist measures to make its point. Even more difficult for the U.S. was to determine when an organization that might have indulged in the occasional violent act to attract publicity would become homicidal. These considerations affected how the CTC chose to spend its limited resources in the early 1990s.

As for the FBI, Revell called the assistant director in charge in New York City after Kahane was killed to ask whether there was an international terrorism dimension to the case. The chief FBI representative in New York said no. "I should not have been satisfied with his answer that there wasn't." But Nosair did not fit the pattern of what they had been seeing in the United States. In retrospect, Revell blames himself for not seeing the parallel with Hezbollah, which had started to hit Israeli targets in Latin America. "We saw this with Hezbollah. This was an Islamic movement that was talking about inflicting casualties for its own sake."[86] Revell would also blame the system within the FBI. His man in New York had bureaucratic reasons to want to look at this as a revenge killing linked to the Arab-Israeli conflict, which could be prosecuted as a simple crime. In 1988, a controversy over the FBI's collection of information about a U.S. pro–El Salvadoran left-wing group, Committee in Solidarity with the People of El Salvador (CISPES), had landed the FBI in trouble with the U.S. Congress and the media. Without higher authorization, an FBI officer had collected public information on the activities of CISPES.[87] According to the attorney general guidelines established by Edward Levi in 1976, the FBI could not open a file on a U.S. citizen or permanent resident without evidence that a crime had been committed or was in the process of being committed. The Privacy Act stipulated that the FBI could not collect information on anyone for whom there was no existing file. The effect of this was

that the FBI could not open a file on the activities of the Farouq
mosque, where Rahman preached, without a criminal predicate.
The FBI representative in New York, who had seen the harm that
was done to the careers of the agents directly involved in the CIS-
PES case, decided to be cautious. Well before the Nosair case, FBI
headquarters was aware of these investigative problems and mentioned the matter to the Justice Department.[88] But, as Revell recalls,
"we had to make do."[89]

There would be no structural changes to the U.S. counterterrorism and antiterrorism system, both domestic and foreign, in the four
years of George H. W. Bush's presidency. The president seemed to
be satisfied with the system despite the fact that not all of the recommendations of his vice presidential task force had been implemented. After the Gulf War, Bush did sign one directive on U.S.
port security that reflected sensitivity to at least one of the gaps in
domestic security discovered in the course of his task force's
1985–87 review of U.S. counterterrorism.[90] But there was no cata-
lyst to encourage a harder look at the broken intersection of U.S.
foreign and domestic security. These were issues skated over by the
task force because no real threat seemed to exist against the United
States at home. In the absence of that threat, none of the agencies
had an interest in upsetting the delicate relationships each had established with the others.

During the 1988 campaign, Steven Emerson, a reporter for *U.S.
News & World Report,* obtained a copy of the classified section of
NSDD 207 and concluded, after interviewing various experts, that
"fewer than half of the 42 classified recommendations have ever
been implemented."[91] In mid-October 1988, Emerson called the vice
president's office asking for an explanation. The reporter said that it
was his conclusion that the task force report reflected an effort to
make a "Big Splash" with "no real commitment."[92] On background,
Emerson was told that his sources were wrong. Admiral Holloway
had revisited all of the recommendations in March–April 1987 and

found that they had either been implemented or were "of a continuing nature."[93] Emerson went ahead with his story anyway, entitling it "Bush's Toothless War Against Terrorism."[94] The piece ended with an anonymous "senior counterintelligence expert" opining that "the report was a farce."[95] The story did not become a campaign issue. No one in the press, even after the inauguration, checked whether Emerson's charges were true.

George Bush's leadership as president would be judged on many criteria. But his effectiveness on counterterrorism would not be one of them. International terrorism would not figure at all in the 1992 election. The issue of counterterrorism in general had slipped low on the national agenda.

Burying William Buckley

At the end of December 1991, Hezbollah released its last American hostage, Terry Anderson, and the bodies of William Buckley and Lt. Colonel William Higgins.[96] The denouement of this seven-year ordeal for the surviving hostages, the American people, and the U.S. government had come following the end of the Gulf War. In a futile bid to curry favor with Iran, Saddam Hussein had handed the Dawa prisoners to the Iranians after he took Kuwait in August 1990. The war that followed delayed the effect of the release of the Dawa prisoners on the fate of the hostages. But in May 1991, Iran resumed its efforts to release the Westerners. Hezbollah resisted until it was assured of its political survival in the new Lebanese political order being brokered by Iran and Syria.[97] Hezbollah's chief ally in Tehran, Mohtashemi, did not stand in the way of releasing the Americans. By August 1991, he had become chairman of the Defense Committee of Iran's parliament, Majlis, and apparently no longer felt he needed to obstruct Rafsanjani's foreign efforts, at least not those involving the Western hostages.[98] That August, Edward Tracy, the first U.S. hostage to be released since April 1990, went home, and by the end of the year all of the hostages had been liberated.

The return of Buckley's remains was especially poignant. His capture more than any other event had prompted the U.S. government to begin organizing itself to fight international terrorism. In the months that followed, some top people in the cadre of aggressive counterterrorism officers who had rallied to the cause at the CIA and the FBI retired or moved on to other official responsibilities.

The year 1992 also saw another symbolic victory in the silent struggle against terrorism. In September, Peruvian authorities arrested Abimael Guzman Reynoso, the leader of the Shining Path. The CIA had played a vital yet long undisclosed role in hunting down Guzman, whose organization the State Department described as "the most violent and vicious terrorist group that has ever existed in Latin America." The Shining Path, which controlled the richest coca fields in Peru, financed its operations through drug trafficking. Half of the cocaine sold in the United States came from Peru.[99] Guzman's idiosyncrasies were his downfall. He had particular dietary needs and smoked an unusual tobacco. The CIA devised the strategy: Working with the Peruvians, they identified the grocery stores in the capital city of Lima that supplied these items and then combed through garbage bins in those neighborhoods to locate the appropriate wrappers and containers. This "trashint" (trash intelligence) turned out to be the key to finding Guzman.[100]

With the ending of the hostage drama in Beirut, the neutralization of ANO, and the capture of Guzman, there was talk in the CIA of shutting down the CTC because the terrorism problem had been "solved."[101] An era had ended in U.S. counterterrorism.

CHAPTER NINE

The New Terrorism

JUST BEFORE EIGHT O'CLOCK in the morning on January 25, 1993, a man in his mid-twenties walked down the double row of cars waiting to enter the CIA's main entrance and began shooting through windows and windshields. "It was a pretty horrifying experience to witness," recalled Robert Smith, a U.S. Senator from New Hampshire, who was in his car on Virginia State Highway 123 about fifty feet away.[1] Agency officials typically viewed returning to headquarters from an overseas mission as a respite from danger. "It isn't the place you expect to go to and die," said one officer to the *New York Times*.[2] But two CIA employees died in their cars that morning and three were wounded.

There were no immediate suspects. Although many commuters besides Senator Smith had seen the attack, the local police, the FBI, and the CIA's Office of Security had only a vague physical description to go by. After shooting off several rounds of his rifle, the young man sprinted away to a car that he had parked nearby. No one recognized him, yet there was some concern that he might be a disgruntled employee. Equally popular was the theory that he was a foreign terrorist. "It doesn't appear to be a group terrorist kind of thing, but it's something in people's minds," one anonymous CIA official told the press.[3]

One of those at the agency who had to consider whether this was the first terrorist act ever directed at the CIA on U.S. soil was Winston Wiley, the new deputy chief of the Counterterrorist Center (CTC). Lanky and owlish, Wiley had a reputation as a comer on the analytical side of the agency, and he was also known for an excellent sense of timing. He had run a startup team in the Directorate of Intelligence before taking over the Persian Gulf unit. He was not in that job more than a couple of months before Saddam Hussein invaded Kuwait and everyone in the NSC started caring what he and his group of smart young analysts had to say. But when Wiley accepted the position as Steve Richter's deputy at CTC in 1992, his colleagues wondered whether he had made his first bad career move. "Terrorism was considered a dead issue," recalls Wiley. After six years of achievement, CTC was suddenly a CIA backwater. Fred Turco and his team had finished off the Abu Nidal Organization and fingered Abimael Guzman of the Shining Path before leaving. Meanwhile, Carlos the Jackal was on the run, the PLO was engaged in the Middle East peace process, and Western European extremists were either dead or had lost their ideological focus with the collapse of the Soviet Union. Wiley had wanted to get some experience in the Directorate of Operations and had hoped for a job in the counternarcotics business. When he was offered the CTC job instead, he felt he couldn't refuse. Wiley joined the CTC in November 1992.[4]

The incoming Clinton administration shared the expectation that counterterrorism would not be a major focus of U.S. foreign policy. "Terrorism," recalls Leon Fuerth, who would be Vice President Gore's influential assistant for national security affairs for the entire eight-year period of the administration, "was a problem elsewhere in the world."[5] As evidence of this new view, half of the members of the NSC staff who covered terrorism were let go.[6] On the few occasions that he talked about foreign policy in the campaign, the Democratic nominee had said that "no national security issue is more urgent" than assisting the development of stability and freedom in the former Soviet Union.[7] The administration also inherited the problem of stability in Somalia and faced a humanitarian crisis in Haiti and a political one in the former Yugoslavia. With the hostages home from Beirut, no one was talking about terrorism. Soon after his inauguration, President Clinton took his cabinet and his top advisors to Camp David, where he explained that even with those challenges, he did not consider foreign policy among his top five concerns in the first hundred days of his administration. The new president focused his team on achieving an economic recovery plan, a health care plan, welfare reform, political reform, and a national service program. When journalists pointed out to his cocky young political advisors that foreign policy seemed absent, they replied, "That's why he is president and George Bush isn't."[8]

The young and youthful members of the Clinton team were self-conscious about this being the first post–Cold War presidency. Their priorities reflected a yearning among many Americans, on the left and the right, for a "peace dividend" following the long, expensive slough of a fifty-year struggle with the Soviet Union. Clinton had explicitly promised a cut in the defense budget and assured his listeners on the campaign trail that intelligence would bear some of those cuts. The rapid collapse of the Soviet Union was interpreted by many as a repudiation of CIA analyses that had systematically exaggerated Soviet power, especially Moscow's economic strength. Clinton's vow to cut $7.5 billion over five years from the intelligence budget, which was estimated at $29 billion in 1993, therefore did not become a campaign issue and may even have helped him with the voters.[9]

Clinton's nominee for the CIA directorship, W. James Woolsey, was opposed to any cuts in the intelligence budget, but shared the belief that terrorism would not be a major issue for the intelligence community. In his Senate confirmation hearing, Woolsey noted that the world was still a dangerous place. "Yes, we have slain a dragon," he said. "But we now live in a jungle filled with poisonous snakes. And in many ways, the dragon was easier to keep track of."[10] He pointed to threats from the proliferation of weapons of mass destruction and ethnic violence, but not terrorism. Among the new missions for the CIA, he believed, was the more active collection of economic intelligence to make American business more competitive.[11]

On the matter of the intelligence budget, Congress sided more with the president than with his hawkish CIA appointee. The chairman of the Senate Select Committee on Intelligence, Dennis DeConcini, a Democrat from Arizona, was even more committed to cutting the intelligence budget than the new president. DeConcini wanted to punish the CIA for its analytical mistakes in the Cold War and the recent Gulf War. In 1992 he had successfully spearheaded a drive to cut $1.6 billion from the intelligence budget and intended to do the same in 1993. Outgoing DCI Robert Gates warned that the effect of another round of budget cuts would be "real damage to the intelligence capability of the country." But DeConcini disagreed. "Common sense tells me," he said, "that intelligence shouldn't cost as much as it once did." "I'm sure that the world may be no less a dangerous place than it once was, but to me that means that information is easier to get now."[12]

The relaxation of vigilance could also be seen among domestic law enforcement. The FBI component of New York City's Joint Terrorism Task Force (JTTF), the first of its kind in the country, was taking fewer risks. The JTTF was an experiment in partnering local and federal agencies, including the New York Police Department, the FBI, the Immigration and Naturalization Service, the FAA, the Bureau of Alcohol, Tobacco, and Firearms, and the U.S. Marshals Service, to pursue terrorism investigations. When a dispute arose over the quality of an informant close to Sheikh Omar Abdel Rahman—a resident of Brooklyn and the spiritual leader of the radical Al-Gama'a al-Islamiyya—the FBI dropped the informant. The Sunni Al-Gama'a al-Islamiyya had never killed any Americans, but had been very radical and very violent in Egypt. In the United States, it was viewed as just another exile organization that had imported its petty political disputes to this country. The penetration agent was good but a little too much trouble given the FBI's assessment of the importance of the target. Emad Salem was let go in July 1992.[13]

The CIA shooting in January 1993 suggested that terrorism might not be a completely dead issue. Three days after the incident, the roommate of a Pakistani man named Mir Amal Kansi reported him missing to police. A police search of their apartment turned up evidence that Kansi had bought a ticket to Pakistan the day after the shootings. He was long gone. The CIA had no better sense of who he was, though now there was clearly an Islamic connection, and some began to wonder whether the Pakistani government, whose relations with the United States had soured after the USSR pulled out of Afghanistan in 1988, was somehow behind this.[14] It would take an even bloodier event in early 1993 to start the process of convincing intelligence officials and policymakers to accept that terrorism could be a post–Cold War problem.

The courtly FBI director William Sessions liked to have his office television set tuned in to CNN with the volume turned down. "It was something I was criticized for," he recalls good-naturedly. (Sessions was no more popular with the incoming Clinton team at Justice than he had been with the Bush Justice Department.) On February 26, 1993, CNN was reporting an explosion at the World Trade Center with at least five people dead and hundreds suffering from smoke inhalation. Sessions assumed that a conspiracy was behind the attack and thought at first that it involved Balkan terrorists.[15] About an hour after the explosion, a group calling itself the Serbian Liberation Army claimed credit.[16] The Clinton administration had taken a tougher stand on Serbia's aggression toward Bosnia, and this might have provoked a violent reaction from extremists. The Joint Terrorism Task Force in New York immediately took the lead in the investigation.

At the CIA, the first reports from New York suggested that the explosion might have been caused by mechanical failure.[17] That theory was soon discarded. The CTC, however, did not then spend much time considering a Balkan link. Already investigating Islamist ties to Kansi, the CIA was ready to accept a Middle Eastern explanation for the attack on the World Trade Center.

Within hours, the FBI realized how wrong it had been to let Emad Salem go. His parting words when he received his last payment had been, "Don't call me when the bombs go off."[18] Salem had not known about the plot against the World Trade Center, but he knew the key conspirators and had given the FBI all of their names months before the attack. A matter of hours after the bombing the FBI was investigating the Rahman group and the Farouq mosque on Atlantic Avenue in Brooklyn. A forensic breakthrough helped confirm that this group of extremists was involved. The left axle of the bombers' van had survived the blast. On it was inscribed a vehicle identification number, which the FBI used to trace the van to a car rental agency. The night before the attack, a man named Mohammed Salameh had called the rental agency to report a stolen van. Salameh was known to be among Rahman's inner circle. Salameh, it turned out, was also a clumsy conspirator. Incredibly, on February 27 he returned to the rental company to claim his down payment. FBI agents were waiting for him.[19]

From Salameh and Salem, the FBI reconstructed details of the attack. Under the operational leadership of a Pakistani named Ramzi Yousef, Nidal Ayyad, Mohammed Salameh, Mahmud Abouhalima, and Eyad Ismoil had plotted to bring down the World Trade Center by filling a rented Ford Econoline van with fertilizer and a timed fuse and parking it in the garage below the complex. The bureau was able to capture Ayyad and Ismoil in addition to Salameh, but the rest had already disappeared.

Yousef, the chief planner, was a skilled terrorist. Besides building the bomb, he had plotted his own escape. Paying cash and using an alias, he had bought a first-class ticket on Pakistan International Airlines to Karachi for late on the same day as the bombing. With the

FBI still looking in the wrong direction, he would board his delayed flight just after midnight on February 27. Before the U.S. government understood that he was the key to the conspiracy, Yousef was safely in his hometown of Quetta, Pakistan.[20]

The CIA had little to offer the FBI in its investigation. The agency had been monitoring Rahman since the assassination of Anwar Sadat in 1981, when Rahman emerged as spiritual guide to Al-Gama'a al-Islamiyya, a radical offshoot of the Muslim Brotherhood and a fierce opponent of the secular leadership in Egypt. After Rahman moved to the United States in 1991, the CIA investigated the ties he retained to Al-Gama'a al-Islamiyya in Egypt.[21] The CIA had more information that might have caused the FBI to look harder at the possibility that the Rahman group would turn some of that violence against Americans. The Brooklyn mosque seemed to have a connection to a violent domestic group that had attracted the CIA's attention before February 1993. Al Fuqra was a Pakistani Islamic organization with lines into African-American communities in Colorado and New York.[22] In 1989, Al Fuqra had been involved in the killing of a Black Muslim minister in Tucson, Arizona.

Having realized its mistake, the FBI reactivated Emad Salem as a penetration agent near Rahman and would ultimately give him $1.5 million in cash and other compensation.[23] Over the next few months, Salem provided leads for investigators, thereby saving thousands of lives. In June, Salem reported that far from being deterred by the FBI's new attention to domestic terrorism, the sheikh's inner circle was plotting a series of dramatic terrorist attacks. On what the FBI came to describe as the Day of Terror, Rahman and his disciples planned to bomb the George Washington Bridge, the United Nations building, the Holland Tunnel, and the Queens Midtown Tunnel. "A scheme and a plan so horrible, so monstrous, so vicious, that if it had been successful, the lives of every person in this city and in this nation would be changed forever," a prosecutor in this case would later conclude.[24] The FBI subsequently arrested Sheikh Rahman and eleven of his followers, all of whom were convicted in December 1995 of plotting terrorism.

The investigation of the World Trade Center bombing and the breaking up of the Day of Terror plot initiated what would be a gradual process of transforming the Clinton administration into as active a foe of terrorism as the Reagan administration had been. At the White House, W. Anthony Lake, the president's new assistant for national security affairs, was the first key policymaker to focus his attention on terrorism. A former professor of international relations at Mount Holyoke College, Lake had both an academic and hands-on understanding of the national security system. Between 1969 and 1970, he had been part of Henry Kissinger's cadre of bright young staffers at the NSC. Lake left the NSC after a year to protest U.S. involvement in Cambodia. He returned to government in the Carter administration as a member of Cyrus Vance's State Department. Those two stints coincided with periods in which terrorism had attracted some high-level attention. Before the World Trade Center bombing, however, Lake had assumed that terrorism would not be a problem that the Clinton NSC would need to spend much time on.

The bombing was a wake-up call to Lake that the U.S. government was woefully unprepared to deal with serious terrorist attacks at home. Lake was not a soothsayer: He did not predict a major attack in the near future. Nevertheless, he noticed that there was nothing like the NSC to monitor, improve, and defend U.S. domestic security. "There was no bureaucratic box," he said, in which to put a domestic terrorist attack.[25] The duties of the FBI, local police, the Federal Emergency Management Agency, and the CIA were not clearly spelled out. It would take two years, but Lake would make sure that this defect was redressed.

A notch lower than Lake at the NSC was another individual who saw the World Trade Center bombing as an opportunity to repair a long-standing problem. The phenomenon of Richard Clarke belongs more appropriately to the British system, where high-ranking civil servants inhabit Whitehall for entire careers, acquiring a more detailed understanding of how to make government work than any of the elected officials who are around for only a few years. Richard Clarke had joined the executive branch in the Ford administration, serving in the Pentagon and then in the State Department's Bureau of Politico-Military Affairs under Jimmy Carter and Ronald Reagan. He quickly earned a reputation for doggedly pursuing his policy convictions with nearly inexhaustible energy. As a player in the State Department's Bureau of Intelligence and Research, Clarke had pushed to send Stinger missiles to the Afghan rebels in their fight against the Soviets. In the first years of the George H. W. Bush administration, Clarke was assistant secretary of state for politico-military affairs. During the transition from the Bush to Clinton administrations, Clarke had briefed Tony Lake on Somalia.[26] Lake had been favorably impressed and invited Clarke to stay on as chief of a catchall office in the Clinton National Security Council that dealt with global issues. For a year, Clarke had handled a similar portfolio for the Bush NSC. Terrorism was to be part of his global affairs portfolio for Tony Lake, though by no means the most important issue. Clarke was asked to chair what had been the Coordinating Sub-Group (CSG) of the Bush administration, which handled terrorist crises. Over the next two years, Clarke would increasingly spend more time on terrorism, until it ultimately overshadowed his other duties, with the result that the CSG became known as the Counterterrorism Security Group, and its old name disappeared.

The attacks on the CIA and the World Trade Center did not seem to fit the traditional pattern of terrorist activity. The Sunni radicals behind them could not be tied to any particular country. At CTC, Richter and Wiley set up a new Islamic extremists section to monitor and plan operations against this new breed of freelance terrorists, including members of Al-Gama'a al-Islamiyya.[27] By far most of the CTC's activities, however, were still directed at Hezbollah.

This Iranian-backed group had been responsible for hundreds of deaths, and the agency still mourned the loss of its entire station in Beirut, including the irreplaceable Bob Ames, in a Hezbollah attack in 1983.

Hezbollah had returned to the headlines in 1994, suggesting that the terrorism problem in the post–Cold War world would still involve the state-sponsored variety. In July 1994, Hezbollah staged two bloody attacks that were reminders of its global reach. Nearly one hundred died and over two hundred were injured when a bomb exploded beside the Jewish Community Center in Buenos Aires on July 20. A week later, bombs went off simultaneously in front of the Israeli Embassy and the headquarters of the Joint Israeli Appeal in London, with no deaths but about a score injured. The Argentine government blamed Iran for planning the massacre on the streets of Buenos Aires.[28] And although the British did not issue a public warning against Tehran, the Clinton administration concluded that all of these attacks had been state-sponsored. "Groups like Hezbollah that wreak havoc and bloodshed must be defeated," said Clinton's first secretary of state, Warren Christopher, in congressional testimony at the end of July. "And Hezbollah's patron, Iran, must be contained."[29] In response to this activity, the CTC paid a great deal of attention to Hezbollah's chief of operations, Imad Mugniyah. Born in 1962, Mugniyah was credited with having planned the bombing of the Marine barracks in Beirut as well as most of Hezbollah's subsequent attacks. Preferring the shadows, Mughniyah never issued statements and avoided having his picture taken. Despite the absence of international celebrity, Mughniyah was at the time considered the CIA's principal terrorist target.[30]

Three months after the Hezbollah attacks in Buenos Aires and London, a wave of terrorist attacks began inside Israel. The perpetrators were members of Hamas, a violent Palestinian group that sought the destruction of Israel. Iran was but one of the sources of assistance for Hamas, which raised funds in the United States. Meanwhile, the Israeli government warned Washington that Hezbollah had its own cells operating in America.[31] Concern over these cells, which were believed to be designed to raise funds, much as the ANO cells in the Midwest had raised money for Abu Nidal in the 1980s, focused the Clinton administration on the problem of terrorism finance. Lake believed that terrorist fund-raising was a useful means of penetrating and neutralizing these organizations. "It was the softest part of the target," recalls Lake. And the United States, because of its immense and powerful banking sector, enjoyed a comparative advantage in studying the flow of terrorism finance.[32]

In late January 1995, President Clinton issued an executive order to "block all property, including bank deposits" of Hamas and Hezbollah and outlawed any fund-raising by them in the United States. "Fundraising for terrorism and use of the U.S. banking system for transfers on behalf of such organizations," wrote Clinton in a message to Congress announcing these measures, "are inimical to American interests."[33] In his message, Clinton pointed out that the bombings in Buenos Aires, London, and Israel "threaten to disrupt the peace process."[34]

Lake was not able to obtain approval for covert action against bank accounts linked to terrorist activity. The national security advisor hoped to siphon money out of the accounts or otherwise sabotage them. The Treasury Department, however, put up very stiff resistance. Any clandestine attempts to mess with Hezbollah's or Hamas's bank accounts, Treasury representatives argued, would threaten "the sanctity of the U.S. banking system." "I usually sought consensus or to win; this one I lost," Lake recalls.[35]

Not all covert action against terrorists was blocked in the early years of the Clinton administration. The World Trade Center investigations led to the first renditions of terrorists since the Fawaz Yunis operation in 1987. In the spring of 1993, after Emad Salem reported to the FBI that coconspirator Mahmud Abouhalima had returned to his native Egypt, the Egyptians tracked him down.[36] Using a civilian aircraft and with the consent of the Egyptian government, the CIA arranged for Abouhalima to be returned to the United States to stand trial. Over the next twelve months, the CIA staged two other renditions.[37] Each one required the president to sign a finding that went to congressional intelligence overseers. On at least one occasion, the president's White House counsel, Lloyd Cutler, argued against a rendition on the grounds that it was in violation of international law.[38] In the crudest terms, opponents argued that renditions verged on being state-sponsored abductions.

The Clinton team's growing appreciation of the change in terrorism tactics also brought the revival of yet another aspect of the Reagan war on terrorism. At Clarke's urging, Lake sponsored the first attempt at improving U.S. antiterrorism measures since 1986. The NSC assembled a legislative package incorporating some of the recommendations from Vice President Bush's task force. Called the Omnibus Counter-Terrorism Bill of 1995, the bill amended the Electronic Privacy Act of 1968 to allow law enforcement officers to place wiretaps on individuals who had many telephones—so-called roving wiretaps—and to collect information on which telephone numbers a target is dialing and from which telephones the suspect is receiving telephone calls. Clinton's Republican predecessors had viewed these changes as necessary, but neither Ronald Reagan nor George H. W. Bush had tried to legislate them.

Lake and Clarke did not view this problem in partisan terms. Although his own privacy had been violated by the Nixon administration after he had come out against the invasion of Cambodia, Lake saw the reforms that followed Watergate and Vietnam as weakening the bureau's ability to collect information on the new terrorists. The Levi guidelines of the mid-1970s required that a link to a foreign government be established or evidence of a crime be found before a file could be opened on an individual. Designed to discourage political witch hunts without harming legitimate counterspy operations, the guidelines severely complicated investigations of terrorists who did not have state sponsors.

"I got religion," Lake recalled in explaining why he became a strong supporter of this legislation. He was not the only one. His deputy, Samuel R. Berger, who would replace Lake in Clinton's second term, also shared this concern about the new terrorism. So, too, did the NSC senior director for intelligence programs, George J. Tenet, who in 1997 would become director of central intelligence.[39]

Lake had started a series of breakfast seminars, inviting experts on various aspects of foreign policy to join him. One of these involved a group of terrorism specialists, which included Brian M. Jenkins, who had been influential on George Shultz in 1984. Jenkins had a similar effect on Clinton's national security advisor. In the 1980s, when helping to define conventional wisdom on the terrorism threat, Jenkins had explained that terrorists were unlikely to plot mass casualty incidents because these detracted from the main mission of recruiting converts. Jenkins explained to Lake that he was seeing something new. The freelancers did not seem to have a political agenda. Unlike the PLO, which had sworn off international terrorism as it was drawn into a political process, these Islamists did not appear to be affected by the same inducements and deterrents. They also did not need any states to sponsor them.[40]

The ideological preferences of the new administration would actually facilitate the gradual acceptance of this new kind of terrorism as a major national security concern. Lake and his associates were globalists who believed that there were international issues—such as hunger and disease—that transcended old-fashioned power politics but were nonetheless significant factors in determining whether the world would be a secure or insecure place. This was what President Clinton described as the darker side of globalism, to which terrorism also belonged.[41] The legislative package was set to be introduced in early 1995.

Capturing Ramzi Yousef

On Saturday, January 6, 1995, following up on an earlier report of a fire in a Manila apartment complex, the Philippine police discovered a bomb-making laboratory, where they found manuals, precursor chemicals, and a computer hard drive with incriminating information. They arrested Abdul Hakim Murad, who told the police that his chief, Ramzi Yousef, planned to bomb, in a simultaneous orgy of terror, twelve planes bound for the United States over the Pacific. A veteran of warfare in Bosnia, Yousef had called the plot Operation Bojinka.[42] Murad also explained that he had been trained to fly an airplane into CIA headquarters in Langley and that Yousef also had a scheme to kill the Pope, who was due to arrive in the Philippines in mid-January.[43]

Because of the time difference, it was still Saturday morning, January 6, when the Philippine government informed the White House of the intelligence from Murad and the materials found in the apartment. Despite its being the weekend, the senior NSC chiefs were at their desks. Dick Clarke carried the information into Tony Lake. Lake wanted to ground all of the U.S. flights over the Pacific. "Get me the secretary of transportation," Tony Lake barked into his phone before he realized that he did not know the man's name. "Who the hell is the secretary of transportation?" he asked Dick Clarke, who was standing nearby.[44] The secretary, Federico Pena, could not be found, and Lake later recounted the confusion: "To my frustration, which led to incredulity, we were unable to locate the secretary of transportation. His department was closed that day, and there was no answer even on his central telephone number." So the men decided that the planes could be grounded by order of the president to the FAA. "It was only hours later," Lake recalled, "that we reached [Pena] to get his formal approval of the FAA's action."[45]

Washington had received information about the Bojinka plot only a few weeks after a plot to kill hundreds of people in Paris had been foiled by the French government. The episode had begun with what seemed like a routine hijacking of an Air France jet by Algerian extremists. The terrorists were members of the Groupes Islamiques

Armées (the Armed Islamic Groups, known as GIA). The GIA had taken up arms in January 1992 after the main Islamic Party, the Islamic Salvation Front (FIS), had won 80 percent of the vote in the first round of parliamentary elections and the Algerian regime then canceled the second round. The GIA became a brutal adversary in a war that would claim at least sixty thousand lives in its first few years.[46] Until December 1994, however, the GIA's methods had not included hijacking. "There was a lot of information predicting that this would happen," recalls Mona Yacoubian, a leading Arabist, who was the North African analyst at the State Department's Bureau of Intelligence and Research.[47] What no one had predicted was that the GIA would attempt to use a plane for a suicide attack on Paris. Despite the warning, the GIA managed to take control of a flight out of Algiers. When the plane landed in Marseilles and the hijackers demanded the plane be refueled, the French government learned that the hijackers intended to blow the airplane up over the capital. To prevent this, a French counterterrorism force stormed the plane, rescuing all of the hostages.[48]

The incident drew U.S. intelligence interest, but no one at CTC or in Clarke's group at the NSC saw the distant outlines of a new pattern emerging among these post–Cold War terrorists. In Battery Park City, over the Pacific, and in Paris, the Islamists were trying to kill as many people as possible. In the 1970s, the PLO and the Marxist groups had used terrorism as theater to inspire an overreaction by the target state and attract more followers. In the 1980s, Hezbollah staged the first mass casualty events but still with a regional political agenda. What seemed to be appearing now was another shift in terrorist tactics: acts of wanton slaughter with no discernible political aim.

In Washington in early 1995, the significance of the GIA attack was that it represented a spillover of the Algerian struggle into European affairs, a concern that the U.S. intelligence community had had for some time. "The tactical [innovation]," recalls Yacoubian, "was

lost [on us]." At the CTC, Winston Wiley recalled reading about the
GIA's innovation in tactics. But he filed it in the same place he
would put the report on Yousef's conversation with Murad about attacking CIA headquarters. "It was [a matter of] 'oh shit, oh dear.'"[49]

Six weeks after the GIA assault in France and a month after Murad was picked up in Manila, U.S. intelligence caught up with Murad's chief, Ramzi Yousef. Responding to a report in *Newsweek* of a $2
million reward for information leading to his capture, Istaique
Parker, a South African student who was working for Yousef in Pakistan, turned him in to the U.S. embassy in Islamabad. Yousef had
trained Parker to place suitcases laden with explosives on United
Airlines trans-Pacific flights originating in Bangkok, but at the last
moment his conscience intervened and he backed out of the plan.
The information from Parker led to a guest house where Pakistani
officials with Americans behind them arrested an unsuspecting
Yousef.[50]

At the time that Parker walked into the U.S. embassy, the NSC
had been working on another rendition, which was proving difficult.
Plans for that operation made it easier to move rapidly when the opportunity to take Yousef arose.[51] The only snag came when the Pentagon declared that it could not provide a plane to return Yousef to
the United States. The terrorists snatched in 1993–1994 had been
sent to the United States on civilian aircraft arranged by the CIA.
Those aircraft had been able to land at friendly air bases for refueling. Yousef had been picked up in Pakistan, and it would be advan-
tageous to bring him to the U.S. without any stops, requiring an
airplane capable of being refueled in the air, which only the military
could provide. Finally, the Pentagon agreed to supply the requisite
aircraft. After the operation, the Defense Department submitted a
bill of $12 million to the FBI. John O'Neill, the FBI representative
on the NSC committee that had planned the renditions, was
shocked. He was told, however, that if the military had really expected the FBI to pay it would have submitted a bill for $100,000.

By asking for $12 million, the military was delivering a message that next time, the FBI or CIA should think twice before requesting military participation in a rendition.

A month after Yousef landed in the United States, an event halfway around the world signaled that not only were terrorists in this new age seeking to kill as many people as possible, they also had access to weapons that made such terrible acts easier to accomplish. On March 20, 1995, members of the Aum Shinrikyo sect set off canisters of sarin gas on three different lines in the Tokyo subway, killing twelve people and injuring 3,769. Anthony Lake's reaction captured how many in the administration were feeling: "We [had] crossed the threshold to the era of high-tech terror, including the use of weapons of mass destruction."[52] Lake's response was intellectual as much as practical. "I would later bore people by constantly referring to the concept of "the nexus," Lake recalled.[53] The nexus was the combination of terrorist aims and weapons of mass destruction.

Discouraging to Lake and the NSC was that no one knew much of anything about this sect. Subsequent investigation would turn up that Aum Shinrikyo had 50,000 members, most of whom were in Russia and not Japan, and apparently controlled $1 billion in assets with offices in Bonn, New York, Moscow, and Sri Lanka.[54] Richard Clarke found that neither the CIA nor the FBI had anything in their files on this group.[55] The U.S. government was to learn later that this group had tried to infect hundreds of U.S. sailors with bubonic plague. But either because the strain of the bacterium was too weak or their delivery mechanism failed, no one became infected, though the cult's anti-American bent was clear. Nevertheless the new freelance terrorism had attained a new level of seriousness. "We are seeing a transformation of the terrorist network from nation states to self employment," an unidentified intelligence official told the *New York Times* in the days following the attack on the Tokyo subway.[56] The CIA later learned that Aum Shinrikyo had been able to obtain all of the components needed to produce the sarin gas legally.[57]

However shocking this development, the new terrorism was still viewed as a foreign phenomenon. However, on the morning of April 19, 1995, Americans learned to their horror that terrorists could successfully execute a mass casualty event at home. Shortly after 9 A.M., a bomb inside a rented truck exploded in front of the Alfred P. Murrah Federal Building, in Oklahoma City, killing 169 people. Never had so many people died in a terrorist attack on U.S. soil. This was ten times the number that had been killed in the still-unsolved La-Guardia Airport bombing of twenty years earlier. Given the climate of the times, it was first assumed that Islamic extremists were involved. And Oklahoma City had a large Muslim population. Two days later, a home-grown white supremacist, Timothy McVeigh, was charged with the terrorist attack. Shortly thereafter, two of his conspirators were also in custody. These men were anarchists whose hatred of centralized authority had evolved into a murderous fury.

The Yousef case, the incident in the Tokyo subway, and the Oklahoma City bombing accelerated plans to restructure the counterterrorism bureaucracy over which Lake and Clarke had been mulling in the wake of the World Trade Center bombing two years earlier. In June 1995, President Clinton signed PDD-39, the first formal presidential decision directive dealing with counterterrorism since Ronald Reagan launched the first war on terrorism in 1986. PDD-39 instructed Attorney General Janet Reno to chair a cabinet committee to review vulnerabilities of U.S. government facilities and critical national infrastructure to terrorist acts. The directive stressed that there was "no higher priority than preventing the acquisition of this capability [weapons of mass destruction] or removing this capability from terrorist groups potentially opposed to the U.S."[58]

The directive also dealt firmly with the U.S. military's reluctance to assist in renditions. "When terrorists wanted for violation of U.S. law are at large overseas, their return for prosecution shall be a matter of the highest priority." So that the U.S. military understood its responsibilities, the directive added that "return of suspects by force may be effected without the cooperation of the host government" and "agencies directed to participate in the . . . conduct of counterterrorist operations shall bear the costs of their participation, unless otherwise directed by me." There would be no more bills from the Pentagon to the FBI for renditions.[59]

The directive also formalized the administration's interest in learning more about terrorism financing. At Lake's urging, the CIA was instructed to expand its efforts against foreign terrorist financiers. The CTC created a special Terrorism Financial Links [TFL] unit, over Winston Wiley's mild objections. Wiley was skeptical of the idea that following the money would prevent any future terrorist attack. However, the national security advisor was persistent, as was Richard Clarke. So Wiley took his best expert on the Sunni radicals and elevated him to head the new unit. As chief of the Islamic Extremists section, Michael Scheuer had impressed many at the agency by rapidly piecing together the materials on the Bojinka plot as they came in from Manila and other CIA stations. At Wiley's suggestion, David Cohen, the CIA's deputy director for operations, made him chief of the TFL unit.[60]

The Clinton administration also pushed forward with its effort to improve offensive and defensive measures against terrorism at home. In February 1995, even before the Tokyo subway attack and Oklahoma City, the Clinton administration introduced the Omnibus Counter-Terrorism Act of 1995.

The legislation was the most serious attempt to date to create a comprehensive antiterrorism capability in the United States in peacetime. To the surprise of Clinton's national security team, the country was not ready to adopt it. Despite its roots in the recommendations of a Republican administration, this Democratic proposal met with crippling opposition from left and right in the House of Representatives.

The measure stalled in the Republican-controlled House. Conservative Republicans joined with some liberal Democrats in successfully opposing the $2.1 billion package. This resistance did not let up after the Oklahoma City bombing in April. Even after the Senate passed a revised version of it overwhelmingly in June 1995, the House leadership refused to bring it to a vote.[61]

Opposition to the bill was not limited to Congress. The *New York Times* attacked the Clinton initiative for its "intrusive new surveillance powers for law enforcement agencies." The *Times* believed that the FBI "already has ample authority to pursue terrorists" and that the bill was asking Americans to surrender too much of their civil liberties. "Diminishing American liberties," the editorialists concluded, "is not the solution to terrorism."[62]

For months, Clinton tried to use the public reaction to the Oklahoma City bombing to persuade the House to legislate some antiterrorism measures. A year later, a much weaker bill was passed, which allocated only an additional $1 billion to counterterrorism and dropped the authorization to the FBI to expand its ability to tap the telephones of suspected terrorists and the mandate to put taggants in explosive powder to make it easier to trace. "It's kind of the world turned upside down," observed Senator Orrin G. Hatch. "I remember years ago when the conservatives voted to increase wiretap authority and the liberals raised concern about it, and now it's the liberals who want to expand the authority and some conservatives who are concerned about it."[63] In the House, Representative Tom Coburn argued that the threat of terrorism should not lead lawmakers to forget first principles: "There is a greater fear in this country, and that is fear of our own government."[64] This debate was a reminder of how deep-seated was public mistrust of measures that enhanced federal intelligence powers, especially in the area of counterterrorism.

Iranian Terrorism

The new terrorism still seemed more of a potential threat than an actual one. As the administration enhanced its capabilities to monitor

Sunni extremists like Ramzi Yousef and Sheikh Rahman, it still faced a serious challenge from a nation that used terror as an instrument of foreign policy. In 1995, for reasons that remain obscure, the Iranians launched an unexpected and aggressive campaign to intimidate the Clinton administration. "They were pinging us," recalls Kenneth Pollack, who was working on Persian Gulf issues in the NSC at the time.[65] During the Cold War, U.S. and Soviet submarines would play games of cat and mouse, using their sonars to indicate when an adversary had been spotted. In wartime, of course, the two sides would be using depth charges instead. Roger Cressey, later Clarke's deputy at the NSC, was then at the Pentagon. He remembers the sense that the Iranians were "casing us."[66] No one in the Clinton White House could predict whether Iran was preparing for some kind of low-intensity warfare. Hezbollah was apparently not involved in their surveillance operations, just the Iranian secret service.

Hezbollah was involved, however, in another high-profile threat to U.S. national security. In the fall of 1995, the CIA learned in Sudan of a fatwa against the life of National Security Advisor Anthony Lake. Richard Clarke went to Lake to convince him to take it seriously. "I had wanted to ignore it, but then I thought of the paperwork for Dick if I were killed," Lake recalls. Lake, who was recently separated from his wife, moved to a safe house with a cache of submachine guns in the basement and was driven to work in an armored car.

The incident produced another moment of black humor. When Lake left the NSC in 1970 over the invasion of Cambodia, Henry Kissinger had authorized wiretaps on his home telephone. A quarter century later, with the presumed fatwa threatening Lake's life, it was thought useful to put surveillance on all of his communications. Two FBI officers subsequently brought to Lake, who now occupied Kissinger's office in the West Wing, written authorization to tap Lake's private telephone. He started signing his name on the form and stopped: "You know there is a certain irony in this." "We know, sir," said the two agents, without a hint of a smile.[67]

The threat from Hezbollah hung over Lake for a few months. "Then it just drifted away," he later recalled.[68] What did not drift away was the sense that Tehran and its allies were testing Washington, perhaps in preparation for a confrontation. The tension continued to rise, causing the CIA station chief in Riyadh to predict in 1996 that something would soon happen to U.S. assets in the Saudi kingdom.

The attack was a suicide truck bombing, much in the style of the attacks on U.S. facilities in Beirut in the 1980s. It was carried out in June 1996, killing nineteen. The target was the Khobar Towers complex that served as housing for U.S. Air Force personnel near Dhahran Air Base. The Clinton administration suspected early on that Hezbollah and Iran were both involved, but because of Saudi reluctance to cooperate in the investigation, proof of Iran's role would not be available to Washington until 1999.[69] The Saudis arrested some suspects within days of the attack but refused to let them be interrogated by U.S. representatives.

Riyadh did not want the U.S. to retaliate against Tehran. A U.S. attack on Tehran might ruin the Iranian-Saudi rapprochement, especially since some of the bombers might be launched from the U.S. air base in the desert kingdom. The Saudis pursued a policy of balancing Iran and Iraq. Since Iraq seemed to be regaining some of its power, especially after Saddam Hussein crushed an incipient rebellion in the North earlier in the year, Riyadh had been pragmatically tightening relations with Tehran. As a result, the Saudis stonewalled as Sessions's successor FBI director, Louis Freeh, who traveled to the country to gain evidence on the bombing and for the FBI to interview the suspects.

In his public remarks after the Khobar bombing, President Clinton did not place blame on any particular terrorist group. At the memorial service for some of the victims, he spoke generally of terrorism as the enemy of the post–Cold War age. "In our time, terrorism is the enemy of peace and freedom. America must not and America will not be driven from the fight against terrorism." Clinton did not let on that he and his government saw this attack as a more traditional challenge from an enemy state, Iran. Instead, he linked the attack to the new terrorism. "We know now painfully that terrorists can strike anywhere," said Clinton, "from a subway in Tokyo to the streets of London, from the sacred ground of the Holy Land to the World Trade Center in New York and Oklahoma City and now in Saudi Arabia."[70]

The terrorist incident had occurred a matter of hours before the president was to fly to Lyon, France, for the meeting of the group of the world's seven great economic powers, the G-7. Terrorism was a topic of discussion, and the U.S. sought very sensible measures to complicate terrorist planning. Washington rallied its allies to deny terrorists a "place to hide," to seize their assets, to complicate terrorist travel by strengthening national borders, and to undermine terrorist communications through improved cybersecurity.[71] Terrorism was also one of the topics at the president's news conference before he left Lyon. One journalist asked whether part of the problem was that the United States was always preparing for the last terrorist attack, not the next one. Clinton had just charged retired Army General Wayne A. Downing with examining what had happened at Dhahran. "We had this huge wave of terrorism in the eighties; it primarily involved something other than bombs, although we had that awful incident in Lebanon," said Clinton in a reflective tone. "And we just learn as we go along. And I'm sure that there will be times in the future when murderous forces outsmart those of us that are trying to stop them. But I believe we will learn something from this." Clinton then again addressed the fact that terrorism and proliferation were the two most important threats facing the United States. "Our generation's time is going to be increasingly occupied with dealing with the terrorists and the people who try to proliferate dangerous weapons—chemical, biological, small-scale nuclear weapons—the drug smugglers and others who try to kill people in this way. It's not the Cold War, it's not World War II, but it's an important part of our struggle to make this a civilized and sane world."[72]

As Clinton was meeting with his counterparts in Lyon, his advisors in Washington were preparing for possible action against Iran. The NSC tasked Richard Clarke to write a political-military plan (pol-mil) for an air strike on Iran in case evidence turned up linking Tehran to the Khobar Towers murders. The pol-mil plan was a Clinton administration innovation. "It was a playbook," recalls Roger Cressey, a staffer in the Pentagon who worked with Clarke on the plan. At the time of the U.S. intervention in Haiti in 1993, Clinton had asked his military advisors for a briefing on the political and diplomatic actions planned to follow the landing of troops, since the plan he had been given did not include these elements. From that point on, the NSC understood that Clinton also wanted to know about the civilian side of any military operation.

The Clinton administration did not reveal its preparations against Iran. The president hinted at a much bigger story when NBC news anchor Tom Brokaw asked him why the U.S. was not trying harder to force the Saudis to help with the investigation. "This is a case with international implications, and we have to cooperate."[73] But the fact that the United States was edging toward war was not picked up by the media.

As the White House examined the military plans, it became increasingly clear that there was no victorious military solution other than invading Iran and toppling the government. Called the Eisenhower option, this was a plan for which there were no backers in the administration, let alone any public support. The public was unaware of the deadly cat and mouse game that had been going on with Iranian intelligence for over two years, that Tony Lake had been living under a death threat, and of the Iranian link to the attack on Khobar Towers. Air strikes were considered, but it was unclear where they would lead. Iran lacked missiles to reach the United States but could deploy Hezbollah to respond against U.S. targets worldwide, perhaps even in the United States.

With military options unsatisfactory, the Clinton administration opted for an audacious covert response. Tehran was to be signalled that Iranian intelligence operatives were being watched and that the Iranian government would be held accountable. U.S. and allied services put tails on the agents who were surveying U.S. installations. These tails were meant to be noticed by the Iranians but not by the public. There had been some discussion of having allies expel these Iranian operatives from their countries, by declaring them *persona non grata,* but in the end it was decided to take a much quieter approach.[74] The operation took place in Europe and the Middle East.[75] Subsequently, there was a dramatic drop in Iranian intelligence and Hezbollah activity.

Although Hezbollah and the Iranians were the major focus of the counterterrorism efforts of the Clinton administration in 1995–96, the CIA had not forgotten about the Sunni freelancers. Winston Wiley was always looking for more money to increase the number of his operations. Since the low-water mark for funding in 1993, CTC had been receiving additional support, but it was never enough. A friend of Wiley's in the agency suggested an intriguing source of additional funding. The CIA had launched a pilot project to exploit emerging technologies to test the idea of a virtual station. The traditional station was a CIA office in a foreign country that managed operations within that country. The virtual station would target a certain issue or country from Washington using computers to link operatives and managers around the world. "I didn't think that the concept was all that functional," recalls Wiley. But the pilot project would come with a chunk of money if the CIA unit's proposal were accepted. In mid-1995, CTC applied for money to upgrade the work of the Terrorism Finance Links unit.[76]

There was another reason to refocus the efforts of the TFL. Information from the field, especially but not exclusively from Sudan, suggested that much of the funding of the new Islamic terrorists came from a single source. Born in 1957, the scion of a large and fabulously wealthy family in the construction business in Saudi Arabia, Osama bin Laden had fought against the Soviets in Afghanistan in the 1980s. During this struggle, bin Laden had worked closely with others in creating fund-raising and training organizations around the Islamic world to recruit and provision an Islamic army. After the battle against the Soviets had been won, bin Laden renamed this network al Qaeda (the base, or the foundation) and began to transform it into an instrument for a much broader jihad, or holy war. Saddam Hussein's invasion of Kuwait soon pitted bin Laden against his own government. Bin Laden bitterly opposed the deployment of U.S. troops in the Saudi kingdom. This brought about his expulsion from Saudi Arabia in 1991 and his move to Sudan, which was under the control of a radical Islamic regime.

Intelligence received by Washington showed prospective terrorists coming to bin Laden in Khartoum, hat in hand for money. Bin Laden would often respond by asking these men to draft or redraft a business plan, as if they were planning to open a factory in Khartoum.[77] He was known around CTC as "the venture capitalist of Terror."[78]

David Cohen, the CIA's deputy director for operations, liked the idea of a virtual station that concentrated on bin Laden. He believed that it would be easier to fund a station and that such a unit would benefit from being able to send cables around the CIA system, which was one of the privileges of a regular station. He was impressed with Wiley's argument that more needed to be done to figure out bin Laden's operations. CTC received the money, and the Osama bin Laden virtual station was born in January 1996. Wiley suggested that Scheuer stay on, and Cohen agreed. His only suggestion was that the unit be housed outside the CIA headquarters building so that, as he explained with a smile and a south Boston accent, the "fuckers could not be pulled into meetings all day long."[79] Scheuer named it after his son: the Alec station.

The formation of the Alec station was not the only sign of innovation in U.S. counterterrorism. In 1995, the directors of the CIA and the FBI were trying to work through their differences to permit greater intelligence sharing. David Cohen, at the CIA, and his counterpart Robert "Bear" Bryant, at the FBI, headed what became known as the "Gang of Eight," who met frequently to discuss inter-agency cooperation. As a result of these efforts, the bureau and the CIA swapped top counterterrorism chiefs—Dale Watson and Jeff O'Connell—to let each see how the other service functioned.[80]

These innovations were coming despite what was an extremely difficult time for the CIA. "Bin Laden was one of hundreds of things to worry about," recalls Cohen.[81] Not only was the agency hurrying to acquire more information on the volatile Balkan situation and the Iranian problem, but CIA director John Deutch, who had succeeded James Woolsey in 1995, faced a severe morale problem, partly of his own making. Deutch and Cohen encountered severe criticism when they systematically closed down unproductive CIA operations that were remnants of the Cold War. They also set up a system for re-viewing future recruitments that some field officers viewed as too re-strictive. Deutch made things worse by his manner—his arrogance was legendary—and by certain actions that left the impression of not backing his officers in the field. In 1996, for example, the CIA was caught trying to recruit a Russian general. When the general in-formed his embassy, Moscow complained to the Clinton administra-tion, and Deutch wanted the CIA to issue a formal apology to the Russian government. "When the DCI suggests giving an apology," recalls an officer who opposed the idea, "you can imagine the ef-fect."[82] Intelligence services do not usually apologize for doing their jobs. In the Deutch era, which lasted until December 1996, a greater number of lawyers were routinely invited to participate in covert ac-tion planning meetings. This, too, sent a negative message, which was not at all encouraging of the energetic approach needed for chal-lenges like Osama bin Laden.

A Glimpse into al Qaeda

About ten months after the formation of the station, the CIA ac-quired its best glimpse to date into the structure of bin Laden's organization when Jamal Ahmed al-Fadl walked into a U.S. embassy in an African capital.[83] "He was the Oleg Penkovskiy of terrorism," recalls Lloyd Salvetti, who was Cohen's executive officer.[84] Penkovskiy was a joint U.S.-British penetration agent in the Soviet military intelligence service, the GRU, who provided the finest insight into Kremlin politics and military policy obtained by any human agent in the Cold War. Al-Fadl was not a U.S. penetration. He had already left bin Laden, but he had an encyclopedic knowledge of what he called al Qaeda, or the base.

Born in 1963 in Sudan, Al-Fadl spent two years as a student in the United States. He had worshipped at the Farouq mosque in Brooklyn, raising money and recruits for the Afghan war against the Soviets. In the late 1980s, he went to fight in Afghanistan. Al-Fadl explained that bin Laden was as much an organizer of terror as he was a financier. In 1990, Al Fadl had attended the training camp that bin Laden had established in Afghanistan, where members of the group had taken bayat, that is, an oath of allegiance, to jihad in the presence of bin Laden. These holy warriors came from around the Islamic world and from Islamic communities in Western countries. In 1991, Al-Fadl followed bin Laden to Khartoum, where he managed some of his commercial affairs. Al-Fadl described to U.S. intelligence the web of companies that bin Laden had established in Sudan to finance terrorism. What also become increasingly clear was that bin Laden was increasingly interested in being more than the money man for jihad, that he saw himself as the emir, or leader, of a movement.[85]

Bin Laden was no longer in Sudan when al-Fadl defected. In May 1996, bin Laden had moved himself and the headquarters of al Qaeda to Afghanistan. The Saudi terrorist had left Sudan because he no longer felt welcome. Since the early 1990s, the radical Islamic regime in Khartoum had welcomed representatives from several terrorist organizations, including Hamas, Hezbollah, and Al-Gama'a al-Islamiyya. Hassan al-Turabi, the spiritual leader of Sudan's ruling

National Islamic Front, had visions of uniting all Muslims under a pan-Islamic council. Bin Laden was one among many radicals whom he cultivated. Hezbollah's mysterious chief of operations, Imad Mugniyah, also spent time in Khartoum.

The Sudanese government, however, had some pragmatists who were not prepared to take on the world to achieve this dream. In 1994, the Sudanese gave up Ilich Ramirez, the notorious Carlos the Jackal, to the French. The CIA played as significant a role in the capture of the Jackal as it had two years earlier in nabbing Guzman in Peru. Acting on information from the CIA, the French had obtained the cooperation of the Sudanese authorities. Ramirez had been living in Khartoum for a year, having lost his Syrian sanctuary at about the same time as the Abu Nidal Organization.[86]

Sudan's commitment to bin Laden was stronger, but ultimately not unshakeable. The Sudanese government first came under serious pressure to expel bin Laden after the attempted assassination of Egyptian president Hosni Mubarak at the Organization of African Unity conference in Ethiopia in June 1995 implicated an Al-Gama'a al-Islamiyya cell in Khartoum. The United Nations imposed sanctions, and throughout the last half of 1995 and into 1996, the Clinton administration did what it could to persuade the Sudanese to stop providing sanctuary to international terrorists. While these discussions continued, the administration pulled out all U.S. diplomatic personnel in February 1996 out of concern for their safety.[87] Not long after the Americans left the country, the Sudanese asked bin Laden and many of his followers to follow suit. Khartoum's concerns about growing international isolation, especially at a time when it was looking for foreign investment in its oil industry, played a role in this request. Perhaps a contributing factor as well was al-Turabi's increasing rivalry with bin Laden. When he first arrived in Sudan, the tall Saudi bin Laden was not a "rock star," but by 1996 he had gained a larger international profile than his Sudanese host.[88] In any case, by the late spring of 1996, Osama bin Laden was gone from Africa.

As bin Laden was leaving Sudan, the Clinton administration was facing two incidents at home that seemed to signal that international terrorism had become an intractable domestic problem. In July 1996 a bomb went off at Centennial Plaza at the heart of the Olympic complex in Atlanta, where the 1996 games were being held. Also in July, TWA flight 800 fell out of the skies after an explosion over Long Island. In the end, international terrorism was shown to have been responsible for neither incident. The Atlanta bombing was the work of Eric Rudolf, a white supremacist in the mold of Timothy McVeigh, and the TWA tragedy was produced by a faulty fuel line. Yet these incidents increased concerns in the Clinton administration about vulnerabilities in the U.S. antiterrorism system. Following the TWA tragedy, Clinton tasked Vice President Gore with looking into airline security, particularly in view of the assumption that a bomb had brought down the plane. The president also tried to revive those measures that House Republicans had stripped from the antiterrorism bill that he had signed in April. This effort failed again at the hands of congressional partisans. The National Rifle Association pressured its allies in Congress to prevent any special identification being placed in black powder for fear that it represented the first step in preventing access to explosives. Meanwhile, Speaker of the House Newt Gingrich threw the authority of his office against any effort to expand the FBI's ability to investigate terrorists. Doubtful of the threat that terrorism posed, he decided to sacrifice any major improvement of the U.S. antiterrorism system for another opportunity to criticize the president and the first lady, who were in the midst of a reelection campaign. Citing some communications between the FBI and the Clintons in one of the many scandals that House Republicans had charged them with, Gingrich explained that the Filegate matter was "a major factor in stopping us from being able to give them the wiretap authority they seek."[89]

These efforts by the Right to politicize antiterrorism undermined the administration's efforts to shore up domestic security, but they had no discernible political effect on Clinton's popularity. In November 1996, he easily won a second term.

The first term had educated this administration about the role that terrorism would play in the post–Cold War world. The second term would provide ample opportunities to demonstrate those early lessons. Clinton and his national security team, however, would never again attempt to legislate antiterrorism measures at home. The political climate remained too hostile, and despite his considerable charisma, the president decided not to invest any more political capital in this effort. Increasingly, Clinton would see the solution in a quiet struggle largely fought abroad by the CIA. The first year of the second term brought a counterterrorism victory that suggested that the CIA was up to the task. The State Department's program of offering huge bounties in exchange for information on fugitive terrorists also played a role in capturing the CIA assassin Mir Aimal Kansi in June 1997. Having learned about the $2 million reward, some men in Kansi's inner circle approached the U.S. embassy in Karachi with an offer to reveal Kansi's location. Having decided that the information was credible, the CIA approached the Pakistani government. For the Pakistanis, Kansi was a lone wolf. Having no interest in protecting him, the Pakistanis led the raid on a hotel in central Pakistan to which Kansi's bodyguards had pointed. On June 15, 1997, Kansi was taken and flown to the United States.[90]

It had been four years since Kansi had killed the CIA commuters. Since that time, Winston Wiley had kept Kansi's wanted poster on his door. "It was a reminder that we would not stop looking for him." With Kansi finally coming to the United States to face trial, Wiley wanted to see his quarry. "I wanted to see what he looked like." The small, timorous man who was taken off the C-41 in an orange jumpsuit wearing handcuffs and leg-irons was a disappointment. This was no mastermind. "He was a nothing . . . To call him a lone wolf is to insult wolves."[91] The CIA threw a triumphal public event in the auditorium called the bubble to mark this success. After some difficult years in managing the transition from the Cold War to a world of new targets, the agency was prepared for some rejoicing. Following some set speeches, the deputy director of operations, David Cohen, had only three words to add: "Aren't we great!" he said in terms that summed up the exuberance of the group and the moment.[92]

The capture of Kansi, like that of Ramzi Yousef two years earlier, showed that the U.S. government could track down freelance terrorists. So, too, did a series of extensive operations against Al-Gama'a al-Islamiyya in 1996–97. When in January 1996 a federal judge gave Sheikh Rahman a life sentence, Al-Gama'a al-Islamiyya threatened to attack U.S. "interests and people." In the months that followed, the CIA worked closely with the Egyptian government, whose president had been targeted for assassination by Al-Gama'a al-Islamiyya in 1995, to detain key members of that terrorist affiliate of al Qaeda. The U.S. government used its newly honed rendition capabilities to nab Al-Gama'a al-Islamiyya terrorists in Azerbaijan and Albania and hand them over to the Egyptians. The Al-Gama'a al-Islamiyya would launch one more major operation. In November 1997, its terrorists opened fire on European tourists visiting the ancient ruins at Luxor, in central Egypt, killing sixty. But thereafter, the Al-Gama'a al-Islamiyya was considered by the CIA a much diminished organization.[93]

Hidden among the recommendations in the final report of Vice President Gore's aviation security commission, which appeared in February 1997, was a warning that the United States would need its terrorist-tracking skills even more in the future:

> The Federal Bureau of Investigation, the Central Intelligence Agency, and other intelligence sources have been warning that the threat of terrorism is changing in two important ways. First, it is no longer just an overseas threat from foreign terrorists. People and places in the United States have joined the list of targets, and Americans have joined the ranks of terrorists. The bombings of the World Trade Center in New York and the Federal Building in Oklahoma City are clear

examples of the shift, as is the conviction of Ramzi Yousef for attempting to bomb twelve American airliners out of the sky over the Pacific Ocean. The second change is that in addition to well-known, established terrorist groups, it is becoming more common to find terrorists working alone or in ad hoc groups, some of whom are not afraid to die in carrying out their designs.[94]

Ironically, though its report offered this prescient assessment of future threats from suicide terrorists not linked to any state, the Gore commission revealed by its recommendations the limits that still prevented the country from adopting a thoroughgoing domestic antiterrorist strategy. Over the course of its deliberations, the Gore commission had watered down its recommendations for improving airline security. The commission did recommend that security personnel at airports be trained better and paid more and pushed for more bomb-sniffing dogs and technologically advanced imaging equipment for screening bags. But under pressure from the airlines, which had consistently fought a rearguard action against what they considered expensive and unnecessary security upgrades since the late 1960s, the commission decided not to require even more far-reaching changes in airport security. The consultant Brian M. Jenkins, who had been named to the commission, later admitted that there had been pressure from the airlines.[95] Even in this volatile threat environment, domestic security remained the stepchild of counterterrorism. The challenge for the Clinton administration would be to continue improving U.S. counterterrorism abroad while not neglecting defenses at home.

CHAPTER TEN

Clinton Versus
bin Laden

"WHEN I CAME INTO OFFICE, I thought of terrorists as a rogues' gallery with many portraits, none of which stood out from any of the others," said Leon Fuerth, the vice president's chief national security aide.[1] On February 23, 1998, Osama bin Laden ensured that for the remaining three years of Clinton's second term, his portrait would dominate all the others in the terrorist portrait gallery. As head of an alliance of Islamist groups in Egypt, Pakistan, and Bangladesh, he issued a joint declaration of war on the United States, its friends, and its interests. "The ruling to kill Americans and their allies–civilians and military–is an individual duty for every Muslim who can do it in every country in which it is possible to do it." The group said that these measures were designed to eliminate American and allied influence in Saudi Arabia and to remove all Western troops from "all the lands of Islam, defeated, and unable to threaten any Muslim."[2] In August 1996, a London newspaper with Iraqi backing had published a statement from bin Laden in which he vowed to kill the American occupiers of Saudi Arabia.[3] At that time, bin Laden had been toying with the Clinton administration after the Khobar attack. He was not a suspect in the attack, and later evidence suggested that there was no serious link. Iran and its terrorist client Hezbollah were at the time still in a better position than bin Laden to challenge his enemy. By 1998, however, bin Laden was making the challenge himself.

In 1997, the CIA's Alec station had begun work on a plan to capture bin Laden in his new Afghan sanctuary. Probably with the connivance of the Pakistani intelligence service, the ISI, bin Laden had taken up residence in May 1996 near the Pakistani border in the eastern part of the province. By mid-1997, bin Laden had moved south to the area around Kandahar. This was the heartland of the Taliban, the most Islamist of the armed groups fighting over Afghanistan. Although bin Laden and the Taliban leader Mullah Muhammed Omar shared a commitment to hostile political Islam, they had initially eyed each other warily. But after the Taliban took Kabul and installed themselves as the government of the country, an alliance developed. The CIA then turned to the anti-Taliban tribal groups, which they had originally contacted for the rendition of Mir Kansi, to assist in any future operation against bin Laden.[4]

In reaction to bin Laden's 1998 declaration of war, the Clinton administration approved using the Taliban's enemies—which became known by the shorthand of "tribals"—to capture the Saudi terrorist, and a specific plan was drawn up. The preparations were meticulous. After mapping bin Laden's compound at Tarnak Farms, a desert location not far from the airport in Kandahar, in southern Afghanistan, the CIA built a scale replica at a secret site in Florida. Bin Laden was to be grabbed at the compound and taken by the tribals to an airfield used during the Kansi rendition. The CIA rehearsed the operation in the third week of May 1998, and the counterterrorism specialists felt confident that it had a good chance of succeeding. Jeff O'Connell, Winston Wiley's successor at CTC, put the odds at 30 percent. CIA senior management, however, considered those odds overly optimistic. At the NSC, Richard Clarke also doubted that the plan could succeed. Responding to

Clarke's misgivings and those of the CIA's senior managers, George Tenet decided in late May 1998 that the operation was not ready.[5]

May 1998 was a hectic time for the Clinton administration, whose attention was drawn to another issue in South Asia. On May 11, the newly elected Hindu nationalist government in India made good on an election promise and detonated five nuclear devices. The Indian tests set off a confrontation with rival Pakistan. Ignoring a request from Washington to show restraint, Islamabad responded on May 29 with five underground nuclear tests of its own. "I cannot believe," said President Clinton in reaction, "that we are about to start the twenty-first century by having the Indian subcontinent repeat the worst mistakes of the twentieth century."[6] In late May, as the NSC contemplated whether to stage a dramatic rendition of bin Laden from Afghanistan, the administration cautioned India and Pakistan not to come any closer to the nuclear brink. The Pakistanis had not bothered to disguise their final preparations for their nuclear tests from U.S. spy satellites, resulting in a series of calls from the Oval Office to Islamabad offering additional financial assistance if the Pakistanis showed restraint.[7] Now that the Pakistanis had gone ahead, the Nuclear Nonproliferation Act, as amended in 1994, and the Arms Export Control Act of 1994 complicated future U.S. efforts to enlist them in a policy of squeezing the Taliban. These laws mandated that the United States automatically slap sanctions, with no end date, on any nonnuclear state that tested a nuclear device. These sanctions involved curtailing all trade credits, military sales, loans from private sources and international lenders, and loan guarantees to U.S. companies doing business with the offending state.[8] Commenting on this policy, former national security advisor Robert McFarlane said that this was "a nonsensical framework of sanctions . . . offering no incentives for restraint or intellectual solutions to Pakistan's problems."[9] The law left little room for the Clinton administration to maneuver. "I recall meetings where we went down checklists to ensure that we had cut every bilateral tie with Pakistan," says Leon Fuerth.[10] It would be difficult to ask Pakistan to ignore a U.S. military operation in neighboring Afghanistan while the United States was pushing the country to the brink of economic default and ending all military-to-military contacts.[11]

With Pakistan unavailable as a back channel to Kabul, the Clinton administration approached the Saudis in the hope that they could convince the Taliban to expel bin Laden. Saudi Arabia was one of only three countries—Pakistan and the United Arab Emirates being the other two—that recognized the Taliban regime. Crown Prince Abdullah agreed to help and sent the chief of Saudi intelligence to meet Mullah Omar, the head of the Afghan regime. Mullah Omar then promised to hand over bin Laden. It was an empty promise.[12] By this time, bin Laden was reportedly paying the Taliban between ten and twenty million dollars a year in return for providing him sanctuary. Mullah Omar was not about to sacrifice his meal ticket. In September 1998, he would tell the Saudis that he had changed his mind and would not hand over bin Laden.[13]

As these new efforts were taking place, the White House reorganized its counterterrorism bureaucracy. The Counterterrorism Security Group (CSG), which Clarke chaired, received budgetary authority and was given policymaking responsibilities. Presidential Decision Directive-62, which Clinton signed in June 1998, also created the position of national counterterrorism coordinator. Clarke became the first coordinator, and though he was not given the status of a principal—the peer of a cabinet secretary or the national security advisor—he was permitted at the national security advisor's discretion to attend principals' meetings. With National Security Advisor Sandy Berger an ally and friend, Clarke would henceforth attend all principals' meetings where bin Laden or terrorism was discussed. The participants at these highly sensitive terrorism discussions were known as the Small Group.[14]

"We Are at War"

As the United States learned more about al Qaeda, it discovered that bin Laden's network had been targeting the United States for a decade. In 1992, bin Laden's associates had participated in an attempted attack on U.S. Air Force personnel in Yemen. A year later, al Qaeda played a role in the "Black Hawk Down" incident that killed eighteen U.S. soldiers in Mogadishu, Somalia.[15] But for all the fatwas and operational tidbits picked up in the mid-1990s, neither bin Laden nor his associates had ever been known to actually execute a major terrorist incident. If one carried out a rough comparison between the lethality of Hezbollah's attacks on U.S. targets since 1983 and those of al Qaeda, there was no question which terrorist organization represented the greatest threat to U.S. national security.

All of that changed at three o'clock in the morning (EDT) on August 7, 1998, when the White House Situation Room relayed news to Gayle Smith, the new special assistant to the president for Africa, that two huge bombs had gone off within minutes of each other in front of the U.S. embassies in Nairobi, Kenya, and Dar es Salaam, Tanzania. Early casualty reports were vague—ultimately 257 people would be lost in these incidents—but the simultaneity of these attacks indicated that a sophisticated terrorist organization was responsible. As veteran CIA officer Milt Bearden explained at the time, "Two at once is not twice as hard. Two at once is 100 times as hard."[16] Clarke immediately called a five o'clock meeting of the CSG for that morning, where he explained to Smith that the attack bore bin Laden's signature.[17]

A week later, U.S. intelligence formally informed President Clinton that it could prove that bin Laden was behind the attacks. "This one is a slam dunk, Mr. President," Clarke recalls George Tenet saying.[18] Later, in hearings before the 9/11 Commission, Tenet explained the source of his confidence in August 1998: "You did have authority, direction, and control through some means—very, very quickly—and there were named individuals."[19] Al-Fadl had purchased a satellite phone for bin Laden in 1996, and both the National Security Agency and the British, who had tightened counterterrorism cooperation with Washington in the mid-1990s, were able to intercept his calls.[20] On the day of the bombing and the following day, faxes claiming to be from the perpetrators of the crime had arrived at press bureaus in France, Qatar, and the United Arab Emirates. The fax number used had been in recent contact with bin Laden's satellite phone. A few days after the bombing, conspirator Muhhamed Rashed Daoud al-Owali called a telephone number in Yemen to request money. He had been expected to die in the Nairobi bombing but at the last minute had lost his nerve and jumped from the truck. That same day, bin Laden called the same number in Yemen using his satellite phone.[21] From Afghanistan, other intelligence indicated that bin Laden had arranged a meeting for August 20 to discuss the attacks.[22]

Al Qaeda had targeted other U.S. installations that August. In the spring, the United States had successfully persuaded the Albanian government to extradite three members of the Egyptian Islamic Jihad, an al Qaeda affiliate headed by bin Laden's operations chief Ayman al-Zawahiri, to Cairo. In July, al-Zawahiri had vowed revenge, and in mid-August there was dramatic evidence that the U.S. embassy in Tirana would be the next one hit.[23] Some technical information gathered by the CIA at the last minute allowed the Albanian government to arrest an al Qaeda terrorist on August 13 before he was set to blow up the embassy.[24] Equally serious plots to blow up the U.S. embassies in Kampala, Uganda, and Abidjan, Ivory Coast, were subsequently disrupted.[25]

Faced with cascading reports of activity related to bin Laden's networks, Clarke established a Threat Subgroup, chaired by his deputy and populated by desk chiefs from all relevant agencies, to share information and "separate the wheat from the chaff."[26] The goal was similar in concept to the fusion center that Vice President Bush's commission had recommended in 1986. In periods of high threat, the group would meet daily. Meanwhile, the president formally approved the capture operation that had been tabled in May.

The intelligence tip-off to a meeting of bin Laden and his associates on August 20 presented an opportunity for even more dramatic action. On August 14, Tenet and Clarke raised the possibility of killing bin Laden, and they received strong support from National Security Advisor Sandy Berger. With the intelligence very convincing, the president agreed. Clinton then gathered a small group of advisors to approve specific targets, with the idea of inflicting damage to bin Laden's network and possibly killing bin Laden himself. To keep these meetings a secret, Clinton had his secretary of state and the other members of the group keep to their public schedules.[27] The administration selected three terrorist training sites around Khost, south of Kabul, and the al-Shifa pharmaceutical plant near Khartoum, in Sudan.[28] A CIA team had secretly taken soil samples from around the plant and found chemical precursors for the nerve gas VX.[29] Gayle Smith recalls that "the intelligence wasn't 100 percent, but it seemed conclusive . . . If the information on al Shifa had gotten out and the Clinton administration had done nothing, we would never have heard the end of it."[30] Clinton had an unmistakable objective in using these cruise missiles. "I assure you they were not delivering an arrest warrant," recalled Sandy Berger. "The intent was to kill bin Laden."[31]

On August 20, U.S. submarines launched seventy-nine cruise missiles at the four sites in Afghanistan and Sudan. Operation Infinite Reach was the largest U.S. military response to a terrorist attack since the El Dorado raid on Libya in the Reagan administration. For the first time in over a decade, the American people were being told that a terrorist threat required a U.S. military response. "The information now in our possession is convincing," Clinton explained in his weekly radio broadcast taped less than twenty-four hours after the start of U.S. military operations. "Behind these attacks [in East Africa] were the same hands that killed American and Pakistani peacekeepers in Somalia, the same hands that plotted the assassinations of the Pope and President Mubarak of Egypt. I'm referring to the bin Laden network of radical groups, probably the most dangerous nonstate terrorist actor in the world today."[32]

The results of Infinite Reach were just as disappointing as those of El Dorado Canyon. Although the CIA estimated that about thirty al Qaeda members died in the attacks on the Khost region, bin Laden was not among them.[33] Indeed, the CIA was never able to determine whether the original intelligence that had occasioned the attack was correct.[34] In one very important respect, the results were worse for the Clinton administration than El Dorado Canyon had been for Ronald Reagan. This attack was greeted with an unexpected media frenzy that spread doubt about the president's fitness for this new struggle.

Within hours of the attack, there were allegations that the operation had been designed less to punish international terrorists than to distract the American public from the president's personal political problems. Three days before the bombing, President Clinton had testified under oath about his relationship with an intern, Monica Lewinsky. The testimony was the latest chapter in the running inquisition of the Clintons led by special prosecutor Kenneth Starr. Making matters worse, a popular film suggested a strategy behind the president's actions. In December 1997, Hollywood had released *Wag the Dog*, a dark comedy staring Dustin Hoffman and Robert DeNiro about a sex-obsessed president whose advisors concoct a fake war in Albania to distract the voters from a scandal in the midst of a reelection campaign.

While Speaker Gingrich publicly supported the operation, calling it "the right thing to do at the right time," some Republicans in the Senate subtly gave credibility to the *Wag the Dog* explanation. "I just hope and pray," said Senator Dan Coats, of Indiana, "the decision that was made was made on the basis of sound judgment and made for the right reasons, and not made because it was necessary to save the president's job." Senator Arlen Specter used a variation of the old "when did you stop beating your wife" smear to make the same point. "I'm not going to suggest ulterior motives," he said. "I especially want to know the reason for doing it now." Meanwhile, television commentators expressed their doubts even less subtly. When the Sudanese complained that al-Shifa made baby food and not VX, it only fed public skepticism of the attack.[35]

The president's real and alleged personal indiscretions had accelerated a trivialization of news begun with the end of the Cold War and the Gulf War. These two great historical events had spawned twenty-four-hour news coverage, which, coupled with the popularization of cable television and the Internet, reduced the daily news cycle from hours to minutes. Information, however banal, was needed to fill these cycles.

Although the public response to the missile strikes would make the Clinton administration extremely reluctant to attempt a second strike, the planning against bin Laden did not stop. Clarke offered his "Political-Military Plan *Delenda*" to National Security Advisor Berger. Delenda, an homage to the Roman Empire's commitment to destroying Carthage (*Carthago delenda* is Latin for "Carthage must be destroyed"), was a multilevel plan for neutralizing the "bin Laden network," using covert action, diplomacy, and a sustained bombing campaign of associated sites in Afghanistan.[36]

When information was received placing bin Laden in a particular home on the night of December 20, 1998, the Clinton White House organized for a decision. The outcome, however, was a "no go." The Pentagon needed six hours between receiving a presidential order and the cruise missiles reaching their target.[37] In this particular case, the U.S. military concluded that there was not enough time: bin Laden had probably already left the target area.[38] Meanwhile, the administration considered covert action employing its tribal allies. On December 24, 1998, the president signed a memorandum of notification, a document that provided specific authority to the CIA to engage in covert action, which allowed the tribals to kill bin Laden if a capture proved impossible.[39] The message sent to the rebels was simple: "From the American president down to the average man in the street, we want him [bin Laden] stopped."[40]

A few weeks earlier, George Tenet had tried to rally all U.S. intelligence agencies around this new mission. "We are at war. I want no resources or people spared in this effort, either inside CIA or the Community."[41] Clarke agreed with this dramatic assessment of the challenge facing the U.S. government. He hoped for the same commitment from the Pentagon. Although they were less familiar with the terrain, U.S. special forces were better trained for a capture mission than the Afghan rebels. But the generals, especially the chairman of the Joint Chiefs of Staff, H. Hugh Shelton, were reluctant to risk the Delta Force on this desert mission. Memories of the failed hostage rescue in Iran in 1980 acted as a deterrent. Strongly seconded by Michael Sheehan, the State Department's coordinator for counterterrorism and a former Green Beret, Clarke would expend a lot of energy in the coming months trying to persuade the Pentagon that this was a war in which risks had to be taken.[42]

The August missile attacks rendered the Khost training facilities unusable, forcing Bin Laden to open a new one some months later. But like Reagan's assault on Libya, the attacks had no deterrent effect on America's enemy. Bin Laden continued to receive proposals for new attacks against U.S. targets from international jihadists and was as interested in them as ever. Indeed, the failed attack probably intensified his hunger for violence. Some time after Operation Infinite Reach, a group came to bin Laden with the idea of blowing up a U.S. destroyer, the USS *Sullivans*, as it refueled in the Yemeni port of Aden. Ultimately, the operation against the USS *Sullivans* would fail in January 2000, but bin Laden liked the concept, and al Qaeda would later try again to hit a U.S. destroyer in the port of Aden.[43]

From another terror entrepreneur came an even more audacious proposal that would involve an attack on U.S. soil. The idea for what would become the "Planes Operation" had come from Khalid Sheikh Mohammed. Mohammed, who was captured in Pakistan in March 2003, would later tell U.S. interrogators that as early as 1996 he had begun thinking that old-fashioned terrorist tactics made no sense in international jihad. Mohammed was at that time an unaffiliated international jihadist, who had helped finance his nephew Ramzi Yousef's 1993 World Trade Center and 1995 Bojinka plots. He brought this new idea to bin Laden in 1998 in the hope that al Qaeda would provide men and cash so that under his supervision the operation could come to fruition. Perhaps waiting for proof that Mohammed could be trusted, bin Laden took a few months to agree. Then he suggested a group of four jihadists, two Saudis and two Yemenis, to fly the planes.[44]

Bin Laden's planning remained hidden from Washington. The U.S. government had no human spy close enough to him to report on these conversations about future terrorist attacks. By late 1998, technical means were also no longer as useful a source as they had been in providing information on al Qaeda's operations. A leak in the *Washington Times* just after the East Africa bombings had alerted bin Laden to the vulnerability of his satellite phone. Since then, he had stopped using it, depriving Washington of a useful way of monitoring his activities. "This was a big deal," recalls a senior counterterrorism expert. There was still signals intelligence. The National Security Agency intercepted calls made by Islamist agents on GSM (global services for mobile) cell phones. The location of a GSM cell phone cannot be pinpointed, something known to al Qaeda. Bin Laden's agents would routinely flip from cell phone to cell phone, not only thereby complicating interception, but also requiring additional warrants for listening in when the individual was a U.S. citizen. The agents also talked in a code that U.S. eavesdroppers were still trying to learn. "We lacked the Capt'n Crunch decoder ring," says an official who read these intercepts. The al Qaeda operatives would talk about watermelons and a wedding party. Only later would U.S. intelligence figure out that "wedding party" meant "an attack."[45]

As bin Laden was working out the details of the Planes Operation and the attack on the USS *Sullivans* with Mohammed and others, the Clinton administration was on the verge of launching another missile strike on bin Laden's new headquarters.[46] "The TLAMS [cruise missiles] were twirling in their tubes" a few more times that year. In each case, the intelligence was not strong enough to ensure good odds of hitting bin Laden. Collateral damage was expected, but if al Qaeda were decapitated, then the operation could be explained to a skeptical American public as a success.

It was the assessment of the 9/11 Commission that the best opportunity to strike at bin Laden with cruise missiles came in May 1999. Spies in Afghanistan reported bin Laden's movements over a period of five days. Staff officers at the CIA and the Pentagon later recalled the intelligence being as good as one could expect. It was, in a word, "actionable." Nevertheless, at the time, George Tenet was not satisfied with it and refused to recommend an attack. In the Clinton White House, if the DCI opposed an attack, it did not happen. In his public and private testimony, Tenet could not recall the reasons for his caution in 1999.[47]

The Plan

In the six months since the East African bombings, the Clinton administration came to the conclusion that under present circumstances the military option for dealing with bin Laden was not viable. The administration then went on a diplomatic offensive to deny bin Laden his Afghan sanctuary. In July 1999, the U.S. imposed sanctions on the Taliban and worked hard to convince its allies to pressure the Taliban to turn over Osama bin Laden. As a result, the UN Security Council "strongly" condemned the Afghan government for sheltering terrorists and, in an unprecedented move, named Osama bin Laden and called on the Taliban to expel him.[48] The counterterrorism community in Washington—the planners and policymakers in the CSG and the intelligence collectors and operators at the CIA—looked for ways to improve the chances of a successful military strike if he could not be dislodged from Afghanistan. The intelligence on bin Laden's daily activities had to improve. Information from the tribals was almost impossible to verify, and it was not always fresh. And a way had to be found to shorten the period between the acquisition of targeting information and U.S. military action against bin Laden.

At the CIA, George Tenet concentrated on intelligence collection. Following India's nuclear tests in May 1998, Tenet had impaneled a special investigative committee under retired admiral David Jeremiah to investigate how the Indians had managed to surprise the U.S. intelligence community. Delhi had run a sophisticated deception operation, but Tenet understood that U.S. intelligence shared some of the blame for not seeing through it. Among Jeremiah's conclusions, which he delivered to the CIA director in early June, was that the community needed more spies, or in the jargon, human intelligence. "Our human intelligence capacity," he contended, "is seriously limited."[49] The admiral criticized senior management at the CIA for not taking enough risks to secure better intelligence. Courage was something that Jeremiah also expected to see more of from intelligence analysts. Before the tests, no one had seriously challenged the conventional wisdom that the Indians would not risk the political consequences of a nuclear test. Now he recommended that analysts be exposed to more contrarian views and that the neat compartments, or stovepipes, that channeled specific kinds of intelligence from the collector to the policymaker be broken down to permit more all-source studies and critiques. Although the Jeremiah report was in response to a different intelligence failure, Tenet took the first recommendation to heart in thinking about how to avoid additional surprises like the East African bombings from bin Laden.

"Intelligence collection is the necessary prerequisite to any actions we could take to try to eliminate the terrorist threat posed by bin Laden and his al-Qaeda organization," Tenet reported to the 9/11 Commission six years later. In the spring of 1999, the CTC developed a strategy for acquiring the intelligence to capture bin Laden. Called simply The Plan, its prime objective was "to acquire intelligence about bin Laden by penetrating his organization. Without this effort, the United States could not mount a successful covert action program to stop him or his operations." In addition to looking at ways that the agency could expand its technical collection within Afghanistan, the CIA launched an aggressive recruitment program in the United States to find the people with the temperament, intelligence, and language skills to go out into the Third World and cultivate agents.[50] The CIA already had human sources reporting on bin Laden, but it needed more, and they had to be closer to him.

Meanwhile, in 1999 at the NSC, Clarke's team was looking for ways to launch quicker military strikes against bin Laden. The weakened relationship with Pakistan and the absence of close relations with neighboring Turkmenistan, Uzbekistan, and Tajikistan meant that a U.S. commando attack would have to be flown in from long distances, increasing the risks and again lengthening reaction time.

Despite this activity, one very important assumption about the nature of the threat and what to do about it remained largely unexamined. Faced with accumulating information since 1996 that bin Laden was seeking to acquire weapons of mass destruction, no one asked whether he might look for another way to kill large numbers of Americans. The counterterrorism community associated the threat of a mass casualty event with the use of weapons of mass destruction (WMD): chemical, biological, or nuclear weapons. Given the assumption that even al Qaeda was a number of years away from acquiring a significant WMD capability—despite bin Laden's best efforts—the community did not assume that a very bloody attack in the territorial United States was imminent. Instead, the U.S. government, at least, scrambled to fix urgent security lapses at its installations abroad.[51] Caught up in the daily grind of finding creative solutions to the tactical problems of fighting a global network—what one Clarke aide described as "drinking from a fire hose"—the group never took the time to rethink its strategic assumptions.[52] Clarke's Delenda and the CIA's Plan, admirable though they were, only reinforced this conventional wisdom. Meanwhile, the agencies with domestic jurisdictions drank from the same source. Neither the Justice Department, which had responsibility for both the FBI and the Immigration and Naturalization Service, nor the White House undertook any examination of domestic antiterrorism defenses in 1998–99.[53] After seeing its antiterrorism package watered down in 1996, the administration apparently had no stomach to fight with the Republican-controlled House over this again. Events in late 1999 would soon challenge this conventional wisdom, without, however, overturning it.

The Millennium Plots

In 1987, FBI director William Webster had emphasized four reasons why the U.S. homeland had been largely immune from a terrorist attack, including distance and the fact that American installations overseas were easier targets.[54] As the century was about to turn, U.S. intelligence was no longer as confident. Serious high-level concern about a "millennium attack" on the United States began with an intercepted telephone call in Jordan. On November 30, 1999, Abu Zubaydah, who would later lead a resistance organization in Iraq, called a Palestinian terrorist and said, "The time for training is over." Acting on this tip, the Jordanian arrested the Palestinian and fifteen others.[55] Zubaydah's group had been preparing to blow up several tourist sites in Jordan.

George Tenet was convinced that more terrorist attacks were coming. The CIA warned the administration to expect "between five and fifteen terrorist attacks against American interests both here and overseas." Tenet entered into discussions with the heads of twenty foreign intelligence services to mount a worldwide effort to prevent these terrorist attacks. Thirty-six terrorists were identified, of whom twenty-one were neutralized, either through arrest and rendition, detainment in the foreign country, or blanket surveillance. These U.S. disruption operations occurred in eight countries on four continents.[56]

Two weeks later, on December 14, an alert customs official asked a suspiciously nervous Arab man entering the United States at Port Angeles, Washington, after driving off a ferry from Victoria, British Columbia, to step out of his car. Thirty-two-year-old Ahmed Ressam panicked and ran from his car. In the trunk, U.S. customs agents found explosives. Ressam was an Algerian extremist who had resided illegally in Montreal. Although not formally a member of al Qaeda, he had trained for jihad in Afghanistan and had met Abu Zubaydah. He now wanted to do his part in the crusade by exploding a large car bomb at Los Angeles International Airport. The Clinton White House only later learned that his target was in Los Angeles. In December 1999 it was assumed to have been Seattle.[57]

Clinton was very engaged in the process. He read the intelligence that was sent to him and asked for more. The system for informing the president was imperfect. At times, the CIA would share with Clinton terrifying tidbits that had already been checked out and discarded by the twenty-four-hour fusion center established by Clarke's team at the NSC.[58] A few unnecessary scares took place in the Oval Office because of this. But at least none of the counterterrorism specialists doubted that they had the president's attention.

On December 8, a week before Ressam was picked up, Clinton's foreign policy team had instructed Clarke's team to prepare plans to frustrate bin Laden's plots. Chaired by Sandy Berger, the Small Group continued to follow up this intelligence and provided policy

guidance on a daily basis to the president. Concerned that bin
Laden might have chemical or biological weapons, all U.S. embassies received quantities of Cipro—an antidote to anthrax poison-
ing—and the department started the bureaucratic process of
procuring masks for all diplomats.[59]

Once the millennium had passed without incident, the daily meetings on the threat, at the principals level and the deputies level, became less frequent, though the concern of another bin Laden attack
did not end. Seeing this experience as an opportunity to improve
U.S. security in a more permanent way, Richard Clarke had his
deputies produce an after-action report that listed the lessons of the
"Millennium Plot" scare and provided recommendations. The
Ressam story had illustrated the importance of involving the Canadians and, by extension, the Mexicans in any effort to tighten U.S.
borders. Clarke visited Ottawa in the winter of 2000 to discuss better coordination in counterterrorism with Canadian officials. As a result, one of the recommendations developed by his team was that all
of North America be viewed as a common counterterrorism zone.[60]

In March, Clinton's foreign policy team accepted all of Richard
Clarke's twenty-nine proposals for improving domestic security. Besides the initiative to create a North American common zone, these
included a program to observe whether foreign students enrolled in
humanities courses might be surreptitiously studying nuclear
physics, another to increase the number of Arabic translators at the
FBI so that the bureau would have real-time access to intercepts of
suspect conversations, and a third to facilitate the use of classified information in immigration cases and new staffing requirements that
put more immigration agents at the FBI-led Joint Terrorism Task
Forces (JTTF). Clarke wanted there to be a JTTF at each of the
FBI's fifty-six offices. Reflecting the overwhelming concern about
WMD, the proposals also included special detectors at border crossings to track any movements of these special weapons into the country and having people at those crossings at all times. If implemented,

these proposals would have raised the country's antiterrorism system to an unprecedented level.[61]

The public learned about some of these measures two months later. Clinton used a speech to the class of 2000 at the Coast Guard Academy to unveil this new program. "In responding to terrorist threats, our own strategy should be identical to your motto: *Semper paratus*–always be ready." To raise the level of readiness, the Clinton administration requested $9 billion for counterterrorism funding in the 2001 budget, an increase of 40 percent over three years. At the Coast Guard Academy, Clinton announced the request for another $300 million "to fund critical programs to protect our citizens from terrorists, to expand our intelligence efforts, to improve our ability to use forensic evidence, to track terrorists, to enhance our coordination with state and local officials, as we did over New Year's to protect our nation against possible attacks."[62]

Before a group of reporters a week before the Coast Guard Academy speech, the president had reiterated his hope that Osama bin Laden would be captured.[63] In private, Clinton's frustration was growing at the inability of either the CIA or the Pentagon to provide him with realistic options to eliminate bin Laden and the leadership of Al Qaeda. "You know," the president said to the chairman of the Joint Chiefs of Staff, General Hugh Shelton, "it would scare the shit out of al Qaeda if suddenly a bunch of black ninjas rappelled out of helicopters into the middle of their camp."[64]

The essential problem remained the lack of precise intelligence on Bin Laden's location. The CIA reported up to a 50 percent increase in the number of its spies "operating against the terrorism target" and a similar increase in reports specifically on bin Laden and al Qaeda.[65] But this was still not enough to give the administration what it wanted. The problem was finding him. In the spring of 2000, a joint CIA-Pentagon project, code-named Afghan Eyes, began a search for an overhead capability that could provide real-time streaming images of the Afghan countryside. By the end of June,

Berger's Small Group blessed the project, which involved deploying an unmanned drone called the Predator. The first Predator flew over Afghanistan on September 7, 2000.

A little over a month after the Predator had taken the hunt for Bin Laden to a new level of technology, the master terrorist provided the Clinton administration with yet another reason to stop him. At midday on October 12, 2000, the USS *Cole,* a destroyer that formed part of the force deployed for a potential missile strike against al Qaeda, was attacked in Yemen's Aden harbor. While the ship was being guided to its moorings by local craft, a small boat darted from the shore laden with C-4 explosives. On approaching the vessel, the crew of two stood up and bowed as they detonated the explosive device. The explosion blew a sixty-by-eighty-foot hole in the side of the destroyer, killing seventeen sailors in the engine room and mess, where lunch was being served. Only good luck prevented the bomb from igniting the ordnance only yards from the engine room. As the Department of Defense's internal investigation of the attack later concluded, al Qaeda had found a "seam in the fabric of efforts to protect our forces." Since the 1996 attack on Khobar Towers, the U.S. military had beefed up security at its installations. No similar effort had been made to protect forces in transit.[66]

Initial reports described the event as an accident, but within hours, the Middle East and counterterrorism experts in the NSC had no doubt it was the work of bin Laden.[67] The president and his closest aides were less sure or at the very least wanted better evidence before publicly accusing bin Laden. In the words of Clarke's deputy, Roger Cressey, they wanted proof that "the mothership had ordered the attack."[68] In August 1998, the U.S. intelligence community had been able to hand the president an intercepted message from bin Laden's satellite telephone that linked him to the tragedy. This time, there wasn't any similar intelligence. "Although we consumed every bit of intelligence we had," recalled Secretary of State Madeleine Albright, "we never had a comparable break again."[69] Once again, bin Laden did not take credit for the blast. He had made it part of the code of al Qaeda not to claim responsibility for an attack. "By claiming credit," he had explained to CNN's Peter Arnett in May 1997, "we were told that the group will earn the wrath of the target state . . . Why claim credit and become identified and then hunted down?"[70] Meanwhile, the Yemeni government, reflecting its complicated relationship with bin Laden, insisted that an accident had caused the explosion.

In a public statement from the White House Rose Garden on the afternoon of October 12, the president made clear that international terrorism had struck again but did not hint at any prime suspect. "If, as it now appears, this was an act of terrorism, it was a despicable and cowardly act. We will find out who was responsible and hold them accountable."[71]

Washington immediately applied diplomatic pressure on the Yemeni government to help with the investigation, and within days, there was limited cooperation.[72] By mid-November, increasingly strong evidence reached Washington that seemed to confirm a link to al Qaeda. The Yemenis had arrested two men, Jamal al Badawi and Fahd al Quso, who admitted under interrogation that they were local representatives of al Qaeda.[73]

On November 11 and again two weeks later, Berger and the counterterrorism coordinator, Richard Clarke, briefed Clinton that it looked as if al Qaeda was behind the attack on the *Cole*. Neither the FBI nor the CIA, which were cooperating on the investigation, was prepared to conclude definitively that al Qaeda was behind the attack. At the end of December a highly classified slide presentation prepared by the CIA for Berger's Small Group featured the conclusion that the agency had "no definitive answer on [the] crucial question of outside direction of the attack—how and by whom."[74] Part of the problem was that the Yemenis refused to allow U.S. investigators to witness the interrogations of Badawi and Quso and would not turn over any relevant telephone logs, so that everything the U.S. received was secondhand.

The two detainees did, however, provide the first evidence of a link between the local al Qaeda organization and bin Laden. They identified a man they knew as "Khallad" as the individual from whom they had received operational guidance. Khallad was actually Tawfiq bin Attash, who had already come to the attention of U.S. intelligence. An important al Qaeda source, run jointly by the FBI and the CIA, reported that "Khallad" was bin Laden's "run boy."[75] In December 2000, this source identified "Khallad" from a picture supplied by the Yemenis.

Still sensitive to the unwarranted criticism of his *Wag the Dog* attacks in 1998, President Clinton told his advisors that this evidence was not strong enough justification for launching a second attack on bin Laden in Afghanistan. The president felt he needed evidence that could stand up in the court of public opinion.[76] In his 2004 memoirs, Clinton insists that he established this standard because the options he was given were only for a major military operation, "a large-scale bombing campaign against all suspected al Qaeda campsites or a sizable invasion." Clinton wrote that he almost approved a missile strike in October against bin Laden but backed down when the CIA recommended at the last minute that the intelligence on his location was unreliable.[77] His counterterrorism experts in the National Security Council cannot recall this mission.[78]

Secretary of State Madeleine Albright and Defense Secretary William Cohen appealed to the president's caution. Albright, who had argued for the U.S. intervention in the Balkans, did not argue out of any discomfort over using force in international relations. Her concerns were tied to the ongoing Middle East peace process, which had just taken a turn for the worse following Ariel Sharon's visit to the Temple Mount in September 2000. She worried that a bombing campaign against Afghanistan that was not founded on solid evidence of bin Laden's complicity would further inflame Arab public opinion. What the CIA and FBI provided did not even convince the secretary of state of a link between the al Qaeda organization and the *Cole* attack. Cohen's concerns apparently reflected some anxiety that an attack would undermine the regime in Pakistan, which had recently expanded its cooperation with Washington.[79]

The unwillingness of key policymakers to exploit the *Cole* incident to prepare another attack on bin Laden frustrated the counterterrorism and regional specialists at the NSC. Badawi and Quso had admitted being members of al Qaeda, even if the actual order for the attack could not be definitively traced back to Afghanistan. At the deputies level there were theories to explain this reluctance. Some believed that because the Middle East peace process was in high gear—President Clinton had personally intervened to bring about an agreement between Yasir Arafat and the new Israeli prime minister, Ehud Barak—there was reluctance to attack another Islamic country. In case the administration changed its mind, Clarke and his team developed a political-military plan for a strike on twelve targets in Afghanistan, all linked to al Qaeda command, control, or training.[80] The strikes would probably not kill bin Laden. The problem of getting good enough intelligence to locate bin Laden in time for a missile strike remained, and there was still reluctance on the part of the CIA and the military to send special forces teams into Afghanistan. The one option that was not discussed was invading Afghanistan, taking bin Laden, and toppling the Taliban.[81] That option had not been on the table even after the embassy bombings in 1998 or during the millennium scare of 1999, and certainly was not a viable consideration in the election year of 2000. In any case, none of the military options against al Qaeda were seriously considered in the final months of the Clinton administration.

Disliking his options and still wary of the value of the intelligence from Yemen, the president was very careful in public not to pin the blame on bin Laden for the attack on the *Cole*. In one of his last interviews before leaving office, Clinton left the issue to the incoming administration. "I do believe he was behind some other attacks on our people and that people affiliated with him have been involved in other attacks. But we're investigating this. We're still running down some of the leads . . . I think we will know . . . I have absolutely no doubt that President-elect Bush will continue to pursue the investigation and, when the evidence is in, will take appropriate action. And when that happens, I will support him in doing so."[82]

The clock ran out on the Clinton administration before the president could order a second military response against al Qaeda and its Afghan hosts, the Taliban. Despite this lack of military activity, the *Cole* incident stimulated discussion about U.S. vulnerability to this new wave of terrorism. Embedded in its report to Defense Secretary Cohen, the USS *Cole* Commission concluded that combating terrorism was "so important" that it required "complete unity of effort at the level of the Office of the Secretary of Defense," which the commission believed would be best achieved by creating a new position at the assistant secretary level to work the terrorism problem.[83]

In the last weeks of the administration, al Qaeda itself provided yet one more stimulus to action. In November and December 2000 a serious threat surge coincided with the Islamic holiday of Ramadan. The United States and its allies subsequently detected and broke up cells preparing attacks against targets in the Persian Gulf, which included U.S. installations.[84]

Although the U.S. government appeared to have handled the Ramadan threats as successfully as the millennium plots, the counterterrorism community knew that it could do better. The CIA's Counterterrorist Center developed ideas about ways to make the country stronger. Much as Bill Casey had warned Ronald Reagan fifteen years earlier when the problem had been Iranian-sponsored Hezbollah in Lebanon, the CTC cautioned that there was no "silver bullet" to solve the country's principal terrorist problem. Instead, the CTC recommended focusing on the problem of denying bin Laden his Afghan sanctuary. Eliminating their safe havens had been an important part of the success against the Abu Nidal Organization and Carlos the Jackal in the late 1980s and early 1990s. Although it may not have been thinking about those old cases, the CTC suggested more vigorous covert action in Afghanistan to squeeze the Taliban and provoke Kabul to deploy the Arab Afghans in battles against a U.S.-sponsored opposition. Its recommendations were contained in what became known as the "Blue Sky" memo, which appears not to have reached the president or Sandy Berger. [85] These recommendations were left for the next administration.

Richard Clarke also worked on some recommendations in December 2000.[86] The Florida recount was over, and George W. Bush had won the closest U.S. presidential election in history. With a changing of the guard at the NSC likely, Clarke wanted to summarize what had been achieved in the struggle against bin Laden and what more needed to be done.

Clarke justifiably felt some pride at what the U.S. counterterrorism community had been able to do about bin Laden. By 1996, the U.S. government had identified the new wave of non-government-sponsored terrorism, singling out bin Laden as its most virulent practitioner and indicting him for murder following the East Africa bombings. Within the CIA and the FBI there were units dedicated to the chase, and next to collection of intelligence for supporting military operations, U.S. spies spent most of their energy seeking information on al Qaeda. The United States had coordinated international pressure for his expulsion from the sanctuary that allowed him to continue his deadly planning. In a joint effort, the CIA and the military were developing an unmanned vehicle that could spot and then kill this man. A still classified number of al Qaeda plots had been disrupted overseas.

Yet Clarke believed that more not only could be done but had to be done. He recalled the Abu Nidal case as a great U.S. counterterrorism success. For Clarke this achievement could be repeated against al Qaeda. The organization might not be completely eliminated—its chief might remain at large as Abu Nidal had—but it would no longer have any significant offensive capability. Having in mind the timetable of that old operation, Clarke suggested three to five years as the time frame for achieving this goal.

In retrospect, the memory of the Abu Nidal case also had a limiting effect on Clarke's imagination. Although he had seen evidence that bin Laden was seeking weapons of mass destruction, evidently to kill lots of Americans, Clarke estimated the likely lethality of an al Qaeda attack in the short term at no greater than the worst terrorism of the 1980s.

These intellectual blinders also affected how he considered the threat to domestic U.S. targets. Clarke explained in his December 2000 strategy memorandum that al Qaeda maintained a presence in the United States and cited evidence of al Qaeda involvement in the Manhattan plots involving Sheikh Rahman. Yet he did not predict any imminent attacks here and did not argue for domestic antiterrorism agencies to maintain a degree of high alert. What he wanted was additional funding to ensure that "bin Laden's organizational presence in the United States will . . . be uncovered fully." It was as if he was looking for more bankers like the ANO's Zein al-Abdeen Hassan Isa and not bin Laden's suicide hijackers.

For all of its success in detecting the new jihadism and identifying bin Laden, the Clinton administration had not been able to figure out bin Laden's operational methods. It did not understand that he would not wait to acquire sarin gas or biological weapons to attempt a spectacular attack. Lacking any evidence of the "Planes Operation," the U.S. intelligence community also assumed that bin Laden's next big attack would most likely occur abroad.

The inability of counterterrorism specialists to imagine a near-term attack on U.S. soil was not the only reason for lack of domestic preparedness as the Clinton administration came to an end. Since 1998, the president had chosen to fight his duel with bin Laden almost entirely in secrecy. Despite the occasional presidential reference to trying to bring bin Laden to trial, the public had no idea of the trigger mechanism that the administration had built to destroy this man if it could find him.

It was a curious misstep by Clinton, who was otherwise so sensitive to the need to enlist the public in a national initiative. In 1998, for example, he had rallied a reluctant public behind an interventionist policy in Kosovo. Was it the country's almost sarcastic reaction to the retaliatory strikes against bin Laden in the summer of 1998 that caused his reluctance in this instance? Clinton did refer to terrorism in later speeches, but his administration did not attempt any sustained public education on the issue. Whatever the reason, as Clinton left office, the public had little understanding of the stakes in fighting this new terrorist phenomenon. When in the hard-fought presidential campaign of 2000 neither George W. Bush nor Clinton's vice president, Al Gore, cited counterterrorism as a priority of the next administration, the public accepted this omission. Too ill-prepared by their leaders, the American people did not ask, "What about bin Laden?"

There was less reason for the air of complacency that had settled over the U.S. Congress in 2000. The House and Senate leadership were kept informed of the hunt for bin Laden and the administration's concerns about al Qaeda. Yet they, too, seemed to view bin Laden as a faraway threat.

As a result, George W. Bush would come to power without any public or congressional pressure to do something about Osama bin Laden and al Qaeda. The incoming administration could, if it wished, turn its gaze.

CHAPTER ELEVEN

George W. Bush and bin Laden

ON PAPER, OSAMA BIN LADEN had much to fear from the incoming administration. George W. Bush's team included several veterans of the most successful period in U.S. counterterrorism. The new secretary of state, Colin Powell, had been national security advisor during the campaigns against Abu Nidal and the Shining Path's Abimael Guzman. Dick Cheney, the incoming vice president, had been defense secretary in the first Bush government, and below these men were veterans of the Reagan war on terrorism Eliott Abrams and Paul Wolfowitz.

The new president also chose to keep the Clinton counterterrorism team in place. Richard Clarke remained as the National Security Council's counterterrorism expert; George Tenet stayed as CIA director. Louis Freeh's term as FBI director had been mandated by Congress to last ten years. He would be staying anyway.

Five days after Bush's inauguration, Richard Clarke recommended to his new boss, national security advisor Condoleezza Rice, that the administration not waste any time in taking up the issue of what to do next about bin Laden. "We *urgently* need such a Principals level review on the al Qida network," he wrote on January

25, 2001.[1] In earlier briefings Clarke had warned Rice that al Qaeda was "not some narrow, little terrorist issue that needs to be included in broader regional policy." Instead, al Qaeda was a transnational threat that should drive policies across a number of regions.

Clarke raised two decisions deferred by the Clinton administration that now seemed to require a quick presidential decision. Would the United States provide additional assistance to the Northern Alliance that was fighting the Taliban and its al Qaeda allies in Afghanistan? Fearing that the Northern Alliance would collapse as a viable force without this help, Clarke argued for a decision before fighting resumed after the winter thaw. Afghanistan's neighbor Uzbekistan also faced a challenge from jihadists and was already receiving U.S. assistance, and while the Clinton administration had considered giving it more, it had left office without doing so.

Less urgent but equally important were three additional matters highlighted by Clarke. He wanted the Bush team to reconsider U.S. options in regard to both Pakistan and the Taliban. The Clinton administration's efforts to coax the Pakistanis and threaten the Taliban to shut down bin Laden's sanctuary had clearly failed, and the effort to shut down al Qaeda's headquarters had stalled. Clarke also wanted the new administration to consider increasing the CIA's counterterrorism budget and funding an expansion of the State Department's assistance program for foreign counterterrorism efforts. Finally, Clarke raised the issue of responding to the attack on the USS *Cole*.

In trying to persuade the new foreign policy team to take al Qaeda seriously, Clarke emphasized bin Laden's efforts to "drive the U.S. out of the Muslim world" and "to replace moderate, modern, Western regime[s] in Muslim countries with theocracies modeled along the lines of the Taliban."[2] Despite his experience in handling the millennium plots in 1999, Clarke did not mention any imminent domestic threat. In January 2001, al Qaeda's potential to reach inside the United States was not uppermost in Clarke's mind.

Although he forwarded to Rice a memorandum written in late 2000 on al Qaeda that concluded that the organization was "present in the United States" and was "attempting to develop or acquire chemical or radiological weapons," Clarke chose not to highlight either point in his appeal for President George W. Bush's attention.[3] Consistent with how he viewed the problem at that moment, Clarke also did not stress what the new administration might do to strengthen U.S. antiterrorism capabilities. The twenty-nine domestic security recommendations approved in principle by the Clinton NSC in 2000 had not been included in any documents turned over to the Bush transition team, and Clarke did not use his first formal memorandum on al Qaeda to raise them with Rice.[4]

What Clarke did share with Rice in January 2001 was the multiyear program he had designed in consultation with the CIA in late 2000 for dealing with al Qaeda. The goal was "to roll back the al Qida network to a point where it no longer pose[s] a serious threat to the U.S. or its interests, as was done previously to robust terrorist groups such as the Abu Nidal Organization and the Japanese Red Army." Although al Qaeda was a serious threat, the CIA and Clarke still believed that a three-to-five-year time frame for achieving this goal was acceptable. But they needed more money. At current levels of funding, U.S. countermeasures against al Qaeda "will prevent some attacks but will not seriously attrit their ability to plan and conduct attacks."[5]

Rice did not react to the January 2001 memorandum and attachments as Clarke had hoped. No meeting of the president and his top advisors was arranged to discuss al Qaeda. Instead, the Bush national security council demoted the hunt for bin Laden from the level of the principals to that of the deputies. In a return to the structure of the George H. W. Bush administration, Condoleezza Rice decided to have the interagency counterterrorism group report to the deputies committee, as the CSG had done in the early 1990s. Clarke had earlier relied on a close relationship with Clinton's national security advisor, Sandy Berger, to bring him into the inner decision-making circle. With Berger gone, Clarke reverted to being just another NSC senior director, which in the highly feudal world of the federal government meant that he was not even on the level of the deputies of other departments.

In part, the new team's handling of Richard Clarke reflected a change in style. The Bush administration wanted to restore some order to the messiness of U.S. foreign policy. Even Clinton loyalists conceded that the former president had been a kind of enfant terrible, fascinated and fascinating in policy discussions. Self-confident and curious, Bill Clinton wanted a great deal of input before making a decision. This contributed to a flexible decision-making system, but also one in which important things fell through large cracks. John F. Kennedy had run the same kind of ship with similar results. Often, policies were not fully staffed. In "Washington speak," it meant that not all of the departments knew their responsibilities and were on board to do what was necessary to implement the president's wishes. At the height of the Cuban missile crisis, President Kennedy expressed surprise that a missile system that he had wanted removed from Turkey in 1961 was still there in October 1962.

The downplaying of counterterrorism also reflected a change in substance. Unpersuaded that the problem was imminent and the threat urgent, Condoleezza Rice consigned the question of what to do next about al Qaeda to a slow interagency process. The Bush team linked Osama bin Laden to the general problem of U.S. interests in South Asia. Any intensification of covert action against the Taliban was put on hold pending a review of U.S. policy toward Afghanistan.[6] The president sent mixed signals on how he wished this review to turn out. On the one hand, he had little patience for the options available to his predecessor. In what would become a famous phrase, the president said that he "was tired of swatting flies." Others in his administration reinforced this prejudice against isolated missile strikes in retaliation for terrorist acts, the games of "tit-for-tat." Yet this impatience did not breed any sense of urgency. In the first months of 2001, Bush watched as his national security team suspended action on new covert measures to assist the Northern Alliance in Afghanistan.

Unlike the widespread impression of a laissez-faire "Dubya," the new president was not passive in foreign policy. It was just that his priorities were elsewhere. His team saw China, nuclear proliferation, and the faltering peace process in the Middle East as greater concerns than terrorism. Some foreign policy issues were fast-tracked by the new administration; the new terrorism in South Asia was just not one of them.

One foreign policy matter stood out from all others. Described as "the keystone of the administration's foreign policy," ballistic missile defense absorbed more of the Bush foreign policy team's attention than any other issue in the first half of 2001.[7] Since March 1983, when Ronald Reagan first spoke publicly of his long-held desire to use technology to put the nuclear genie back into its bottle, the dream of building a defense shield that could prevent enemy ballistic missiles from reaching the United States became a cherished plank in the Republican Party's platform. Ironically, the Anti-Ballistic Missile (ABM) Treaty of 1972 with the Soviet Union, which restricted U.S. development of an antiballistic system, had been negotiated by another Republican president, Richard Nixon.

The issue did not did go away with the disappearance of the Soviet Union. Polls consistently showed that the U.S. public believed that an antimissile shield already existed, a fact that made opposition to technology that might enhance it seem illogical. In the 1990s, a group within the Republican Party seized upon this public misunderstanding and used Congress to revive missile defense as an important national security issue. In the spring of 1999, both the Senate and the House passed measures by huge majorities calling for the U.S. to deploy a missile shield as soon as possible. As evidence of how popular this national security issue had become, the margin was ninety-seven to three in the Democratic-controlled Senate.

Clinton did not see the issue as purely a matter of domestic politics. In August 1998, the North Koreans tested a missile to put a satellite into orbit. Forty years earlier, the launch of the Sputnik satellite had revealed that the Soviet Union was well on the way to putting nuclear warheads on missiles that could reach U.S. targets. The North Korean test failed, however, and unlike the Soviets, the North Koreans were never going to have enough nuclear missiles to survive a U.S. nuclear attack. Nevertheless, the regime, which was clearly starving its people to be able to build a puny strategic force, was neurotic and unpredictable enough to make a suicide attack plausible.

Working closely with Ambassador-at-Large and Special Advisor to the Secretary of State Strobe Talbott, who had been a Rhodes scholar with Clinton at Oxford in 1968, the president had used some of his last year in office trying to convince Moscow to work with him on building for both countries a limited missile defense system that would make it possible to screen out a small attack from a country like North Korea.[8] The Clinton plan involved negotiating an amendment to the ABM treaty to permit a limited system with more than one terminus.

Clinton's effort to find a compromise satisfied neither of the major stakeholders in the debate. Congress felt that the administration was not doing enough, while the Russians suspected that this new policy was directed at gaining some kind of strategic advantage over them and attempted to stonewall. In the summer of 2000, with polls showing that 58 percent of Americans supported some kind of missile defense, both political parties mentioned the program in their platforms. The Democrats advocated a limited system directed at "states of concern." The Republicans promised something more robust and criticized the Clinton administration for being "hopelessly entangled in its commitment to an obsolete treaty signed in 1972."[9]

In the presidential campaign, Governor Bush vowed to take the United States out of that treaty and build a system that could cover all fifty states.

Once in office, George W. Bush moved quickly to sweep away the Clinton compromise. His administration revealed that it wished to start breaking ground for a new missile defense installation in Alaska in June 2001. Construction was supposed to take a year, and according to the ABM treaty, the United States had to give Moscow six months' notice before unilaterally withdrawing. Bush raised missile defense at his first meeting with Russian president Vladimir Putin, in June 2001. This was the summit that went so well that the president made a rookie mistake by saying that he had "looked into Putin's soul" and liked what he saw. Putin was not as extravagant in his praise of the missile defense issue and had strong words for the president. In July, Condoleezza Rice, who spoke Russian and had been a Soviet expert in the George H. W. Bush NSC, led a follow-up mission to Moscow. On the president's behalf, Rice made clear that the Kremlin could not expect to exercise a veto over the construction in Alaska. The administration would go ahead regardless of the success of bilateral diplomacy.[10]

On a much lower plane, the Bush administration gradually addressed Osama bin Laden and al Qaeda. When the deputies got around to discussing terrorism in April 2001, Clarke encountered skepticism from Paul Wolfowitz, Rumsfeld's deputy at the Department of Defense. The deputy secretary of defense doubted that bin Laden was a terrorist mastermind and wondered whether he should remain the obsession of U.S. counterterrorism. Clarke later recalled that Wolfowitz asserted that al Qaeda was a less-professional terrorism organization than the Iraqi intelligence services.[11] It was a curious error by a foreign policy specialist. Wolfowitz had been an assistant secretary of defense in 1990–91 when Saddam Hussein had contracted terrorist work out to the PLO rejectionists like Abu Nidal because of the ineffectiveness of his own services. Few intelligence veterans of the Gulf War had anything but contempt for Iraqi intelligence capabilities.

Wolfowitz's assessment of bin Laden was more considered, though ultimately just as wrongheaded. His views reflected a school of thought building outside government that bin Laden was overrated as a threat. The evidence unearthed at the U.S. trial of four of the conspirators indicted for blowing up the U.S. embassies in Nairobi and Dar es Salaam suggested to some foreign policy experts that al Qaeda was "at times slipshod, torn by inner strife, betrayal, greed, and the banalities of life that one might find in any office." "Before the embassy bombings trial," observed Benjamin Weiser, of the *New York Times,* "Osama bin Laden loomed large in the American psyche, a villain of unimaginable evil and sophisticated reach . . . In some ways, though, it was an image created because so little was known about how he worked." The public testimony of al-Fadl and of the four bombers suggested that bin Laden could be miserly and would on occasion refuse to support missions. These details suggested some organizational inefficiencies and a limit on the dedication of bin Laden and some of his associates.[12]

The Pentagon's reluctance to accept bin Laden as a major threat was a serious setback to Clarke's effort to make the hunting down of this man as important a priority for the new administration as it had been for the old one. The carefully crafted PDD-39, the presidential directive that had tethered the Pentagon to counterterrorism in 1995, had lapsed with the change in administrations. The leadership of the NSC did not attempt to outmaneuver Wolfowitz by referring the issue to a higher level. At the moment, no intelligence from Afghanistan raised the possibility of a successful strike on bin Laden, so the issue did not require any immediate action.

Despite the administration's preference for other foreign policy issues, al Qaeda refused to go away. A wave of intelligence reports in the late spring and early summer that al Qaeda was planning some kind of spectacular attack bumped the issue from the deputies level up to that of the main Bush national security players. Most of the intelligence pointed to an assault on a U.S. installation overseas, but there were vague references to the possibility of something happening in the United States. In May 2001, a source volunteered to the FBI that al Qaeda was planning a coordinated attack on London, Boston, and New York. In mid-May, an anonymous tip was phoned in to a U.S. embassy, probably in the United Arab Emirates, warning of a future attack in the United States by bin Laden's group.[13] Most of the warnings were of attacks on U.S. installations abroad. In late May, Clarke advised National Security Advisor Rice to ask the CIA whether anything more could be done to disrupt these plots. "When these attacks occur, as they likely will," wrote Clarke to Rice and her deputy on May 29, "we will wonder what more we could have done to stop them."[14]

These warnings of possible attacks drew Condoleezza Rice's attention to al Qaeda as had nothing else since January. The national security advisor arranged a seminar discussion on al Qaeda with Tenet and Clarke and the head of the CTC, Cofer Black, on May 29. She now wanted to know how to take the offensive against bin Laden. Five months earlier, Clarke had shared with her a CIA plan that had been worked up at the end of the Clinton administration, but it had made no impression. In May, the CIA and Clarke told Rice that by disrupting al Qaeda operations abroad, the U.S. intelligence community was taking the offensive. Rice knew very little about al Qaeda and asked what leverage, if any, the United States had in dealing with either bin Laden or the Taliban. In response, Clarke explained that bin Laden was essentially undeterrable.[15]

The Bush administration had still not made up its mind as to what policy to pursue toward the Taliban. At various levels there was a stubborn belief that the Taliban might yet be turned against bin Laden. Secretary of State Powell did not share this view, believing instead that U.S. policy should be to overthrow the Taliban. The Clinton administration had left office believing that there was little to be gained from engagement with the Taliban but had not taken the step in adopting the policy of regime change. Over the summer of 2001, discussion of what to do about bin Laden bogged down over consideration of a multipart strategy that began with giving Mullah Omar one last chance.[16]

Clarke and the counterterrorism specialists in the CIA grew frustrated at the policy process established by Rice. Nothing in the first six months indicated that the new foreign policy team shared their concern about al Qaeda. A case in point was their handling of the *Cole* issue. Both the CIA and the FBI continued to work the problem, following up leads that in the next few months would bring them very close to the heart of the bin Laden conspiracy, but George W. Bush's top advisors sent a signal that this case had slipped in importance. "They showed no interest in following up the *Cole*," recalls Clarke's deputy Roger Cressey.[17]

The impatience of the Clinton holdovers, however, had more to do with a desire to move to the next stage in undermining the Taliban—through supporting either the anti-Taliban Pashtun tribes or the Tajiks and Uzbeks of the Northern Alliance—than with any sixth sense about any near-term threat posed by bin Laden to the U.S. homeland. Clarke and the CSG were no longer issuing the kinds of warnings about possible attacks at home that they had at the end of 1999, when the Ressam case had shown that there were al Qaeda sleeper cells in the United States.

The consensus in the U.S. intelligence community—which Clarke shared—was that al Qaeda was probably planning to attack a U.S. installation, likely an embassy, on or around July 4. On June 22, the CIA and the State Department each warned their own personnel at all U.S. embassies of the possibility of an imminent terrorist attack. That same day, the Pentagon established the highest possible "threat protection condition level" for U.S. forces in six countries, and the U.S. Fifth Fleet left the port of Bahrain for the safety of open waters. The CIA warning included the prediction that it would be an al

Qaeda terrorist attack. A State Department decision to protect Saudi visa applicants indicated the pervasive belief that the problem was abroad. Concerned that a terrorist attack on the U.S. embassy in Riyadh would kill hundreds of Saudis waiting in line at the consular office, the department established a Visa Express program so that Saudis could obtain visas at travel agencies, dispersing the applicants, though at the same time making it easier for terrorists to enter the United States.[18]

U.S. efforts in overseas counterterrorism were stepped up as well. According to the 9/11 Commission, "disruption operations against al Qaeda-affiliated cells were launched involving 20 countries." Collaboration with foreign services led to the detainment of "several terrorist operatives." The countries most likely to be hit were believed to be Saudi Arabia, Israel, Bahrain, Kuwait, Yemen, and Italy.[19]

With Clarke asserting that these warnings had "reached a crescendo," top administration officials were briefed on June 30 that bin Laden was planning "High-Profile Attacks." The CSG pointed to six separate reports with warnings from al Qaeda personnel of an imminent attack. Clarke's group alerted foreign response teams to deploy to a foreign terrorist site within a matter of hours.[20]

Although the administration and its counterterrorism specialists considered a foreign attack more likely, there were echoes of this heightened concern at home. The FBI advised federal, state, and local law enforcement agencies to "exercise extreme vigilance," but there was no mechanism in place to coordinate any domestic preparations, nor could the FBI provide any actionable information for local police or intelligence officers to use. The FBI believed that it lacked any "information indicating a credible threat of terrorist attack in the United States." It had no Emad Salems or any other major penetration in an al Qaeda cell through whom to test the master assumption that the imminent threat was abroad.

Despite the apparent successes abroad, the CIA and the CSG were dissatisfied with the Bush administration's response to these warnings. While the experts did what they could in the field, the White House did not create the kind of interagency war room that had been set up by the Clinton NSC in late 1999 to monitor the millennium threats. Some in the Pentagon, especially Deputy Secretary of Defense Paul Wolfowitz, openly doubted that these threats were real. In April, Wolfowitz had argued that bin Laden was more inefficient than Clarke believed. This time, Wolfowitz suggested that the warnings might be a deliberate deception, a symphony carefully orchestrated by bin Laden to test U.S. reactions, much as the Iranians had been "pinging" U.S. security systems in 1995. DOD did not provide an explanation, however, for why bin Laden thought he should be testing these systems. CIA director Tenet felt he had to intervene personally to convince the NSC not to take Wolfowitz's theory seriously. While the State Department, the FBI, and the U.S. military issued very strong warnings of possible attacks, the mixed signals that the White House was itself sending so worried Cofer Black's team at CTC that there was discussion of a mass public resignation to force the U.S. government to go on an even higher level of alert.[21]

This internal debate reached the attention of influential *New York Times* columnist Thomas Friedman in June 2001. In his satirical "memoir from Osama," Friedman imagined a memorandum from the Saudi terrorist who was rejoicing at his success in shutting down the *Cole* investigation and minimizing through intimidation the U.S. presence in Arabia. Friedman used the satire to criticize the administration for being too distracted by the missile defense issue to think twice about bin Laden. But even Friedman did not believe that bin Laden had goals greater than hitting U.S. targets overseas. "But the great thing is that Donald Rumsfeld is so obsessed with getting his missile-shield toy," Friedman has bin Laden saying, "he's been telling everyone that deterrence doesn't work anymore against people like us. So they need a missile shield instead. And Bush just repeats it. I love it, because we are not going to attack America's strength at home. We are going to attack soft U.S. targets abroad through shadows."22

Al Qaeda Sleepers in the United States

Indeed, the U.S. itself had become a soft target. As Friedman's article went to press, there were al Qaeda sleeper agents in the United States preparing for the "Planes Operation." All but one of the fifteen men who would provide the "muscle" during the hijackings had arrived in the United States and were living in southern Florida, joining gyms and staying in shape. Three of the four pilots—Mohammed Atta, Marwan al-Shehi, Ziad Jarrah—who had been in the country taking flight lessons for over a year, were traveling as first-class passengers on cross-country flights to observe when the flight crews opened the cockpit doors and other details that would facilitate the operation. These men also tested airport security, carrying onboard the box cutters, knives, and mace that they would later use to kill the pilots and subdue the flight attendants. The fourth pilot, Hani Hanjour, who had been in the United States about nine months, was still taking flight lessons. Atta, who was the operational leader, was about to fly to Spain in July to receive his final briefing from the al Qaeda leadership. D-day for the "Planes Operation" had yet to be decided. Atta would soon learn that bin Laden worried about having so many of his operatives in the United States at once and was impatient for the attacks to occur. Bin Laden expected the targets to be the Pentagon, each of the twin towers of the World Trade Center, and the White House.23

By the end of July, the tempo of the warnings subsided, and the CSG and the CIA concluded that bin Laden might have decided to delay the attack or attacks. The FBI continued to warn of a possible attack and even began discussing the need for ready response teams should something occur within the United States. Yet the bureau remained on the defensive. It did not put in motion any operations in Muslim-American communities to increase the available intelligence on al Qaeda's intentions. In July, at the request of the CSG, the FAA sent a vague warning to the aviation community of the existence of reports pointing to imminent terrorist attacks in the Middle East but gave no guidance and did not suggest that domestic travel might be targeted.[24]

The August 6 PDB

President Bush awoke early in Crawford, Texas, to go for a four-mile run. Once the sun rose, the temperature could easily surpass one hundred degrees in the shade. It was a treat for the president to be able to run outside, and he did not want to pass up the opportunity. When the president was in Washington, D.C., the Secret Service required him to confine his running to a treadmill. Bush had a lot to think about on his run. Four days earlier, on the eve of his departure for a month in Texas, the president had met with specialists on the stem cell issue. Researchers had found that the cells of the tiniest human embryos were extremely useful in pathbreaking research on cures for diseases like Alzheimer's that had so far resisted existing treatments. Because it involved human embryos, admittedly ones only days old, the issue challenged this "pro-life" presidency.

They "told me," Bush later recalled to ABC News, that "there were enough existing stem cell lines to do serious research to determine whether or not embryonic stem cell research could live up to its potential."[25] The information gave him a possible compromise on this politically charged issue. He would ban federal support for any newly created stem cell lines but permit work on a portion of those already in existence. The issue had become the most important of this young presidency, and Bush was scheduled to devote his first televised address to the nation, on August 9, to stem cell research.

The speech, which was being worked on by a small group, was very closely held.[26]

If the president wanted to think about foreign policy that morning, his administration's principal foreign policy initiative, a new military and strategic relationship with Russia, was moving into high gear. Defense Secretary Donald Rumsfeld was due to arrive in Moscow in a few days armed with reasons why Putin should accept Washington's decision to end the ABM treaty of 1972. "We all tend to be rooted somewhat into our past," said the boyish seventy-one-year-old who had headed the Congressional Commission to Assess the Ballistic Missiles Threat to the United States in the late 1990s.[27] The administration was already thinking of announcing its withdrawal from the ABM treaty in November, and the president expected to host Putin for a summit at that time in Crawford, where the Russians might agree to make that withdrawal mutual.[28]

When Bush returned from his run, he had a call on the Balkans from Condoleezza Rice.[29] Some progress had been achieved at peace negotiations between the Macedonian government and ethnic Albanians. Since March 2001, Albanian insurgents, members of the National Liberation Army, had been clashing with Macedonian authorities over linguistic and economic rights for the country's Albanian minority. In June, the Bush administration had intervened in the conflict by freezing assets belonging to those thought to be financing the guerrillas and then offering a U.S. envoy to broker a peace agreement. On August 5, the parties had agreed that the Macedonian police would hire one thousand ethnic Albanians.[30]

The president was also given the news of the day in a highly classified daily report called the president's Daily Brief (PDB). Franklin Roosevelt was the first president to receive a daily intelligence update. Called the Magic Summary in 1941, it contained the latest intercepted Japanese diplomatic messages. In the early Cold War, presidents stopped receiving the intelligence community's most sensitive information in a regular daily form. But after the disastrous

Bay of Pigs operation in Cuba, President John F. Kennedy insisted on a more orderly system of receiving the best the CIA had to offer. What was called the "President's Intelligence Checklist" for him became under Johnson and every president after him the presidential Daily Brief.[31] How each president absorbed this information was as idiosyncratic as whether they took cream in the coffee they might be sipping at the same time. When President Clinton read his PDBs, he would cover them with marginal notations: "What's this? Need more on this."[32] Perhaps from his father, who had been director of central intelligence, the new president brought with him to the Oval Office a strong respect for the CIA and the importance of intelligence. George W. Bush wanted to see analyses as well as raw intelligence traffic, and expected the PDB to have the most relevant information available. For all previous presidents the PDB was always bound with the seal of the president. Bush was so impatient for new information that his PDBs often came in loose-leaf binders so that pages could be faxed to the White House minutes before the volume was handed to the president. Bush also liked to have a personal briefing every morning from a CIA officer based on the PDB. The briefing was designed to allow for give-and-take. When the president was in Washington, that briefing was often given by George Tenet himself. At the CIA, they started calling Tenet "the color commentator" because he was in the Oval Office to amplify whatever the analysts had placed in the PDB.[33]

George Tenet was not in Crawford on August 6, and a lower-level CIA official was on hand to present Bush the PDB.[34] What the president received that day was a curiously weak report on the bin Laden threat to the U.S. homeland. Throughout the summer, Clarke's group had continued reporting to Rice about a series of warnings indicating the possibility of an al Qaeda attack, a few of which hinted at something in the United States. The FBI had received weeks earlier some information about planning here. None of that appeared in the item prepared for President Bush. Instead, the

CIA provided him with information much of which any reader of the *New York Times* or Simon Reeve's excellent 1999 book on Ramzi Yousef, *The New Jackals,* could have known. New tidbits included an FBI report of suspicious activity "consistent with preparations for hijackings or other types of attacks, including recent surveillance of federal buildings in New York." From the CIA was a reference to the anonymous warning phoned into a U.S. embassy in May. Curiously, the president was assured that the FBI had undertaken "seventy full field investigations throughout the U.S. that it considers bin Laden-related," and the CIA was working with the FBI to try to corroborate the May phone call.[35]

Members of the CSG later speculated that this item was a well-intentioned attempt by some CIA officials, where frustration with the administration's halfhearted response to the bin Laden threat was rife, to send a message. They were right. This brief was not in response to any specific presidential request. It was, in the words of one official responsible for the product, a deliberate effort to gather all of the available information pointing to an al Qaeda threat to the United States in one place and tie it "up in a bow." The effect was supposed to be a "hair on fire" message that would move the president to take the al Qaeda threat more seriously.[36]

The message misfired badly. President Bush found the item uninformative. It did not raise his pulse, let alone set his hair on fire. In his interview with the 9/11 Commission, the president explained that it "told him that al Qaeda was dangerous, which he said he had known since he had become president."[37] Unlike President Clinton, who had a habit of jumping on even second-rate reporting, the president did not instruct Rice, Tenet, or Attorney General John Ashcroft to find out more or to deliver reports on these ongoing investigations to him personally.

Later, Bush administration officials would point to the August 6 PDB as evidence of the lack of actionable intelligence. Yet it was clear that the president had been shielded from the ongoing debate on bin Laden between the counterterrorism specialists at the CIA and the NSC and the Department of Defense and his national security advisor. Far better organized than the Clinton administration in the way in which it methodically moved issues from the deputies level to the president for decision, the Bush system required that the principals take an issue seriously for it to get the president's attention. In the Clinton administration, the president's uncontrollable curiosity, and his eagerness to be a jack-of-all-trades, meant that at any given moment he might reach into the bureaucracy to learn more about an issue. Bush did not operate that way before September 11. Because Rice, Powell, and Ashcroft did not consider al Qaeda to be a matter of the highest consideration, the president devoted his attention in Crawford to the issues of stem cell research, missile defense, and his first vacation since the inauguration.

It is heartbreaking in retrospect to consider that well below the attention of the president and the other principals, U.S. investigators were getting tantalizingly close to the heart of the "Planes Operation" plot in August 2001. For some time the CIA had been interested in information about a jihadist operational group that had met in the Malaysian capital of Kuala Lumpur in January 2000. The group included an experienced operative Tawfiq bin Attash, alias Khallad, who would later be implicated in the *Cole* attack. Also identified as part of the group were two new men, Khalid al Mihdhar and Nawaf al Hazmi. In winter 2000 the CIA learned that Mihdhar and Hazmi were headed toward the United States. Hazmi arrived in Los Angeles in January 2000 and Mihdhar received a U.S. visa in March. From that point the trail went cold. The CIA officers involved turned to other queries and no one at the agency bothered to ask the FBI to pursue the leads. In May 2001, over a year later, a CIA official working at the FBI was doing what he could to figure out where al Qaeda might strike in the summer of 2001. He decided to review the old intelligence at his home service, CIA, on the meeting in Kuala Lumpur and on Mihdhar and Hazmi. The CIA officer decided to bring this material to the attention of the FBI team working on the *Cole* bombing and an FBI analyst detailed to the Alec station at CTC. That analyst, identified only as "Mary" in the 9/11 report, worked with an FBI colleague on the *Cole* investigation to bring the names of Mihdhar and Hazmi to the attention of the State Department and the FBI. She saw the information that Mihdhar had received a visa in March 2000 to come to the United States and that Hazmi had actually arrived in January. Contacting the Immigration and Naturalization Service, she learned that Mihdhar had been issued two visas. He had left the United States in June 2000 but had just returned through New York on July 4. It was assumed Hazmi had also left in June 2000 but had not returned. Her FBI colleague "Jane," in the *Cole* investigation, alerted the FBI field station in New York that Mihdhar, a man with jihadist connections, was around, and that he should be found and interviewed. Although "Jane" took the time to call an agent in the New York office, she assigned only "routine" importance to the cable that she drafted recommending this course of action. In the language of the FBI, a routine cable meant that the corresponding office had thirty days to act. The cable reached the New York office on August 28, 2001.[38]

This low-level investigation had come close to identifying Mihdhar before he returned to the United States on July 4 and before he boarded his flight on September 11. The problem that prevented his identification was not bureaucratic squabbling between the CIA and the FBI. The decade-long efforts to improve intelligence sharing had worked. What hampered a complete fusion of FBI and CIA information were regulations and a division of labor that separated some expertise from relevant information.

Zacharias Moussaoui represented another lost opportunity in the summer of 2001. A French national who had attended an al Qaeda training camp, Moussaoui had entered the United States in February 2001. After first taking flying lessons at Airman Flight School in Oklahoma, he moved to Minnesota. There he attracted the attention of the FBI in mid-August for his jihadist beliefs and his desire to pilot a wide-body jet without having any real flight experience. Subsequent investigation turned up a bank account with $32,000. The FBI took him into custody in August. Like the investigation of Mihdhar, the work on Moussaoui ran into legal and regulatory snags. Unless it could be proven that he was acting on behalf of a foreign power, Moussaoui's effects—especially his laptop computer—could not be subject to a search. Established to facilitate counterespionage operations against foreign intelligence agents, the rules governing Foreign Intelligence Surveillance Act (FISA) warrants were unavailable for use against freelance or NGO-sponsored terrorists. A criminal warrant might have been obtained, but the local FBI office doubted that it had probable cause for one. On August 18, the bureau wired for help from French and British intelligence in the hope that evidence of a link to a foreign power could be established. French liaison information that Moussaoui had once been in touch with Chechen rebels touched off a debate over whether Chechen terrorist groups qualified as a foreign power for the purposes of FISA. This issue was not resolved before September 11.[39]

The FBI's investigation of Moussaoui did reach CIA director George Tenet. On August 23 he received a briefing summarized as "Islamic Extremist Learns to Fly." The FBI explained that this French citizen wanted to fly a 747 on a simulated flight from London to New York, had paid for the training in cash, and was asking peculiar questions about which doors could be opened in a plane during flight. Tenet described the climate of that sticky summer by "the system was blinking red." Nevertheless, like the FBI, the CIA did not coordinate this information with the other leads that summer. Moussaoui was an FBI case and, more importantly, he was already in custody.[40]

As detailed in the 9/11 Commission report, these were leads that "could have derailed" bin Laden's "Planes Operation" if acted on more effectively.[41] Even if al Qaeda had opted to press on with the attack despite U.S. knowledge of Mihdhar, Hazmi, and Moussaoui, had these cases been more fully exploited, the principals might have taken the threat of a domestic attack more seriously and launched a coordinated effort to strengthen U.S. antiterrorism screening at U.S. airports in early September.

The formal meeting of the principals to discuss al Qaeda finally occurred on September 4, 2001, a few days after President Bush returned from his Texas ranch. The 9/11 Commission determined that President Bush had not been told about any of the summer's intelligence leads. As preparation for this meeting, Clarke wrote to Condoleezza Rice, "Decision-makers should imagine themselves on a future day when the CSG has not succeeded in stopping al Qaeda attacks and hundreds of Americans lay dead in several countries, including the U.S."[42] Clarke reminded Rice that the Arab world was watching how the U.S. handled the *Cole* tragedy. "The fact that the USS *Cole* was attacked during the last administration does not absolve us of responding for the attack."[43] Once again, Clarke drew upon the analogy to Abu Nidal. Osama bin Laden was an overseas problem that over a period of years could be weakened. Clarke believed that the U.S. government had the luxury to implement a multiyear strategy to eliminate al Qaeda. Clarke told his staff that his hope was to do to bin Laden's group what his predecessors in the late 1980s had done to the ANO: to leave it broken, to discredit its leadership, to eliminate any effective financing, and to render it incapable of carrying out operational attacks against the United States or U.S. interests.[44] These goals had been achieved without capturing or killing Abu Nidal, and the same might be true with bin Laden.

The intelligence community had been too uninterested to provide strategy assessments of the threat; CSG had been too busy to ask. After twenty years in the business, Clarke had become jaded. "They give us lemons and we have to make lemonade," he had told his deputy.[45] No one was sitting back thinking how al Qaeda might attack and questioning the conventional wisdom that they would likely attack abroad.

The records of the September 4 meeting are sparse. Participants recall that there was little discussion following presentations by George Tenet and Richard Clarke on the bin Laden threat. The president again showed no concern at the lack of urgency displayed by his team. The summer threats appeared to have passed. At issue was how to deal with the sanctuary that gave bin Laden the opportunity to plan attacks against the United States. There was no sense that a domestic awareness campaign was required. The set of proposals for strengthening antiterrorism at home adopted but never implemented by the Clinton administration was never discussed. When Rice told President Bush that this new sanctuary strategy would take three years to undermine al Qaeda, he accepted it.[46]

The only disagreement involved a tactical weapons system for counterterrorism. The president passively observed a catfight between the CIA and the Defense Department over who would pay for and therefore run the Predator program. He never intervened to demand a resolution. Acting as a recording secretary but not as an advisor, Condoleezza Rice noted that there was no decision. In the mid-1980s, Ronald Reagan would emerge from principals meetings on terrorism furious that a decision had not been reached on an issue of importance to him. Apparently, the bin Laden problem on September 4 had not risen to that level of significance for George W. Bush.

The president spent the next few days taking care of his first state visitor, President Vicente Fox, of Mexico. Meanwhile, the buzz in Washington was that Bush's aides wanted him to focus more on the economy. The unemployment rate had risen to 4.9 percent. Recent polls indicated that the American people viewed their new president as more tentative than decisive, and there was discussion of the size of the cue cards that he seemed to need. The Bush team felt that in the coming fall he would need to turn these impressions around by showing leadership on the economy. None of the pundits mentioned any challenges from Afghanistan.[47]

In the bureaucratic weeds miles from the president, the Moussaoui investigation was stalled, and the low-level inquiry into Mihdhar and Hazmi, which had not attracted any high-level attention, had slowed. The U.S. government was looking the other way. At 8:20 A.M. on September 11, American Airlines Flight 77 took off from Dulles International Airport with Nawaf al Hazmi, Khalid al Mihdhar, Majed Moqed, Salem al Hazmi, and Hani Hanjour

aboard. An hour and seventeen minutes later, at 9:37 A.M., with hijacker Hani Hanjour at the controls, the plane was crashed into the
west wall of the Pentagon, killing all 64 aboard and 125 on the
ground. Less than an hour earlier, two planes that had taken off
from Boston, headed for Los Angeles, were crashed by their hijackers into the north and south towers of the World Trade Center, toppling them in the resulting fire. A fourth hijacked plane missed its
appointed target after the passengers attacked the hijackers, causing
them to drive the plane into a Pennsylvania field.

September 11

Ken Pollack, the former NSC director for the Near East, had left the
White House with most of the Clinton national security group.
When he saw the CNN coverage of the attacks on the World Trade
Center, he called his friend Roger Cressey, who was still at the NSC.

"No chance it was the Iraqis?"

"No."

"It was bin Laden, wasn't it?"

"Uh-huh."

Then with gallows humor, he added, "Lucky it wasn't Hezbollah." Pollack then rang off, knowing that his friend had many more
important things to do than to revisit Richard Clarke's controversial
decision to talk up the bin Laden threat when to others, the Iranians
and their terrorist allies seemed to be a greater concern.[48]

Amidst the anger and sadness of that day was an intense sense of
frustration in Clarke's shop that despite three years of concentrating
on bin Laden, the U.S. government had been unable to prevent him
from killing thousands of people, destroying a New York landmark,
and delivering a blow to the heart of the U.S. military.

No one could point to any particular operation that had been bun-
gled or piece of intelligence that had been missed. Clarke and many

in the CIA wondered about the nine months that had been lost educating the new administration, while the new administration wondered why they had not received better warning from the intelligence community. Within roughly a month, the United States was at war with both al Qaeda and the Taliban, and Congress had passed the Patriot Act, containing many of the antiterrorism provisions suggested by the commission headed by the president's father in 1985–86 and again by the Clinton administration in 1995–96. Thirty years after Yasir Arafat awakened them to international terrorism, the American people sadly had to accept they could be attacked at home. Now they had to enact the serious antiterrorism precautions that they and their government had long sought to avoid.

CONCLUSION

Blind Spots and 9/11

WHAT WENT WRONG? It could not be said that the United States was unaware of the dangers of terrorism. For over half a century before 9/11, U.S. intelligence had considered the problem of detecting and neutralizing foreign terrorists. For thirty years, Washington had monitored the activities of international terrorists from the Middle East. For fifteen years, a high-level group within the Central Intelligence Agency had operated solely against foreign terrorists. For a decade, top American policymakers had identified new terrorism as self-financing groups intent on killing as many people as possible. And for a little over three years, the national security elite of the U.S. government had singled out Osama bin Laden and his al Qaeda network as the most dangerous of these new terrorists.

Yet on September 11, 2001, al Qaeda shrewdly exploited weaknesses in U.S. defenses and carried out a series of terrorist acts in which 3,000 people died. The terrorists had studied our domestic airline security. They had learned airline passengers could bring knives of a certain length and box cutters on board and that commercial pilots liked to keep cockpit doors open in the first ten minutes of flight. Al Qaeda's choice of conspirators also reflected serious preparation. Bin Laden's lieutenants had observed that terrorists with Saudi passports could gain entry to the United States more easily than nationals of other Arab countries. Not wishing to take any additional chances, with two notable exceptions, the chief plotters did not involve anyone in the operation who had a terrorist profile.

For most of the last half-century, terrorism was a blind spot for the U.S. government. As we have seen, Americans are reluctant participants in campaigns against terrorists in peacetime. Intelligence and military leaders have traditionally disliked counterterrorism, which involves dirty operations that call for dealings with unsavory types and which since the intelligence reforms of the 1970s have placed U.S. participants in legal jeopardy. Policymakers have disliked these operations because if they leak, they are hard to explain to the American people. Politicians have similarly seen little gain from antiterrorism measures. There are no domestic constituencies in peacetime for longer lines at airports, more government intrusion into communications, and enhanced police powers. U.S. business, the American Civil Liberties Union, and the National Rifle Association share a commitment to reducing government intrusion. The American public, who are more pragmatic than any single-interest lobby, share an aversion to unwarranted state intrusion. Our traditions and our system of divided government make us especially vulnerable to a determined terrorist enemy in peacetime.

The tortuous story of airline security is a case in point. In the 1960s, the American public and U.S. government were willing to put up with a monthly rate of hijacking that appears almost absurd in the context of the post-9/11 world. At the time, all of the private-sector lobbies, including initially the Air Line Pilots Association, opposed even the most limited security measures. Pilots were the first to seek congressional assistance, but it was not until the harrowing hijacking in 1972 that the federal government instituted mandatory searches of passengers and carry-on luggage. A spate of airline bombs later in the 1970s was not enough to force mandatory inspection of checked luggage. Even the explosions on Pan Am 103 in 1988 and TWA 800 in 1996, which was thought to have been brought down by a bomb, did not spark tighter luggage screening because of a widespread belief that the main threat was abroad and that the cost of implementing such a change was too great.

An unbroken line of presidents, both Democrat and Republican, saw domestic security measures as a potential political liability. An increase in airline protection, for example, would involve a fight with the airlines and their main federal ally, the FAA. And leaving aside the issue of airline security, counterterrorism itself held political dangers for a U.S. president. "As you know, there's very little we can do (that hasn't already been done) without incurring far more negatives than pluses," suggested a staffer in the Ford administration in 1975. "Any presidential involvement in this subject invites terrorists to target the United States and latent domestic dissidents to move into action."[1] This sentiment was present at the upper levels of all U.S. administrations until September 11, 2001.

From the late 1960s, controversy surrounded any domestic fight against saboteurs or terrorists. The techniques developed in World War II by the X-2 branch of the OSS and the FBI required the systematic surveillance of individuals and their communications. Perfectly suited to the climate and exigencies of wartime, these measures were incompatible with the rights and protections that Americans expect in peacetime. The U.S. intelligence community's effort to continue such surveillance unconstitutionally in the undeclared Cold War—usually with presidential approval—had the effect of tainting the counterterrorism mission. In reaction to the revelations of CIA and FBI overreaching and misdeeds in the 1970s, the U.S. government established rules that made domestic intelligence gathering on potential terrorists even harder and deepened the reluctance of subsequent administrations to enlist Americans in the fight against terrorists. The Iran-Contra scandal of the late 1980s only deepened public suspicion of counterterrorism and those that practiced it.

In spite of these political restrictions, for decades the U.S. government seemed to get the balance about right between risks to the United States and the costs of additional security. No passengers died in the hijackings of the 1960s and early 1970s. When the perception of the danger increased, the Nixon administration with the unexpected assistance of the Castro regime in Havana cured the hijacking epidemic. The 1980s brought a deadlier threat to U.S. installations and Americans traveling abroad. After an initial stumble, the Reagan administration reacted with an energetic and largely successful counterterrorism program, which the George H. W. Bush administration completed. By the early 1990s, the main terrorism entrepreneurs of the 1970s and 1980s, Abu Nidal and Carlos the Jackal, had been thoroughly neutralized, and Peru's murderous Abimael Guzman was in jail.

But the end of the Cold War ushered in a more virulent strain of terrorism, which Washington found difficult to counter. Abu Nidal and Carlos the Jackal had benefited from socialist sanctuaries and cynical secular Arab regimes that used them as pawns in their Cold War games. With the collapse of the Soviet empire, these sanctuaries disappeared, but the forces of nationalism and religious chauvinism unleashed by the decaying of the old authoritarian regimes had a darker side. The Soviet failure in Afghanistan inspired a generation of young Islamic men and clerics to see in armed struggle a successful means of advancing their religious and cultural mission. Struggles in Bosnia, Kosovo, and Chechnya allowed these fighters to see additional combat. What the penetrating American political scientist Samuel Huntington called the clash of civilizations was the mother's milk of this new lost generation, which substituted religious certitudes for Marxist-Leninist doctrine. Meanwhile, the globalization of information technology meant that these groups could communicate and coordinate even without state sponsorship.

This new enemy required a new strategy. Yet to varying degrees, both the Clinton and George W. Bush administrations tried to fight the new jihadists as Reagan and Bush's father had fought an earlier generation of terrorists. The Clinton administration, which emptied think tanks full of people sensitive to issues of globalism, understood that a more serious terrorist threat had emerged without knowing exactly what to do about it. Indeed, there is a parallel between how the Reagan administration managed the threat from international terrorism and how the Clinton team responded. Like Reagan, Clinton elevated the struggle with terrorism to the presidential level and shared some of his concerns with the American people. He discussed the virulence of the new terrorism and identified Osama bin Laden as its most dangerous practitioner. And like Reagan, Clinton chose to fight this struggle abroad, though his administration did more than Reagan's had to improve U.S. domestic security.

Clinton's efforts to move antiterrorism legislation in 1995 and 1996 were serious, but in retrospect even they seem half-hearted. He never forced congressional Republicans to pay any political price for their opposition and did not return to the issue seriously after his re-election in 1996. At no time did Clinton signal to the American public and the news media that antiterrorism was a priority of his administration on a par with health care or balancing the federal budget or even NATO enlargement. It was only with the revelations of the 9/11 Commission that the public came to realize how much energy Clinton and his top advisors had invested between August 1998 and January 2001 in trying to kill bin Laden and destroy his organization.

The Clinton administration's choice of counterterrorism tactics against bin Laden also reflected an unwillingness to break out of the policies of the 1980s. Debates within the Clinton NSC over how and when to bomb bin Laden and his camps were reminiscent of the policy discussions about Muammar Gadhafi a decade earlier. Suggestions that U.S. special forces be used instead of U.S. bombers were rejected, and there was no serious discussion of invading Afghanistan.

This lack of creativity was not entirely the fault of the policymakers. The political environment of the 1990s era discouraged risk-taking and innovation. The country craved a breather, a respite from foreign entanglements, after two generations of Cold War. The American people and the U.S. armed forces, which since Vietnam had taken its cues from public opinion, had no stomach for any greater military activity. Meanwhile, partisan attacks on the president in his role as commander in chief—Clinton was the target of almost relentless Republican criticism for not having served in the Vietnam War—weakened his ability to set his administration's foreign policy agenda. Despite these difficulties, Clinton could have tried to mobilize the American people for a confrontation with the Taliban, but he did not. Instead, the administration accepted that an invasion of Afghanistan was politically impossible.

The administration of George W. Bush did not wish to continue even a limited duel between Washington and al Qaeda. Much as the officials of the George H. W. Bush administration had toned down the Reagan war on terrorism, the new Bush team in 2001 consciously took the bin Laden problem out of the Oval Office. George W. Bush never publicly mentioned bin Laden, just as his father had tried not to mention Hezbollah. The struggle was confined instead to the intelligence community. There is evidence that the Bush team was prepared to give the CIA whatever it needed in fighting terrorism. But it was in no hurry to do so, and in its first months, the administration did not believe that the president needed to spend much of his valuable time on the issue.

In 1989, the first Bush administration's underplaying of the terrorism issue reflected an effort to cope with the consequences of Iran-Contra and not a different assessment of the significance of international terrorism. The policy shift between Clinton and George W. Bush, however, reflected a disagreement over the nature of the terrorist threat. The new president's advisors missed the implications of the change in terrorism of the 1990s and refused to accord bin Laden the same importance that they gave to the Russian and Chinese leadership. The Bush team seemed to discount the threat from a terrorist group that didn't have a state sponsor. "Al Qida is not some narrow, little terrorist issue that needs to be included in broader regional policy," Richard Clarke had warned in January 2001, fearing that the new administration might adopt the thinking on terrorism characteristic of the Cold War.[2] Whatever chance there was to put the American system on alert in time to stop al Qaeda's "Planes Operations"—by warning the traveling public and forcing the airlines and border-control agencies to take serious, intrusive measures—was lost in the Bush administration's stubborn refusal to understand that the world of 2001 was different from that of 1993.

As a result, in the summer of 2001, the U.S. government was not on full alert. With U.S. intelligence unable to penetrate bin Laden's inner circle or acquire enough information to pinpoint him for an assassination attempt, the country's domestic security system stood as the last line of defense against the September 11 plot. Weak to begin with, that system failed. Information about two of the future hijackers did not reach the airlines in time to prevent Khalid al Mihdhar and Nawaf al Hazmi from boarding American Airlines Flight 77. What threat information was passed to the airlines by the FAA, though dramatic, was vague and was read in a climate of complacency. The struggle with al Qaeda, which had been carried on by the upper tier of the U.S. government, was almost completely unknown to the press and the remainder of the U.S. elite, let alone to the American people. There had been no national conversation about the new terrorism and what it meant for how we must lead our lives. The few voices that raised the issue were viewed as extremists, catastrophists, or authoritarians with a hidden agenda.

Did anyone get it right? The American counterterrorism community understood after 1998 that the new terrorism represented a vital threat to U.S. interests. Yet even they did not see it as something that would kill thousands of people in 2001. Richard Clarke, who deserves more credit than any other individual for trying to keep busy policymakers focused on the new threat, was not himself completely free of the models of the 1980s. In 2000–01 he assumed that Washington still had three years to neutralize bin Laden before he could launch a major attack on U.S. territory. Even those considered alarmists in the U.S. government worried primarily about a terrorist attack with weapons of mass destruction. Bin Laden was thought to be a few years from having that capability. No one assumed that al Qaeda would press forward with a mass casualty event that required only conventional weapons.

Have We Learned?

In the wake of the tragedy, the U.S. government attacked Afghanistan and with the assistance of the Northern Alliance overthrew the Taliban regime; Congress passed the Patriot Act; and the Bush administration established a federalized airport security and Terrorist Threat Integration Center (TTIC), an interagency effort to integrate all U.S. government information and analysis on terrorists and terrorism.[3] Meanwhile, the FBI launched an effort to upgrade its internal records system, first by replacing a computer system that belonged in a museum and not in a modern investigative agency. Finally, Congress created a Department of Homeland Security to coordinate the twenty-two agencies responsible for aspects of domestic protection and terrorism prevention.

Some of these measures were long overdue. The Patriot Act included quite a few of the provisions in the Clinton administration's Counter-Terrorism Bill of 1995. The requests for roving taps, access to telephone pen registers (the record of numbers dialed on a telephone), trap/trace powers (involving records on incoming calls), records from common carriers and hotels on terrorist suspects, and the use of national security letters to obtain information on terrorism financing had been discussed a decade earlier and dropped by Congress. The George W. Bush administration pushed the boundaries of some of these measures beyond where the Clinton administration believed it could go in the mid-1990s, but the spirit was the same. These reforms permitted the FBI to undertake investigations of terrorists with the same tools available for detecting and neutralizing foreign spies.

TTIC was an updated version of the terrorism "fusion center" suggested by Vice President Bush's task force in 1986. In its responsibility to build a database of all known and suspected terrorists entered in U.S. government registries, it also harked back to the SHAEF G-2, CI War Room that tracked Nazi saboteurs and agents in 1945. The spirit of cooperation between the CIA and the FBI had been improving since the mid-1990s, but TTIC represented the highest profile yet given to U.S. government sharing in terrorist information and analysis. Following the publication of the 9/11 Commission's recommendations, President Bush renamed TTIC as the National Counterterrorism Center by executive order in August 2004. In December 2004 this change was formalized in the Intelligence Reform and Terrorism Prevention Act.

The most dramatic of all structural changes came at the end of 2004, when again at the recommendation of the 9/11 Commission, Congress created the post of director of national intelligence (DNI). This change ended the CIA director's nearly sixty-year reign as the president's principal intelligence advisor. The commission made this recommendation because the nineteen directors of central intelligence, including the incumbent Porter Goss, never had the power their title implied. Lacking control over the budgets of all intelligence services but the CIA, DCIs historically found it difficult to marshal the resources of the U.S. intelligence community. The new DNI has more budget authority but perhaps not enough to control all of the components of the U.S. intelligence community. In February 2005, President Bush nominated longtime diplomat John D. Negroponte to the post. Until somebody has held the job for a while, it will remain an open question whether this new office will be a centralizing force

in intelligence or yet another bureaucratic layer between raw information and policymaking.

The U.S. captures of the mastermind of the 9/11 attack, Khalid
Sheik Muhhamed; a key al Qaeda planner, Abu Zubaydah; as well
as bin Laden's operations chief in the Persian Gulf, Abd al-Rahim al-
Nashiri; and his Southeast Asian chief, Omar al-Farouq, represent
major gains in the war on al Qaeda. So, too, does the death in
Afghanistan of bin Laden's military chief, Mohammed Atef. In background discussions, U.S. officials describe al Qaeda as having been
disrupted. But the fact that bin Laden remains at large suggests a
limitation on U.S. capabilities. Even with Afghanistan under the rule
of a friendly government, its borderlands with Pakistan remain a
sanctuary for al Qaeda. Moreover, since 2002, a new threat has appeared in the form of groups allied with al Qaeda but not centrally
controlled by bin Laden. These groups have attacked Western targets in Madrid and Bali with considerable loss of life.

The least successful aspect of the Bush administration's approach
to counterterrorism since 9/11 has been its public awareness program. The Department of Homeland Security introduced an ineffectual warning system that assigned a color to the level of terrorist
threat existing in the United States. Citizens had no way of knowing
what changes in these threat levels meant for how they should conduct their lives. If the color changed from yellow (elevated) to orange (high), should they keep their children at home? The color
coding did have significance for local police, but since most threats
are not to small or medium-sized American cities, these warnings involve more wasted effort than anything else. The presidency has
also not been as effective a bully pulpit as it could be. After deftly
rallying the nation in the few weeks after the attacks, President Bush
then used his credibility to outline the magnitude of the new threat.
In 2002–03, this effort was conflated with an effort by the administration to justify a renewed hard line on Saddam Hussein and ultimately an invasion of Iraq. By 2004, this focus on fear became a
centerpiece in the president's reelection campaign.

This public awareness campaign created confusion and public disquiet. The blurring of the threat posed by Saddam Hussein—an old-fashioned threat from an aggressive power with hegemonic aspirations in a region of interest to Washington—with the threat posed by violent jihadism has weakened domestic understanding of the struggle. At a time when Americans should be united behind their government, there are severe divisions. The politics of fear have also prevented a serious national conversation about the true dimensions of the threat. The public has no idea of the tradeoffs between security and freedom. Their elected representatives speak of doing everything necessary to protect them, while each political party argues that it is more likely than the opposition to keep the nation secure.

In truth, we live in a period of greater uncertainty than the Cold War, when the two main protagonists, no matter how much they huffed and puffed, played by certain rules. The jihadists, however, cannot be deterred with a threat of nuclear retaliation. But there is a limit to what they can do to us. Unlike the Kremlin, al Qaeda can never possess sufficient force to destroy our civilization.

The American public should be informed that the terrorists cannot win any war against the United States. The struggle will take years and involve the cooperation of other countries. At home, we need to discuss the appropriate balance between privacy and security. This discussion should have taken place in the 1990s. Had this happened, the public might well have permitted Washington to build a better security screen in time to detect the "Planes Operation." Now the issue is the moral authority of counterterrorism. The public needs to participate in decisions either to extend the Patriot Act or not to. The story of the costs and benefits of allowing the FBI to carry out internal intelligence activities needs to be aired. The costs of the overreaction to J. Edgar Hoover's excesses should figure prominently in that story.

A mature discussion of terrorism would not look like what we saw in the 2004 campaign. In the fall, a *New York Times Magazine* article by Matt Bai drew controversy by suggesting that the Democratic nominee, John F. Kerry, did not believe that the struggle against terrorism should be described as a war. Republicans jumped on this as evidence that Kerry was not up to the task of fighting bin Laden. A more careful reading of the article showed that Kerry, or at least the author, was arguing that terrorism is something that has to be lived with, which is not the same thing as saying it is something that has to countenanced as hijacking was in the 1960s.

If indeed this is a war, how does it end? Once the threat of al Qaeda has diminished, does that mean that we can dismantle the array of new institutions set up after 9/11 to monitor, analyze, and destroy that organization? Will we again enter the period of bureaucratic malaise of the early 1990s, when there were calls to eliminate the CIA's counterterrorism center? As long as the United States remains an object of envy and there are adversaries who wish us harm, there will be terrorism.

The restructuring of the U.S. intelligence community in late 2004 was the most dramatic sign that 9/11 had changed how the U.S. government would handle counterterrorism. But restructuring can provide only part of the solution. The shift in policy between the Clinton and Bush administrations illustrates what can happen when top policymakers lose interest in an issue or do not grasp its essence. George Tenet, the DCI, was said to have a good relationship with George W. Bush. He shared Richard Clarke's concerns about al Qaeda, and his CIA had formulated a set of plans to deal with al Qaeda, the most recent in December 2000.[4] Yet he failed to convince President Bush and National Security Advisor Rice to invest more time and energy in the problem before September 2001. It is hard to believe that the president would have reacted differently even had the post of director of national intelligence existed in September 2001.

Historically, what we often refer to as intelligence failures are policy failures. According to an apocryphal, but completely plausible, story, when Secretary of State Henry Kissinger complained about some such intelligence failure, a high-level intelligence analyst interjected, "But we warned you, sir." "Yes," replied Kissinger, "but you didn't persuade me." If the policymakers refuse to accept what their intelligence services give them, who is at fault?

Mandating that presidents be more astute in understanding threats is an impractical solution. The problem is how busy people in Washington can learn to spot trouble before it happens. Here the past is instructive. Between 1969 and 1998, with few exceptions, policymakers routinely downplayed the warnings from alarmists in their counterterrorism shops. Time and again, policymakers had to be shocked into changing their minds. Until the harrowing Southern Air hijacking of 1972, the Nixon administration opposed mandatory passenger screening; until the Beirut bombings of 1983–84, the State Department did not have a policy of reinforcing U.S. embassies; until the Abu Nidal airport massacres of 1985, the CIA opposed the creation of a special counterterrorism unit. With only a few hundred lives lost, the costs of being reactive were relatively small and did not cause lasting political damage. In September 2001 the costs became high and politically unacceptable. Until that point, it was assumed that in the short term, terrorists could not hit the United States with devastating effect.

Given its size and inescapable bureaucratic sluggishness, does the U.S. government always have to be reactive? Can it be nimble enough to anticipate threats? Al Qaeda is now on everyone's to-do list. But what about the next group of jihadists or another brand of terrorist? Even the most gifted counterterrorism analysts misunderstood al Qaeda's operational tactics. Embedded in the mission of the TTIC and now the National Counterterrorism Center is all-source analysis of terrorist entities. Such analysis was not undertaken by the CTCs of the 1980s and 1990s and their equivalent at the FBI. The FBI failed to hire any group of terrorism analysts, and those at the CIA, though skilled, focused primarily on analyses needed for current CIA operations.

A second innovation in the new reforms is a source of some optimism: that the analysis that gets done will be better. Congress created the Intelligence Community Scholarship Program. The armed services have traditionally paid for promising young men and women to obtain an education in return for a commitment of service for a number of years. Now future intelligence analysts and operatives have the opportunity to attend undergraduate and graduate institutions to learn the languages and skills required in the struggle against Islamic extremism.

The history of U.S. intelligence is littered with mistakes and misjudgments caused by a lack of expertise. Through the 1960s, the clandestine service of the CIA was turned inside out by those who believed that the KGB had penetrated their organization. The counterintelligence officers who led this hunt not only did not know the Russian language, but lacked a detailed understanding of the Soviet intelligence system. Their belief that the CIA was penetrated was based on an assessment of a Soviet defector, whom they assumed had been sent intentionally by Moscow. The Kremlin never trusted any intelligence officer enough to send him or her on a long-term mission to live in the United States and operate as a false defector. A similar lack of expertise characterized U.S. assessments of the Soviet military and the Soviet economy. Throughout the first half of the Cold War, the team that wrote national intelligence estimates on the Soviet Union did not include a single expert on Russian history or one who could read or speak Russian. More recently, the CIA's analyses of Saddam Hussein reflected a misjudgment of the man and his willingness to admit that he had destroyed his stocks of chemical and biological weapons.

For too long, the CIA and the FBI have rewarded generalists over specialists. Career enhancement has gone to those who can be moved from one specialty to another until they reach senior management positions. In this atmosphere, expertise in the politics and society of a single country or even an area is devalued. The State Department, in contrast, has traditionally rewarded expertise. Accordingly, in the run-up to the Iraqi war, the analyses of Hussein's weapons of mass destruction program done by the State Department's Bureau of Intelligence and Research were more accurate than those produced by any other component of the U.S. intelligence community.

The struggle against al Qaeda is part of a longer engagement with radical Islam. Islam is the principal religion of two billion people—approximately one-fourth of the world's population—speaking dozens of languages and spread over five continents. Sensing that the Kremlin understood the developing world better than Washington, in the 1960s the United States began programs like the Peace Corps and devised strategies to win the "hearts and minds" of young people in the third world. As it turned out, the Soviets were far less adroit than Washington had imagined, but so, too, was the United States. This time, it appears that the United States faces a more dexterous adversary whose message attracts many adherents, some of whom are willing to sacrifice their lives in its name. Killing the leadership of this movement is less important in the long run than in killing its ideology and drying up its source of recruits. Besides nimble counterterrorism abroad and reasonable antiterrorism at home, future successes will depend on pragmatic foreign policy and public diplomacy that provides young Muslims in the Middle East, Africa, and Asia with a tangible alternative to violence.

We want to avoid the mistakes of the past. As this book has shown, terrorism was long treated as a speck in Uncle Sam's eye. It was an irritant, a distraction from the "real" or strategic threats to the country. There were periods of engagement and then relaxation. In the mid-1970s and again in 1992, we thought we had defeated the problem. But terrorism is an issue linked to more than one man's hatred of our society. It is a tactic that will be used again and again by weaker enemies who lack substantial military power. We should not allow the ultimate victory over bin Laden, which is only a matter of time, to dissuade us from maintaining a long-term capability to deal with terrorism at home as well as abroad.

And there is yet another useful lesson to pull from our recent past. This country is very successful when it focuses on a problem. In the

Cold War, we sustained a concentration on the Soviet threat for over a generation. Yet even in that victorious struggle there were moments when our leaders exaggerated the threat to our security, causing us to overbuild our military and to impose unnecessary restrictions on our liberty. Overreacting to a threat can be as harmful as ignoring it. As part of a searching national conversation about terrorism there should be sensitivity to the realities of the threat. Should we pay the huge pricetag to defend all commercial aircraft against the possibility that terrorists might fire portable rockets against them? Should we make it difficult for first responders to know whether a burning rail-car contains hazardous materials because tagging these cars might help a terrorist target chemical cargoes?

No one said fighting an invisible enemy who can strike at his own choosing would be easy. But greater public engagement is likely to create more national resolve and unity. And should there be another terrorist attack on U.S. soil, and chances are there will be, the terrorists would cause sorrow but not confusion and self-doubt. There can be no stronger weapon in our arsenal than national self-discipline.

NOTES

Preface

1. This argument is skillfully developed in John Costello's *Days of Infamy* (New York: Pocket Books, 1994).

Chapter One

1. Omar Bradley, *A Soldier's Story,* pp. 467, 469.

2. Heron (Stuyvesant Wainwright, Jr.) to Berding, SCI Headquarters, 12 AG, December 20, 1944. Record Group 226, Entry 139, Box 89, National Archives, College Park, MD [NARA].

3. Lt. Colonel Lord Rothschild and JIGGER (Herbert Bechtold), "Rocquencourt; Abwehr II–SD Sabotage Depot," October 8, 1944. Record Group 226, Entry 108a, Box 166, NARA. Two sources pointed these dumps out to X-2 and the British JIGGER (Herbert Bechtold) and Peter Shagen.

4. Supreme Headquarters Allied Expeditionary Force, Counter Intelligence War Room London, "The German Intelligence Service," April 1945, William J. Donovan Collection, Military History Institute, Carlisle, Pennsylvania.

5. H. Montgomery Hyde, *Secret Intelligence Agent: British Espionage in America and the Creation of the OSS* (New York: St. Martin's Press, 1982), p. 67.

6. Norman Holmes Pearson, foreword to John C. Masterman, *The Double Cross System* (New Haven: Yale University Press, 1974), p. xiv.

7. Ibid., pp. 112–126.

8. AD/I to D.S.C., "48917 C.E. Organisation," March 12, 1943, Hyde Collection, 3/29, Churchill College, Cambridge, UK; William Stephenson took

credit for establishing X-2 in correspondence and interviews with the author. On January 23, 1984, for example, he sent the following telegram: "I suggested to Donovan that he establish his own OSS Counter Intelligence Office in London, to establish continuous contact with British C.I. and that Jimmy Murphy would be a good choice to run it." In old age Sir William was an unreliable witness. Two strokes, one in 1950 and the second in the early 1960s, muddled his recollection of the past. See Timothy Naftali, "INTREPID's Last Deception: Documenting the Career of Sir William Stephenson," *Intelligence and National Security* (July 1993). But in this particular instance, Sir William's memory served him well. James Murphy gave an interview to the X-2 War Diary officer in late August 1944, in which he laid out Stephenson's responsibility. On the basis of what Murphy had told him, the War Diary officer, Gerstle Mack, wrote, "In August 1942 Mr. Stephenson of the British Security Coordination discussed the problem [the need for an American Section V] with authorities in the American intelligence services, proposed the establishment of a civilian CE agency under OSS jurisdiction, and suggested that Mr. Samuel Foxworth, head of the New York office of FBI, should be placed at the head of the CE Division." Proof of Murphy's responsibility for this information comes from a marginal note: "Information given verbally to the War Diary Officer by Mr. James Murphy, 28 August, 1944." The discovery of Gerstle Mack's rough draft was a boon. In the final version of the introductory chapter to the X-2 War Diary, Stephenson's personal responsibility was edited out. The diary section contains the following instead: "The American intelligence services discussed the problem with Mr. Stevenson [sic] in August 1942, and the establishment of a civilian CE agency under OSS jurisdiction was proposed," RG 226/99/80, NA. At the end of the war, the OSS history office compiled a complete history of the organization's 13 main branches, based in part on the War Diaries completed by the operational branches. This version returns to the thrust of the Murphy interview, without any of the detail: "In August 1942, therefore, representations were made by the British which strongly suggested an arrangement between the British and American agencies that would provide a more restricted and secure channel for the handling of CE information." U.S. War Department, *War Report of the OSS (Office of Strategic Services)*, I:188, Declassified 1975, Washington, D.C., 1976.

9. Timothy J. Naftali, *X-2 and the Apprenticeship of Modern American Counterespionage*, Unpublished manuscript, 1993, Harvard University Archives.

10. J. Felix Cowgill interview (February 1984). Colonel Cowgill headed Section V, the counterespionage branch of MI6, from 1939 until his resignation in December 1944. Cowgill would be outmaneuvered by H. A. R. [Kim] Philby, his erstwhile protégé who was ultimately unmasked as a Soviet agent.

11. Timothy J. Naftali, *X-2 and the Apprenticeship of Modern American Counteres-*

pionage, Unpublished manuscript, 1993, Harvard University Archives; Federico D'Amato interview (1991). D'Amato was a CIA contact from 1943 until his retirement in the 1970s from the leadership of the Italian police.

12. Timothy J. Naftali, *X-2 and the Apprenticeship of Modern American Counterespionage,* Unpublished manuscript, 1993, Harvard University Archives.

13. D. G. White interview (April 13, 1984).

14. "History of the Counter Intelligence War Room, March 1–November 1, 1945," RG 226, Entry 176, Box 2, NARA.

15. Ibid.

16. Norman Holmes Pearson, Note, April 2, 1945, Record Group 226, Entry 119, Box 15, NARA.

17. Memorandum for the President, March 23, 1945, RG 226, Entry 162, Box 7, OSS Records, National Archives. The report itself is in the PS File, Box 171, FDR Library, Hyde Park, NY.

18. George C. Marshall to SHAEF Fwd., personal for Eisenhower, March 31, 1945. Eisenhower Mss., Cable File, Quoted as # 2377, *The Papers of Dwight David Eisenhower, the War Years: IV,* Alfred D. Chandler, Jr., Editor (Baltimore: The Johns Hopkins Press, 1970).

19. Eisenhower to George C. Marshall for FDR, March 31, 1945. Quoted as #2377, *The Papers of DDE, the War Years: IV* (Baltimore, 1970).

20. Stephen E. Ambrose, *The Supreme Commander: The War Years of General Dwight D. Eisenhower* (New York: Doubleday & Company, 1970), p. 625.

21. Eisenhower to the Combined Chiefs of Staff, April 14, 1945. Number 2413, *The Papers of DDE, the War Years: IV.*

22. Otto Skorzeny Name File, RG 263, NARA; "Nazi's Arch-Killer Captured by Yanks," *New York Times,* May 18, 1945.

23. Scott Miler interview (December 19, 2004) (Miler was deputy director of the CIA's CI Staff); Richard Helms interview (1991). Richard Helms averred that every U.S. postmaster general from the Truman administration through the Ford administration had approved this operation.

24. James Critchfield interview (August 17, 2001). Scott Miler interview (December 20, 2004).

25. Nikolai Khokhlov, *In the Name of Conscience: The Testament of a Soviet Secret Agent* (New York: David McKay, 1959), p. 246; John Barron, *KGB: The Secret Work of Soviet Secret Agents* (London: Hodder and Stoughton, 1974), p. 311.

26. Christopher Andrew and Oleg Gordievsky, *KGB: The Inside Story of Its Foreign Operations from Lenin to Gorbachev* (New York: HarperCollins, 1990), p. 426.

27. Nikolai Khokhlov, p. 246.

28. Telephone conversaton with David Murphy (December 30, 2004).

29. Anatoli Sudoplatov, Jerrold L. Schecter, Pavel Sudoplatov, and Leona P. Schecter, *Special Tasks: The Memoirs of an Unwanted Witness, A Soviet Spymaster*

(Boston: Little, Brown, 1994), p. 245. We know much less about the U.S. sabotage program. In the late 1940s and early 1950s, the CIA's Office of Policy Coordination trained so-called stay-behind agents to remain in Soviet-occupied Europe in the event that the Kremlin launched an invasion. See Evan Thomas, *The Very Best Men, Four Who Dared: The Early Years of the CIA* (New York: Simon & Schuster, 1995), pp. 36–37.

30. Christopher Andrew and Vasili Mitrokhin, *The Sword and the Shield: The Mitrokhin Archive and the Secret History of the KGB* (New York: Basic Books, 1999), p. 360.

31. Ibid.

32. Ibid.

33. The twenty-five-year-old Stashinsky suffered remorse after killing Ukrainian resistance leader Stefan Bandera. Barron, *KGB: The Secret Work of Soviet Secret Agents,* p. 315.

34. Christopher Andrew and Vasili Mitrokhin, *The Sword and the Shield*, pp. 378–379.

35. Walter Lippmann, "Terrorists and Spies," *Washington Post,* March 4, 1954.

36. CIA, National Intelligence Estimate 11-7-63, "The Clandestine Introduction of Weapons of Mass Destruction into the United States," March 13, 1963. There is a handwritten note on the cover page, indicating that President Kennedy read this. National Security File, National Intelligence Estimates File, "11-63, USSR." Box 2, Lyndon Baines Johnson Library [LBJL].

37. Robert McNamara telephone conversation (February 20, 2004).

Chapter Two

1. UPI, "Gunman Is Foiled in Jet Hijacking," *New York Times,* July 13, 1968; UPI, "Plane Hijacker Is Held in Miami," *New York Times,* July 14, 1968.

2. FAA, "Chronology of Hijackings of US Registered Aircraft," November 7, 1972, "Hijackings Part II," NSC 331, Nixon Materials Project, NARA.

3. Robert D. McFadden, "Airlines Trying Number of Ways to Foil Hijackers," *New York Times,* Jan. 20, 1969.

4. Bob Sayre memo, February 21, 1968, Country File, National Security File (NSF), Cuba, "Hijacked Airliners," LBJL.

5. Quoted in "Eastland Says Courts, Not Laws, Are at Fault," *Washington Post, Times Herald,* July 14, 1968.

6. "Hijackings Worry Cubans in Miami," *New York Times,* July 7, 1968.

7. The doors were also made to be collapsible to permit rapid in-flight recompression between the cockpit and the cabin. In addition, cockpit doors were routinely left open during takeoffs and landings, the two most dangerous periods in a flight.

8. John Sibley, "Airline and FAA Officials Seek Means to Counter Hijackers," *New York Times,* July 18, 1968; Andrew Wilson, "Air Hijackings Stirring Wide Concern," *Washington Post, Times Herald,* Aug. 14, 1968.

9. Claude Koprowski, "Airlines Study Anti-Hijacking Plan," *Washington Post, Times Herald,* Jan. 24, 1969.

10. "Deterring the Hijackers," *Washington Post, Times Herald,* July 20, 1968.

11. John Sibley, "Airline and FAA Officials Seek Means to Counter Hijackers," *New York Times,* July 18, 1968.

12. "Federal Agents Ride Planes in Effort to Stop Hijackings," *New York Times,* July 20, 1968.

13. Ben Funk, "Jet Forced to Cuba with Gun, Grenade," *Washington Post, Times Herald,* July 18, 1968.

14. Enclosure to Walt W. Rostow, "Message to the Senate for Signature by the President," September 6, 1968, "Convention on Offenses and Certain Other Acts Committed on Board Aircraft," Office Files of Ernest Goldstein, Box 10, LBJL.

15. DOS cable, "El Al Aircraft Hijacking," July 24, 1968, NSArch-CT.

16. "European Pilots Boycott Algeria over Hijacking of Israeli Plane," *Washington Post, Times Herald,* August 14, 1968.

17. Alvin Shuster, "Hijacking and What Can Be Done about It," *New York Times,* Aug. 18, 1968.

18. Reuters, "Cuba Willing to Sign Accord on Air Hijacks," *Washington Post, Times Herald,* Sept. 22, 1968.

19. Rostow to LBJ, September 7, 1968, Memos to the President, NSF, Box 39 (1 of 2), "Volume 93 September 1–11 [1 of 2]," LBJL.

20. CIA intelligence information cable, July 7, 1967, Country File, Box 54, "Guatemala Memos & Misc., Vol. II," LBJL.

21. Bowdler to Rostow, "Guerrilla Problems in Latin America," July 5, 1967, Intelligence File, NSF, LBJL.

22. Rostow to LBJ, July 11, 1967, Country File, NSF, Box 54, "Guatemala Memos & Misc., Vol. II," LBJL; Bowdler to Rostow, "Our 4:30 Meeting on Subversion in Latin America," July 5, 1967, Intelligence File, NSF, Box 2, "Guerrilla Problem in Latin America," LBJL. In 1967, the U.S. Department of Defense gave the Guatemalan army $1 million for helicopters and communications assistance for the counterinsurgency action, and the State Department gave $324,000 to support the reorganization of the police. The U.S. intelligence community also provided assistance, but the amount of this assistance remains classified.

23. CIA intelligence information cable, July 7, 1967, Country File, NSF, Box 54, "Guatemala Memos & Misc., Vol. II," LBJL.

24. Ibid.

25. CIA intelligence memorandum, "Assassination of US Ambassador to

Guatemala," Aug. 29, 1968, Country File, NSF, Box 54, "Guatemala Cables [1 of 2], Vol. II, 1/66–11/68," LBJL.

26. CIA intelligence memorandum, "The Communist Insurgency Movement in Guatemala," September 20, 1968, Country File, NSF, Box 54, "Guatemala Cables [1 of 2], Vol. II, 1/66–11/68," LBJL.

27. CIA intelligence memorandum, "Assassination of US Ambassador to Guatemala," August 29, 1968, Country File, NSF, Box 54, "Guatemala Cables [1 of 2], Vol. II, 1/66–11/68," LBJL.

28. White House Situation Room to Tom Johnson, "[Excised] on the Assassination of US Ambassador to Guatemala [excised]," August 29, 1968, Country File, NSF, Box 54, "Guatemala Cables [2 of 2], Vol. II, 1/66–11/68," LBJL.

29. Bowdler memo to Rostow, March 8, 1968, Country File, NSF, Box 54, "Guatemala Memos & Misc., Vol. II," LBJL.

30. CIA intelligence information cable, March 7, 1968, Country File, NSF, Box 54, "Guatemala Memos & Misc., Vol. II," LBJL.

31. Peter Jessup to the chairman and members of the President's Foreign Intelligence Advisory Board [PFIAB], "Minutes of 303 Meetings for Past 90-Day Period," June 4, 1968, Intelligence File, NSF, Box 2, "303 Committee," LBJL. The "platter" quotation came from Secretary of State Dean Rusk.

32. Ibid. On citation regarding the role of the 303 Committee, see Bromley K. Smith draft memo to LBJ, "Need for White House Representation on 303 Committee," March 24, 1966, Department of State, Foreign Relations of the United States, 1964–1968, Volume XXXIII:538; see also Thomas Karamessines, DDP of CIA, memo to all staff chiefs and division chiefs, "Criteria for 303 Committee Submissions," September 30, 1967, FRUS, 1964–1968, XXXIII:586–588.

33. Telephone conversation with Peter Jessup (February 2, 2004); Peter Jessup, who was secretary of the 303 Committee in 1968–69, could not recall any retaliatory covert operation against Cuba or the Guatemalan terrorists after the Mein killing.

34. Saunders to Rostow, "Mid-East Terrorism," November 11, 1967, Name File, NSF, Box 7, "Saunders Memos [1 of 2]," LBJL.

35. Ibid.; CIA intelligence memo, "The Arab-Israeli Confrontation—Autumn 1968," September 23, 1968, Country File, NSF, Box 104, "Middle East [1 of 3], Vol. II, 4/68–1/69," LBJL; CIA special report, Weekly Review, "Anti-Israeli Arab Terrorist Organizations," October 4, 1968, Country File, NSF, Box 142, "Israel Memos [2 of 4], Vol. X, 6/68–11/68, LBJL.

36. Saunders to Rostow, "Mid-East Terrorism," November 11, 1967, NSF Name File, Box 7, "Saunders Memos [1 of 2]," LBJL.

37. CIA special report, Weekly Review, "Anti-Israeli Arab Terrorist Organizations," October 4, 1968, Country File, NSF, Box 142, "Israel Memos [2 of 4],

Vol. X, 6/68–11/68; Saunders to Rostow, "Mid-East Terrorism," November 11, 1967, NSF Name File, Box 7, "Saunders Memos [1 of 2]," LBJL; CIA intelligence memo, "The Arab-Israeli Confrontation–Autumn 1968," September 23, 1968, Country File, NSF, Box 104, "Middle East [1 of 3], Vol. II, 4/68–1/69," LBJL.

38. Office of National Estimates, memo for the director of the CIA, "The Jordan Regime: Its Prospects and the Consequences of Its Demise," December 13, 1966, Country Files, NSF, "Jordan Memos, Vol. III, 12/66–5/67," Box 146, LBJL.

39. James Critchfield interview (August 18, 2001).

40. CIA special report, Weekly Review, "Anti-Israeli Arab Terrorist Organizations," Oct. 4, 1968, Country File, NSF, Box 142, "Israel Memos [2 of 4], Vol. X, 6/68–11/68," LBJL.

41. Ibid.

42. Ibid.

43. DOS cable, "El Al Aircraft Hijacking," July 24, 1968, NSArch-CT.

44. Beirut cable to DOS, "Possibility of Arab Terrorist Activities in US," October 16, 1968, Country File, NSF, Box 149, LBJL.

45. Ibid. (a marginal note on the document indicates that this information was forwarded to the White House Situation Room with a suggestion from NSC staffer Harold Saunders that it go to the Secret Service); telephone conversation with Harold Saunders (February 15, 2004).

46. Peter Jessup to chairman of PFIAB and members, "Minutes of 303 Meetings for Past 90-Day Period," June 4, 1968, Intelligence File, NSF, Box 2, "303 Committee," LBJL. Peter Jessup, who was the secretary of the 303 Committee at the time, does not recall any new covert action against the PLO in 1968–69. Telephone conversation with Peter Jessup (February 2, 2004).

47. Reuters, "US Jet with 113 Hijacked to Syria by 2 Young Arabs," *New York Times,* August 30, 1969.

48. James Reston, "The Impotence of Power," *New York Times,* September 11, 1970.

49. Quoted in "Rogers Condemns Diversion of Plane as Act of Piracy," *New York Times,* August 30, 1969.

50. Cuba provided food for its unexpected guests, and the Cubans seemed to be doing all they could to get the planes and the passengers back into the air safely. The hijackers usually stayed behind in Cuba, though in recent years, the Castro regime had started sending back hijackers who had done the deed for money and not ideology.

51. Quoted in Robert Lindsey, "US Moving on Two Fronts in Effort to Halt Sharp Increase in Plane Hijacks," *New York Times,* September 5, 1969.

52. Shaffer quoted in ibid.

53. John Shaffer discussed the history of the task force and the system it recommended in a press conference on September 11, 1970. See "Hijackings, Part 2," NSC 331, Nixon Materials Project (NMP)–National Archives and Records Administration [NARA].

54. Richard Witkin, "Stopping the Hijackers," *New York Times,* November 1, 1969.

55. Quoted in Robert Lindsey, "US Moving on Two Fronts in Effort to Halt Sharp Increase in Plane Attacks," *New York Times,* September 5, 1969.

56. Acting Secretary of State to Nixon, "Aircraft Hijacking," October 2, 1969, "Hijackings, Part 2," NSC 331, NMP-NARA.

57. Kissinger to Nixon, "TWA Hijacking," September 21, 1969, "Hijackings, Part 2," NSC 331, NMP-NARA. Nixon scribbled his approval on this document. The United States opposed the election of Syria to the UN Security Council and alerted the Soviets and other governments that it would seek stronger diplomatic sanctions against Damascus if the Syrians did not release the men.

58. Shultz to Nixon, September 15, 1969; Kissinger to Shultz, "Hijacking of Aircraft," September 22, 1969, "Hijackings, Part 2," NSC 331, NMP-NARA; "US Seeks Pacts on Air Hijackers," *New York Times,* Sept. 19, 1969.

59. Ibid.

60. Alexander Haig, Jr., interview (January 23, 2004).

61. Kissinger to Nixon, "TWA Hijacking," September 21, 1969, "Hijackings, Part 2," NSC 331, NMP-NARA.

62. Kissinger to Peter Flanigan, "Possible Actions Against Countries Which Are Uncooperative on Hijacking," "Hijackings, Part 2," NSC 331, NMP-NARA.

63. Kissinger to Nixon, "Aircraft Hijacking," October 15, 1973; DOS to the president, "Aircraft Hijacking," October 2, 1973, "Hijackings, Part 2," NSC 331, NMP-NARA. Kissinger summarized a report from the acting secretary of state. The acting secretary of state spoke of FAA work on a system of detection but said nothing about perfecting the process.

64. The first airport-wide trial, at New Orleans International Airport, did not occur until July 1970.

65. "4 Jets Hijacked; One, a 747, Is Blown Up," *New York Times,* September 7, 1970.

66. U.S. embassy, Amman, cable to DOS, September 7, 1970, "Jordan, Vol. V, July 1/70–September 30/70," NSC, CO: Middle East, Box 615, NMP-NARA.

67. The administration recognized that it would be in a difficult position if the terrorists had asked for Sirhan Sirhan's release, since Washington expected the Israelis and its allies to release the prisoners requested by the PFLP. Kissinger to Nixon, "Status of Mid-East Hijackings," undated (from context,

appears to be from September 7, 1970), "Hijackings, Part 2," NSC 331, NMP-NARA.

68. This remained the FBI approach to hostage incidents throughout the period under review in this book.

69. DOS, Operations Center, Situation Report [Sitrep] #4, September 8, 1970, 1600 hours, "Hijacking," NSC 330, NMP-NARA.

70. DOS, Operations Center, September 7, 1970, 1800 hours, "Hijacking," NSC 330, NMP-NARA; Kissinger to Nixon, "Hijacking Status," September 9, 1970, NMP-NARA.

71. Kissinger to Nixon, "Status of Mid-East Hijacking," undated (transmittal form for this document, #21799, places it on September 7, 1970), "Hijackings, Part 2," NSC 331, NMP-NARA.

72. Ibid.

73. Kissinger to Nixon, "Your 4:30 Meeting on the Hijackings," September 8, 1970, "Hijackings, Part 2," NSC 331, NMP-NARA.

74. Memo for the president, "Aircraft Hijacking," September 10, 1970, "Hijackings, Part 2," NSC 331, NMP-NARA.

75. Meeting with Bipartisan Leadership, September 11, 1970, "Hijackings, Part 2," NSC 331, NMP-NARA.

76. Laird to Kissinger, "Actions to Prevent Airline Hijacking," September 10, 1970, "Hijacking," NSC 330, NMP-NARA.

77. Laird to Kissinger, "DOD Comments on Draft Statement Concerning Hijacking Proposed for the President," September 10, 1970, "Hijackings, Part 2," NSC 331, NMP-NARA.

78. Laird annotation of draft presidential statement (cover letter, Brig. Gen. Robert E. Pursley to Brig. Gen. Haig, is dated September 11, 1970), "Hijackings, Part 2," NSC 331, NMP-NARA.

79. H. R. Haldeman, *The Haldeman Diaries: Inside the Nixon White House* (New York: Putnam, 1994), pp. 192–193, September 10, 1970, entry.

80. Laird memo to Kissinger, "Use of Military Personnel as Guards on U.S. Flag Air Carriers," September 12, 1970, "Hijackings, Part 2," NSC 331, NMP-NARA. The secretary of defense was concerned that this use of U.S. military personnel violated the legal principle of *posse comitatus,* which prohibits the employment of the military in domestic law enforcement. Laird recommended that the military sky marshals be formally detailed to the FAA. It is not clear from the file whether this ever happened. What is clear is that President Nixon made his decision without concern over the applicability of the principle of *posse comitatus.*

81. Kissinger to Peter Flanigan, "Possible Actions Against Countries Which Are Uncooperative on Hijacking," October 31, 1970, "Hijackings, Part 2," NSC 331, NMP-NARA.

82. Kissinger memo to the president, "Hijacking Status," September 9, 1970, "Hijackings, Part 2," NSC 331, NMP-NARA. From the memo, it appears that Nixon was told about these military movements after the orders were issued.

83. Ibid.

84. Kissinger to Nixon, "Mid-day Situation Report on Hijacking Situation," undated (but cover note is dated September 9, 1970, 3 P.M.), "Hijacking, Part 2," NSC 331, NMP-NARA.

85. Ibid.

86. John O'Connell interview (October 2003).

87. Kissinger to Nixon, "Hijacking Situation Report—10:30 A.M. Sunday Morning," September 13, 1970, "Hijackings, Part 2," NSC 331, NMP-NARA.

88. John O'Connell interview (October 2003).

89. Kissinger to Nixon, "Evening Report on the Hijacking Situation," September 15, 1970, "Hijackings, Part 2," NSC 331, NMP-NARA.

90. "Talking Points for Briefing Selected Members of Congress," "Jordan, Vol. V, July 1/70–September 30/70 [2 of 2]," NSC 615, NMP-NARA; Kissinger memo for the President, "Jordanian Request for Assistance," September 20, 1970, NSC 615, NMP-NARA; Alexander M. Haig, Jr., interview (January 23, 2004); Jack O'Connell interview (October 22, 2003).

91. Helmut Sonnenfeldt to Kissinger, "Additional Comments on the Soviet Position on Jordan," September 19, 1970, "Jordan, Vol. V, July 1/70–September 30/70 [2 of 2]," NSC 615, NMP-NARA.

92. Alexander M. Haig, Jr., interview (January 23, 2004); memo for the President, "Meeting on Jordan," September 22, 1970, "Jordan, Vol. V, July 1/70–September 30/70 [2 of 2]," NSC 615, NMP-NARA This document appears to place the authorization to Israel on September 21.

93. Kissinger memo for the President, "Use of U.S. Land-Based Air over Jordan," September 22, 1970, "Jordan, Vol. V, July 1/70–September 30/70 [2 of 2]," NSC 615, NMP-NARA; memo for the President, "Meeting on Jordan," September 22, 1970, "Jordan, Vol. V, July 1/70–September 30/70 [2 of 2]," NSC 615, NMP-NARA.

94. Jeffrey D. Simon, *The Terrorist Trap: America's Experience with Terrorism* (Bloomington: Indiana University Press, 1994), pp. 102–103.

95. Interview with Alexander M. Haig, Jr., (January 23, 2004).

96. Kissinger to Peter Flanigan, "Possible Actions Against Countries Which Are Uncooperative on Hijacking," October 31, 1970, "Hijackings, Part 2," NSC 331, NMP-NARA.

97. Ibid.

98. Ibid.

99. CIA research study, "International and Transnational Terrorism: Diagnosis and Prognosis," April 1976, NSArch-CT.

100. Melvin H. Levine to Kissinger, "International Efforts to Stop Air Piracy," June 13, 1972, "Hijackings, Part 2," NSC 331, NMP-NARA.

101. Macomber, DOS, to Carlucci, "Western Airline Hijacking," June 10, 1972, "Hijackings, Part 2," NSC 331, NMP-NARA.

102. Robert Oakley interview (February 7, 2004); Harold Saunders, telephone interview (February 15, 2004); Frederick Turco interview (February 5, 2004); Stansfield Turner interview (December 10, 2003).

Chapter Three

1. Jeffrey D. Simon, *The Terrorist Trap: America's Experience with Terrorism* (Bloomington: Indiana University Press, p. 106.

2. Rogers to Nixon, "Measures to Combat Terrorism," September 18, 1972, Subject File, NSC, "Cabinet Committee on Terrorism [September 1972–July 1973]," Box 310, NMP-NARA; Nixon Tapes, Tape 771–2, September 6, 1972. I am grateful to Craig Daigle, a graduate student in the history program at George Washington University, for allowing me to quote from his draft transcript of this meeting.

3. Nixon Tapes, Tape 771–2, September 6, 1972.

4. Rogers to Nixon, "Measures to Combat Terrorism," September 18, 1972, Subject File, NSC, "Cabinet Committee on Terrorism [September 1972–July 1973]," Box 310, NMP-NARA.

5. Ibid.

6. CIA, Weekly Situation Report on International Terrorism, September 15, 1972, WHSF – SM & OF; David R. Young, "Files of the Working Group of the Cabinet Committee to Combat Terrorism," Box 28, NMP-NARA. In January 1973, the CIA produced a report on the Munich massacre: "The Black September Attack at the Munich Olympic Games," ibid. Only the title of this report has been declassified. The CIA also produced a list of individuals linked to the PLO: "Persons Involved with Fedayeen." Vols. I and II are located in Box 26 of the working group files and also remain classified.

7. Nixon Tapes, Tape 771–2, September 6, 1972, Craig Daigle, draft transcript.

8. Nixon Tapes, Tape 772–6, September 7, 1972.

9. Nixon Tapes, Tape 771–7, September 6, 1972.

10. Simon Reeve, *One Day in September: The Full Story of the 1972 Munich Olympic Massacre and the Israeli Revenge Operation "Wrath of God"* (New York: Arcade, 2000), pp. 152–153.

11. Ibid., p. 153.

12. Nixon Tapes, Tape 783–25, September 19, 1972. Dixon also predicted

that Soviet efforts at détente were a fraud and would lead to an ultimatum against the United States in 1973 or 1974. Nixon chose to ignore that information.

13. Nixon Tapes, Tape 784–7, September 21, 1972.

14. Nixon Tapes, Tape 786–5, September 25, 1972.

15. Alexander Haig, Jr., interview (January 23, 2004).

16. Haig to Ehrlichman, September 23, 1972, "Cabinet Committee on Terrorism [September 1972–July 1973]," NSC 310, NMP-NARA.

17. Alexander Haig, Jr., interview (January 23, 2004); *Haldeman Diaries*, p. 386, December 22, 1971, entry.

18. *Haldeman Diaries*, p. 504, September 16, 1972, entry.

19. John W. Dean, telephone interview (May 4, 2004).

20. Nixon Tapes, Tape 804, October 18, 1972.

21. Richard Witkin, "Hijacking Victims Returned as Cuba Holds 3 Suspects," *New York Times,* November 13, 1972.

22. "FBI Hit for Shooting Hijacked Jet's Tires," *Washington Post, Times Herald,* November 14, 1972; Frank Munger, "Recalling an Earlier Day of Terror," *Cincinnati Post,* September 13, 2001.

23. Frank Munger, "Recalling an Earlier Day of Terror," *Cincinnati Post,* September 13, 2001.

24. John Dean was not told that his name had been forged. John Dean, telephone interview (May 4, 2004).

25. Richard Witken, "Stopping the Hijackers," *New York Times,* November 1, 1969.

26. Quoted in Robert Lindsey, "Passengers on Hijacked Jet Recall Anger, Fear, Humor and a Sense of Doom," *New York Times,* November 14, 1972.

27. "FBI Hit for Shooting Hijacked Jet's Tires," *Washington Post, Times Herald,* November 14, 1972.

28. "Flying with Terror," *New York Times,* November 14, 1972.

29. Quoted in Stuart Auerbach, "ALPA Chief Assails Gunfire," *Washington Post, Times Herald,* November 16, 1972.

30. Quoted in Richard Witkin, "Head of FBI Says He Ordered Hijacked Plane's Tires Shot Out," *New York Times,* November 15, 1972.

31. Ibid.

32. Rogers to Nixon, "Action Against International Terrorism," January 8, 1973, "Cabinet Committee on Terrorism [September 1972–July 1973]," NSC 310, NMP-NARA.

33. "Flying with Terror," *New York Times,* November 14, 1972.

34. Richard T. Kennedy to Kissinger, "Status of USG Actions Against Terrorism," November 25, 1972, "Cabinet Committee on Terrorism [September 1972–July 1973]," NSC 310, NMP-NARA.

35. Victor Zorza, "Ultimate Threat: Nuclear Skyjack," *Washington Post, Times Herald,* November 15, 1972.

36. Rogers to Nixon, "Combating Terrorism," June 27, 1973, "Cabinet Committee on Terrorism [September 1972–July 1973]," NSC 310, NMP-NARA.

37. Rogers to Nixon, "Actions to Combat International Terrorism," November 7, 1972, "Cabinet Committee on Terrorism [September 1972–July 1973]," NSC 310, NMP-NARA.

38. "Arabs Are Hardest Hit in U.S. Visa Screening," *Washington Post, Times Herald,* October 17, 1972. Attorneys for Abdeen Jabara, who had been Sirhan Sirhan's lawyer, later claimed that in 1972–73 their client was under electronic surveillance as a result of Operation Boulder. Jabara lived in Detroit, and his lawyers claimed that Operation Boulder had a domestic component and was directed primarily at Arabs and Arab Americans. The FBI subsequently admitted the monitoring but did not describe it as part of Operation Boulder. See Ronald Kessler, "FBI Admits Monitoring Mich. Lawyer," *Washington Post,* February 5, 1975; Bill Richards and La Barbara Bowman, "Slaying of Alon Activated US Watch for Terrorists," *Washington Post, Times Herald,* July 4, 1973; Paul Magnusson, "NSA Tapped Six Overseas Messages by Attorney for Sirhan, FBI Reveals," *Washington Post,* August 3, 1977.

39. Rogers to Nixon, "Combating Terrorism," June 27, 1973, "Cabinet Committee on Terrorism [September 1972–July 1973]," NSC 310, NMP- NARA.

40. "Tough Agreement to Discourage Hijacking and Punish Violators Signed by Cuba, US," *Wall Street Journal,* February 16, 1973.

41. Bush cable to secretary of state, February 5, 1972, NSC, CO: Africa, Sudan, Vol. I (2 of 3), NSC 745, NMP-NARA.

42. Ibid.

43. David Tucker, *Skirmishes at the Edge of Empire: The United States and International Terrorism* (Westport, Connecticut: Praeger, 1997), p. 9. Tucker was able to consult Armin Meyer's unpublished memoir of the Khartoum incident. Meyer argued that the working group had already made this shift in thinking, encouraged by Kissinger.

44. Ibid.

45. Richard D. Lyons, "President Declares Killers Must Be Brought to Justice," *New York Times,* March 3, 1973.

46. David B. Ottaway, "Arafat Implicated in Envoy's Death," *Washington Post, Times Herald,* April 5, 1973; Jim Hoagland, "Killers May Have Shifted Plans," *Washington Post, Times Herald,* March 9, 1973; Harold Saunders, telephone interview (February 15, 2004); Robert Oakley interview (February 7, 2004).

47. CIA special report, Weekly Review, "Anti-Israel Arab Terrorist Organizations," October 4, 1968, Country Files, NSF, "Israel Memos [2 of 4], Vol. X, 6/68–11/68," Box 142, LBJL.

48. Saunders and Richard T. Kennedy to Kissinger, "Follow-up on Murders in Khartoum," undated, NSC, CO: Africa, Sudan, Vol. I, NSC 745, NMP-NARA. This is Kissinger's copy, on which he initialed his approval of the suggested policy.

49. Henry Tanner, "Accusation in Khartoum," *New York Times,* March 7, 1973.

50. Memorandum of conversation, Nixon and Abdel Rahman Abdullah, "Security Help to Sudan," March 6, 1973; Rogers to Nixon, "Security Assistance to Sudan," March 9, 1973, NSC, CO: Africa, Sudan, Vol. I, NSC 745, NMP-NARA.

51. Henry Tanner, "Accusation in Khartoum," *New York Times,* March 7, 1973.

52. Robert Oakley interview (February 7, 2004).

53. Harold Saunders telephone interview (February 15, 2004).

54. Jim Hoagland, "Change of Mood in Sudan," *The Washington Post, Times Herald,* July 29, 1973; "Trial in Sudan," *The Washington Post, Times Herald,* December 12, 1973; "Sudan Starts Trial of Eight Arab Guerrillas," *Washington Post,* June 2, 1974; Jim Hoagland, "Sudan Releases Envoys' Killers to PLO," *The Washington Post;* Bernard Gwertzman, "Guerrillas Freed by Sudan Reported Jailed in Egypt," *The New York Times,* June 29, 1974.

55. Ibid.

56. Scowcroft to Walters, "Talking Points for Meeting with General Walters," October 23, 1973, NSC CO: Middle East, "Palestinian [July 1973–July 1974]," Box 139, NMP-NARA. The United States informed the Israelis of this contact with the PLO a month later. Memcon, Israeli ambassador Simcha Dinitz to Scowcroft, November 26, 1973, NSC CO: Middle East, "Palestinian [July 1973–July 1974]," Box 139, NMP-NARA.

57. Simon Reeve, *One Day in September: The Full Story of the 1972 Munich Olympics Massacre and the Israeli Revenge Operation "Wrath of God"* (New York: Arcade Publishing, 2000), pp. 203–205.

58. Robert Oakley interview (February 7, 2004).

59. Beirut cable to Assistant Secretary of State Atherton, April 22, 1974, Section 1, NSC CO: Middle East, "Palestinian [July 1973–July 1974]," Box 139, NMP-NARA.

60. Robert Oakley interview (February 7, 2004).

61. Beirut cable to Atherton, April 22, 1974, Section 1, NSC CO: Middle East, "Palestinian [July 1973–July 1974]," Box 139, NMP-NARA.

62. Beirut cable to Atherton, April 22, 1974, Section 2, NSC CO: Middle East, "Palestinian [July 1973–July 1974]," Box 139, NMP-NARA.

63. Beirut cable to secretary of state, May 23, 1974, 1:05 P.M., Section 2, NSC CO: Middle East, "Palestinian [July 1973–July 1974]," Box 139, NMP-NARA.

64. Reeve, *One Day in September,* pp. 203–207.

65. John O'Connell interview (October 22, 2003).

66. Harold Saunders telephone interview (February 15, 2004).

67. Ibid.

68. Secretary of State cable to U.S. embassy, Beirut, May 1, 1974, Section 2, NSC CO: Middle East, "Palestinian [July 1973–July 1974]," Box 139, NMP-NARA.

69. Beirut cable to Secretary of State, May 23, 1974, 12:31 P.M., Section 2, NSC CO: Middle East, "Palestinian [July 1973–July 1974]," Box 139, NMP-NARA.

70. Nixon comments on Kissinger, Kenneth R. Cole to Nixon, "Actions to Combat International Terrorism," July 24, 1973, "Cabinet Committee on Terrorism [September 1972–July 1973]," NSC 310, NMP-NARA.

Chapter Four

1. General Ernest Graves, assistant general manager for military applications of the Atomic Energy Commission, memo to Mahlon E. Gates, manager of the AEC's Nevada's Operations Office, "Responsibility for Search and Detection Operations," November 18, 1974, cited in Jeffrey T. Richelson, "Defusing Nuclear Terror," *Bulletin of the Atomic Scientists,* March/April 2002.

2. Quoted in Richard Homan, "Algeria, US Resume Relations, Cut Off During '67 Mideast War," *Washington Post,* November 13, 1974.

3. Minutes of 121st meeting of the Working Group/Cabinet Committee to Combat Terrorism (WG/CCCT), November 10, 1976 (November 19, 1976), NSArch-CT. This meeting included a CIA historical briefing on the evolution of Palestinian terrorist groups. The date in parentheses is that on which the document was created.

4. Joseph Frichett, "PLO Purging Dissident Extremists," *Washington Post,* December 2, 1974.

5. Seymour Hersh, "Huge CIA Operation Reported in US Against Anti-war Forces, Other Dissidents in Nixon Years," *New York Times,* December 22, 1974.

6. Jack Anderson and Les Whitten, "CIA's Files Said to Support Denials," *Washington Post,* January 9, 1975.

7. Quoted in John Prados, *Lost Crusader: The Secret Wars of CIA Director William Colby* (New York: Oxford University Press, 2003), p. 295.

8. Philip W. Buchen to Scowcroft, "Cabinet Committee to Combat Terrorism," January 7, 1975, NSArch-CT; Buchen to John O. Marsh, undated, NSArch-CT. This is Buchen's original, with Marsh's reply scribbled on it. The idea seems to have come from Buchen, the White House counsel. At that time John O. Marsh was Ford's assistant for congressional liaison. "Under present

circumstances," Buchen wrote in an informal note to Marsh, "I suggest we should question the continuance of this Committee and its Working Group." Marsh replied, "I think you're on the right track."

9. James Adams email to the author, June 16, 2004.

10. Loch K. Johnson, *A Season of Inquiry: Senate Intelligence Investigation* (Lexington: University Press of Kentucky, 1985), pp. 153–155.

11. James Adams, telephone interview (June 16, 2004).

12. CIA research study, "International and Transnational Terrorism: Diagnosis and Prognosis," April 1976, NSArch-CT; "Two Rockets Fired at Israeli Jet in Paris," *New York Times,* January 14, 1975. One rocket hit a nearby Yugoslav airliner but did not explode, and the second hit a storage facility. No one was killed. The PLO denounced the attack as "a conspiracy against the Palestinian cause and people."

13. Minutes of 94th meeting of the WG/CCCT, October 15, 1975 (October 20, 1975), NSArch-CT.

14. Quoted in Jeffrey T. Richelson, "Defusing Nuclear Terror," *Bulletin of the Atomic Scientists,* March/April 2002.

15. John R. Emshwiller, "In Atom-Bomb Scare, Federal NEST Team Flies to the Rescue," *Wall Street Journal,* October 21, 1980.

16. Thomas O'Toole, "AEC Seeking to Cut Peril of Atom Threat," *Washington Post,* May 27, 1974 (second of two articles).

17. John R. Emshwiller, "In Atom-Bomb Scare, Federal NEST Team Flies to the Rescue," *Wall Street Journal,* October 21, 1980.

18. Ibid.; Jeffrey T. Richelson, "Defusing Nuclear Terror," *Bulletin of the Atomic Scientists,* March/April 2002.

19. Quoted in Jeffrey T. Richelson, "Defusing Nuclear Terror," *Bulletin of the Atomic Scientists,* March/April 2002.

20. CIA, Weekly Situation Report on International Terrorism, December 17, 1974, CIA FOIA Electronic Reading Room.

21. Minutes of 121st meeting of WG/CCCT, November 10, 1976 (November 19, 1976), NSArch-CT.

22. CIA research study, "International and Transnational Terrorism: Diagnosis and Prognosis," April 1976, NSArch-CT. In the Carter, Reagan, and George H. W. Bush administrations, CIA analysts stopped drawing this distinction between international and transnational terrorism. Instead, the agency focused on whether terrorism was state sponsored.

23. CIA, Weekly Situation Report on International Terrorism, December 17, 1974, CIA FOIA Electronic Reading Room. In the section on terrorist threats and plans, it lists a general warning that "the Fatah leadership expects that the PFLP may mount a terrorist operation in West Germany."

24. Henry Kissinger, *Years of Renewal* (New York: Simon and Schuster, 1999), pp. 1047–1048.

25. Ibid., p. 1048; minutes of 118th meeting of the WG/CCCT, September 29, 1976 (October 6, 1976), NSArch-CT.

26. Minutes of 111th meeting of the WG/CCCT, June 16, 1976 (June 21, 1976), NSArch-CT. Minutes of 112th (June 30), 113th (July 21), 114th (August 4), and 118th (September 29) meetings indicate that no progress had been made in the investigation; see also George Bush, with Victor Gold, *Looking Forward: An Autobiography* (New York: Bantam, 1988), pp. 169–170.

27. Kissinger, *Years of Renewal*, p. 1047.

28. Kupperman to John O. Marsh, counselor to the president, November 19, 1975, NSArch-CT.

29. Minutes of 93rd meeting of the WG/CCCT, October 1, 1975 (October 6, 1975), NSArch-CT.

30. Mike Duval to Jack Marsh, November 28, 1975, NSArch-CT.

31. Mike Duval, meeting on LaGuardia Airport explosion, Cabinet Room, 6:30 P.M., December 30, 1975, NSArch-CT; McLucas, FAA, to Ford, December 30, 1975, NSArch-CT.

32. Quoted in CIA, Weekly Situation Report on Terrorism, January 6, 1976, NSArch-CT.

33. Ibid.

34. FAA, "Explosions, Sabotage, Devices Found U.S. Aircraft/Airports," undated (probably December 1975), NSArch-CT; FAA, "Civil Aviation Security, Security Alert," December 30, 1975, NSArch-CT.

35. McLucas, FAA, to Ford, December 30, 1975, NSArch-CT.

36. Handwritten notes, dated December 30, 1975, NSArch-CT. Ford may have explained to those in the Cabinet Room in which direction he hoped to take U.S. antiterrorism policy, but this does not appear in these notes.

37. Richard Lally, FAA, to chiefs of Air Transportation Security Divisions, January 1, 1976, NSArch-CT.

38. Ibid.

39. Minutes of 99th meeting of the WG/CCCT, January 14, 1976 (January 19, 1976), NSArch-CT.

40. Jim Cannon to Ford, "Secretary Coleman's Report on LaGuardia Bombing," January 23, 1976, NSArch-CT.

41. Peter Harclerode, *Secret Soldiers: Special Forces in the War Against Terrorism* (London: Cassell, 2000), pp. 85–89.

42. Minutes of 99th meeting of the WG/CCCT, January 14, 1976 (January 19, 1976), NSArch-CT. During a report on the OPEC incident, the CIA representative at this meeting recalled an earlier prediction.

43. CIA memo for the WG/CCCT, "Study on the Japanese Red Army," December 23, 1974, CIA FOIA Electronic Reading Room.

44. Robert Fearey, attachment to cover letter, "Intermediate Terrorism Study," January 22, 1976, NSArch-CT.

45. Ibid.

46. Kupperman to Cherne, May 19, 1976, NSArch-CT; Cherne to Kupperman, July 19, 1976, NSArch-CT.

47. Minutes of 109th meeting of the WG/CCCT, May 27, 1976 (June 10, 1976), NSArch-CT.

48. Ibid.

49. Ibid. At this meeting, in 1976, Giuliani raised the importance of the U.S. government's speaking with one voice as it responded to press questions during an international terrorist incident and suggested that "a model plan be worked out."

50. James B. Adams, telephone interview (June 16, 2004). Adams was the FBI's assistant to the director for investigations, the third-ranking official in the bureau, from 1974 to 1978, then associate director from 1978 to 1979.

51. C. L. Sulzberger, "The Antiterrorist League," *New York Times,* April 14, 1976.

52. Quoted in Jon Nordheimer, "Reagan Asserts Law Aids 'The Criminal Defendant,'" *New York Times,* May 27, 1976.

53. Minutes of 111th meeting of the WG/CCCT, June 16, 1976 (June 21, 1976), NSArch-CT.

54. See Jack Anderson and Les Whitten, "Terrorists Get Missiles," *Washington Post,* May 14, 1976; Jack Anderson, "Terrorist 'Fish' in a Sea of Tourists," *Washington Post,* May 16, 1976.

55. Mike Duval to Dick Cheney, "Terrorism," June 21, 1976, NSArch-CT.

56. Ibid.

57. NSDM 340, Port Security, Ford Library.

58. Minutes of 114th meeting of the WG/CCCT, August 10, 1976, NSArch-CT. L. Douglas Heck was the first chairman with the rank of ambassador.

59. Mike Duval to Dick Cheney, "Terrorism," June 21, 1976, NSArch-CT.

60. Jeffrey D. Simon, *The Terrorist Trap: America's Experience with Terrorism* (Bloomington: Indiana University Press, 1994), pp. 110–120.

61. James B. Adams, telephone interview (June 16, 2004).

62. Peter Kornbluh, *The Pinochet File: A Declassified Dossier on Atrocity and Accountability* (New York: New Press, 2003), pp. 346–355.

63. Minutes of 118th meeting of the WG/CCCT, September 29, 1976 (October 6, 1976), NSArch-CT. There was another suspicious political death in Washington, D.C., in February 1941. Questions remain whether a Soviet assassin killed Soviet defector Walter Krivitsky in Capitol Hill's Bellevue Hotel. Soviet-era intelligence materials opened in the 1990s, however, suggest that Krivitsky committed suicide.

64. James B. Adams, telephone interview (June 16, 2004).

Chapter Five

1. Quoted in Tom Wicker, "Talking Tough on Terrorism," *New York Times,* July 20, 1976.

2. William Greider and Richard Harwood, "Hanafis Surrender, Free 134 Hostages After Talks with 3 Moslem Envoys," *Washington Post,* March 11, 1977; Ben A. Franklin and David Binder, "3 Islamic Diplomats Bridge Gap to Gunmen," *New York Times,* March 12, 1977.

3. "3 Islamic Diplomats Bridge Gap to Gunmen," *New York Times,* March 12, 1977; J. Y. Smith and Laura A. Kiernan, "Life Sentences Sought for Hanafis," *Washington Post,* August 31, 1977.

4. General William Odom (ret.) interview (February 27, 2004).

5. Ibid.

6. Memorandum, "Executive Comments on Senate Bill 2236," January 11, 1978, NSArch-CT; Executive Committee on Terrorism, "The United States Government Antiterrorism Program," June 1979, Vice President's Task Force on Counterterrorism, George H. W. Bush Library.

7. General William Odom (ret.) interview (February 27, 2004).

8. Stansfield Turner interview (December 10, 2003).

9. Frank C. Carlucci interview (December 4, 2003); Stansfield Turner interview (December 10, 2003).

10. Frank C. Carlucci interview (December 4, 2003).

11. "Bombs in New York City Kill 1, Injure 8; Threats Force Evacuations of Buildings," *Wall Street Journal,* August 4, 1977; Herbert Hadad and Leo Standora, "One Killed as Bombs Disrupt New York," *Washington Post,* August 4, 1977.

12. Herbert Hadad and Leo Standora, "One Killed as Bombs Disrupt New York," *Washington Post,* August 4, 1977.

13. Oliver B. Revell, executive assistant director, investigations, FBI, "Terrorism: A Law Enforcement Perspective," Unpublished monograph. The author is grateful to Mr. Revell for sharing this paper with him; Arnold H. Lubasch, "Woman Is Charged in FALN Blast," *New York Times,* September 8, 1977.

14. David Burnham, "8,000 Pounds of Atom Materials Unaccounted For by Plants in US," *New York Times,* August 5, 1977.

15. Thomas O'Toole, "4 Tons of A-Metal Missing," *Washington Post,* August 5, 1977.

16. "Around the Nation: Terrorists in San Francisco Target City's Tourist Industry," *Washington Post,* September 3, 1977.

17. Joanne Omang, "Two Groups Claiming Bomb Credit Well Known in Miami's Little Havana," *Washington Post,* September 8, 1977.

18. Arthur T. Hadley, "America's Vulnerability to Terrorism: Carter Sides with the Optimists in Government Dispute," *Washington Post,* December 4, 1977.

19. Paul Hoffman, "Bonn Is Told 3 Planes Will Be Blown Up to Avenge Terrorists' Death," *New York Times,* November 6, 1977; Peter Harclerode, *Secret Soldiers: Special Forces in the War Against Terrorism* (London: Cassell, 2001), pp. 367–382.

20. Quoted in David Binder, "Javits Criticizes Administration Efforts on Terrorism," *New York Times,* November 14, 1977; David Binder, "US Revises Antiterrorist System, but Some Questions Persist," *New York Times,* January 9, 1978.

21. Quoted in David Binder, "Javits Criticizes Administration Efforts on Terrorism," *New York Times,* November 14, 1977.

22. Memorandum, "Executive Comments on Senate Bill 2236," January 11, 1978, NSArch-CT.

23. William E. Odom to Stu Eizenstat, Jack Watson, November 15, 1977, NSArch-CT.

24. "Bill to Cut Flights to Hijack Havens Unveiled," *Washington Post,* October 25, 1977.

25. Arthur T. Hadley, "America's Vulnerability to Terrorism: Carter Sides with Optimists in Government Dispute," *Washington Post,* December 4, 1977. For more information on the debate see David Binder, "US Revises Antiterrorist System, but Some Question Preparedness: Congressional and Government Specialists Say New Lines of Command Are Too Diffuse," *New York Times,* January 9, 1978; David Binder, "Antiterrorist Policy of US Held Weak," *New York Times,* April 23, 1978.

26. Brian Michael Jenkins, "Terrorism in the 1980s," Rand Corporation, December 1980.

27. CIA, National Foreign Assessment Center, "Patterns of International Terrorism: 1980," June 1981, NSArch-CT. UN Resolution 242 had been passed in the wake of the Six Day War of June 1967.

28. Harold Saunders, telephone interview (February 15, 2004); Moshe Brilliant, "Begin Is Adamant on Palestinians as Vance Hints at a Shift by PLO: Premier Declares Israel Will Exercise Veto," *New York Times,* August 9, 1977; Robert Keatley, "US Move for Direct Dealings with PLO Could Bring a Confrontation with Israel," *Wall Street Journal,* August 9, 1977.

29. Arthur T. Hadley, "America's Vulnerability to Terrorism: Carter Sides with Optimists in Government Dispute," *Washington Post,* December 4, 1977; David Binder, "US Revises Antiterrorist System, but Some Question Preparedness: Congressional and Government Specialists Say New Lines of Command Are Too Diffuse," *New York Times,* January 9, 1978; David Binder, "Antiterrorist Policy of US Held Weak," *New York Times,* April 23, 1978.

30. Harclerode, *Secret Soldiers,* pp. 409–411; William Odom interview (February 27, 2004).

31. Kenneth Turan, "Film Cost $18 Million, Eight Years," *Washington Post,* March 10, 1977.

32. Anthony Quainton interview (September 30, 2003).

33. Ibid.

34. Ibid.

35. Ibid.

36. Warren Christopher to Carter, September 21, 1978, Document 3272, Declassified Documents Reference Series.

37. Ibid.

38. Cyrus Vance to Carter, December 4, 1978, Document 0214, Declassified Documents Reference Series.

39. Anthony Quainton interview (September 30, 2003).

40. John K. Cooley, *Libyan Sandstorm: The Complete Account of Qaddafi's Revolution* (New York: Holt, Rinehart, and Winston, 1982), p. 186.

41. Anthony Quainton interview (September 30, 2003).

42. Edward C. Burks, "Spotlight on Ribicoff," *New York Times,* May 21, 1978; "Senators Seek to Legislate Sanctions Against Terrorism," *Washington Post,* February 5, 1979.

43. Annie M. Gutierrez to Stuart Eizenstat, "Ribicoff's Bill on Terrorism," January 12, 1978, NSArch-CT.

44. Ibid.

45. Ibid.

46. Ibid.

47. General William Odom (ret.) interview (February 27, 2004).

48. Jimmy Carter, *Keeping Faith: Memoirs of a President* (New York: Bantam, 1982), p. 457.

49. Ibid.

50. Anthony Quainton interview (September 30, 2003).

51. Ibid. The executive committee, which had been established to bring the principals into the discussion of terrorist acts, would also not be used.

52. Richard Burt, "The New Strategy for Nuclear War: How It Evolved," *New York Times,* August 13, 1980; General William Odom (ret.) interview (February 27, 2004).

53. General William Odom (ret.) interview (February 27, 2004).

Chapter Six

1. Public Papers of the President: Ronald W. Reagan, Vol. 1.

2. Rowland Evans and Robert Novak, "Never Again," *Washington Post,* January 21, 1981.

3. Alexander M. Haig, Jr. interview (January 23, 2004).

4. Anthony Quainton interview (September 30, 2003).

5. The following attended besides President Reagan: the vice president; the secretary of state; the secretary of defense; the attorney general; the directors

of the FBI, the NSA, and the CIA; Edwin Meese; James Baker; the assistant to the president for national security affairs; and the head of the Secret Service. See Richard V. Allen, "Meeting with Interagency Working Committee on Terrorism," January 24, 1981, "Terrorism [1 of 9]," Bush vice presidential records, National Security Affairs, George H. W. Bush Library (hereinafter GHWBL), College Station.

6. Alexander M. Haig, Jr., interview (January 23, 2004). Meese also recalled the relationship between the men as difficult: "Al had formidable abilities, and a temperament to match. My impression was that he saw himself as the only professional among a group of amateurs." Edwin Meese III, *With Reagan: The Inside Story* (Washington, D.C.: Regnery Publishing, 1992), p. 65.

7. Edwin Meese interview (December 8, 2003).

8. Ibid.

9. General William Odom (ret.) interview (February 27, 2004).

10. For a sense of how CIA old-timers saw the role of the Soviet Union in international terrorism, see Harry Rositzke, "If There Were No KGB, Would the Scale and Intensity of Terrorism Be Diminished?" *New York Times,* July 20, 1981.

11. Nancy Bearg Dyke to Vice President Bush, "Meeting on Terrorism with National Security Council Advisors—1:30 P.M. Today," January 26, 1981, "Terrorism [1 of 9]," Bush vice presidential records, National Security Affairs, GH-WBL, College Station.

12. Ronald Reagan, "Russians," May 25, 1977, *Reagan, In His Own Hand,* Kiron K. Skinner, Annelise Anderson, and Martin Anderson, eds. (New York: The Free Press, 2001), pp. 33–35; Reagan, "Namibia, I," and "Namibia, II," July 9, 1979, *Reagan, In His Own Hand,* pp. 190–193.

13. Reagan, "Terrorism," November 16, 1976, *Reagan's Path to Victory, The Shaping of Ronald Reagan's Vision: Selected Writings,"* Kiron K. Skinner, Annelise Anderson, and Martin Anderson, eds. (New York: The Free Press, 2004), pp. 94–95; Reagan, "Counterintelligence," January 19, 1979, *Reagan's Path to Victory,* pp. 409–410.

14. Reagan, "Terrorism," November 16, 1976, in *Reagan's Path to Victory,* Skinner et al., eds., pp. 94–95.

15. Reagan, "Peace," August 18, 1980, *Reagan, In His Own Hand,* Skinner et al., eds., p. 483.

16. Reagan, "Terrorism," November 16, 1976, *Reagan's Path to Victory,* Skinner et al., eds., pp. 94–95.

17. Quoted in Hedrick Smith, "An Assertive America," *New York Times,* January 28, 1981.

18. Michael Getler, "Soviets and Terrorist Activity: World of Shadows and Shading," *Washington Post,* February 7, 1981; Editorial, "Haig at the Helm," *Wall Street Journal,* January 30, 1981.

19. Editorial, "Haig at the Helm," *Wall Street Journal,* January 30, 1981.

20. Alexander M. Haig, Jr., interview (January 23, 2004). For that speech, see Reagan, "Peace," August 18, 1980, *Reagan, In His Own Hand,* Skinner et al., eds., p. 483.

21. Alexander M. Haig, Jr., interview (January 23, 2004).

22. Richard Halloran, "Proof of Soviet-Aided Terror Is Scare," *New York Times,* February 9, 1981; Judith Miller, "US Study Discounts Soviet Terror Role: A Draft CIA Report, Now Being Reviewed, Finds Insufficient Evidence for Direct Help," *New York Times,* March 29, 1981; George Lardner, Jr., "Assault on Terrorism: Internal Security or Witch Hunt?" *Washington Post,* April 20, 1981; Philip Taubman, "US Tries to Back Up Haig on Terrorism," *New York Times,* May 3, 1981; Tom Wicker, "The Great Terrorist Hunt," *New York Times,* May 5, 1981; Leslie H. Gelb, "Role of Moscow in Terror Doubted: US Intelligence Officials Say Haig Based Accusation on Decade-Old Information," *New York Times,* October 18, 1981.

23. Quoted in Christopher Andrew and Vasili Mitrokhin, *The Sword and the Shield: The Mitrokhin Archive and the Secret History of the KGB* (New York: Basic Books, 1999), p. 380. Haddad was agent "Natsionalist."

24. Alexander M. Haig, Jr., interview (January 23, 2004); William Odom interview (February 27, 2004); Edwin Meese III interview (December 8, 2003); John Poindexter interview (November 24, 2003); Robert Oakley interview (February 7, 2004).

25. John Poindexter interview (November 24, 2003).

26. Anthony C. E. Quainton to the executive secretary, "Meeting of the Interdepartmental Group on Terrorism–March 12, 1981," March 12, 1981, "Terrorism [1 of 9]," Bush vice presidential records, National Security Affairs, GHWBL, College Station. In the fourteen months before he left, Quainton had used the working group to maintain federal readiness for various terrorist scenarios. In May 1981, for example, Washington jointly trained with the Canadian government in an antiterrorism exercise. The scenario was that the U.S. consul general in a Canadian city, his wife, and a houseguest were seized by five terrorists and taken to the consulate. The hostage takers requested the release of ten prisoners in the United States who were "known Croatian terrorists" and also demanded $100,000 in gold for of each hostage. These exercises were designed to help formulate a set of guidelines for U.S. officials involved in hostage incidents overseas. The working group had also sought to assist the Reagan administration in preparing a public affairs strategy to avoid the debilitating effect of the Iranian hostage incident in any future crisis. Finally, Quainton's group had encouraged the administration to assist foreign police in raising their counterterrorism capabilities.

27. Robert L. Earl to Admiral Holloway, "Subject: The Interdepartmental Group on Terrorism (IG/T)," November 12, 1985, NSC, Counterterrorism

and Narcotics, "NSDD 207: Responses to Issue Papers [Earl, Robert]," Box 91956, Ronald Reagan Library. Among the eleven permanent members of the Interdepartmental Group were the Department of State, the Office of the Vice President, the NSC, the Department of Justice, the FBI, the Department of the Treasury, the Joint Chiefs of Staff, the Department of Energy, the CIA, and the FAA. Later, a representative from the Drug Enforcement Agency and the national intelligence officer for terrorism (NIO/T) from the CIA were added.

28. Ibid.

29. Blind memo to Admiral Holloway (probably by Robert Earl), "Subject: Comments on NSC Changes on 'Consensus' Draft of Issue #3," November 12, 1985, NSC, Counterterrorism and Narcotics, "NSDD 207: Responses to Issue Papers [Earl, Robert]," Box 91956, Ronald Reagan Library; emphasis in the original.

30. NSDD 30, signed by President Reagan on April 10, 1982, established the TIWG. The White House scheduled the first meeting of the group for April 20, 1982. See William P. Clark, "Managing Terrorism Incidents," April 10, 1984, Office of the Vice President, National Security Affairs, Donald P. Gregg Files, Task Force on Terrorism File, Combating Terrorism Task Force [1 of 7], GHWBL, College Station.

31. L. Paul Bremer, Executive Secretary, Department of State, to participants of SIG/Libya, March 11, 1981, SIG on Libya Folder, Near East and South Asia Affairs Directorate, Box 91144, Ronald Reagan Library.

32. Richard V. Allen to the President, "National Security Meeting, Friday May 22, 1981," [No date], NSC Meeting on Libya May 22, 1981, Folder, Near East and South Asia Affairs Directorate, Box 91144, Ronald Reagan Library.

33. Raymond Tanter, "Libyan Contingencies and U.S. Options," [Cover Note is dated November 4, 1981], IG on Libya November 13, 1981, Near East and South Asia Affairs Directorate, Box 91144, Ronald Reagan Library.

34. Tanter to Allen, "Interagency meetings on Libya and NSC Staff Paper—'Libyan Contingencies and US Options,'" November 13, 1981. IG on Libya November 17, 1981, Folder, Near East and South Asia Affairs Directorate, Box 91144, Ronald Reagan Library.

35. Raymond Tanter to Allen, "IG on Libya, October 1, 1981," September 29, 1981, IG on Libya October 1, 1981, Folder, Near East and South Asia Affairs Directorate, Box 91144, Ronald Reagan Library; Robert C. MacFarlane to NSC, OSD, CIA, "Study of Soviet Responses to U.S. Military Actions Against Libya," November 18, 1981, NSC Meeting–Libya 12/7/81 (2/2) Folder, Near East and South Asia Affairs Directorate, Box 91144, Ronald Reagan Library.

36. L. Paul Bremer to James W. Nance, The White House, "Preliminary Libyan Response to Protest," December 11, 1981, NSC Meeting–Libya 12/7/81 (2/2) Folder, Near East and South Asia Affairs Directorate, Box 91144, Ronald Reagan Library.

37. Alexander M. Haig, Jr., interview (January 23, 2004); William Odom interview (February 27, 2004); John Poindexter interview (November 24, 2003).

38. Magnus Ranstorp, *Hizb'allah in Lebanon: The Politics of the Western Hostage Crisis* (New York: St. Martin's, 1997), pp. 25–59 passim.

39. Ronald Reagan, *An American Life* (New York: Pocket Books, 1990), p. 443.

40. Ibid.

41. Quoted in John M. Goshko, "Reagan Condemns Bombing, Vows to Pursue Peace," *Washington Post*, April 19, 1983.

42. Quoted in ibid.

43. Theodore Draper, *A Very Thin Line: The Iran-Contra Affairs* (New York: Simon and Schuster, 1991), pp. 120–121.

44. Reagan, *An American Life*, p. 453.

45. Quoted in David C. Wills, *The First War on Terrorism: Counter-Terrorism Policy during the Reagan Administration* (Lanham, Md.: Rowman and Littlefield, 2003), p. 64.

46. Ibid.

47. Cited in Judge Royce C. Lamberth's decision in *Peterson v. The Islamic Republic of Iran*. At the March 23, 2004, public hearing, former Reagan navy secretary John Lehman endorsed Admiral Lyons's recollection that this decrypt existed and that it had been available to elements of the U.S. intelligence community before Hezbollah attacked the Marine barracks.

48. NSDD 109, October 23, 1983, Executive Secretariat, NSC: Records: NSDDs, "NSDD 109," Box 91291, Ronald Reagan Library.

49. Ibid.

50. Richard Armitage public testimony, National Commission on the Terrorist Attacks Upon the United States, March 24, 2004.

51. John Poindexter interview (November 24, 2003).

52. A few days later, a hotel in Baalbek frequented by Hussein Mussawi, the leader of the Islamic Amal faction of Hezbollah, was added to the target list.

53. Quoted in David Ignatius and Gerald F. Seib, "Top Suspect in Beirut Blast Emerges," *Wall Street Journal*, November 4, 1983.

54. Bernard Gwertzman, "US Is Now Facing Lebanon Decision," *New York Times*, November 18, 1983.

55. John Poindexter interview (February 17, 2004).

56. Caspar Weinberger, *Fighting for Peace* (New York: Warner Books, 1990), p. 162; see the account in Robert Timberg, *The Nightingale's Song* (New York: Simon and Schuster, 1995), pp. 338–340.

57. John Poindexter interview (February 17, 2004).

58. Ibid.

59. Reagan, *An American Life*, pp. 463–464.

60. John Poindexter email to the author (February 19, 2004).

61. Philip A. Dur and Donald R. Fortier to McFarlane, "Countering Future Terrorist Attacks Against US Forces and Facilities in Lebanon," November 21, 1983, Executive Secretariat, NSC: Records: NSDDs, "NSDD 109," Box 91291, Reagan Library. This is a cover sheet to a memo of the same name from McFarlane to Casey, Weinberger, Shultz, and Vessey.

62. Robert Timberg, *The Nightingale's Song,* pp. 340–341.

63. John Poindexter interview (February 17, 2004).

64. Robert Timberg, *The Nightingale's Song,* pp. 340–341.

65. Quoted in Joseph E. Persico, *Casey: From the OSS to the CIA* (New York: Viking, 1990), p. 315.

66. Stansfield Turner interview (December 10, 2003). Admiral Turner believes that he transferred Ames from the DO to the DI in 1977.

67. Fred Turco interview (February 5, 2004); Stansfield Turner interview (December 10, 2003); Jack O'Connell interview (October 22, 2003); Frank C. Carlucci interview (December 4, 2003).

68. Joseph E. Persico, *Casey,* pp. 316–317.

69. Magnus Ranstorp, *Hizb'allah in Lebanon,* p. 91.

70. Department of State, "Patterns of Global Terrorism: 1983," September 1984, NSArch-CT.

71. Report of the Congressional Committee Investigating the Iran-Contra Affair, 100th Congress, 1st Session, November 1987, p. 160.

72. George Shultz interview (November 18, 2003).

73. "NSDD of April 3, 1984 on Combatting Terrorism," in McFarlane to Meese, "Background Material on Terrorism," August 15, 1984, NSArch-CT.

74. "NSDD of April 3, 1984 on Combatting Terrorism," in McFarlane to Meese, "Background Material on Terrorism," August 15, 1984, NSArch-CT.

75. Oliver "Buck" Revell interview (January 31, 2004).

76. Robert Timberg, *The Nightingale's Song,* p. 342.

77. Secretary of state cable to field, September 11, 1984, NSArch-CT.

78. CIA report, "Alert Items," September 20, 1984, NSArch-CT.

79. Stephen Engleberg, "US Ship Was Set for Lebanon Raid: Official Says Aircraft Carrier Was Prepared to Counter Anti-American Terror," *New York Times,* November 27, 1984; Vice President's Task Force on Combating Terrorism, *Terror Group Profiles* (Amsterdam: Fredonia Books, 2002), p. 17.

80. Information on this meeting comes from the notes taken by Oliver North; see entry for September 21, 1984, Oliver North Notebooks, National Security Archive.

81. CIA report, "The Islamic Jihad," September 25, 1984, NSArch-CT.

82. Oliver North notes entry for September 21, 1984, Oliver North Notebooks, National Security Archive.

83. Ibid.

84. George Shultz recalled that this intelligence came to his attention on September 22; see Shultz, *Turmoil and Triumph: My Years as Secretary of State* (New York: Scribner, 1993), pp. 647–648. Poindexter cannot recall when North told him about it; John Poindexter interview (February 17, 2004). Oliver North recalls that the information was available before the attack; conversation with Oliver North (May 28, 2004).

85. George Shultz, *Turmoil and Triumph*, p. 648; John Poindexter interview (November 24, 2003).

86. Quoted in Francis X. Clines, "Intelligence Cuts by Predecessors Had a Role in Blast, Reagan Says," *New York Times,* September 27, 1984.

87. Frank C. Carlucci interview (December 4, 2003); Stansfield Turner interview (December 10, 2003).

88. Frank C. Carlucci interview (December 4, 2003).

89. Oliver North notes of 0920 meeting with president, re Beirut bombing, September 27, 1984, Oliver North Notebooks, National Security Archive.

90. Philip A. Dur memo to McFarlane, "A Summary of the Intelligence on the September 20, 1984 Attack on the Beirut Embassy," September 28, 1984, NSArch-CT. Dur suggested that McFarlane send the memo "Lebanon: The Hizballah" to President Reagan.

91. Quoted in David Hoffman, "Reagan Telephones Carter on Beirut Remarks," *Washington Post,* September 29, 1984.

92. George Shultz, telephone interview (March 3, 2004).

93. Minutes of NSPG meeting, "Response to Terrorist Activity in Lebanon," October 3, 1984, NSArch-CT. All direct quotations from the discussion come from this document.

94. Quoted in Stephen Engleberg, "US Ship Was Set for Lebanon Raid," *New York Times,* November 27, 1984.

95. George Shultz, *Turmoil and Triumph*, pp. 648–649.

96. Quoted in Bernard Gwertzman, "Bush Challenges Shultz's Position on Terror Policy," *New York Times,* October 27, 1984.

97. Caspar Weinberger, *Fighting for Peace*, pp. 441–442. Weinberger gave this speech on November 28, 1984.

98. Oliver North note, "1800 Call from Adm Moreau," October 30, 1984, Oliver North Notebooks, National Security Archive.

99. North and Dur to McFarlane, "National Security Decision Directive (NSDD) on Support to the Government of Lebanon in Planning for Counter-Terrorist Operations," October 31, 1984, NSArch-CT.

100. Oliver North note, November 1, 1984, Oliver North Notebooks, NSArch-CT. National Security Archive.

101. McFarlane to Vice President Bush et al., "National Security Decision Directive Support to the Government of Lebanon for Counter-Terrorist Operations," November 2, 1984, NSArch-CT.

102. Robert Oakley interview (February 7, 2004).

103. Oliver North note on TIWG meeting, November 10, 1984, Oliver North Notebooks, National Security Archive.

104. Theodore Draper, *A Very Thin Line*, p. 14.

Chapter Seven

1. Don Gregg to Bush, December 5, 1984, Office of the Vice President [OVP], National Security Affairs, D. P. Gregg Files, Task Force on Terrorism Files, GHWBL. Helms had invited Gregg to lunch on December 5 to discuss "in some detail" a *New York Times* article of December 4 by Thomas L. Friedman, "Israel Turns Terror Back on the Terrorists, but Finds No Political Solution." Gregg enclosed a copy of the article for Bush.

2. Don Gregg to Bush, December 5, 1984, OVP, National Security Affairs, D. P. Gregg Files, Task Force on Terrorism Files, GHWBL. The date of the meeting is handwritten on Gregg's memo.

3. George Bush diary, "Notes 12/15/70–2/8/71," UN Ambassador Papers, GHWBL. In an entry for January 5, 1971, Bush wrote, "I had a long CIA briefing from Dick Helms after lunch. He is a friend and I think this will prove to be helpful."

4. "Memo for the Record–September 28, 1972," George Bush diary, "Notes 1/5/72–11/30/72," UN Ambassador Papers, GHWBL.

5. Don Gregg to Bush, December 5, 1984, OVP, National Security Affairs, D. P. Gregg Files, Task Force in Terrorism Files, GHWBL. The date of the meeting, initialed approvingly by Bush, is handwritten on Gregg's memo.

6. Joseph E. Persico, *Casey: From the OSS to the CIA* (New York: Viking, 1990), p. 429.

7. Ibid.

8. Robert Oakley interview (February 7, 2004).

9. This information comes solely from Bob Woodward's *Veil: The Secret Wars of the CIA, 1981–1987* (New York: Simon and Schuster, 1987), pp. 395–397. Woodward's theory about the Fadlallah incident shifted. In 1985, he had asserted in the *Washington Post* that a rogue Lebanese element trained as a result of the November 1984 finding had arranged the bombing.

10. Quoted in Persico, *Casey*, p. 430.

11. John Poindexter interview (November 24, 2003); Fred Turco interview (February 5, 2004).

12. Cable, DOS, Armacost to U.S. embassies in Ankara, Islamabad, Tokyo, Bonn, London, Canberra, and Paris, January 14, 1985, NSArch-CT.

13. Ibid.

14. Ibid.

15. Ibid.

16. Poindexter, "Notes from CPPG Meeting, March 13, 1985," NSArch-CT.

17. Cable, (DOS), Armacost to U.S. embassies in Ankara, Islamabad, Tokyo, Bonn, London, Canberra, and Paris, January 14, 1985, NSArch-CT.

18. Nicholas Platt (executive secretary, DOS) to McFarlane, January 15, 1985, NSArch-CT.

19. Minutes of NSPG meeting, "Response to Threat to Lebanon Hostages," January 18, 1985, NSArch-CT.

20. Ibid.

21. Poindexter to Reagan, "Meeting with the National Security Planning Group," January 17, 1985, NSArch-CT.

22. Armacost (DOS) immediate delivery to U.S. embassies in Ankara, Islamabad, Tokyo, Bonn, London, Canberra, and Paris, January 14, 1985, NSArch-CT.

23. Magnus Ranstorp, *Hizb'allah in Lebanon: The Politics of the Western Hostage Crisis* (New York: St. Martin's, 1997), p. 34.

24. Minutes of NSPG meeting, "Response to Threat to Lebanon Hostages," January 18, 1985, NSArch-CT. Given that details of the four options were redacted from the declassified document, the argument that these two options involved attacks on Iranian targets is a matter of conjecture by the author based on the character of the Pentagon's objections, the nature of the problem facing the United States at that moment, and the fact that there is general evidence that the Reagan administration did discuss possible air strikes on Iran or Iranian targets in Lebanon.

25. John Poindexter interview (February 17, 2004).

26. Minutes of NSPG meeting, "Response to Threat to Lebanon Hostages," January 18, 1985, NSArch-CT.

27. Ibid.

28. Ibid.

29. Ibid.

30. "Hostage Locating Task Force: Terms of Reference," undated (context suggests prior to February 13, 1985), NSArch-CT. Levin, who escaped on February 13, is described as still a hostage.

31. John Poindexter, "Notes from CPPG Meeting, March 13, 1985," NSArch-CT.

32. "Hostage Locating Task Force: Terms of Reference," undated (context suggests prior to February 13, 1985), NSArch-CT. Levin, who escaped on February 13, is described as still a hostage.

33. Ibid.

34. John Poindexter, "Notes from CPPG Meeting, March 13, 1985," NSArch-CT.

35. Ibid.

36. "Talking Points," undated (context suggests prior to March 13 CPPG meeting), NSArch-CT.

37. John Poindexter, "Notes from CPPG Meeting, March 13, 1985," NSArch-CT. Political difficulties within the Lebanese government increased the vulnerability of the U.S. legation. Members of the Lebanese army were standing guard around the embassy, but in recent days there was evidence that factional fighting within the Christian Phalange movement—which supported the Lebanese government—made it likely that these troops would be withdrawn.

38. "Talking Points," undated (context suggests prior to March 13 CPPG meeting), NSArch-CT.

39. Ibid.

40. Report, Vice President's Task Force on Combating Terrorism, Counsel's Office, John Schmitz Files, "Terrorism-General," V.P. Papers, GHWBL. These assumptions are spelled out and accepted in the task force report.

41. CIA, "The Shias: Potential for Terrorism," *Terrorism Review*, March 15, 1984, CIA FOIA Electronic Reading Room.

42. DIA terrorism summary, March 18, 1985, NSArch-CT.

43. "Talking Points," undated (context suggests prior to March 13 CPPG meeting), NSArch-CT.

44. Magnus Ranstorp, *Hizb'allah in Lebanon,* p. 214, n. 30.

45. Ibid, p. 36.

46. "Talking Points" (circa March 19, 1985), NSArch-CT. The document mentions the possibility of a Syrian rescue attempt but did not handicap the likelihood of success.

47. Oliver North Notebooks, NSArch-CT.

48. John Poindexter interviews (November 24, 2003; February 17, 2004).

49. *Report of the Congressional Committees Investigating the Iran-Contra Affair,* 100th Congress, 1st Session, November 1987, p. 165.

50. For a superb reconstruction of the policymaking during the tense seventeen days of the TWA 847 incident, see David C. Wills, *The First War on Terrorism: Counter-Terrorism Policy During the Reagan Administration* (Oxford: Rowan and Littlefield, 2003), pp. 89–137.

51. Minutes of NSPG meeting, "Response to Threat to Lebanon Hostages," January 18, 1985, NSArch-CT. Casey described this operation as part of his briefing. The name of the mediating state or group is redacted.

52. John Poindexter interview (February 17, 2004).

53. Ronald Reagan, *An American Life* (New York: Pocket Books, 1990), pp. 498–499.

54. Ibid.

55. "Excerpts from the President's Address Accusing Nations of 'Acts of War,'" *New York Times,* July 9, 1985.

56. Entry for June 27, 1985, quoted in Reagan, *An American Life,* p. 496.

57. Ronald Reagan, *An American Life,* p. 511.

58. Edward D. Sargent, "$5 Million Qaddafi Loan to Go to Toiletry Firm; Farrakhan Says Company Will Hire Blacks," *Washington Post,* May 4, 1985.

59. E. R. Shipp, "Chicago Muslim Gets Qaddafi Loan," *New York Times,* May 4, 1985; Editorial, "The Qaddafi Connection," *New York Times,* May 7, 1985.

60. Joe Pichirallo, "Plot Against Libyans Probed; Grand Jury in Alexandria Calls Qaddafi Supporters," *Washington Post,* May 30, 1985.

61. David B. Ottaway, "US Expels Libyan Tied to Terrorism," *Washington Post,* June 6, 1985.

62. Quoted in Henry Kamm, "Qaddafi Menaces Reagan on Sudan; Tells Western Reporters That President's 'Nose Will Be Cut' If He Interferes," *New York Times,* April 11, 1985.

63. CIA, "Libya: Qaddafi's Prospects for Survival," August 5, 1985, James Stark Files, Libya (3) Box 91095, Ronald Reagan Library.

64. The terms *Rose* and *Tulip* come from Woodward, *Veil,* p. 411.

65. John M. Poindexter to Reagan, April 10, 1986, "Supplemental Finding on Libya Covert Action," Donald Fortier Files, Libya (2 of 12), Box 91673, Ronald Reagan Library. This remarkable document, which was declassified in March 2001, summarizes the goals of the July 1985 finding for President Reagan.

66. Bob Woodward, *Veil,* p. 411.

67. Ibid. In his book *The First War on Terrorism,* David C. Wills assumes that neither finding was signed in July; however, the April 1986 finding makes clear that what was called "Tulip" was signed in July. Wills, *The First War on Terrorism,* pp. 172–175.

68. John Poindexter to the author, March 2004.

69. John Poindexter interview (February 17, 2004).

70. John Poindexter interview (February 17, 2004); Wills, *The First War on Terrorism,* p. 172.

71. Blind memorandum, "Libya," Donald Fortier Files, Libya (2 of 12), Box 91673, Reagan Library.

72. Wills, *The First War on Terrorism,* pp. 172–175.

73. CIA, "Near East and South Asia Review: The Levant and North Africa in 1986," December 6, 1985, CIA Electronic FOIA Archive.

74. David C. Wills, *The First War on Terrorism,* p. 175.

75. Ronald Reagan, *An American Life,* pp. 501–502.

76. Robert McFarlane memo for George Shultz, "Israeli-Iranian Contact," July 13, 1985, Document 70, in Peter Kornbluh and Malcolm Byrne, eds., *The Iran-Contra Scandal: The Declassified History* (New York: New Press, 1993).

77. Ibid.

78. Ronald Reagan, *An American Life,* p. 506.

79. Robert McFarlane memo for George Shultz, "Israeli-Iranian Contact," July 13, 1985, Document 70, in Peter Kornbluh and Malcolm Byrne, eds., *The Iran-Contra Scandal: The Declassified History* (New York: New Press, 1993).

80. George Shultz cable to Robert McFarlane, "Reply to Backchannel No. 3 from Bud," July 14, 1985, Document 71, in Peter Kornbluh and Malcolm Byrne, eds., *The Iran-Contra Scandal: The Declassified History* (New York: New Press, 1993).

81. Reagan, *An American Life,* p. 506.

82. Lou Cannon, *President Reagan: Role of a Lifetime* (New York: PublicAffairs, 2000), p. 546. Although there is controversy over whether Reagan gave prior approval to this first sale of U.S. TOW missiles, Cannon says it was cleared up through reference to Reagan's diaries, to which the Tower Commission investigating the Iran-Contra scandal had access. The sections from the president's diary quoted in Reagan's memoirs seem to substantiate this as well.

83. Cannon, *President Reagan,* p. 534.

84. Unless otherwise noted, this account of the *Achille Lauro* case is based on David Wills's superb reconstruction; see Wills, *The First War on Terrorism,* pp. 139–161. See also Vlad Jenkins, "The *Achille Lauro* Hijacking (A) and (B)," studies C16-88-863.0 and C16-88-864.0 written in 1988 for the Case Program at Harvard's John F. Kennedy School of Government.

85. David C. Wills, *The First War on Terrorism,* p. 149.

86. John Poindexter interview (February 17, 2004).

87. Ibid.

88. Ronald Reagan, *An American Life,* p. 509.

89. Kornbluh and Byrne, eds., *The Iran-Contra Scandal,* pp. 394–395.

90. Bob Woodward, "CIA Anti-Qaddafi Plan Backed; Reagan Authorizes Covert Operation to Undermine Libyan Regime," *Washington Post,* November 3, 1985; Stephen Engleberg, "Reagan Approval Reported on Plan to Weaken Libya; Covert CIA Operation Would Reportedly Help Countries That Oppose Qaddafi," *New York Times,* November 4, 1985.

91. Bob Woodward, "CIA Anti-Qaddafi Plan Backed; Reagan Authorizes Covert Operation to Undermine Libyan Regime," *Washington Post,* November 3, 1985.

92. "CIA Plan's Leak Probed; Reagan 'Concerned' about Libya Report," *Washington Post,* November 4, 1985.

93. "Libya Belittles Reported Plan to Oust Qaddafi," *Washington Post,* November 5, 1985.

94. John M. Poindexter to Reagan, "Supplemental Finding on Libya Covert Action," April 10, 1986, Donald Fortier Files, Libya (2 of 12), Box 91673, Ronald Reagan Library. This document discusses the fate of the July 1985 finding.

95. Statement of Ambassador Edward Marks, Deputy Director, Counter-Terrorism Programs, Office for Counter-Terrorism and Emergency Planning, Department of State Before the House Committee on Foreign Relations, Concerning HR 2822, June 25, 1985, Bush Presidential Records; National Security Council, Richard Canas Files, "Combating Terrorism: Department of State Report (1985) [2of 2] [OA/ID CF01573]," GHWBL.

96. NSDD 180, Civil Aviation Anti-Terrorism Program, July 19, 1985, declassified 1995.

97. David C. Wills, *The First War on Terrorism*, p. 114.

98. Executive Committee on Terrorism, "The United States Government Antiterrorism Program, An Unclassified Summary Report," June 1979, Office of the Vice President, National Security Affairs, "Terrorism," GHWBL.

99. Marginalia on "Issue Paper No. 1 . . . Subject: National Program for Combating Terrorism," undated (during VP task force investigation, 1985–1986), Counterterrorism and Narcotics, NSC, "NSDD 207 NSC Staff: Craig Coy; Robert Earl" (1), Box 91956, Reagan Library.

100. George Shultz interview (November 18, 2003).

101. John Poindexter interview (November 24, 2003).

102. Memorandum for Senior Review Group, Admiral J. T. Holloway III, April 10, 1987, NSC Office of Counterterrorism and Narcotics, "Program Review of the Vice President's Task Force on Combating Terrorism, March–April 1987," (4), Box 91956, Reagan Library. The Senior Review Group included Oliver Revell, the FBI's executive assistant director for investigations; Robert Oakley, the State Department's ambassador at large for counterterrorism; Richard Armitage, the assistant secretary of defense (ISA); future governor of Oklahoma Francis A. Keating II, then the assistant secretary for enforcement; Associate Attorney General Steven Trott; Matthew V. Scocozza, assistant secretary, Police and International Affairs, Department of Transportation; Lt. General John H. Moellering, assistant to the chairman, JCS; Rear Admiral John Poindexter (later Donald Fortier), the deputy national security advisor; and Charles Allen (later Duane Clarridge), of the CIA.

103. John Poindexter interview (February 17, 2004).

104. Doug Menarchik to Donald Gregg, "Holloway Meeting with Carlucci," 1986 (exact date unclear), Counterterrorism and Narcotics, NSC: General: Vice Presidential Task Force NSC Staff (1), Box 91956, Reagan Library.

105. Duane R. Clarridge with Digby Diehl, *A Spy for All Seasons: My Life in the CIA* (New York: Scribner, 1997), p. 324. The details of this finding remain classified.

106. Oliver "Buck" Revell and Dwight Williams, *A G-Man's Journal: A Legendary Career in the FBI–From the Kennedy Assassination to the Oklahoma City Bombing* (New York: Pocket Books, 1998), pp. 292–294.

107. The CPPG retained its responsibility for making foreign policy recom-

mendations to the president and NSC principals, including those on matters touching on counterterrorism, and the TIWG remained an ad hoc institution that could be convened to deal with any particular terrorism crisis.

108. Robert B. Oakley, "International Terrorism: Current Trends and the U.S. Response," U.S. Department of State, Bureau of Public Affairs, May 1985, NSC, Richard Canas Files, "Combating Terrorism, Dept. of State Report (1985)" (1 of 3), Bush Presidential records, GHWBL.

109. Report, Vice President's Task Force on Combating Terrorism, Counsel's Office, John Schmitz Files, "Terrorism-General," V.P. Papers, GHWBL.

110. Ibid.

111. Duane R. Clarridge, *A Spy for All Seasons*, pp. 319–320; Fredrick Turco interview (February 5, 2004).

112. Fredrick Turco interview (February 5, 2004).

113. William Webster interview (December 10, 2003).

114. Duane R. Clarridge, *A Spy for All Seasons,* pp. 319–320.

115. Fredrick Turco interview (February 5, 2004).

116. Ibid.

117. Ronald Reagan, *An American Life,* p. 511.

118. Ibid.

119. John Poindexter interview (February 17, 2004).

120. Ibid.

121. NSDD 205 (with military and intelligence annex), January 8, 1986, declassified 1991.

122. Ibid.; John Poindexter interview (February 17, 2004).

123. However, two U.S. Air Force pilots were killed in the attack.

124. Ronald Reagan, *An American Life,* p. 519.

125. Revell and Williams, *A G-Man's Journal,* p. 312.

126. Fred Turco interview (February 5, 2004).

127. CIA, "Libya: Reviewing Terrorist Capabilities," Terrorism Review, August 10, 1988, CIA FOIA Reading Room.

128. James Stark to Donald Fortier, James Stark Files, "Operations/Targetting (2)," Box 91747, Reagan Library.

129. "Next Steps to Deter Further Libyan Terrorism," undated (from context, April 18 or 19, 1986), Donald Fortier Files, "Libya (Fortier File) [7 of 12]," Box 91673, Reagan Library.

130. CIA, NID, "Lull in Abu Nidal Attacks," July 16, 1986, CIA FOIA Electronic Reading Room; CIA, "Libyan Terrorism in 1986," Terrorism Review, April 9, 1987, CIA FOIA Electronic Reading Room.

131. Oliver L. North, Robert L. Earl, and Craig P. Coy memo to Alton G. Keel, "Crisis Pre-Planning Group (CPPG) Meeting," November 3, 1986, Craig Coy Files, "Syria (2 of 3)," Box CPC–1; FBI–098, Ronald Reagan Library.

132. General William Odom (ret.) interview (February 27, 2004). General William Odom became director of the NSA in 1985. Admiral Poindexter recalls that this step was taken in late 1985 or early 1986 after President Reagan signed the first presidential finding on the Iran initiative. Secretary of State Shultz told Poindexter that he "did not want to be involved in any way and didn't want to see anything about it." John Poindexter to the author, June 30, 2004. Shultz recalls that conversation in much the same way. Telephone conversation with George Shultz, telephone interview (March 4, 2004). He had just returned from a trip overseas in December 1985 and was angry to learn that in his absence President Reagan had signed an order making lie detector tests mandatory for administration officials. Shultz believed that the order was directed at the State Department because some officials in the White House did not trust him with classified information. When Shultz threatened to resign, Reagan rescinded the order. The conversation with Poindexter came amidst this controversy. Shultz recalls telling Poindexter that he did not wish to know any of the operational details of the Iran initiative. Shultz explains that he made this request because he was sure that "if anything leaked, it would be blamed on me and I did not want that to happen." In retrospect, Shultz regrets that he asked to be cut out of this information.

133. William Webster interview (December 10, 2003); Oliver "Buck" Revell interview (January 31, 2004).

134. Theodore Draper, *A Very Thin Line: The Iran-Contra Affairs* (New York: Simon and Schuster, 1991), p. 391.

135. John Poindexter interview (February 17, 2004); Edwin Meese III, *With Reagan: The Inside Story* (Washington, D.C.: Regnery Publishing, 1992), p. 255.

136. Magnus Ranstorp, *Hizb'allah in Lebanon,* p. 98.

137. Frank Carlucci interview (December 4, 2003).

138. Ibid.

139. Ibid.

140. Ibid.

141. Ibid.

142. Fred Turco interview (February 5, 2004); Fred Turco, telephone interview (February 15, 2004).

143. Robert B. Oakley, Barry Kelley to Frank C. Carlucci, "Syria and Iran," March 16, 1987, NSArch-CT.

144. Robert Oakley interview (February 7, 2004).

145. Frank C. Carlucci interview (December 4, 2003); Robert Oakley interview (February 7, 2004).

146. CIA notes, 12:15 P.M., March 30, 1987, NSC Office of Counterterrorism and Narcotics, "Program Review of the Vice President's Task Force on Combating Terrorism, March–April 1987 (4)," Box 91956, Ronald Reagan Library.

147. "FBI Meeting: 12:00 NOON Meeting," NSC Office of Counterterrorism and Narcotics, "Program Review of the Vice President's Task Force on Combating Terrorism, March–April 1987 (4)," Box 91956, Ronald Reagan Library.

148. Ibid.

149. Ibid.

150. "Department of Transportation: Friday, April 3, 1987," NSC Office of Counterterrorism and Narcotics, "Program Review of the Vice President's Task Force on Combating Terrorism, March–April 1987 (4)," Box 91956, Ronald Reagan Library.

151. Ibid.

152. Philip W. Haseltine to Rodney B. McDaniel (executive secretary, NSC), May 20, 1986, NSC Office of Counterterrorism and Narcotics, "Program Review of the Vice President's Task Force on Combating Terrorism, March–April 1987 (4)," Box 91956, Ronald Reagan Library.

153. Ibid.

154. "Talking Points," attachment to briefing memo for the vice president, June 1, 1987, NSC, Counterterrorism and Narcotics, "General: Vice Presidential Task Force NSC Staff (2)," Box 91956, Ronald Reagan Library.

155. State Department, "The Abu Nidal Terror Network," July 1987, NSArch-CT. This classified study was probably based on information from the CTC.

156. Ibid.

157. Fred Turco, telephone interview (February 24, 2004).

158. State Department, "The Abu Nidal Terror Network," July 1987, NSArch-CT.

159. Ibid.

160. Ellen Harris, *Guarding the Secrets: Palestinian Terrorism and a Father's Murder of His Too-American Daughter* (New York: Scribner, 1995), pp. 99–100.

161. Ibid., pp. 301–302.

162. Fred Turco, telephone interview (February 15, 2004).

163. This account of the Carter visit to Damascus comes from an interview with Robert Oakley (February 7, 2004), who was briefed on the Carter visit after the fact.

164. Mark Perry, *Eclipse: The Last Days of the CIA* (New York: Morrow, 1992), pp. 191–194; Fred Turco, telephone interview (February 24, 2004).

165. Mark Perry, *Eclipse,* pp. 192–193.

166. Patrick Seale, *Abu Nidal: A Gun for Hire* (New York: Random House, 1992), pp. 290–291.

167. Ibid., pp. 291–292.

168. Ibid., pp. 296–301.

169. William Webster interview (December 10, 2003).

170. Revell and Williams, *A G-Man's Journal,* pp. 317–318.

171. William Webster interview (December 10, 2003); Oliver "Buck" Revell interview (January 31, 2004); Revell and Williams, *A G-Man's Journal,* pp. 313–326.

172. David Ignatius, "Policy Vacuum: A Clear Plan to Handle Terrorism Still Eludes Divided Reagan Camp; Some Doubt Value of Force; Priority of Saving Lives Leaves US Few Options; Successes Go Unpublicized," *Wall Street Journal,* June 20, 1985.

173. Fred Turco, telephone interview (February 24, 2004).

174. Ibid.

175. CIA, Terrorism Review, October 6, 1988, CIA FOIA Electronic Reading Room.

176. Ibid.

177. CIA, "Lebanon: Hizballah at the Crossroads," Near East and South Asia Review, August 26, 1988, CIA FOIA Electronic Reading Room.

178. Ibid.

179. CIA, Terrorism Review, October 6, 1988, CIA FOIA Electronic Reading Room.

Chapter Eight

1. Fred Turco, telephone interview (February 15, 2004).

2. Fred Turco interview (February 5, 2004); Mark Perry, *Eclipse: The Last Days of the CIA* (New York: Morrow, 1992), p. 462, unnumbered note to p. 171; Craig R. Whitney, "Terrorism Alert: A System Shows Gaps," *New York Times,* March 21, 1989. The information was passed in a form that permitted wide distribution. At the bottom of these classified intelligence reports there was an unclassified alert that could be torn off and shared with people who did not hold security clearances. The unclassified alert was known as a tear line report.

3. Fred Turco interview (February 5, 2004).

4. Ibid.

5. Ibid.

6. Oliver "Buck" Revell interview (January 31, 2004); Oliver "Buck" Revell and Dwight Williams, *A G-Man's Journal: A Legendary Career in the FBI—From the Kennedy Assassination to the Oklahoma City Bombing* (New York: Pocket Books, 1998), pp. 314–315, 370. The Operational Sub-Group (OSG) had emerged from the Bush task force's Senior Policy Group. It was renamed CSG after the Iran-Contra scandal to emphasize that it had a "coordinating" and not an "operational" role.

7. Ruth Marcus and John Goshko, "Bush Vows to 'Punish Severely' Perpetrators of Pan Am Bombing," *Washington Post,* December 30, 1988.

8. Telephone conversation with Oliver "Buck" Revell, July 15, 2004.

9. Mark Perry, *Eclipse,* pp. 174–175.

10. George Shultz interview (November 18, 2003).

11. Brent Scowcroft testimony, Joint House and Senate Select Intelligence Committee, Hearing on Iraq, September 18, 2002.

12. Robert M. Gates, *From the Shadows: The Ultimate Insider's Story of Five Presidents and How They Won the Cold War* (New York, Simon and Schuster, 1996), pp. 458–459.

13. Christopher Andrew, *For the President's Eyes Only: Secret Intelligence and the American Presidency from Washington to Bush* (New York: Harper Collins, 1995), pp. 503–536.

14. Fred Turco interview (February 5, 2004); Oliver "Buck" Revell interview (January 31, 2004); Ambassador David Miller interview (February 13, 2004).

15. Fred Turco interview (February 5, 2004).

16. Oliver "Buck" Revell, telephone interview (July 15, 2004).

17. Fred Turco interview (February 5, 2004); Brent Scowcroft testimony, Joint House and Senate Select Intelligence Committee, Hearing on Iraq, September 18, 2002.

18. Fred Turco interview (February 5, 2004).

19. CIA, DI, Terrorism Review, June 1, 1989, declassified July 7, 1999, CIA FOIA Electronic Reading Room.

20. CIA, DI, Terrorism Review, December 14, 1989, declassified July 7, 1999, CIA FOIA Electronic Reading Room.

21. Joint House and Senate Select Intelligence Committee, Hearing on Iraq, September 18, 2002.

22. Oliver "Buck" Revell, telephone interview (July 15, 2004).

23. Fred Turco interview (February 5, 2004); Ambassador David Miller interview (February 13, 2004).

24. Magnus Ranstorp, *Hizb'allah in Lebanon: The Politics of the Western Hostage Crisis* (New York: St. Martin's, 1997), pp. 116–133.

25. Brent Scowcroft testimony, Joint House and Senate Select Intelligence Committee, Hearing on Iraq, September 18, 2002.

26. Telephone conversation with Fred Turco, February 24, 2004.

27. Ambassador David Miller interview (February 13, 2004). Boykin is currently deputy undersecretary of defense for intelligence.

28. Ibid.

29. Neither James Baker in *The Politics of Diplomacy* (New York: Putnam, 1995) nor George Bush and Brent Scowcroft in their joint memoir, *A World Transformed* (New York: Knopf, 1998), mention the hostage issue.

30. Elaine Sciolino, "Reports Indicate Mounting Efforts to Free US Hostages in Lebanon," *New York Times,* March 6, 1990.

31. Thomas L. Friedman, "Bush Denies Any Deal with Iran for Release," *New York Times,* April 23, 1990.

32. Youssel M. Ibrahim, "Arabs Fear End of Cold War Means a Loss of Aid and Allies," *New York Times,* March 6, 1990.

33. Ihsan A. Hijazi, "Carter Says Syria Aids on Hostages; Ex-President Tells of Promise by Assad to Spur Efforts to Gain Their Release," *New York Times,* March 16, 1990.

34. Quoted in Ihsan A. Hijazi, "Signs of Hope for Lebanon Hostages," *New York Times,* February 27, 1990.

35. Thomas L. Friedman, "Bush Denies Any Deal with Iran for Release," *New York Times,* April 23, 1990.

36. "Iran and Syria Discuss Efforts to Free Hostages," *New York Times,* March 5, 1990.

37. Elaine Sciolino, "Washington Talk: Hoax Shows the Limits of Personal Diplomacy," *New York Times,* March 13, 1990. Thomas Friedman would make this point a month later when the first hostage release in 1990 hit a snag; see Thomas L. Friedman, "Militants Delay Hostage's Release; Say Move Is a Result of US Refusal to Send Diplomat," *New York Times,* April 20, 1990.

38. George H. W. Bush, NSD 26, "US Policy Toward the Persian Gulf," October 2, 1989, George H. W. Bush Library (GHWBL).

39. The "Iran by means of the PFLP-GC" theory to explain the Pan Am 103 disaster was already in the press; see Steve Emerson and Brian Duffy, "The High-Tech Terrorist," *New York Times,* March 18, 1990.

40. Ihsan A. Hijazi, "Iranian Official Says All Hostages May Be Freed within 10 Months," *New York Times,* March 19, 1990.

41. Thomas Friedman, "Militants Delay Hostage's Release; Say Move Is a Result of US Refusal to Send Diplomat," *New York Times,* April 20, 1990.

42. Minutes of meeting of the NSC Deputies Committee, April 19, 1990, NSArch-CT.

43. "Summary of Conclusions of Deputies Committee," April 19, 1990, NSArch-CT.

44. Youssef M. Ibrahim, "US Hostage Move Annoys Militants; Refusal to Send Diplomat Is Called 'Cowboy Behavior' in Group's Statement," *New York Times,* April 21, 1990.

45. Quoted in Youssef M. Ibrahim, "Syrian Official Says He Expects Release of Hostage," *New York Times,* April 22, 1990.

46. Brent Scowcroft to Bush, April 29, 1990, "Possible Release of Hostage Frank H. Reed," NSArch-CT.

47. Ibid.

48. Youssef M. Ibrahim, "Iran Indicates It Will Seek Release of More Hostages If US Responds," *New York Times,* April 24, 1990.

49. Ihsan A. Hijazi, "Iran Reportedly Gave Weapons to Obtain US Hostage Release," *New York Times,* April 23, 1990; Ranstorp, *Hizb'allah in Lebanon,* pp. 119–133. Dislike of any opening to the hated West was only one of the reasons why Hezbollah was inclined to reject requests from the new Iranian leadership. The Hezbollah leadership was determined to compel the return of their fellow fighters in prisons in Kuwait and Israel. The Dawa group in Kuwait included family members of some leading Hezbollah figures. The Shia militias within the Hezbollah movement also considered the hostages as currency in the dispute over the future shape of the Lebanese state. Like their rival, the pro-Syrian Amal group, Hezbollah saw the rapprochement of Iran and Syria as a possible threat to its interests. Despite requests from their sponsors for a cease-fire, the two groups continued to fight through 1989 and much of 1990.

50. Magnus Ranstorp, *Hizb'allah in Lebanon,* pp. 79–80.

51. Patrick Seale, *Abu Nidal: A Gun for Hire* (New York: Random House, 1992), pp. 307–312; Ihsan A. Hijazi, "Abu Nidal's Rivals Seem to Be Gaining; Dissidents Within Palestinian Militant's Group Now Say They'll Follow Arafat," *New York Times,* June 24, 1990.

52. Fred Turco, telephone interview (February 24, 2004).

53. Ellen Francis Harris, *Guarding the Secrets: Palestinian Terrorism and a Father's Murder of His Too-American Daughter* (New York: Scribner, 1995), p. 16; Fred Turco, telephone interview (July 11, 2004).

54. Ellen Francis Harris, *Guarding the Secrets,* passim.

55. Oliver "Buck" Revell, telephone interview (July 15, 2004).

56. Ibid.

57. Fred Turco interview (February 5, 2004).

58. Ellen Francis Harris, *Guarding the Secrets,* pp. 187–193.

59. CIA, Terrorism Review, January 10, 1991, CIA FOIA Electronic Reading Room.

60. Ibid.

61. Ambassador David Miller interview (February 13, 2004).

62. Ibid.

63. William Sessions interview (December 12, 2004).

64. CIA, Terrorism Review, April 4, 1991, CIA FOIA Electronic Reading Room.

65. Fred Turco interview (February 5, 2004).

66. Oliver "Buck" Revell interview (January 31, 2004).

67. William Baker interview (May 25, 2004).

68. Ibid.; Fred Turco interview (February 5, 2004); Fred Turco, telephone interview (July 11, 2004).

69. Fred Turco, telephone interview (July 11, 2004).

70. Fred Turco interview (February 5, 2004).

71. Allen Gerson and Jerry Adler, *The Price of Terror: The Lessons of Lockerbie for a World on the Brink* (New York: HarperCollins, 2001), p. 88.

72. Fred Turco interview (February 5, 2004).

73. Oliver "Buck" Revell, telephone interview (July 15, 2004).

74. Fred Turco interview (February 5, 2004).

75. David Miller interview (February 13, 2004).

76. Fred Turco interview (February 5, 2004).

77. Ibid.

78. Both Oliver Revell and Bill Baker attempted to improve the quality of FBI analysis but encountered opposition to increasing the number of analysts. Oliver "Buck" Revell, telephone interview (July 15, 2004); Bill Baker interview (May 25, 2004).

79. Fred Turco interview (February 5, 2004).

80. Daniel Benjamin and Steven Simon, *The Age of Sacred Terror: Radical Islam's War Against America* (New York: Random House, 2002), pp. 3–7.

81. CIA, Terrorism Review, CIA FOIA Electronic Reading Room.

82. CIA, Near East and South Asia Review for April 24, 1987, CIA FOIA Electronic Reading Room.

83. Ibid.

84. Fred Turco interview (February 4, 2004).

85. Fred Turco, telephone interview (February 15, 2004).

86. Oliver "Buck" Revell interview (January 31, 2004).

87. Ibid.; Judge William Webster interview (December 10, 2003).

88. Ibid.

89. Ibid.; Oliver "Buck" Revell, telephone interview (July 15, 2004).

90. NSD 57, "US Port Security Program," May 7, 1991, GHWBL.

91. Notes of telephone conversation, October 17, 1988, 6:25 P.M., Vice President's Press Office, Press Office Files, Task Force on Terrorism [DA/ID 14970], GHWBL.

92. Ibid.

93. Notes, undated, Vice President's Press Office, Press Office Files, Task Force on Terrorism [DA/ID 14970], GHWBL.

94. Steven Emerson, "Bush's Toothless War Against Terrorism," *U.S. News & World Report,* October 31, 1988.

95. Ibid.

96. David Binder, "CIA Officer's Body Returned from Beirut," *New York Times,* December 28, 1991.

97. CIA, Terrorism Review, June 27, 1991, CIA FOIA Electronic Reading Room.

98. Magnus Ranstorp, *Hizb'allah in Lebanon,* p. 106.

99. Clifford R. Krauss, "U.S., Mindful of Setbacks in Past, Offers

Guarded Praise of Capture," *The New York Times,* September 14, 1992; James Brooke, "Peru's Shining Path Is Decapitated," *The New York Times,* September 20, 1992.

100. Background information from a former U.S. official.

101. Fred Turco to author, July 13, 2004.

Chapter Nine

1. B. Drummond Aynes, Jr., *New York Times,* January 26, 1993.

2. Neil A. Lewis, "Tranquil Campus of CIA Is Shaken by Killings of Two," *New York Times,* January 27, 1993.

3. Ibid.

4. Winston Wiley interview (December 20, 2004).

5. Leon Fuerth interview (December 21, 2004).

6. Winston Wiley interview (December 20, 2004).

7. Elaine Sciolino, "Senior CIA Analyst Admits Discord over Russia," *New York Times,* February 4, 1993.

8. Thomas L. Friedman, "Clinton Keeping Foreign Policy on a Back Burner," *New York Times,* February 8, 1993.

9. Neil A. Lewis, "Bigger Battle Expected on Spy Budget," *New York Times,* February 1, 1993.

10. Ibid.

11. Douglas Jehl, "CIA Nominee Wary of Budget Cuts," *New York Times,* February 3, 1993.

12. Neil A. Lewis, "Bigger Battle Expected on Spy Budget," *New York Times,* February 1, 1993.

13. Peter Lance, *1000 Years for Revenge, International Terrorism and the FBI: The Untold Story* (New York: Regan Books, 2003), pp. 35, 88–94.

14. Douglas Jehl, "Search Is Widening in CIA Shootings," *New York Times,* February 11, 1993.

15. William A. Sessions interview (December 12, 2003).

16. Peter Lance, *1000 Years for Revenge,* p. 132.

17. Winston Wiley interview (December 20, 2004).

18. Peter Lance, *1000 Years for Revenge,* p. 134.

19. Ibid., pp. 138–142.

20. Ibid., pp. 131–32; 137.

21. Winston Wiley interview (December 20, 2004).

22. Ibid.

23. Peter Lance, *1000 Years for Revenge,* pp. 150–152.

24. Cited in Lance, *1000 Years for Revenge,* p. 149.

25. Anthony Lake interview (December 15, 2004).

26. Anthony Lake, *Six Nightmares: The Real Threats to American Security* (Boston: Little, Brown & Co., 2000), p. 56.

27. Winston Wiley interview (December 20, 2004).

28. "Argentina Linked Iranian Diplomats to Blast," *New York Times*, August 9, 1994.

29. Tim Weiner, "Iran and Allies Are Suspected in Bomb Wave," *New York Times*, July 29, 1994.

30. Lloyd Salvetti interview (December 1, 2004); Winston Wiley interview (December 20, 2004).

31. Richard W. Stevenson, "Bombing in London Hits Israeli Embassy," *New York Times*, July 27, 1994. Israeli Prime Minister Yitzhak Rabin warned of Hezbollah cells in the United States, Latin America, and Europe.

32. Anthony Lake interview (December 15, 2004).

33. William Clinton, "Message to Congress on Terrorists Who Threaten to Disrupt the Middle East Peace Process," January 23, 1995, Presidential Papers: William J. Clinton, 1995.

34. Ibid.

35. Anthony Lake interview (December 15, 2004).

36. Lance, *1000 Years for Revenge*, pp. 148–149.

37. Background information from a former U.S. official.

38. Richard A. Clarke, *Against All Enemies: Inside America's War on Terror* (New York: Free Press, 2004), p. 144.

39. Anthony Lake interview (December 15, 2004).

40. Ibid.

41. William J. Clinton, *My Life*, pp. 890–891.

42. Peter Lance, *1000 Years for Revenge*, p. 200.

43. Simon Reeve, The *New Jackals: Ramzi Yousef, Osama Bin Laden and the Future of Terrorism* (Boston: Northeastern University Press, 1999), pp. 71–93.

44. Richard A. Clarke, *Against All Enemies*, p.93.

45. Anthony Lake, *Six Nightmares*, p. 55.

46. Mona Yacoubian, "Algeria's Struggle for Democracy," Council on Foreign Relations, Studies Department, Occasional Paper Series, No. 3, 1997. See also Daniel Benjamin and Steve Simon, *The Age of Sacred Terror: Radical Islam's War Against America* (New York: Random House, 2002), pp. 195–198.

47. Mona Yacoubian, telephone interview (December 5, 2004).

48. Alan Riding, "25 Hurt as Siege by Algerians Is Ended," *The New York Times*, December 27, 1994.

49. Winston Wiley interview (December 20, 2004).

50. Peter Lance, *1000 Years for Revenge*, pp. 284–293; Lloyd Salvetti interview (December 1, 2004).

51. Background information from a former U.S. official.

52. Lake, *Six Nightmares*, p. 27.

53. Anthony Lake interview (December 15, 2004).

54. Lake, Six *Nightmares*, p. 55.

55. Richard A. Clarke, *Against All Enemies*, p. 156.

56. Tim Weiner, "U.S. Intelligence Officials Baffled over Possible Motives," *New York Times*, March 21, 1995.

57. John Deutch, DCI, "Worldwide Threat Assessment Brief to the Senate Select Committee on Intelligence," unclassified prepared brief, February 22, 1996.

58. William Clinton, "US Policy on Counterterrorism," June 21, 1995. The declassified version is heavily sanitized.

59. Ibid.

60. David Cohen interview (November 16, 2004); Winston Wiley interview (December 20, 2004).

61. "Anti-Terrorism Bill Is Stalled in Congress," *New York Times*, December 19, 1995.

62. "The Wrong Answer to Terrorism," *New York Times*, March 13, 1996.

63. Stephen Labaton, "Senate Easily Passes Counterterrorism Bill," *New York Times*, April 18, 1996.

64. "House Strips New Powers from Terrorism Bill," *CQ Weekly*, March 16, 1996.

65. Kenneth Pollack interview (December 1, 2004).

66. Roger Cressey interview (December 6, 2004).

67. Anthony Lake interview (December 15, 2004).

68. Ibid.

69. Kenneth Pollack, *The Persian Puzzle: The Conflict Between Iran and America*, pp. 280–286.

70. William Clinton, "Remarks at the Memorial Service at Patrick Air Force Base, Florida, for American Servicemen Killed in Saudi Arabia," June 30, 1996, Public Papers of the Presidents: William J. Clinton, 1996.

71. William Clinton, "The President's Radio Address," June 29, 1996, Public Papers of the Presidents: William J. Clinton, 1996; in his remarks upon arriving, President Clinton stated that he had about forty specific proposals to make to achieve those goals. William Clinton, "Remarks with President Jacques Chirac of France on the G-7 Response to Terrorism and an Exchange with Reporters at Lyons," June 27, 1996, Public Papers of the Presidents: William J. Clinton, 1996.

72. William Clinton, "The President's News Conference in Lyons," June 29, 1996, Public Papers of the Presidents: William J. Clinton, 1996.

73. William Clinton, "Interview with Tom Brokaw of MSNBC's "Inter-Night," July 15, 1996, Public Papers of the Presidents: William J. Clinton, 1996.

74. Anthony Lake interview (December 15, 2004).

75. Richard A. Clarke, *Against All Enemies*, pp. 120–121.

76. Winston Wiley interview (December 20, 2004).

77. Ibid.

78. Rohan Gunaratna, *Inside al Qaeda: Global Network of Terror* (New York: Berkley Books, 2003), pp. 21–71; *The 9/11 Commission Report: Final Report of the National Commission on Terrorist Attacks upon the United States* (New York: W.W. Norton & Company, 2004), pp. 55–59; Winston Wiley interview (December 20, 2004).

79. David Cohen interview (November 16, 2004).

80. Lloyd Salvetti interview (December 1, 2004). As Cohen's executive officer, Salvetti was one of the organizers of these meetings.

81. David Cohen interview (November 16, 2004).

82. Background information from a former U.S. official.

83. *The 9/11 Commission Report*, p. 109.

84. Lloyd Salvetti interview, (December 1, 2004).

85. Benjamin Weiser, "Ex-Aide to Bin Laden Describes Terror Campaign Aimed at U.S.," *New York Times,* February 7, 2001; Jamal Al-Fadl Testimony, February 6, 2001, *United States v. Usama Bin Laden,* US District Court, Southern District of New York, S(7) 98 Cr. 1023.

86. John Follain, *Jackal: The Complete Story of the Legendary Terrorist, Carlos the Jackal* (NY: Arcade, 1998), pp. 193–228.

87. Barbara Crossette, "Fearing Terrorism, US Plans to Press Sudan," *New York Times,* February 2, 1996.

88. Benjamin and Simon, *The Age of Sacred Terror,* pp. 109–115; 132–133; Gayle Smith interview (January 7, 2005); Rohan Gunaratna, *Inside al Qaeda,* pp. 39–51.

89. "F.B.I. Blamed for Lack of Bill on Terrorism," *New York Times,* August 5, 1996.

90. Ronald Kessler, *The CIA at War: Inside the Secret Campaign Against Terror* (New York: St. Martin's Griffin, 2003), pp. 172–173; Lloyd Salvetti interview (December 1, 2004).

91. Winston Wiley interview (December 20, 2004).

92. Lloyd Salvetti interview (December 1, 2004).

93. Coll, *Ghost Wars,* pp. 376–377; background information from a former U.S. official; Benjamin and Simon, *The Age of Sacred Terror,* p. 150; Douglas Jehl, "Islamic Group Vows Revenge on Americans," *New York Times,* January 22, 1996.

94. White House Commission on Aviation Safety and Security, February 12, 1997.

95. "Airlines Fought Security Changes," *Boston Globe,* September 20, 2001. The most expensive involved bag-matching. No bag would be boarded unless the ticket holder was present on the aircraft. This precaution would, of course, be of no value against a suicide bomber. What makes the commission's deci-

sion evidence of the lack of urgency is that in September 1996, the commission indicated that it was prepared to require this measure. But by the release of its findings and recommendations in February 1997, that recommendation had been dropped.

Chapter Ten

1. Leon Fuerth interview (December 21, 2004).

2. Osama bin Laden, "Statement: Jihad Against Jews and Crusaders," February 23, 1998, in Barry Rubin and Judith Colp Rubin, eds., *Anti-American Terrorism and the Middle East: A Documentary Reader* (New York: Oxford University Press, 2002), pp. 149–151.

3. Osama bin Laden, "Declaration of War," August 1996, ibid., pp. 137–142.

4. Steve Coll, *Ghost Wars: The Secret History of the CIA, Afghanistan, and Bin Laden: From the Soviet Invasion to September 10, 2001* (New York: Penguin Press, 2004), pp. 327–328; 340–342; *The 9/11 Commission Report: Final Report of the National Commission on Terrorist Attacks Upon the United States* (New York: W.W. Norton & Company), pp. 63–65; 110–114.

5. *The 9/11 Commission Report*, pp. 110–114, and background information from a former U.S. official.

6. John F. Burns, "Arms Race Feared," *New York Times*, May 30, 1998.

7. Ibid.

8. Katharine Q. Seelye, "Congress May Lift Ban on Wheat Sales to India and Pakistan," *New York Times*, June 15, 1998; David E. Sanger, "Despite A-Test, U.S. Won't Bar Pakistan Bailout," *New York Times*, July 22, 1998; Barbara Crossette, "New Curbs Set for Pakistan and India," *New York Times*, October 3, 1998.

9. Robert C. McFarlane, "Pakistan's Catch-22," *New York Times*, May 30, 1998.

10. Leon Fuerth interview (December 21, 2004).

11. Recognizing its error, the U.S. Congress passed an omnibus bill in November 1998 that allowed the Clinton administration to waive some of the sanctions, including the curtailment of military-to-military training programs. The ban on arms sales, trade credits, and U.S. and private lending remained. Steven Erlanger, "U.S. to Lift Some Sanctions Against India and Pakistan," *New York Times*, November 7, 1998.

12. *The 9/11 Commission Report*, p. 115.

13. *The 9/11 Commission Report*, pp. 121–122.

14. Richard A. Clarke, *Against All Enemies: Inside America's War on Terror* (New York: Free Press, 2004), pp. 167–171; background information from a former U.S. official.

15. NSC Memorandum, "Strategy for Eliminating the Threat from the Jihadist Network al Qida: Status and Prospects" (December 2000), www.gwu.edu/~nsarchiv/ (accessed February 12, 2005).

16. Tim Weiner, "Sophisticated Terrorists Post Daunting Obstacle," *New York Times,* August 13, 1998.

17. Gayle Smith interview (January 7, 2005); Clarke, *Against All Enemies,* p. 181.

18. Clarke, *Against All Enemies,* p. 184.

19. "Transcript: Wednesday's 9/11 Commission Hearings, March 24, 2004, www.washingtonpost.com, viewed January 4, 2005.

20. See Steve Coll, *Ghost Wars,* p. 319, for information about U.S. interception capabilities; for evidence of British interception see UK Government, "Responsibility for the Terrorist Atrocities in the United States, September 11, 2001 (October 4, 2001)," in Barry Rubin and Judith Colp Rubin, eds., *Anti-American Terrorism and the Middle East: A Documentary Reader* (New York: OUP, 2002), pp. 214–216. Coll's source for his assertion appears to be softer than most in his excellent book, and it may well be that the British supplied the bulk of the signals intelligence from this telephone tap. On Fadl's role see Jamal Al-Fadl Testimony, February 6, 2001, *United States v. Usama Bin Laden,* US District Court, Southern District of New York, S(7) 98 Cr. 1023. Information on the tightening of Anglo-American work on bin Laden comes from the British "Review of Intelligence on Weapons of Mass Destruction: Report of a Committee of Privy Counsellors," [The Butler Report], London: The Stationary Office, 2004, pp. 31–33 and background information from a former U.S. official.

21. UK Government, "Responsibility for the Terrorist Atrocities in the United States, September 11, 2001 (October 4, 2001)," in Barry Rubin and Judith Colp Rubin, eds., *Anti-American Terrorism and the Middle East: A Documentary Reader* (New York: OUP, 2002), pp. 214–216.

22. Clarke, *Against All Enemies,* p. 184.

23. Philip Shenon, "U.S. Halts Business at Embassy in Albania," *New York Times,* August 15, 1998; background information from a former U.S. official.

24. Ibid.

25. *The 9/11 Commission Report* [CK pp.].

26. Roger Cressey to author (January 4, 2005); Clarke, *Against All Enemies,* p. 217.

27. Madeleine Albright, *Madam Secretary: A Memoir* (New York: Miramax Books, 2003), p. 364.

28. Ibid., p. 364.

29. Rohan Gunaratna, *Inside Al Qaeda: Global Network of Terror,* updated edition (New York: Berkley Books, 2003), p. 63.

30. Gayle Smith interview (January 7, 2005).

31. *Washington Post,* "Full Transcript of Wednesday's Hearing by the National

Commission on Terrorist Attacks Upon the United States," March 24, 2004, www.washingtonpost.com (accessed December 21, 2004).

32. William Clinton, "The President's Radio Address," August 22, 1998, Public Papers of the Presidents of the United States: The Administration of William J. Clinton, 1998 (Washington, DC: USGPO, 1999).

33. *The 9/11 Commission Report,* p. 117.

34. Background information from a former U.S. official.

35. Todd S. Purdum, "Critics of Clinton Support Attacks," *New York Times,* August 21, 1998; Frank Bruni, "Wagging Tongues in 'Incredibly Cynical Times,'" *New York Times,* August 21, 1998.

36. *The 9/11 Commission Report,* p. 120.

37. For this statement by Samuel Berger, see the *Washington Post,* "Full Transcript of Wednesday's hearing by the National Commission on Terrorist Attacks Upon the United States," March 24, 2004, www.washingtonpost.com (accessed December 21, 2004).

38. *The 9/11 Commission Report,* p. 131.

39. Ibid., pp. 131–132.

40. Ibid., p. 132.

41. Ibid., p. 357. The commission cited the community's tepid reaction to this message as evidence of "some of the limitations of the DCI's authority over the direction and priorities of the intelligence community, especially its elements within the Department of Defense."

42. Ibid., pp. 134–137. On Sheehan, see Albright, *Madam Secretary,* pp. 369–370.

43. *The 9/11 Commission Report,* p. 152.

44. Ibid., p. 154.

45. Background information from former U.S. officials.

46. *The 9/11 Commission Report,* p. 140.

47. Ibid. The 9/11 Commission suggested that Tenet's caution may have been a by-product of the mistaken bombing of the Chinese Embassy in Belgrade, which had just occurred.

48. UNSC Resolution 1267, October 15, 1999, Rubin and Rubin, eds., *Anti-American Terrorism and the Middle East,* pp. 219–220.

49. CIA Press Release, "Jeremiah Press Conference," June 2, 1998, www.cia.gov (accessed January 7, 2005).

50. George Tenet, "Written Statement for the Record of the Director of Central Intelligence Before the National Commission on Terrorist Attacks Upon the United States," March 24, 2004.

51. Steve Coll, *Ghost Wars,* p. 367; *The 9/11 Commission Report,* p. 343. Winston Wiley telephone conversation (January 10, 2005). The British Joint Intelligence Community more than likely expressed the U.S. view as well in its July 1999 conclusion that "the indications of terrorist interest in CBRN materials

[WMD] have yet to be matched by a comparable amount of evidence about possession and intent to use CBRN." "Review of Intelligence on Weapons of Mass Destruction: Report of a Committee of Privy Counsellors," [The Butler Report], London: The Stationary Office, 2004, p. 33.

52. Paul Kurtz telephone conversation (January 3, 2005).

53. Gayle Smith interview (January 7, 2005) on the U.S. counterterrorism successes of 1998–2000.

54. See Chapter 7, p. 193.

55. *The 9/11 Commission Report,* pp. 174–175; Clarke, *Against All Enemies,* p. 205.

56. George Tenet, "Written Statement for the Record of the Director of Central Intelligence Before the National Commission on Terrorist Attacks Upon the United States," March 24, 2004.

57. *The 9/11 Commission Report,* pp. 177–179.

58. Roger Cressey interview (December 6, 2004).

59. Madeleine Albright, *Madam Secretary,* p. 373.

60. Roger Cressey interview (December 6, 2004); Paul Kurtz telephone conversation (January 3, 2005).

61. *The 9/11 Commission Report,* pp. 186–187; Clarke, *Against All Enemies,* p. 219.

62. William Clinton, "Commencement Address at the United States Coast Guard Academy in New London, Connecticut, May 17, 2000, Public Papers of the Presidents: William J. Clinton, 2000.

63. William Clinton, "Remarks on the Employment Report and an Exchange with Reporters," May 5, 2000, Public Papers of the Presidents of the United States: William J. Clinton, 2000.

64. *The 9/11 Commission Report,* pp. 188–189.

65. George Tenet, Written Statement for the Record of the Director of Central Intelligence Before the National Commission on Terrorist Attacks Upon the United States, March 24, 2004.

66. DoD USS *Cole Commission Report,* January 9, 2001, Executive Summary. www.defenselink.mil (accessed November 27, 2004).

67. Kenneth Pollack interview (December 1, 2004); Roger Cressey interview (December 6, 2004).

68. Roger Cressey interview (December 6, 2004).

69. Madeleine Albright, *Madam Secretary,* p. 375.

70. Cited in Gunaratna, *Inside Al Qaeda,* p. 46.

71. William J. Clinton, "Remarks on the Attack on the U.S.S. *Cole* and the Situation in the Middle East," October 12, 2000, Public Papers of the Presidents: William J. Clinton, 2000–2001.

72. Kenneth Pollack, who was director for the Persian Gulf at the NSC, recalls four reasons complicating U.S.-Yemeni cooperation on the *Cole* investiga-

tion: (1) The Yemenis did not want there to be an investigation at all; (2) the Yemeni president was worried about getting into a conflict with bin Laden; (3) the Yemeni president had domestic dissidents to worry about; (4) Yemen is among the most inefficient Arab countries. Kenneth Pollack interview (December 1, 2004).

73. *The 9/11 Commission Report,* p. 192.

74. Ibid., p. 195.

75. Ibid., p. 192.

76. Ibid., p. 193.

77. William J. Clinton, *My Life,* p. 925.

78. Interview with Roger Cressey (December 6, 2004).

79. Richard Miniter, *Losing bin Laden: How Bill Clinton's Failures Unleashed Global Terror* (Washington, DC: Regnery, 2003), pp. 224–227; Albright, *Madam Secretary,* p. 376.

80. Roger Cressey interview (December 6, 2004).

81. Albright, *Madam Secretary,* p. 375.

82. Public Papers of the Presidents: William J. Clinton, "Interview with Mark Knoller of CBS Radio in Dover, New Hampshire, January 11, 2001."

83. DoD USS *Cole Commission Report,* January 9, 2001, Executive Summary.

84. George Tenet, "Written Statement for the Record of the Director of Central Intelligence," March 24, 2004.

85. *The 9/11 Commission Report,* p. 197.

86. NSC Memorandum, "Strategy for Eliminating the Threat from the Jihadist Network al Qida: Status and prospects," [December 2000], www.gwu.edu/~nsarchiv/ (accessed February 12, 2005).

Chapter Eleven

1. Richard A. Clarke to Condoleezza Rice, "Presidential Policy Initiative/Review–The Al Qida Network," January 25, 2001, www.gwu.edu/~nsarchiv/ (accessed February 12, 2005).

2. Ibid.

3. NSC memorandum, "Strategy for Eliminating the Threat from the Jihadist Network al Qida: Status and prospects," (December 2000), www.gwu.edu/~nsarchiv/ (accessed February 12, 2005). Clarke also appended the 1998 Delenda Plan to this document and his January 25, 2001, memorandum to Condoleezza Rice.

4. Background information from a former U.S. official.

5. NSC Memorandum, "Strategy for Eliminating the Threat from the Jihadist Network al Qida: Status and prospects" (December 2000), www.gwu.edu/~nsarchiv/ (accessed February 12, 2005).

6. *The 9/11 Commission Report,* p. 202.

7. Jane Perlez, "Rice on Front Line in Foreign Policy Role," *New York Times,* August 19, 2001.

8. Strobe Talbott, *The Russia Hand: A Memoir of Presidential Diplomacy* (New York: Random House, 2002), pp. 370–399.

9. David E. Rosenbaum, "The Military: Plan for Missile Defense Survives, but in Competing Versions," *New York Times,* August 16, 2000.

10. Jane Perlez, "Rice on Front Line in Foreign Policy Role, *New York Times,* August 19, 2001.

11. Richard Clarke, *Against All Enemies,* p. 231.

12. Benjamin Weiser, "Trial Poked Holes in Image of Bin Laden's Terror Group," *New York Times,* May 31, 2001.

13. *The 9/11 Commission Report,* pp. 255–256. An anonymous call to the U.S. embassy in the United Arab Emirates is mentioned in the PDB of August 6, 2001, reproduced on pages 261–262.

14. NSC email, Clarke to Rice and Hadley, "Stopping Abu Zubaydah's attacks," May 29, 2001, cited in *The 9/11 Commission Report,* p. 256.

15. *The 9/11 Commission Report,* p. 204.

16. Ibid., pp. 205–206.

17. Roger Cressey interview (December 6, 2004).

18. Ibid., pp. 256–257.

19. 9/11 Commission Staff Statement #10, "Threats and Responses in 2001."

20. *The 9/11 Commission Report,* pp. 258–259.

21. Ibid., pp. 259–260.

22. Thomas Friedman, "A Memo from Osama," *New York Times,* June 26, 2001.

23. *The 9/11 Commission Report,* pp. 237, 241–244.

24. 9/11 Commission, Staff Statement #10, "Threats and Responses in 2001," 9/11 Commission Final Report, p. 259.

25. Quoted in Katharine Q. Seelye with Frank Bruni, "A Long Process That Led Bush to His Decision," *New York Times,* August 11, 1001.

26. David Frum, *The Right Man: The Surprise Presidency of George W. Bush,* (New York: Random House, 2003), p. 106–110.

27. Thom Shanker, "Rumsfeld Puts Missile Plan on Table Today in Moscow," August 13, 2001, *New York Times*; James Mann, *Rise of the Vulcans* (New York: Viking, 2004), pp. 240–242.

28. Patrick E. Tyler, "US Sets Deadline for an Agreement on ABM Porposal," *New York Times,* August 22, 2001.

29. Katharine Q. Seelye, "Political Memo: President Is on Vacation, Mostly Not Taking It Easy," *New York Times,* August 7, 2001.

30. "Accord on Police at Macedonian Talks," *New York Times,* August 6, 2001.

31. Christopher Andrew, *For the President's Eyes Only: Secret Intelligence and the American Presidency from Washington to Bush* (New York: Harper Collins, 1995), pp. 266, 311.

32. Anthony Lake interview (December 15, 2004).

33. Background information from a former U.S. official.

34. *The 9/11 Commission Report,* p. 262. Tenet was in Crawford on August 17 but apparently did not brief Bush on bin Laden or al Qaeda that day.

35. *The 9/11 Commission Report,* p. 262.

36. Background information from a former U.S. official.

37. *The 9/11 Commission Report,* p .260.

38. Ibid., pp. 266–272.

39. *The 9/11 Commission Report,* pp. 273–276.

40. Ibid., p. 275.

41. *The 9/11 Commission Report,* p. 272. The quotation comes from the commission's assessment regarding the FBI's inability to detain Mihdhar and Hazmi before September 11.

42. Ibid., p. 212.

43. Ibid.

44. Roger Cressey interview (December 6, 2004).

45. Ibid.

46. *The 9/11 Commission Report,* p. 214.

47. Richard L. Berke and David E. Sanger, "Bush Aides Seek to Focus Efforts on the Economy," *New York Times,* September 9, 2001.

48. Kenneth Pollock interview (December 1, 2004).

Conclusion

1. Mike Duval to Jack Marsh, November 28, 1975, NSArch-CT.

2. Richard A. Clarke, Memorandum for Condoleezza Rice, January 25, 2001, www.gwu.edu~nsarchive (accessed February 12, 2005).

3. Testimony by Winston P. Wiley, chair, Senior Steering Group, Terrorist Threat Integration Center, and assistant director of central intelligence for homeland security, before the Senate Government Affairs Committee, February 26, 2003, www.cia.gov (accessed February 12, 2005).

4. "Strategy for Eliminating the Threat from the Jihadist Network al Qida: Status and Prospects," December 2000, www.gwu~nsarchiv (accessed February 12, 2005).

INDEX